ia College
ndria

Victoria College

Victoria College

A History Revealed

Edited by
Sahar Hamouda
and
Colin Clement

The American University in Cairo Press
Cairo   New York

The American University in Cairo Press
113 Sharia Kasr el Aini, Cairo, Egypt
420 Fifth Avenue, New York, NY 10018
www.aucpress.com

Copyright © 2002 by the Old Victorian Association

All rights reserved. No part of this publication may be reproduced, stored in a retrieval system, or transmitted in any form or by any means, electronic, mechanical, photocopying, recording, or otherwise, without the prior written permission of the publisher.

Dar el Kutub No. 7819/02
ISBN 977 424 756 6

Endpapers: Sketches by schoolmaster Mr. G.S. Shiber, 1905:
Old Victoria College; and the Quad, Victoria College at Siouf.

Designed by the AUC Press Design Center
Printed in Egypt

Contents

Contributors ix

Acknowledgments xi

Preface 1
    Sahar Hamouda

Introduction 5
    Sahar Hamouda and Colin Clement

Chapter One: A School is Born 15
    Sahar Hamouda

Chapter Two: The Reed Phenomenon 63
    Sahar Hamouda

Chapter Three: From War to War 137
    Colin Clement

Chapter Four: Victoria into Victory 187
    Hala Halim

Appendices

A. Middle East in Miniature, reflections by Douglas
   Haydon, and a biographical note by his son 245

B. Pupils' list and school management, November 1902 251

Contents

C. Lord Cromer's address at the laying of the foundation
stone, Siouf, 24 May 1906 ... 253
D. Staff list, first year at Siouf, 1908–9 ... 256
E. Note on Victoria College, submitted to the Special
Mission to Egypt, by four former pupils, 1920 ... 258
F. The Balkan adventures of Ibrahim el Masry ... 263
G. Random notes by Malek Hanna on Mr. Lias, Mr. Reed,
and Amin Osman ... 268
H. Letter from the Daira of her Sultanate Highness
the Princess Nimatallah to Mr. Reed; list of clothes for
the Nabil Mohamed Tewfik Tousson ... 278
I. Emir Abdulillah's letter to Mr. Reed, 1933 ... 280
J. Percy Bolton's obituary in *The Victorian*, 1946 ... 284
K. Letter of authorization from Princess Emina Fazil to
Mr. Reed, 1934 ... 286
L. Speech Day 1926: excerpts of speeches by Lord Lloyd,
Ahmed Ziwer Pasha, and Sir Henry Barker ... 288
M. Invitation to Old Victorian Dinner, 1942, held in honor
of HRH Emir Abdulillah ... 293
N. Victoria College application form of Ayesha Osman, 1927 ... 295
O. Telegram from Asadig Assenussi, 1952 ... 296
P. Letter from the Royal Hashemite Diwan, 1953 ... 297
Q. Invitation from His Majesty King Hussein I to the
1981 Annual Reunion in Amman ... 298
R. Victoria College: Meanings in its Architecture,
by Mohamed Awad ... 299

Contents

S. Programme of the memorial service for His Majesty the
late King Hussein ibn Talal of Jordan, 19 March 1999 ... 307
T. Letter from Her Majesty Queen Nour to the
Old Victorian Association, April 1999 ... 308
Bibliography ... 309
Notes ... 311
Index ... 317

Contributors

SAHAR HAMOUDA is an associate professor in the Department of English Language and Literature at the University of Alexandria.

COLIN CLEMENT worked as a teacher at Victoria College in the 1980s and has lived some twelve years in Alexandria, working as a writer and translator.

HALA HALIM studied English and comparative literature at Alexandria University and the American University in Cairo. She is now a doctoral candidate in comparative literature at the University of California, Los Angeles.

Acknowledgments

The authors would like to express their warmest thanks to the following people:

Nicolas Anagnostaras; the late Mr. Fouad Awad; Mrs. Zizi el Baroudi; Mr. Antoine Bassili; Mr. Hafez Bassoumi; Dr. Mohamed Ezzat; Ambassador Mahmoud el Falaki; Mr. Mansour Hassan; Mr. Magdeldin Idrissi; Mr. Armand Kahil; Mr. Mustafa Kamel; Dr. Azza Kararah; Mr. Usama Kassem; Dr. Nawal Khalafallah; Dr. Peter Lewin; Mr. Fathi Loutfi; Mr. Ismail el Mahdi; Mr. Sadek el Mahdi; Mr. Mohamed el Mekabati; Mr. Akram el Nakeeb; Mrs. Moheiba el Nahhas; the late Mr. Stephen Nimr; Mr. Mohamed Nofal; Mr. Adnan Pachachi; the late Mr. Ibrahim Sadek; Mr. Mustafa el Sakkaf; Mrs. Dea el Sakkaf; Mr. Tewfik Saleh; Dr. Nadia el Shazly; Mr. Nicholas Stamboulieh; Dr. Oswald Weisz; and Mr. Omar Zulfikar for granting extended interviews and for sharing memories and information.

At Victory College:

Mr. Mustafa el Medani, headmaster, for permission to locate and research the school archives, and Suleiman Abdel Moneim for extending assistance in locating and retrieving archival material.

In England:

The late Mr. Michael Barker for Sir Henry Barker's speeches, and for sharing his knowledge of the history of the Alexandria Schools Trust Charity and granting access to archival material on the institution; Mr. Charles Hamdy for an extended interview and his family for their hospitality; Mr. Christopher Haydon for personal papers and photos concern-

ACKNOWLEDGMENTS

ing the school, and for the notes that were written by Malek Hanna on the school, and on Mr. Lias, Mr. Reed, and Amin Pasha Osman, for an earlier project begun by Douglas Haydon; Dr. George Kardouche for bringing over material from England, providing contacts in the UK, and coordinating meetings; Mrs. Rider for Mr. Rider's notes toward a memoir; and Mr. R.M.Thomason for Mr. Price's letters and photos.

For photographs:

Dr. Mohamed Awad; Mr. Jean Chamas; Dr. Alex Ghorayeb; Mr. Abd el Aziz el Ikiabi; Mr. Armand Kahil; Mr. Ibrahim el Kerdani; Mr. Omar Koreish; Mr. Fathi Loutfi; Mr. Waguih el Mehelmi; and Mr. Mohamed Nofal.

Dr. Mohamed Awad for information on families and locations in Alexandria, and for endless general help and advice.

Professor William Cleveland for material on George Antonius' career after leaving the school and also for the Note for the Milner Commission.

Mr. Hani Farag for scanning the photographs and original manuscripts.

Lawyer Nabil Hamdy for his help in obtaining the text of the post-Suez laws concerning ex-foreign schools.

Her Royal Highness Dr. Soad al Sabbah for a generous donation.

Messrs. Phillip Seaton and John Shimwell for their sterling work in tidying up the manuscript.

I knew almost immediately that this school
was a more serious place than any I had attended,
the pressure greater, the teachers harsher, the students
more competitive and sharp, the atmosphere bristling
with challenges, punishments, bullies and risks.
Out of Place, Edward Said

Preface

Sahar Hamouda

Late one April afternoon five elderly men were gathered round what might have been an Edwardian tea table. There was the tea and the bread and butter and jam and the cakes. The five of them, their ages ranging from seventy to eighty, were having what was almost a nursery tea in a room which might have been in Bath or Harrogate in the early years of this [the twentieth] century. In fact the year was 1976 and they were in a hotel in Helwan, south of Cairo, once a small health resort and now also an industrial town. Over their teacups they were discussing a school which had opened in Alexandria in 1902 and its first headmaster, C.R. Lias, who was in many ways an Edwardian figure. The oldest of the five, Abdel Rahman Hamada, had left the school, Victoria College, in 1910, the year Edward VII died. Hamada was the founder of the first effective textile town of Mehalla Kobra. Three of the others were also old Victorians. One was formerly a landowner who devoted much time to youth organisations and boys' clubs. He was the man who took to England the only [Egyptian] cricket team ever to play at Lord's: Fares Sarofeem. A third was a distinguished medical man, Dr. Safwat, and Abdel Rahman's younger brother, who had been in the government service and

PREFACE

> was something of a diplomat, was also present. The conversation turned again and again to the character and leadership of Lias, and this history of Victoria College will be in a large part the story of two men: C.R. Lias and his successor, R.W.G. Reed.

These words were written by Douglas Haydon, the fifth man present. He had been a master at Victoria College from 1928 to 1948. In 1976 he had returned from England to visit Egypt and Alexandria and to collect material for his history of the school. In the same year he asked Malek Hanna, an Old Boy then living in Canada, to write something for him on the school's first two headmasters, Mr. Lias and Mr. Reed, as well as on Amin Pasha Osman, another former pupil (see Appendix G). Mr. Haydon wrote some preliminary notes (see Appendix A) and eight pages covering the years 1897–1919, but he never finished the project.

In 1995 the idea was born once more. Dr. Mohamed Awad, chairman of the Old Victorian Association, thought that a serious and comprehensive history of the school deserved to be written. An older history by Mr. Lias already existed, but it did not go beyond the year 1920. Though it was an accurate reference for dates and figures, it did not bring the pupils, the masters, the school, or Alexandria to life. Dr. Awad wanted a narrative that would explain why Victoria College was the phenomenon it had become, and how it reflected the spirit of Alexandria during the first half of the twentieth century.

He approached seven contributors, whose initial enthusiasm eventually waned, and the number finally dwindled to three. Circulars were sent out to all members of the Old Victorian Association, asking for memories, anecdotes, documents, or information. Old Victorians of today are—as they were in the past—notorious for their laziness in responding to pleas. In 1938 an Old Boy, Charles Issawi, tried to collect subscriptions for the Old Victorian Club in Cairo. In despair he commented, "Like Ysolde I have waited patiently, and like her I have waited in vain": he had received subscriptions from only three Old Boys. Like Ysolde, and like Charles Issawi, we too waited patiently and in vain. The response to our circular was disappointing. A few took the time to write back, and to them a special word of thanks is due here. Also, distinguished alumni of the school and former teachers were asked for either short contributions or to answer a specially prepared interview, but again the response was feeble. Since this history was conceived of as an attempt to bring the school to life and to use, as much as possible, the words of the people involved—people like the Old Boys, the teachers, and the headmasters—a lot of research and contacts had to be made. This was no easy task, since many of those involved are scattered all over the world. Archival material was another stumbling block. Some material and a sizable collection of photographs are in the possession of the Association. At the school itself, and with the kind cooperation of Mr. Mustafa el Medani, the headmaster at the time, some records were finally found, but they are by no means comprehensive. In England some material was available, and thanks are due to Dr. George Kardouche for collecting it and bringing it to Egypt. Also, as noted, we must not forget all those Old Victorians who did take the time to meet with the authors and share their memories of the school.

A history has to be as truthful as it can be. Inevitably, this one relies heavily on documents, and on the words of the people concerned or those related to them. Many of the school records are missing, so those which have not been found will not be mentioned. Names of eminent or colorful alumni will unfortunately have to be omitted from this history if either no documents concerning them survive or if they have not responded to our request for a contribution or an interview. It would have been impossible for us to determine which names to mention and which ones to bypass, or who is more important and who has faded from the limelight. That would have been a most unscientific and subjective method, depending on personal preferences, memory, and hearsay. Sensationalism has had to be sacrificed for the sake of faithfulness and consistency. Thus Old Boys looking for the mention of famous people who went to Victoria College may be disappointed. Many other names have been omitted simply because of space considerations. A quick glance at the student lists compiled by the Old Victorian Association, Alexandria, indicates what a rich mosaic the school was and how much material has had to be left out; indeed, this book simply scratches the surface, and more research should be done in the future.

Preface

A point that has had to be seriously considered is at what date to end the history. Opinion initially favored 1956, when the school was nationalized and its name changed to Victory College. However, the alumni who had graduated from Victory College maintained that they were still Old Victorians and that 1956 was an arbitrary date at which to draw the line. So it was thought worthwhile to look closely at this date and consider how the change affected the school. Also, Victoria College, Cairo, was an important establishment in its own right, but it has no surviving records at all—not even a list of its boys—so any mention of it is effectively limited to the documents we managed to find in the Public Record Office, London.

The course that Douglas Haydon had decided his history would take was undoubtedly the right one. Mr. Lias and Mr. Reed were the two people who made the school what it was. Others, such as the teachers, Sir George Beeton Alderson who provided the bulk of the funds, Sir Henry Barker who was Chairman of the College Council for thirty years, and the pupils themselves, all played important roles. But it was Mr. Lias who took the helm of the school in its first year and steered it through innumerable financial difficulties. It was also he who determined its character. Mr. Reed maintained the principles that Mr. Lias had set, and went even further by stamping it with his own character and raising it to an international standard. In the eleven years between Mr. Reed's death in 1945 and nationalisation in 1956, the school went on riding the wave of success, though it had begun to accept of necessity a slightly different kind of pupil, which reflected the changing conditions of the country and the region. More changes took place in 1956.

This book is neither a sensational list of famous Old Victorians, nor a Dryasdust (to use Carlyle's term) factual account. While we realize that we have uncovered material that would be of significance to Middle East and postcolonial scholars, we have chosen to refrain from commenting, analyzing or taking a particular standpoint. We have tried to set down the facts as we found them and present a review of Alexandrian life in microcosm, written not only for Old Victorians in particular, but for general readers as well. Those interested in education, or in the social history of Alexandria during the first half of the twentieth century, will hopefully find the book worth their while.

Introduction

Sahar Hamouda and Colin Clement

On 22 January 1901, Victoria, Queen of Great Britain and Ireland, Empress of India, died. Some three months later, on 15 April, the foundation stone of Victoria College was laid in the town of Alexandria on the Mediterranean coast of Egypt. The death of the old queen stands as an obvious landmark in the history of Great Britain and, given Britain's international position at the time, in that of the wider world. The early years of the new century witnessed a continued and intensified scramble for overseas possessions and an increasing arms race among the European powers. Turkey, the erstwhile overlord of the eastern Mediterranean, was gradually crumbling. A world war was about to break out. Within the interstices of what threatened to be an uncertain and changing future, Alexandria flourished as a commercial and financial center, a crossroads between east and west, a point of encounter and exchange. When the small British community established the new school, they were reflecting the confidence of this fast-growing city.

During the nineteenth century, British foreign policy had tended to prop up Turkey as a means of checking Russian expansion into the eastern Mediterranean. However, the provinces on the periphery of the Ottoman empire were open to French and British penetration. In North Africa, France occupied Algiers in 1830, making it predominantly European, and proceeded to settle emigrants in the interior. There was an expansion of European trade and the opening of consulates in Morocco; in Tunis, Jews and foreigners were allowed to own land and engage in business activities. In 1839, Britain took Aden, and the British presence in the Gulf began to increase either as a result of naval power or by formal agreements. By the end of the nineteenth century the Trucial States, Kuwait, Bahrain, Oman, and the rest of the Arabian peninsula had all surrendered their foreign affairs to Britain.

Under the energetic and ambitious rule of the viceroy, or pasha, Muhammad Ali (1805–48), Egypt had gained a certain degree of autonomy from the Ottoman Porte, and the pasha's military adventures took him as far as Sudan, Syria, and Arabia. This southern threat to the stability of Turkey was not countenanced by the European powers, which drove him back to Egypt with the concession of hereditary rule. However, while Muhammad Ali's foreign expansion was checked, the very program of modernization that he had instituted in order to create an efficient army capable of such adventures rejuvenated a country that had been underachieving for some three hundred years. Agricultural production, most notably cotton, was improved and expanded, and irrigation was updated. The patterns of state and government were reformed to provide a strict, economical, and effective centralized control. New industries were established, primarily to furnish his army with home-produced materials and supplies. Foreign "experts" and teachers were invited to reside in the country, and Egyptians were sent to Europe to study; the experience and expertise they gained would then be put to the service of the state. Muhammad Ali also introduced a limited system of state education to provide a body of cadres capable of managing the new Egypt. While the country as a whole developed, Alexandria in particular benefitted. The digging of the Mahmoudieh Canal in 1819 provided a constant source of fresh water, and the construction of shipyards and an arsenal reactivated the port and the possibilities of increased maritime trade. From a sleepy hamlet of some 6,000 souls at the beginning of the nineteenth century, Alexandria had grown into a bustling city with an estimated population of 100,000 at the time of the viceroy's death in 1848.

With Egypt newly opened for business, a steady flow of foreigners poured into the country. They came from every profession, from entrepreneurs to laborers, and represented every country around the Mediterranean Sea. The British, of course, were also present. These new arrivals brought with them cultural baggage and modes of living that were to have a profound effect on the renascent country; and their professional activities touched on all aspects of life from commerce to architecture, from law to medicine, and, naturally, education.

Muhammad Ali's initial educational policy, as noted, was limited to forming a group of technicians capable of performing specific tasks for the state and was in no way aimed at the mass of the people. However, his initiatives had the effect of throwing a light on the question of education in general and in what language it would be provided. Basic schooling was and had been for centuries provided by the traditional *kuttab* or quranic school, often attached to a mosque and staffed by sheikhs. The *kuttabs* taught the rudiments of reading and writing and perhaps some arithmetic, but the essential textbook and subject of study was the Quran. Given the sudden growth in the complexity of Egyptian life as a result of economic and industrial expansion, these small institutions were clearly no longer sufficient. Like all other markets, the educational market was growing. Moreover, the modern knowledge that was now sought after had been available only in European languages. Muhammad Ali's response was to establish a school of languages (Madrasat el Alsun) that would train translators to mediate between the foreign teachers and the local students and to prepare translated texts. He also introduced the teaching of Italian into the elite military school within the Cairo citadel, and eventually both Italian and Turkish were taught in government schools. Once again, these initiatives were of restricted scope, but the intense attention paid by the ruler to education and the teaching of foreign languages gave impetus to intellectual life and the value of learning.

In tandem with this locally revived interest in education, a growing number of foreign schools began to be established. These were based on two distinct traditions—the missionary school and the community school. The former was generally an offshoot of some religious brotherhood or sorority whose principal aim was the spreading of its chosen creed. The latter was generally a closed institution designed to cater to the children of one particular ethnic community. In either case they were independent of the state and did not submit to government intervention, though they were sanctioned by it. Both types had, in fact, been present in Egypt for some time. The Greek community had opened a school in Cairo in 1645, which was limited to Greeks and taught no Arabic. In 1732 the Franciscans had established a charity school attached to a church in the Muski district of Cairo. This school accepted Egyptians, both Christian and Muslim, and taught Arabic as well as Italian. For all that it was a religious institution financed by the Roman Catholic church, the Muski school can be considered the first of Egypt's many foreign schools.

Muhammad Ali removed many of the restrictions on the movement, comportment, and activities of Christians in Egypt, and one result was an increase in Roman Catholic missionary schools. Most of these were run by French brotherhoods, since France was the protector of Catholicism in Ottoman lands. In 1836, for example, the Catholic residents of Alexandria called on the Lazaristes and Les Filles de la Charité missionaries to establish a school for boys and another one for girls, permission for which was granted in 1844.[1]

Protestant missionaries were initially less energetic than the Catholics. The British Protestants began in Alexandria with St. Andrew's Church Harbour Mission in 1856, and the following year, a certain Dr. Yule opened a school to convert Jews, and to provide moral guidance to British sailors. There was also a school for girls in the Manshieh district. The Scottish School for Boys, as it became known, was later to have Mr. Douglas Dunlop as its headmaster until he became Inspector in the Ministry of Education in 1889. No official aid was forthcoming from Great Britain, and these Scottish Presbyterians in Alexandria were left to continue alone, since other, earlier-established British Protestant missionary schools elsewhere in Egypt had ceased to function in 1848. It was only after the British occupation of Egypt in 1882 that they resumed their activities. But by the turn of the century there were still only twenty British Protestant missionary schools in the whole country.[2]

The American Protestant missionaries were more active than their British counterparts. Their first schools opened in Cairo in 1855 for boys, and in 1860 for girls. In Alexandria two schools, one for boys and another for girls, were opened in 1856. The American missionary schools quickly spread all over the country, numbering 186 by 1896.[3]

All these missionary schools had a shared concept and practice. Although they accepted Copts, Muslims, and Jews, they were supervised by a church, and religious instruction formed an essential part of the curriculum. Their main aim was to spread their particular brand of Christianity. Within these boundaries, French-language schools remained the most popular, in spite of American competition and even after the British occupation, the main reason being that the French language had taken over from Italian as the *lingua franca* in the first half of the century. It was to retain this dominant position in Egyptian society up to the Second World War, largely, as we shall see, as a result of British indifference to education.

Schools started by the foreign communities had a different purpose. They did not seek to perpetuate a certain creed or win converts, but to preserve the culture and language of the expatriate community. Although they too were often subsidized and supervised by churches, they had no missionary aims, and the pupils were specifically the children of their own community. The first Greek school, which opened in Cairo in 1645, was supported financially by the Greek Orthodox Church. It was not until a Greek community organization was established in Alexandria in 1843 that the Greeks themselves began to properly finance their schools. In the same year the Tossizza School was founded, so called after the Tossizza brothers who had donated generous grants toward its foundation. The Cairo Greek community organization was established in 1856, and from then on the number of Greek schools increased. The Armenian schools, similarly, started under the control of the Armenian Orthodox Church in 1828, and they received special encouragement from Muhammad Ali, who employed a number of Armenians in prominent positions within his administration. The German community was considerably smaller than the rest, so the German schools generally accepted pupils from all nationalities. They were founded as a response to the British missionaries, but ceased operation in 1848. As with the Greeks, it was in Alexandria in 1866 that individual efforts were made to set up schools that would preserve and spread German culture. By 1871 there were two German schools in Alexandria, one for boys and another for girls, and two years later the German schools started in Cairo. St. Charles Borromeo, which fell somewhere between the mission and the community school, was established in Alexandria in 1882; two years later three nuns arrived and work proper began.[4]

Just as it was in Alexandria that the foreign communities began to concentrate their individual efforts to found their own schools, so too it was in Alexandria that the first secular school as such was founded. This was the Italian School, endowed by Said Pasha and placed under the supervision of the Italian government. No church involvement was allowed, the subsidies coming mainly from the Italian government's board of directors, headed by the Consul-General of Italy, the same body that set the constitution of the school in 1871.[5] Owing to the strong presence of French missionary schools in Alexandria, particularly those of the Frères des Ecoles Chrétiennes, there does not seem to have been any attempt to create a French secular school, and the *lycées* were not to come until the twentieth century, though there was the rather strangely named Ecole Anglaise in the Moharrem Bey district, which taught English, French, and Italian.

There were also Jewish community schools, which in Alexandria were extremely satisfactory. There were the Aghion schools, founded by Behor and Isaac Aghion in 1865: the schools were clean, beautifully built, and situated near the seashore. Hebrew, Arabic, French, and Italian were all taught, and education was provided for girls. Half the pupils were born in Egypt; the rest came from within the Ottoman empire, particularly from Morocco and Syria—the Ashkenazim went elsewhere. By 1896 the Aghion School in Alexandria had 257 pupils. The other noteworthy Jewish school was founded by Baron Jacob de Menasce in 1885, and in 1903 it had 125 pupils. Unlike the other community schools, it was essentially secular and lacked a Jewish spirit. However, the wealthier Jews preferred to send their children to Christian schools, in order to distance themselves from the poorer Jews, who went to the Talmud Torah schools and the Alliance Israélite Universelle schools that were opened in Alexandria in 1897.[6]

Whether the schools were founded by missionaries or foreign communities, they remained somewhat exclusive in that the main emphasis was on spreading either religion or the particular language and culture of a community. After the British occupation of 1882 the British authorities made no attempt to copy the existing models. Their policy concerning education differed markedly from that of the French, whose language and schools permeated Egypt until well into the twentieth century (despite the brevity of the French stay in Egypt).

INTRODUCTION

Lord Cromer, British Agent and Consul-General of Egypt, the effective ruler of the country, believed that a little education was an "evil thing" and was inclined to follow "the general policy of His [Britannic] Majesty's Government [which] precluded any direct attempt to establish the influence of British culture."[7] What Lord Cromer "actually did was to appoint an Egyptian Minister of Education and to leave him to work out the educational salvation of Egypt with a British Advisor, who could, it seems, be trusted most effectively to obstruct any schemes but those of his own devising."[8] This "advisor" was Mr. Douglas Dunlop, erstwhile headmaster of the Alexandrian Scottish School, who was to stay in Egypt until 1920. He has been described by Humphrey Bowman, an inspector of schools in Egypt between 1903 and 1918, as "a Scotsman of limited ideas and rigid views."[9] Lord Lloyd, British High Commissioner in Egypt, 1925–29, was equally dismissive, saying that Dunlop's "administration of the educational department could hardly have been described as alight with either insight or imagination."[10] At the beginning of the century the Egyptian Ministry of Public Instruction, to give it its full title, was seen as a stepping stone to the Ministry of Finance. According to Bowman:

> The original system of recruitment [to the Ministry], however advantageous to other branches of the service, had been disastrous to education. It had involved the selection each year of a batch of new schoolmasters, few of them trained in the science of teaching, fewer still with any intention of making education their life work . . . 'Dunlop's young men' as the newcomers were called, arrived in annual batches, callow and inexperienced . . . It can hardly be said that they were ideal schoolmasters.[11]

Indeed, Bowman continues that there was "almost a feeling of discredit at being in the P.I. at all; 'Dunlop's young men' came out to Cairo full of enthusiasm, not for their work, but for early escape from it. Their one ambition was to transfer to another Department as soon as could conveniently be arranged."[12] Many years later, the secretary of the

Association of British Schoolmasters in Egyptian Government Schools, Mr. J. Cryer, wrote the following about Mr. Dunlop:

> I met several Egyptians—teachers and others—who were old enough to remember Dunlop, and they all gave a similar account of him: a bullying administrator who ruled by fear. They also accused him of deliberately retarding Egypt's education for political reasons . . . the impatience with which he brushed aside all proposals for founding an Egyptian University confirms his critics' suspicions. And how can an educationalist who despised the people he was supposed to be educating, and who arouses their hatred, be regarded as anything other than a failure and a misfortune?

As if this were not enough, there was also the financial question. Britain's stated reason for occupying Egypt was to refloat the country's bankrupt economy, and, in consequence, spending on education was reduced. In 1883 some forty-two schools were shut down, and the very notion of free education was abolished. By 1890, however, the Finance Department began to raise the sum of state money spent on education and steadily increased it thereafter. At the beginning of the twentieth century, the educational system in Egypt was divided into three main categories. The *kuttabs* were the most widespread. The state schools, modeled on the French system, were few. There were thirty-two primary schools and three secondary schools in 1900, with Egyptian, British, and French teachers. Finally, there were the private schools, which were affiliated to the Ministry of Waqf (religious endowments), and benevolent societies, Coptic societies, missionaries and foreign communities.[13]

When Victoria College was founded in 1901, there was no dearth of foreign schools in Egypt, or even of those that used English as a medium of instruction, thanks to the missionary efforts of the Americans. There was, however, no school that served the British community, nor did the British authorities show any inclination to establish one. It was thus left to the British community to found its own school, and again it was Alexandria that took the initiative. Yet this was to be, from the outset, a different sort of school. For all that there was a community of British citizens in Egypt, there was no community organization along the lines of those of the Greeks, Italians, and Armenians. These organizations, modeled on the Ottoman *millet* system, were important elements in the cosmopolitan social fabric of nineteenth- and early-twentieth-century Egypt. They were the essential point of insertion into social life for immigrants and provided everything from health care to retirement funds to sports teams to education. The British may have grouped around their sporting clubs and churches, but these were, in general, open to others—of the upper crust, naturally. Prior to 1882, the British settled in Egypt were not sufficiently numerous to require such a structure, and given that the original concept was one of protection from, and a point of collective negotiation with, the indigenous authorities, it seems unlikely that they ever considered it. Being a citizen of the world's greatest power was quite enough. After 1882, the British were also the occupying power. So when a group of British businessmen gathered to found a new British school, it was not within the confines of a structured community organization. Indeed, among the eight promoters of the project there were two non-British citizens, Baron Jacques de Menasce, president of the Austro–Hungarian Chamber of Commerce and of the Jewish Community of Alexandria, and Joseph Saba Pasha, of Syrian origin and Postmaster General of the Egyptian Postal Service. Although the school may have been started primarily for the British, there was an immediate understanding implicit in the fact that it was free from consular, community, and church control; and, perhaps most important, since it was established as a business venture, it would be open to all. And so it was. It attracted the children of royalty, dignitaries, diplomats, magnates, ministers, political refugees, landowners, and very ordinary people. It educated children of all nationalities, not only from all over Egypt, but also from the entire Middle East and beyond. Victoria College gained a reputation that made it the foremost school in the Middle East.

Of course it is pertinent to ask why it was in Alexandria that this secular British school was founded; why this particular school and not any other—British or otherwise—burgeoned into the meeting point of the notables of the Middle East, and why its alumni, even when they came from undistinguished backgrounds, proceeded to have distinguished careers and leave their mark on fields as diverse as the political, cultural, academic, and economic, both in their own countries and internationally. Victoria College was unique, reflecting the multi-ethnic and multicultural nature of a city that was like no other in the Middle East from the mid-nineteenth to the mid-twentieth centuries. But the credit must also go to its headmasters and teachers, who established an educational system that was unprecedented in the entire region. It was unthinkable that the headmaster of one of the Frères schools, in a public address, could have lectured on the virtues of "education for leisure" and "education in leadership," as Mr. Barritt (headmaster 1947–56) did. It was equally unthinkable that the headmaster of another foreign school (let alone a state school) would recommend one of his pupils on the strength of his performance on the cricket field, as Mr. Reed (headmaster 1922–45) did. The importance of Egypt as a whole during the nineteenth and twentieth centuries, together with the significance and special atmosphere of Alexandria as it blossomed from a forgotten provincial backwater into a major cosmopolitan center, plus the superior quality of the headmasters and masters and the multi-ethnicity of the school's pupils—all these factors combined to produce the phenomenon that was Victoria College.

1
A School is Born

Sahar Hamouda

An English school! Large stately buildings, boys playing football. English masters! We were all like one big family.
  Edward Atiyah, An Arab Tells His Story

At 4.30 p.m. on that Alexandrian spring afternoon of 24 May 1906, hundreds of distinguished guests gathered for a grand celebration in the suburb of Domaine de Siouf. The *Egyptian Gazette* reported the event the following morning:

> Among the many notables present among the spectators were his Beatitude Photius II, the Greek Orthodox Patriarch of Alexandria, Yacoub Pasha Artin, Under-Secretary of State to the Ministry of Public Instruction, the Grand Rabbi of Alexandria, Mustapha Pasha Ibadi, Governor of Alexandria, Sir Vincent Corbett, Financial Adviser, Mgr. Kyrollis Goha, Greek Catholic Melchite Patriarch of Antioch, Jerusalem and Alexandria, the Father Superior of the Jesuits, Judges of Mixed Courts, Sir Massie Blomfield [Rear-Admiral in charge of Alexandria Harbor], Baron Jacques de Menasce, president of the Jewish Community of Alexandria, M. Michel Sinadino, vice-president of the Hellenic community, the members of the Diplomatic and Consular Corps, Scheiss Pasha, vice-president of the Alexandria

Chapter 1

Municipality, and a large gathering of officials and prominent representatives of the European and native communities.

They had all come to witness Lord Cromer (British Agent and Consul-General of Egypt, 1900–1907) and Lady Cromer lay the foundation stone of the new buildings of the four-year-old Victoria College. When Baron Jacques de Menasce, introduced by Mr. E.B. Gould, the British Consul-General of Alexandria, as "one of the most influential of the original promoters of our school," addressed the audience in French, he outlined the pressing reasons for the establishment of the school. At the turn of the century, he said, opportunities for education in Alexandria were limited. The choices open to parents were few:

> Confier ses enfants aux établissements religieux, seuls existants alors, et faire ainsi litière de scrupules respectables; ou les envoyer en Europe à grands frais et au prix de cruels déchirements, telles étaient les deux alternatives entre lesquelles on avait à choisir. Et les enfants ainsi élevés, rentraient le plus souvent en étrangers dans le foyer familial, dont ils avaient perdu le contact et oublié la douceur. Dans une ville d'initiative comme Alexandrie, cette situation n'avait que trop duré, et un courant d'opinion finit par se former, en faveur de la création d'une école libre de toute attache confessionelle. Des réunions furent organisées où l'on discuta les divers systèmes d'éducation. Le système qui a fait la part égale entre les exercises de l'esprit et ceux du corps fut unanimement adopté. . . . Un comité internationale fut élu, comprenant des notabilités de cultes et de nationalités différentes.[14]

In fact, the school owed its original concept to Mr. Gould's predecessor, Sir Charles Cookson, who in 1898 first suggested the idea of an English school in Alexandria. Sir Henry Barker, who was later to become the president of the British community in Alexandria and president of Victoria College Council for thirty years, recounted in a speech at an Old Victorian dinner in 1934 that some people favored the idea, but "nobody was keen on providing the cash and many ways of doing so were discussed. Sir Charles had a great brainwave, he said let us make it a limited liability company and then perhaps we shall be able to pay dividends. This had the effect of making subscribers a little less shy and a list was started."

The list comprised the names of leading Alexandrian figures who responded not for altruistic reasons but for practical ones. A number of them did not have sons, or had sons who were already too old for primary school. But they were shrewd enough to realize that investment in the project would cause business to flourish even more in Alexandria, which by the end of the nineteenth century had become a city of no mean stature and was the gateway to Europe, its finance, and its culture. And yet it lacked a school that would prepare its citizens to hold high posts in the administrative, political, financial, and cultural life of Egypt. The marble tablet recording the Domaine de Siouf foundation ceremony of 1906, placed in the dining hall of the school, reads: "Victoria College was founded in memory of Queen Victoria to provide a liberal education for the sons of Egyptians and residents in Egypt." That certainly was the purpose of the establishing of the school and it was also the achievement of Victoria College, but it was not the simple motive behind its founding.

The original founders and early promoters were people who had a vested interest in encouraging business in Alexandria by supplying it with young men who would fill gaps in the financial and professional fields and eventually take over. Sir Charles Cookson was the British Consul-General and Judge Lionel Sandars was in charge of the Native Court. Mr. George Beeton Alderson (later Sir) first came to Alexandria as the representative of an English engineering firm and then joined the firm of Messrs. Allen and Co. In 1864 the firm of Allen, Alderson and Co. was founded and was to become among the most prosperous in Alexandria. It was a key player in the project that purchased a fleet of ships belonging to the late Ismail Pasha and which, in an enlarged and reorganized form, became the Khedivial Mail Steamship and Graving Dock Co. Ltd. When he died in 1926, aged eighty-three, Sir George Alderson's obituary occupied a whole page in a newspaper and started

Chapter 1

thus: "Both the City and Parish of Alexandria have suffered an irreparable loss in the decease of Sir George Alderson KBE who died in his house at Bulkeley, Ramleh, on December 2." Baron Jacques de Menasce, as noted, was the president of the Austro-Hungarian Chamber of Commerce and of the Jewish community in Alexandria, and a member of the Commission d'Examen in the Delegation Municipale. Mr. Henry Barker was the proprietor of a large shipping business, and a member of the committee of the British Chamber of Commerce, of the International Chamber of Shipping, and of the General Produce Association. Mr. Sidney Carver, the great cotton merchant, was vice-president of the Commission Municipale and president of the Commission d'Examen dans la Délégation Municipale. Mr. Harry Pugh Kingham was manager of the Anglo-Egyptian Bank in Alexandria, member of the Municipal Council, chairman of the Kafr al-Zayyat Cotton Co. Ltd., and former president of the British Chamber of Commerce. Mr. Robert Moss was one of the biggest shipowners in Alexandria, and was to become president of the British Chamber of Commerce. Mr. Arthur S. Preston was His Britannic Majesty's Crown Prosecutor in Egypt. Sir Joseph Saba Pasha was the Postmaster General of the Egyptian Postal Service. Dr. Marc Armand Ruffer (later Sir) was the president of the Conseil Sanitaire, Maritime et Quarantenaire d'Egypte—the street that bore his name, Ruffer Street, was changed to Syria Street when street names were arabized after 1956. These men were, as Sir Henry Barker described them in an address to the British community at Victoria College in 1928, a "group of hard-headed, far-sighted business men, who knew what they wanted, and what others wanted and were not afraid to get it. They knew that what they wanted was a school that would give lads an education, as much as possible along English public school lines, which would best fit them for their life in this country."

Since Alexandria was such a cosmopolitan city, it figured that its future leading citizens would be from different religions and nationalities, and therefore it made sense not to limit the school to a certain community, but to "provide for the upper classes in Egypt of all nationalities and creeds a school for the education of their sons which would, so far as possible, follow the lines of an English Public School," as Mr. A.S. Preston, honorary secretary of the Executive Committee, announced at the Domaine de Siouf ceremony. With the exception of Baron de Menasce and Saba Pasha, the founders and early promoters were Englishmen. They may not have had a political aim in founding the school, but a by-product of education at Victoria College was that it made its Arab boys bicultural. Consequently, the English education they received at Victoria College qualified a number of Old Boys to mediate between the Arabs and the British both in the Arab world and in the West. Furthermore, a great number of the boys were to work with British institutions in Egypt and all over the world. Barclay's Bank and Shell in particular offered almost unlimited job opportunities, and when Victoria College started a branch in Cairo during the Second World War, the successive general managers of Shell Ltd. sat on the board of the Cairo school.

Having decided on a limited liability company, the pioneers proceeded to collect subscriptions from British residents in Alexandria, their friends abroad, and various communities in Alexandria. When the subscriptions exceeded £4,000 sterling, the Articles of Association were drawn up and the name "The British Schools of Egypt" was chosen for the project. Dr. Marc Armand Ruffer and Judge Lionel Sandars were sent to enlist the support of Lord Cromer. To their disappointment, he did not countenance the scheme along the lines suggested. He refused to provide any British Authority funds, and suggested that since over £3,000 would go into the buildings, leaving insufficient money for the remaining expenses of the school, it would make more sense to rent a flat or a house to start the school in. His only other suggestion was that an application might be made to the Egyptian government for a "grant in aid," and that an English master in the employment of the Egyptian government schools might be lent for a year, provided that the school pay his salary.

Lord Cromer's refusal to lend any support to the proposed English school must have been based upon his beliefs about how the colonies were to be administered. In 1902 Lord Cromer, in collaboration with Lord Kitchener (Governor-General of Sudan, Sirdar of the Egyptian Army, and Pro-Consul of Egypt 1911–14) and Sir Reginald Wingate (Governor-General of Sudan, Sirdar of the Egyptian Army, and High Commissioner for Egypt 1917–19), used British Authority and government funds to found Gordon College in Khartoum, which later became the University of Khartoum. While Lord Kitchener was in England he called on Britain for money for Gordon College, and £100,000 was subscribed by the British public in two months.[15] However, the purposes of Gordon College were fundamentally different from those of Victoria College. Victoria College aspired to provide a liberal education along English public school lines to the elites of Alexandrian and Egyptian society, regardless of nationality or creed, and to prepare them for leading roles in the country. Gordon College, by contrast, sought to teach Sudanese boys English and mathematics so that they could work as clerks or tax gatherers under British administration but would rise no higher than that, or to teach them a craft in the several workshops attached to the school. They were to be trained to serve the British and not to compete with them. Also, in 1916 the British authorities and government funded the establishment of the English School in Cairo, but again its aim was different from that of the Alexandria project. It was established for the sons of British subjects and allowed only 20 percent of its pupils to be foreigners. In this case, Britain was unstinting in its help, and the Treasury and Foreign Office came forward several times to relieve the English School of its financial difficulties. One of its alumni was the spy George Blake.

Disheartened by Lord Cromer's negative attitude, the project of "The British Schools of Egypt" was temporarily dropped, since Lord Cromer's suggestions of a rented flat, together with a grant from the Egyptian government and the loan of an English master were in no way in accordance with the ambitious scheme the founders had in mind. Some of the subscribers withdrew their money and the sum sank to LE 3,570.544. The death of Queen Victoria in January 1901 prompted the British community in Alexandria to set up a memorial to her. The idea of a hospital was discussed and then abandoned because of a lack of funds, so the project of a school was revived. At this point Mr. G.B. Alderson, "whom in mediaeval times we would have looked upon as the pious founder of our school," as Mr. Lias (the first headmaster) said of him in 1912, stepped in to remove the immediate financial obstacles. He gave a loan of LE 2,500 and a gift of 25,000 square pics[16] in Mazarita overlooking the Eastern Harbor, and the committee changed the name from "The British Schools of Egypt" to Victoria College. An architect, Mr. H.

Favarger, was commissioned to design the buildings, and the contracting company McClure and Dorling was commissioned to carry out the construction. Now that the idea had become a reality, Lord Cromer was willing to sanction it by coming himself to lay the foundation stone on 15 April 1901. An advertisement was placed in *The Times* and other leading English newspapers for a headmaster. It announced a starting salary of LE 500 per annum with no housing arrangements yet, but estimated that a bachelor's living expenses would be in the range of LE 120–150 per annum. The stipulations were as follows: "Candidates should be laymen and have a University degree. They should be between the ages of 25 and 40, and should be prepared to take an active interest in cricket, football and other games." These terms were to determine the character of the school for the next sixty years. The fact that the headmaster had to be a layman meant that no religious discrimination or missionary work would be tolerated; a university degree ensured a high academic standard; comparative youth guaranteed energy in administration and hopefully a liberal and progressive attitude, and sports were instrumental in promoting an *esprit de corps* and healthy pupils. The committee chose Mr. Charles Lias, of King's College, Cambridge, who arrived on board the *Equateur* on 3 August 1902. He was met by Mr. Preston and taken immediately to inspect the premises. The very selection of Mr. Lias was to set firmly in place another feature of the new school and prove that from the beginning it would follow the lines of English public schools so ardently desired by its founders: Mr. Lias had been a schoolfellow of Mr. Preston's at Marlborough College, and the fact that they were both Old Marlburians demonstrated that the ethos of the "school tie" would take root in Alexandria.

The school was scheduled to open in October 1902. However, as Mr. Lias was to say at the first Old Victorian Annual Dinner in 1912, "we live in Egypt and it will not surprise you, those of you who are not already in the secret, that throughout the month of October 1902 Victoria College remained obstinately shut. It had been a cholera year." From 15 October Mr. Ambrose Mustard gave lessons informally in Rue Mariette Pasha, and Lord Cromer arrived on 20 October to inspect the buildings. The teachers recruited were Sheikh Mohamed Hamid to teach Arabic, M. Georges Dumont to teach French, and from England came two scholars from King's College, Cambridge, and former pupils of Mr. Lias: Mr. V.R. Mustard and Mr. Lowick. Within a year the English staff had been reinforced by Mr. Alfred Morrison, late scholar of King's College, Cambridge, and Mr. Aubrey, late scholar of Emmanuel College, Cambridge. The school fees were LE 3 a month and included the midday meal. The schedule was composed of morning and afternoon classes with intervals for dinner and drills, and concluded with football from 4.30 to 5.00 p.m. daily. Sunday was a holiday and Saturday a half-holiday. Religious instruction, though not for examination purposes, was given only at the request of parents, by Sheikh Hamid to the Muslims, by Hakham Harûn to the Jews, and by Archdeacon Ward, the Chaplain of St. Mark's, Alexandria, to the Christians.

Victoria College opened its doors formally on Saturday, 1 November 1902, with twenty-five boys, and on Monday morning one more boy joined. This British school had only one British boy, Edwin Harle, who came from Tanta. He was accommodated in the headmaster's flat, since no arrangements had been made for boarders yet. In his *A Short Account of Victoria College, Alexandria: From its Founding to 1919*, Mr. Lias comments that it "may be said that on that Saturday morning the character of the school was in some degree determined: with the generous assistance of Mr. G.B. Alderson it had been founded by public subscription, it was to be administered on the lines of English Public Schools, and its first boys were to be drawn from Egyptians and various communities whose lot is cast in Egypt." Certainly those twenty-six boys, as they now were, represented five of what in those days were considered nationalities (See Appendix B for this first list of pupils, together with the school management). They were classified according to creed (Muslim/Mohamedan/Musulman, Israelite, Christian) as well as nationality. Under Ottoman rule, Lebanese and Syrians were collectively referred to as Syrians, and this was the classification followed by the school, though hardly any boys came from the political entity that is today called Syria. The majority of "Syrian" boys came from Lebanese families, who were found in abundance in Alexandria and were among its leading citizens. They were mostly Christians who sought either refuge from Ottoman rule or the wealth of Egypt. The first batches of Syrian boys came from families established in Alexandria, Cairo, and

Khartoum, but eventually they came straight from Beirut, Tripoli, or the mountains of Lebanon. There was an English-language educational establishment on Bliss Street in Ras Beirut, the Syrian Protestant College, which was founded in 1866 and was later to change its name to the American University of Beirut: it boasted (and still does) splendid premises and American teachers. Initially, however, the medium of instruction at the Syrian Protestant College was Arabic. Boys from Victoria College went to the Syrian Protestant College and vice versa, and continued to do so for many years. In 1913 Dr. Howard Bliss, its principal, paid a visit to Victoria College and recognized some of his former pupils. He remarked that a few Victoria College boys were now at his college. The Syrians were more adventurous than the Egyptians in sending their sons to the new school. In November 1902 there were only three Egyptians enrolled: Hassan and Yusuf Sirry, the sons of Ismail Bey Sirry, Conseiller à la Cour d'Appel, and Hamid Mansur. Joseph Saba Pasha (whose son Farid died very soon after leaving the school) was of Syrian origin.

Well-known Greek families also preferred the new English school to their community school. There were the Valassopoulos and the Lagonicos, as well as the Rallis, Ambroise Ralli being the president of the Greek community and considered the father of the Municipal Council—he was its vice-president from 1896 to 1906. One of Alexandria's main streets was named Ambroise Ralli after him, and when many of the foreign place names were replaced by Arab names after 1956, became Port Said Street.

However, the Jews (classified as Israelites) were even more farsighted than either the Greeks or the Syrians. Out of the twenty-five boys, ten were Jews. Their parents were anything from middle-class widows to notables like Victor Aghion, representative of the Anglo-Jewish Association in Alexandria, who sent his sons Elie and Fernand there. In December 1902 ten more boys joined the school, of whom nine were Jews (including Aghion's third son, Charles). Although the Menasce and Aghion families founded Jewish community schools in Alexandria, it was these two families that were to patronize Victoria College, in the realization that Italian and French were on their way out and English on its way in.

Chapter 1

That first year was an exciting though difficult one. It was described by Mr. Lias as "the year of spade work and of pioneers, when the old school had but one storey, when the playground was open to the four winds of heaven and also the vulgar crowds of earth." By the second year there were twenty-seven new boys, of whom seven were boarders. The number of boys had become sixty-six, with an increase of forty-one since November 1902. They were now arriving from Cairo, Helwan, Abu Kebir, Kafr al-Zayyat, Desunis, Birkat al-Sab, Asyut, Fayoum, Mit Ghamr, and Mansura. Consequently, adjustments had to be made in the school to accommodate the rising numbers. A new story was added for dormitories (the contractors were again McClure and Dorling), and with the permission of the Municipality of Alexandria the playground was enclosed. When Lord Cromer visited in 1904 he commented that "the boys looked happy and the playground bare." In 1903 a fourth form was added, with the intention of adding a form a year to go up to Sixth Form.

Also, by the second year a kindergarten was built, although there was no certainty that it would open because even then the school was too full and the new classroom would be used to absorb the overflowing numbers. Already by 1904 Mr. Lias was lamenting that the obstacle to a kindergarten was the absence of an English school for girls. Parents would wish their little boys and girls to go to the same kindergarten, but it would be pointless to send girls to Victoria College if there was no English school for girls to go on to. In later years Mr. Reed, as headmaster, was occasionally to accept girls in kindergarten, and in 1933 he was writing that there were "twelve nice little girls in the Kindergarten, the nucleus, as I hope, of a Victoria College for girls." Zeinab Niazi (VC 1936) was one of those girls, and though she did not stay for long at Victoria College and is not therefore, strictly speaking, an Old Girl, she is one of the few instances of an Old Victorian getting married to another Old Victorian: Tarek Hassanein (VC 1938–45). Another of the little girls was Ayesha Osman (VC 1933), the daughter of Old Victorian Amin Pasha Osman (VC 1907–19).

From the 1920s on, Sir Henry Barker would campaign with the British community, with whom he had meetings in Victoria College, to raise funds for an English school for girls. It was not, however, until 1935 that the English Girls' College (EGC) opened. On its Speech Day of 25 June 1936 Sir Henry Barker announced that private subscriptions had amounted to £58,000 sterling in addition to £10,000 from the British government (whose position had become more supportive than in the days of Lord Cromer), a gift of eight acres of land, and the option of a further six from the Municipality of Alexandria. The EGC was consequently able to move into its beautiful buildings in Chatby after it had started out in the Villa Zervudachi in Ramleh in 1935. But Mr. Lias was not going to wait that long to start a kindergarten for boys at Victoria College: one did open in 1904 under his sister, Miss M.T. Lias. In July 1907 it comprised three classes and sixty-six boys.

The management of the school was entrusted to three bodies: the Trustees, who were His Britannic Majesty's Plenipotentiary and Agent General (from December 1914 High Commissioner, and from December 1936, Ambassador), the British Consul-General in Alexandria, and also the president of the British Chamber of Commerce; the General Committee; and the Executive Committee. These two last included British members and leading Alexandrian figures such as H. Barker, G.B. Alderson, H.P. Kingham, Jacques de Menasce, M.A. Ruffer, S.H. Carver, R.J. Moss, A. Ralli, J. Rolo, and Saba Pasha. One reason why the school progressed must have been that they gave the headmaster a free hand in establishing the traditions that were to distinguish it from other schools in Egypt.

Mr. Lias's most important achievement was to revolutionize the examination system. In its first two years the school assessed its boys by setting its own exams, during which Mr. Gould, Sir Charles Cookson's successor as British Consul-General in Alexandria, made a round of the school to make sure that the boys were not getting any assistance. But Mr. Lias was not satisfied with these conditions and realized that parents would want an accredited exam that would qualify their boys for universities abroad, since Egypt did not yet have education on the tertiary level; the Egyptian University did not open till 1908. The exam he chose for his school was the Oxford and Cambridge Joint Board Examination, which was a qualifying exam for English medical and engineering schools, as well as for Oxford and Cambridge, and which was not held in Egypt.[17] The reason for this choice was simple: it was the custom in English public schools, he said, "for the highest form to be examined by outside examiners." This was the exam that public school boys in England generally sat for. Mr. Lias therefore got Mr. Gould to negotiate for holding it at Victoria College. Arabic was included in the language group at Mr. Lias's recommendation to Lord Cromer, who persuaded Mr. Dunlop, Secretary-General to the Ministry of Education, to obtain the consent of the secretaries of the Oxford and Cambridge Board.

The first Joint Board exams were held in July 1906 for the fifth formers, who sat for the Lower Certificate. Mr. Lias described the decision to enter boys "for a difficult examination conducted in what is to most of them a foreign tongue," only five years after the establishment of the school, as an experiment "to be qualified as rash rather than bold." However, the experiment was a great success. Humphrey Bowman, Inspector of Egyptian Primary Schools and later Director of Education in Palestine, superintended the exams, and the results were printed in August. Out of sixteen candidates, ten were awarded certificates, a remarkable achievement, for out of a total of 1046 boys who sat for the exam, 570 passed. The certificates were presented in December 1906 by Mrs. Gould in the presence of parents, masters, and members of the General and Executive Committees. In 1910 they were presented by Sir Eldon Gorst, Lord Cromer's successor. This was the beginning of the ceremony that was to develop into the Speech Day pageant when successive High Commissioners, Prime and other Ministers, clergymen, and anybody who was anybody in Egypt met in Victoria College once a year to hear Anglo-Egyptian pronouncements from the platform. It was Mr. Lias who established this ritual, an account of which would be published in the newspapers the following day, complete with the speeches of the British Consul-General (or High Commissioner or Ambassador, depending on which period in Egyptian history it was), the Prime Minister, the headmaster, various dignitaries, and the names of the boys who had been awarded certificates and/or prizes. Mr. Lias certainly sought to promote his school by giving it status and color. A love of the flamboyant was inherent in his character: in 1909 he asked the Consul of Spain in Alexandria, Señor Vasquez, to come to the school and read the Spanish dictation for the Lower Certificate exam.

The results of the Lower Certificate of 1906 indicated something about life in Alexandria. The seven subjects taken were Greek, French,

English, Arabic, mathematics, English history and geography. Out of the sixteen candidates, fifteen sat for the French exam, of whom seven were placed in the first class and three in the second class. The report of the Secretaries of the Board of Examiners for the unprepared translation and dictation in French read: "the Translation was as a rule exceedingly good; M. Antonius and Valassopoulo deserve especial mention. There was a certain amount of very curious spelling, 'saggacity, orizontally, observating, shined, flied,' and a very strong flavor of French idiom in some of the renderings 'serve himself of them, redressed' etc.; but the work as a whole was extremely satisfactory." By contrast, out of the fifteen who sat for the English exam, only one was placed in the first class and five in the second. The masters who had come all the way from Cambridge must have done a relatively good job in preparing Alexandrian boys for the British examination, but obviously French was more of a mother tongue for them and it influenced their acquisition of the target language. For the next several years their performance in the French exam excelled that of the English exam. The following year, 1907, the same group sat again for the Lower Certificate to prepare themselves for the Higher Certificate. Out of twenty candidates, eleven obtained certificates (satisfactory results compared with the 463 certificates awarded out of a total of 1027 candidates). All twenty boys sat for the French, of whom sixteen were placed in the first class and two in the second. Once more the report of the Secretaries of the Board read, "the results showed a very creditable grasp of idiomatic French. With some of the sets of answers there was little or no fault to find. [In the unprepared translation] the English was generally satisfactory, though there were some renderings which showed that French was the more familiar language." In the English exam only five were placed in the first place and six in the second.

In 1908 the story was repeated. In English, the report for the paper on Chaucer's Prologue, the Prioress's Tale, and the Squire's Tale said that "the bulk of the boys evidently had difficulty with the language; and the literary style of their work was poor . . . With few exceptions the more literary answers were meagre and undiscerning and the spelling was often bad." On the other hand, the examiners thought that French seemed to be the boys' "native language," which, to a great extent, for many

CHAPTER 1

Alexandrians it was, regardless of whether they were Egyptians, Levantines, or foreigners residing in Egypt. But it also seems that M. Dumont was doing an excellent job, for the examiners commended the boys on their fluency and grasp of idiom—which they would have picked up from home and life in Alexandria in general—as well as on their grammar and dictation, which had to be learned at school and which, according to the examiner of 1908, was "far the best 'pile' I have ever looked over." M. Dumont's methods were conventional, for when Edward Atiyah (VC 1918–21) first joined the school, M. Dumont examined him and asked him to write a composition on the horse, then declared it to be *très faible*, leading the boy to complain to Mr. Reed of M. Dumont's "lack of imagination in the choice of composition subjects."[18] However, these conventional methods seemed to have worked wonders. Over the years English improved, but French continued to come more naturally to the boys and one of them even published an article in 1913 in *The Victorian*, the school magazine, in defense of French:

> Le Collège Victoria est essentiellement un collège anglais qui a pour but de suivre les traditions des écoles d'Angleterre. Comme ce collège est situé dans une ville cosmopolite, où l'on rencontre des gens de toutes les nationalités, il est bien naturel que plusieurs langues y soient parlées. Mais il est certain que l'influence française y joue un rôle important. Quelqu'un n'a-t-il pas observé avec justesse que toute personne bien elevée connait le français. C'est donc le français qui est le plus parlé au Collège Victoria.

By the 1940s the tide had turned and French ceased to be the *lingua franca* of Egypt in general and Alexandria in particular. An unnamed classmate of Antoine Bassili's (VC 1942–52), who served as an ambassador of Egypt, was asked by the French master to conjugate the verb *être malade*. The boy dutifully wrote: "je suis malade, tu es *ta*lade, il est *sa*lade." Nevertheless, most Victorians continued to speak French fluently. In 1996 Mr. Armand Kahil (VC 1941–45), Honorary Secretary of the Old Victorian Association from its founding in 1978 to 1998, complained that he was unable to communicate with the members of the Old EGC Association because they could not speak French!

Notwithstanding the inferiority of their English to their French, the first batch of Victorians did extremely well at their studies at school and later on at university. Of those who obtained their certificates between 1908 and 1910, one went to work in the Ministry of Finance in Cairo, a few went into business in Alexandria, and the majority went to universities abroad. M. Antonius (VC 1902–9) went to study law at Toulouse University; G. Antonius (VC 1902–10) was at King's College, Cambridge; G. Valassopoulo (VC 1902–8) studied at King's College, Cambridge, and later obtained a degree in law from Toulouse University; H. Mansour (1902–10) at Ecole de Commerce, Neuchâtel; A.F.S. Nimr (VC 1903–9) at Christ's College, Cambridge; M. Moursy (VC 1904–9) at Pembroke College, Cambridge; S. Naggiar (VC 1905–10) at Trinity College, Cambridge; A.S. Psaltis (1903–6) at the Agricultural School, Giza; A. Nahas (VC 1904–8) at Northwestern University, Chicago; E. Harle (VC 1902–9) at the University of Pennsylvania; and A.R. Hamada (1904–10) at the University of Birmingham. Two years later M. Abaza (VC 1904–12) went to study medicine at Edinburgh University. Of these boys Abdel Rahman Hamada was to become a captain of the textile industry in Egypt, and Mahmoud Abaza one of the most renowned doctors. Two other boys also deserve especial mention: Michael and George Antonius.

Michael was the very first name entered in the school ledger, followed by George and two other brothers. They were the sons of Habib Antonius, a Syrian landowner in Egypt. He must also have had a very adventurous spirit to be the first parent to enter all four of his sons into a school that had just started and to convince other parents to do the same. His sons, especially Michael and George, were a credit to him. Michael Antonius was probably one of the most brilliant scholars that ever went to Victoria College. He was among the first group of Victorians to sit for the Lower Certificate in 1906, when he gained three distinctions. The same group sat for the Lower Certificate again in 1907, and this time Michael gained distinctions in all the eight subjects he sat for. With G. Valassopoulo he was singled out by the examiners for special praise. He also obtained a first class in Testament history through his own effort at home, since the school provided religious instruction but did not prepare the boys for examinations. In a list of 1027 candidates for the Lower Certificate, his achievements were equaled by only one other boy. In 1909 he obtained the Higher Certificate with distinctions in three subjects, at the same time as he obtained the Secondary Certificate of the Egyptian government examination. In the Egyptian exam his place of merit was the sixteenth on the list, and he obtained full marks in Arabic, English and French in the oral part of the examination. He was also head boy. His distinguished career at school was, as Mr. Lias reported,

> followed by an equally distinguished career at Toulouse University, [and he] has returned for a fourth year to read for his *Doctorat*. At the end of his first year he gained a first class in all the six branches of the first year's law course, together with a first prize and an honourable mention for Essays on Law Subjects. At the public distribution of prizes, his good work won for him a special tribute from the Reporter M. César Bru, who expressed himself as "*Très content de décorer un étudiant étranger qui dans une langue, qui lui est étrangère, ne se laisse pas battre par des Français.*"

Michael did the two years' course for the *Doctorat* in one year, and obtained the degree in 1913. On his return to Alexandria, he taught Arabic translation at the school briefly, and started practice as an advocate, but what his career would have been like must remain in the realm of speculation, for his life was tragically cut short in 1920 when he was thirty years old.

His brother George Antonius was also a brilliant boy and succeeded Michael as head boy in the academic year 1909–10. He obtained his Higher Certificate in 1908 with a first class in two subjects and received special praise from the Board for his three English papers. Like Michael, in 1909 he gained the Secondary Certificate of the Egyptian government examination (Emile Cordahi also gained that Certificate with him, while Alexandre Ruppa chose to sit for the *Baccalauréat français* instead, making him the first boy at an English school to gain it). George Antonius proceeded to King's College, Cambridge, and in 1928 he married into a wealthy and intellectual family. Katy Nimr was the sister of his schoolfellow Albert Nimr (VC 1904–8 and Christ's College, Cambridge). Their father, Dr. Faris Nimr, was a Syrian who had taught at the Syrian Protestant College in Beirut (later the American University of Beirut) and had founded the scientific and cultural periodical *al-Muqtataf* in Beirut in 1876. He then came to Cairo in 1887 (according to his grandson and Old Victorian Stephen Nimr), where he continued publication of *al-Muqtataf* and established the daily paper *al-Muqattam* with two other Syrians, Yacub Sarruf and Shahin Makarius, in February 1889. *Al-Muqattam* called for cooperation with the British in Egypt, and both papers grew to be associated with foreign Christian interests.[19]

George Antonius was the first Victorian whose English education made him an anglophile in his career and a mediator between the Arabs and the British. In 1913 he was appointed to the Ministry of Public Works in Cairo. From 1921 to 1930 he held various posts in the civil service of the British Mandate Palestine Government, in the Education Department (under Mr. H.E. Bowman) and in the Secretariat of the British High Commissioner in Palestine. During that period he also went on British government missions to Abdel Aziz Ibn Saud in Arabia and to Imam Yehia of Yemen, in order to secure Arab recognition of the post-Ottoman boundaries between Arabia, Iraq, and Jordan that Britain required. The British government awarded George Antonius a CBE for his services. He continued to mediate between Arab Palestinians, notably the Mufti of Jerusalem, Haj Amin al Husseini, and British officials, and was the secretary of both the Palestinian and the Arab delegations at the London Conference of 1939.

Nevertheless, in his close dealings with the British Antonius grew disillusioned with their dishonest treatment of the Arabs, especially after the Arabs had revolted against the Turks and allied themselves with Britain during the First World War. In 1938 he published his *The Arab Awakening* (London, Hamish Hamilton), which remains the classic reference on Arab nationalism. It was a ground-breaking book in several ways. Antonius had, through personal relations, access to the private correspondence between al-Sharif Hussein of Mecca who, with his son Feisal, had led the Arab revolt, and Sir Henry MacMahon, High Commissioner of Egypt. Antonius published the correspondence, there-

Chapter 1

by revealing for the first time the treachery of the British and the emptiness of their promises of liberty to the Arabs. In no uncertain terms he denounced this treachery and the dishonorable methods of the British, describing all their subsequent dealings, including the Sykes–Picot agreement (1916) and the Conference of San Remo (1922) as a breach of faith that could be explained only in terms of Western greed. In the West's support of Zionism at the expense of the Palestinians he reveals Western ethics to be hollow and deceptive. Without mincing his words, he targets Britain in particular as the perpetuator of an evil that, if not satisfactorily resolved, is likely to escalate in the future. Once more, he sees that Britain's claims to be a civilizing influence are nothing more than a cover for greed and double standards:

> The relief of Jewish distress caused by European persecution must be sought for elsewhere than in Palestine, for the country is too small to hold a larger increase of population, and it has already borne more than its fair share. It is for Great Britain who has taken the lead in this work of charity at Arab expense to turn to the vast resources of her empire and to practise there some of the charity it has been preaching. It is also for the other countries that pride themselves on being civilised and humane to revise the niggardly decisions of the Evian Conference and consent to some of the sacrifices which Arab Palestine has been bullied into making on a scale that has taxed her capacity. The treatment meted out to Jews in Germany and other European countries is a disgrace to its authors and to modern civilisation; but posterity will not exonerate any country that fails to bear its proper share of the sacrifices needed to alleviate Jewish suffering and distress. To place the brunt of the burden upon Arab Palestine is a miserable evasion of the duty that lies upon the whole of the civilised world. It is also morally outrageous. No code of morals can justify the persecution of one people in an attempt to relieve the persecution of another. The cure for the eviction of Jews

from Germany is not to be sought in the eviction of the Arabs from their homeland; and the relief of Jewish distress may not be accomplished at the cost of inflicting a corresponding distress upon an innocent and peaceful population . . . The logic of facts is inexorable. It shows that no room can be made in Palestine for a second nation except by dislodging or exterminating the nation in possession.[20]

But the book was also ground-breaking in an entirely different way. It is the first account of Arab nationalism written by an Arab from the Arab point of view in English, that is, in the language of the colonizer addressed to the colonizer. According to Edward Said, himself an Old Victorian, current postcolonial scholarship is "unthinkable without the earlier work of partisans" like Antonius. In this respect it is a landmark among the very early

> work of intellectuals from the colonial or peripheral regions who wrote in an 'imperial' language, and who set themselves the revisionist, critical task of dealing frontally with the metropolitan culture, using the techniques, discourses, and weapons of scholarship and criticism once reserved exclusively for the Europeans. Their work is, on its merits, only apparently dependent (and by no means parasitic) on mainstream Western discourses; the result of its originality and creativity has been the transformation of the very terrain of disciplines.[21]

Regardless of their political roles, it was obvious that Victoria College was turning out a fine batch of boys, even among those who had thrown in their luck with the school when it first opened in 1902 and had had no past or guarantee to recommend it save the good faith of its founders. By 1904 a library had been started with gifts of money from Mr. Alderson, the National Bank of Egypt, and others and a lending library was formed of 200 volumes. And by 1906 the school was divided into three parts: the Upper School (Form V), the Lower School

Chapter 1

(Forms IV, IIIa, IIIb, II), and the Preparatory School (Divisions 1 and 2). Already the numbers had grown to such an extent that they could no longer be contained in the buildings, and it was decided that larger premises were needed. As usual, the obstacle was funds, and as usual Mr. Alderson stepped in to solve the problem.

He purchased the old site for LE 100,000, and with this sum a new site of about eighteen feddans (approximately eighteen acres) was purchased in Domaine de Siouf. Mr. Lias remarked that "at first sight it may appear that to remove a school not yet four years old from a central position to a distant suburb . . . [is an experiment] qualified as rash rather than bold." These were the identical words he used in the same year to describe the decision to enter Victorians for the Joint Board Examination, and he had the same reason to justify his decision: it was in keeping with the intention to run Victoria College along the lines of an English public school, and so the "Committee resolved to remove the school to a site even more spacious than that which it now occupies, and to give it by the construction of dormitories and masters' houses the normal features of an English boarding school."

Indeed, Mr. Lias was right in describing Domaine de Siouf as "a distant suburb" in 1906. The name Siouf is the plural of the Arabic word *seif* meaning "sword," and refers to an Alexandrian family whose members were so many and so united that the area was named after them. The boundaries of the town of Alexandria ended with Kom el Dikka, and anything beyond was described as "outside Alexandria" or "near Alexandria." In 1900 the Reverend A. Boddy, Chaplain of All Saints' Church, published *From the Egyptian Ramleh*, in which he talks of the Arab villages of Chatby and Bacos. From Sidi Gaber to Montazah stretched the sand dunes that gave that eastern part of Alexandria the name Ramleh (which means "sand" in Arabic). The sand dunes were interspersed with palm groves, Bedouin tents, and the villas of wealthy families. From Bulkeley to Siouf the two main buildings were the Hotel and Casino San Stefano in San Stefano, and the palace of the khedivial mother in Palais, which still retains this name, though it is now in Arabic: El Saraya. In *Ramleh: Als Winteraufenthalt*, also published in 1900, the Archduke of Austria, Erherzog Ludwig Salvator, describes the few other houses of Benaki, Baron de Menasce, Peitretline, and the Hermitage of

Monsieur Laurens, the cigarette factory owner, whose name is still that by which the area is known. Of Siouf in particular, the Archduke stresses its dreamy, picturesque quality. He is enchanted by the Bedouins, goats, and camels that criss-crossed the sand and the feluccas that bobbed on the sea. The Bedouins and palms made him describe Siouf as an oasis. Thus, to Mr. Lias and Alexandrian parents, the removal of the school to Siouf was nothing short of marooning it in the desert.

The laying of the foundation stone of the new buildings in 1906 was an event that caused a far greater furor than had the laying of the foundation stone of the Mazarita buildings in 1901. In the five years that had elapsed, Victoria College had demonstrated that its tenacious grip on life was not simply going to make it survive but would propel it forward. Its boys had not yet gone out into the world to prove their mettle, but the very fact that their numbers were quadrupling was ample testimony to the success of the school. With Mr. Lias's flair and the backing of the whole British presence in Egypt, the laying of the foundation stone on 24 May 1906 turned into a gala affair that "drew a large and representative gathering to Siouf" as the *Egyptian Gazette* reported the following morning. Speeches were given by Mr. Gould, Baron Jacques de Menasce (in French), Sheikh Mohamed Hamid (in Arabic), Mr. A.S. Preston, Mr. Lias, and Lord Cromer. (Lord Cromer's speech appears as Appendix C.) A scroll was signed by Lord and Lady Cromer, and was then laid in the cavity of a stone by Lady Cromer, this marking the conclusion of the ceremony. The school was scheduled to open in 1907, but was delayed for a whole year when, in the process of construction, the tower collapsed. It was opened informally on 15 October 1908,[22] but 27 March 1909 was cause for more celebrations. The school was officially inaugurated by HRH the Duke of Connaught (the third son of Queen Victoria). He was accompanied by the Duchess of Connaught and their daughter, Princess Patricia, and was received at the school by a Guard of Honor of the 4th Battalion Rifle Brigade. After little Janie Preston (daughter of Mr. Preston) had presented bouquets to the Duchess and Princess Patricia, Mr. Gould gave an address of welcome, and the Duke made a soldierlike speech to the boys before presenting them with their certificates. Among them were the head boy, Michael Antonius, and the Cromer Scholar, Emile Cordahi. The Duke then handed Mr. Alderson an address listing the numerous benefactions he, Alderson, had conferred upon the school. The Duke also inspected the buildings, congratulated the matrons, Miss Smith and Miss Grant, on the dormitories; and finally the masters and the architect, Mr. Henri Gorra, were presented to him. Tea was served under the Arches, and the visit commemorated on a marble tablet on which the royal visitors traced their names.

Despite the flamboyance with which the move from Mazarita to Siouf was made, the school suffered at first. Mr. Lias said in his Annual Report of 1908–9:

> To move from Alexandria to Siûf does not seem at first a serious affair, but the habits of the country must be taken into account, and at Alexandria, for schoolboys, seven miles out of town is a long journey. In any case transplanting is a painful process and it is inevitably followed by a setback. Victoria College did not escape the common lot. The number of boys fell. For a moment, undoubtedly, the school suffered from the shock... The School had been transplanted, but it is the same school; a school tradition is taking shape; its pupils, as they go out into the world, find they owe something to the lessons they have learnt.

One problem, that of transportation, was solved by courtesy of the directors of the Ramleh Railway Company. A special tram service was extended, with a new station (called Victoria) at the school doors, and school hours were accordingly fixed, as the old timetable had been, from eight in the morning till four in the afternoon. Until well into the 1960s the tram ride to and from the school was the highlight of the boys' day. Those who cycled to Siouf missed out on some of the fun, and those who were chauffeur-driven were desolate.

In the 1908–9 report, Mr. Lias mentioned something which was to sustain the school through all its vicissitudes and acquire for it the reputation that it had lost no time in building up: a tradition. What exactly was the tradition at Victoria College? The founders had laid down that it must follow the lines of English public schools, which led Mr. Lias to ask what it was that made one school a public school, but not another. "It is not enough," he said in 1904, "to build a schoolhouse, surround it with a playground, appoint a headmaster and announce to the world 'Here is your public school.'" It must have a spirit that has been tried and tested by time, but it must also be capable of adapting to the changing times. That spirit was a combination of an *esprit de corps* and individual responsibility. These were the ideals that Dr. Thomas Arnold, the father of the public school system, had initiated at Rugby, the school of which he had been headmaster. Then there was the question of recreation:

> What of those necessary hours when the boys or girls are resting or at play? For repose and recreation are now universally recognised as even more indispensable to the young than to the old. It is known to be as unwise as it is cruel to chain the children to the desk all day and—still worse—to burden them with endless tasks at night. The question therefore arises, how are the children to be controlled during these invaluable hours of recreation and repose. The choice lies between two systems; there is the French system of *surveillance* and *espionage*; and there is the English system in which the boys . . . are left in some measure to control themselves. What boys do when left to their own devices is better imagined than described.

Dr. Arnold had modified the fagging system and removed its worst abuses, so that the house and monitorial system he implemented at Rugby, and which spread to the other public schools, served to imbue boys with a sense of responsibility rather than tyranny. He had desired to make each house "as it were an epitome of the whole school." Mr. Lias wanted to make each house "an epitome of the home." As he saw it, the public school system

> has been modified in the past and may be modified again, that it is or may be a compromise between the school and the home, that the secret of its strength lies in

Chapter 1

the sense of individual responsibility animating the members of the corporate body, that this spirit has been partly cultivated among the boys themselves, partly through the influence of masters, and finally that this influence may perhaps best be exercised by men who deserve some material reward for work which it is at once difficult and honourable to perform.

Thus, what Mr. Lias wanted for Victoria College was a communal spirit, to be achieved through games and Houses; individual responsibility, to be attained by means of monitors, prefects, and captains; and honorable wages for his masters, some of whom would also be housemasters and form the characters of the boys. Although Englishmen believed that public schools were indigenous to the English climate and could not survive on foreign soil—G.M. Trevelyan, the famous British historian, asserted that it was impossible to imitate either the English parliament or the English public school system overseas—Mr. Lias was confident that with patience and dedication the experiment could succeed. However, he had a problem that was not found in public schools in the England of the nineteenth century. There, the boys were more or less a homogenous group: mainly the sons of upper- or upper-middle-class Protestant English parents. Mr. Lias had a much more heterogeneous lot in Alexandria. The boys came from the four corners of Egypt and the world, and could be anything from Muslims and Jews to Anglicans, Protestants, Presbyterians, Catholics, Copts, or Orthodox Christians. Besides, his school was, when all was said and done, a foreign presence in an occupied land, and it ran the risk of being looked upon as an embodiment of imperial power by the boys themselves or by the Egyptian population. He therefore had to neutralize feelings among the boys inside the school walls. In addition, he had his own philosophy to impress on the boys: "If School boys are to be taught the lessons of life, not only must heads be trained to think, but also hearts to feel." His achievement was to combine what was best in the English public school system with the flavor of the east, which was also heavily cosmopolitan in Alexandria, to produce a unique school. By 1929 its character and success had become so clear that Sir Percy Lorraine, the High Commissioner, was to say on Speech Day:

> This College is an example of a bold experiment. I think I may safely say so, as you educate boys of twenty-two different nationalities under the same roof and with the same teaching staff. It is a brilliant success which has now been universally recognised and respected by all countries, as well as by all those who have been educated in the School and by those who have sent their children to the College to be educated.

Even earlier, in 1914, Lord Meath had paid the school a visit and had said, "the great traditions of Eton were built upon the training of character. Victoria College was the Eton of Egypt." Later, it became known as "the Eton of the Middle East."

Mr. Lias's method of unifying his boys was to implement the House system and games. At the insistence of the founders of the school, games in Victoria College were regarded as important as studies. Mr. Lias himself was in favor of recreation, sports, and drills. In 1904 he was already promoting outdoor activities, and remarked, "It has been said of the Japanese soldier, that when he is not energetically and cheerfully at work, he is energetically and cheerfully at play." This was an ideal he encouraged in the form of drills supervised by two masters and two of the senior boys, Themistocles Checri and Auguste Verni, "who developed into two smart corporals." Games, "that important department of a boy's life," Mr. Lias said in the same year, "have grown into a serious institution. Hockey found its proper place in the season which intervenes between football and cricket, though these two games, as in England, had the larger number of partisans."

Since the old buildings in Mazarita did not have cricket grounds, the Alexandria Cricket Club allowed Victorians to use their ground once a fortnight. In 1904 Mr. P.W. Carver, a member of the Alexandria Cricket Club, donated LE 20 to the school to be used for games: this sum was spent on two asphalt pitches. Football was played more frequently. In the football season of 1909–10 the school played eighteen matches, as opposed to nine cricket matches. In addition to local teams, such as Red Star, St. Andrews, Boys Scouts, Band Boys, "S.Y. Dorothy," Collège St. François Xavier, Mr. Shimmin's XI, Sporting Club, Egyptian Athletic

Club, and Eastern Telegraph Co., there were visitors to Alexandria that the Victorians lost no chance of confronting on the field, such as the cadets of HMS Cumberland. By 1914 there were also boxing lessons, given by Mr. Tookey; fencing, taught by Signor Prucher and riding, by Mr. J. Rowden.

However, it was football, rather than riding or fencing, that fostered the corporate spirit. On the football pitch, the boys had one sole allegiance, regardless of creed or nationality, and that was to the VC badge emblazoned so proudly on their shirts or jackets. In his *An Arab Tells His Story*, Edward Atiyah records how, as a Christian Syrian coming from Sudan, he was full of misgivings about Egyptian Muslims and was taken aback to see some *tarbouches* in Victoria College, rather than boys who looked more English. He was even more surprised to find that the head boy and captain of the First XI was a dark Egyptian Muslim: Amin Osman. The day Victoria College was to play against the Jesuits, their sworn enemies on the Jesuits' ground, the whole school turned out to watch the match and cheer the Victorians; even M. Dumont came along to support his boys; he, "as French master, had special reasons for hating the Jesuits, who were competing with him in teaching Egypt French. Loyalty to the school, therefore, reinforced by professional jealousy, made of him on these occasions a very bellicose spectator."[23] Mr. Lias promised the school a half-holiday if the team scored five goals. When Amin Osman led the Victorian team to victory, the conversion of Edward Atiyah was made complete: "Under the unifying roof of a common school, the Muslim Egyptian, Amin Osman, was dearer to me than all the Syrian Christians of the world."[24]

The House system was started very early in the life of the school: the first mention of it is in 1906, when Mr. Lias refers to Mr. Morrison (1903–10) as having been housemaster for three years at the Boulevard de Ramleh, when the school was still in Mazarita, and for two more years at the new Victoria College site in Siouf, where the resident masters had flats. Mr. Morrison was helped by his sister, for each house had to have a woman to supervise the cleaners and look after the domestic responsibilities of the house. A glimpse of what bedtime was like from the housemaster's point of view can be obtained from the following article in *The Victorian* written in 1914 by Mr. Reed (VC 1911–45). His description is typical of what took place in the dormitories of the new buildings in Siouf just before the lights were turned out:

> Bed time! The story-teller gets up and his satellites scatter, each to his appointed place in the long room; the owner of the tennis-ball dives under a bed to reclaim his strayed treasure; stamps, pressed flowers and all the motley collection, from cartridge-cases to gee-gaws are stuffed into bottomless bags. The master walks down the room. Has this one cleaned his teeth or that one washed his feet? May this boy in the salmon-coloured pyjamas get up early—he has four exams tomorrow? But did he not get up yesterday to work and was he not seen at half past six playing pelota? A wandering locust is hustled out of the window and kneeling figures rise from their prayers to bury themselves under white sheets or gaily-covered bed-covers. The scent of the breezes steals through the open windows; along the Genaclis Road the frogs croak in stertorous antiphone and the crickets chirp a broken chorus. The lights of Bedouin tents stand out like Jack o' Lanthorns against the dark palm-grove behind. Lights out! F. has donned his black night-cap, and Z. has hung up the alarm-clock on the hook. Silence reigns, and the master paces down the darkened room. Well for him if his pupils have opened his heart to the touch of nature and if he can lay down his head with thoughts as free as theirs.

Mr. Lias's wish that the masters' salaries would increase was a difficult one to fulfill. The school suffered from continuous financial difficulties and it was only by the skin of its teeth that it avoided closing down. Unlike most other schools in Egypt, it was neither subsidized nor endowed. In order to stay open, its fees were higher than those of any other school in Egypt. In its early years Victoria College had to rely entirely on donations for any extra necessities. The library continued to be stocked by gifts and donations of sums like LE 10, even from the boys themselves: Maurice Klat, the Cromer Scholar for 1910, gave the moneys of this scholarship to the Library, which bought the *Encyclopaedia Britannica*. The publisher John Murray donated thirteen books. When the school moved to its new buildings, it was Dr. Ruffer who gave the generous gift of the physics and chemistry classes and equipment, and thus natural science became part of the curriculum. The move itself from Mazarita to Siouf was a shock: the numbers of boys dropped, the school fell heavily in debt, and a collapse seemed imminent. In 1920 Mr. Lias published *A Short Account of Victoria College Alexandria: From its Foundation to 1919* with the intention of raising the interest of the friends of the school to fund and endow it. His argument was persuasive:

> The English Public Schools are endowed. The founders of Victoria College laid down that it was to be a Public School. The masters and the boys have done what they could to carry out the intentions of the founders. May they not hope that in a country as prosperous as Egypt, in a town so wealthy as Alexandria, the time has come for them to be given the endowment for which they have looked for so long?

In the same year Lord Allenby, the High Commissioner, issued an appeal for funds to constitute an Endowment Fund. It was hoped that the sum of LE 120,000 would be raised, but the fund reached only LE 41,000. Another source of help was Alfred Viscount Milner, British Secretary of State for the Colonies. On his visit to Egypt after the First World War to investigate the causes of discontent in the country and the demands of the Wafd, he was boycotted by the Egyptians, who wanted to make their point that all dealings had to be made with Zaghloul Pasha, the representative of the Egyptian nation. However, Mr. Lias had other problems on his mind. He wanted money for his school, and so Lord Milner was graciously received at Victoria College. Mr. Lias arranged with two boys, Edward Atiyah and Zahir Sharara, to present Lord Milner with a play they had written, *A Tragedy in Three Acts*, about William Wallace and Edward I of England. The subject itself was an unhappy choice, since it dealt with the Scottish rebellion against English tyranny and occupation, and Lord Milner would not fail to draw a comparison between William Wallace and Saad Pasha Zaghloul. However, Mr. Lias assured Lord Milner that this had not been the intention of the boys, and to further encourage the campaign for funds, four Old Boys—G. Antonius, G. Valassopoulo, A. Nahas, and S. Naggiar—appealed to Lord Milner in a Note which enumerated the merits of Victoria College and the need to have it properly funded (See Appendix E for the Note).

As Chairman of the Rhodes Fund, Lord Milner granted the school a fund of £30,000. These sums at least freed the school from its immediate financial worries, though it was never entirely relieved of them. In 1934 Sir Henry Barker, Chairman of the College Council, said at a Victoria College dinner: "On one occasion I told a friend of mine that I was somewhat worried about the finances of the School, he advised me to pass my job on to some one else, I mildly suggested that it was not easy to do so and that I looked on it as one of the crosses I had to bear. He replied 'Well console yourself it is the Victoria Cross.'"

In order to cope with the multi-ethnicity of his school, Mr. Lias chose as the motto of Victoria College a quotation from Claudian, himself an Alexandrian poet (born circa 370 in Alexandria, died circa 404 in Rome): *Cuncti gens una sumus*, meaning "We are all one people." The motto was approved by the School Committee, and under the influence of Mr. Lias, the housemasters, the sportsfield, and the monitorial system, the boys treated each other as equals and with respect. An Old Boy who signed his article as E.A. in *The Victorian* of 1930 wrote of the application of the motto:

> This is what every boy and every Old Boy feels, that we all belong to the same race, that the only real and natural ties among men are the ties of human fellowship, without distinction of nationality, colour or creed. The great, the unique achievement of Victoria College, placed as it is in a cosmopolitan centre like Alexandria, is to have created for its boys an atmosphere so pure and healthy, so deeply and essentially human, that no germs of national or religious animosity can exist, far less thrive, in it. Nothing gives me a greater pleasure, both as an Old Boy of the School and as one who cherishes the

CHAPTER 1

ideal of human fellowship, than to see a gathering of Old Boys representing some 7 or 8 nationalities and several creeds, brought together by the mutual ties of sincere friendship, the ties that transcend every artificial barrier set up by blind prejudice, fanaticism, snobbery and exclusiveness. I venture to say that in this respect Victoria College is doing greater and nobler work than any other school in the world. In its own way, and within the limits of its purpose, it is furthering the cause upheld by the League of Nations, and preached by all the great idealists of history.

Nevertheless, the ideals of Victoria College could not stand in the face of war when it broke out. The Balkan wars, which took place in 1912–13 between the Balkan alliance and Greece on the one hand, and the Ottomans on the other, was the first time in the College's history that Victorians found themselves arrayed against each other. The Greek Victorians naturally sided with Greece, while other Victorians allied themselves with the Turks. G. Valassopoulo (VC 1902–6) went to the front to work as secretary to the Greek Red Cross Society. Another Greek, A.G. Psaltis (VC 1903–6), who was a good footballer, was wounded at the front. An Egyptian, Ibrahim el Masry (VC 1904–11),[25] was also wounded at the front—only he was fighting on the side of the Turks against the Greeks and Bulgarians.

The year 1912, however, was a fruitful year for Victoria College, despite the casualties of its Old Boys at the front. In 1911 Mr. Ralph Reed, who had in the same year graduated from Wadham College, Oxford, joined the staff. In 1912 he started *The Victorian*, the school magazine. Its first issue appeared in December 1912, with Mr. Reed as editor, and there were to be three issues a year—once every term. The price was three piastres, and the annual subscription was twelve piastres, post free to any part of the world. The publishers were Whitehead and Morris, the same house that published E.M. Forster's *Alexandria: A History and a Guide,* as well as *Pharos and Pharillon.* In addition to providing both the school and the Old Boys with a voice and a means of exchanging news, *The Victorian* contributed to the promotion of trade in Alexandria. An advertisement was placed in it by Davies Bryan and Co., English tailors and outfitters in Cairo, Alexandria, and Khartoum. They sold school uniforms and advertised their "Splendid Selection of Boys' Norfolk Tunic and Sailor Suits in all Sizes and Qualities. Also extra Navy Blue Knickers, Jerseys and Jersey Suits." Tailoring was in British material only. In addition they had towels and linen, and boots and shoes of "English shapes from P.T. 60 a pair." On the opposite page, Robert, Hughes and Co. advertised their "Sporting Goods." By the 1930s, it was Dessberg (whose boys were in the school) in Place Muhammad Ali (later Manshieh Square) that was the major supplier of Victoria College uniforms. In 1929 the editor, Mr. Reed, relinquished his post and decided that one of the boys should be editor and should be assisted by an editorial committee. This, he said, was an indication that the school was growing up and "seeking to express itself, and learning the lessons of self-government."

On 15 May 1912 yet another Victorian tradition was established. A general meeting of Old Victorians was held in the masters' common room at Victoria College. They discussed and approved the formation of a club for Old Victorians, and chose J.D. Barda as honorary secretary and *Alma matris alumni fideles* as motto. Within six months the number of members rose from thirty-three to sixty-one; they held two club days, gave two concerts, played a match on the school Sports Day, and joined in ten cricket matches. They had their first annual dinner in the College dining hall on 27 July 1912, and the organizers, having learned from Mr. Lias to do everything in style, spared no effort to make the dinner a success. In addition to some forty Old Boys, the guests included two members of the Executive Committee, Mr. Preston and Dr. Ruffer. When Mr. Lias stood up to toast the Old Boys, he said, "The most exacting gourmet could not fail to appreciate the skill and artistry of Mr. Karam's chef, kindly lent for the evening; while Bushra Bey Hanna's head waiter added dignity to the occasion." Bushra Bey Hanna was a notable of Asyut who had chaired the General Congress of Copts in Asyut in 1910; his two sons, Willie (VC 1904–11) and Charles (VC 1905–12), both proceeded to Trinity College, Cambridge. George Karam must have had one of the best chefs in Alexandria, for he was one of its wealthiest men. He was originally Syrian and with his two brothers had founded a timber busi-

Chapter 1

ness in Alexandria in 1848. He was president of the Syrian-Greek Orthodox community in Alexandria, and a member of the Board of the Alexandria Water Co., the Comité de Santé et d'Hygiène Publique, the Société d'Enterprises Urbains et Rurales, and the Société de la Bourse Khédiévale d'Alexandrie. The Karams were among the early parents to send their boys to Victoria College; other timber merchants who followed suit were the Stagnis and the Bassilis.

Like Speech Days, Old Victorian annual dinners were to become grand affairs in the future, when the Old Boys became kings and regents, distinguished members of society, had international political, academic, professional, and financial renown, and rubbed shoulders with the prime ministers and ministers who were invited. A dinner in the school's Birley Hall was given in 1938 in honor of Old Victorian Amin Pasha Osman, KBE, Under-Secretary of State to the Minister of Finance, to celebrate the knighthood conferred upon him by King George V. Another dinner was given in his honor in 1943 to celebrate his appointment to the post of Minister of Finance. The British Ambassador, Sir Miles Lampson, who had been elevated to the peerage as Lord Killearn, attended this dinner. In December 1942 a Cairo Old Victorian dinner was held for Old Victorian Emir Abdulillah, Regent of Iraq, who was then visiting Egypt. Among the guests were Lord Killearn; the Egyptian Prime Minister, Mustapha Pasha el Nahas; and the Iraqi Prime Minister, Nuri Pasha el Said.

The Old Boys' Club acquired its own premises in 1913 at 6 Rue Istanbul in Alexandria and by 1929 it had moved to 9 Rue Cherif Pasha. A club was opened in Cairo in 1929, and for that purpose rooms were taken on the first floor of the Savoy Chambers and were furnished by generous donations from Old Boys. Later the club moved to Adly Pasha Street and was burned in the Cairo fire of 1952. The Alexandria club also eventually moved to Mazarita during the Second World War and into a building across the street from the then British Consulate.

For the boys still at school, entertainment was provided, too. Invitations were extended to scholars, either resident in Alexandria or passing through or visiting, to deliver lectures at the school and expose the boys to diverse topics. Harry St. John Philby, the famous British explorer and Arabist who became adviser to King Abdel Aziz Ibn Saud of Saudi Arabia, and was resident British Representative in Transjordan

(1922–24), visited the school to talk about the Empty Quarter in 1933.

The nucleus of the Victoria College Scouts, a proud band of a dozen boys, was also formed in 1912 under Mr. D.E. Preece and Mr. Housden—according to Malek Hanna Ebeid (VC 1911–19), the first troop in Egypt. The establishment of the Boy Scouts so early in Victoria College is another controversial issue. Lord Baden-Powell, founder and Chief Scout, launched the Scout movement between 1907 and 1908. There is no apparent evil in a boyish pleasure in games, but at the same time there is no contradiction between it and "the overall political purpose of British control over India and Britain's other overseas dominions."[26] Lord Baden-Powell was a contemporary of Kipling and influenced by his books; Kipling's "ideas about 'boyology' fed those images directly into a grand scheme of imperial authority culminating in the great Boy Scout structure,"[27] which combined service with fun and churned out servants of the empire. Whether or not Mr. Lias was aware of the imperial side-product of the Boy Scouts, the fact remains that it was another pioneering venture undertaken by Victoria College and eventually spread to all the schools of the country.

The warlike forays of the Scouts turned into reality when the First World War broke out in 1914. Egypt was declared a protectorate and Lord Kitchener, the British Agent and Consul-General, became Minister of War in England. His successor was Sir Henry MacMahon, and under the new protectorate the title British Agent was changed to High Commissioner. Victoria College was opened by Mr. Reed on 14 October 1914; Mr. Lias and six members of staff arrived from England a week later. In February 1915 Sir Henry MacMahon visited the school, and in March it was partially occupied by the French expeditionary force. In April 1915 the whole school was requisitioned for the 17th General Hospital and a return was made to the old buildings in Mazarita, which had housed the Lycée Français (founded in 1909 and described by Mr. Lias in 1912 as "our young and lusty rival") until it moved to its current buildings in Chatby. Though some of the staff were lost to marriage, more numbers were lost to the war. British masters and boys volunteered, while Egyptians were called to military service. In his recollections of the war years, written for Mr. Douglas Haydon's proposed history of the school in 1976, Malek Hanna had the following to say:

Chapter 1

[In 1914–15] it was impossible to replace these good teachers. C.E. Winn, scholar of Trinity, Cambridge, and a double-first in Maths joined the staff—but he was hopeless with discipline and a bad teacher—a poor substitute for Page. Shiber, a Palestinian from Jerusalem, and a graduate in architecture from London, taught Junior Maths. Miss Burgess, a graduate from Manchester University, taught Junior English. Hart, a local Maltese, was supposed to teach Junior French and French Translation, but spent most of his time amusing his classes by telling jokes. Because of the lack of staff, facilities or equipment, some subjects had to be dropped. For a few years no science was taught until Lias recruited a Coptic teacher, Habib Iskander, from the Morcossia Schools, and we had to use the Labs of that school. Art was dropped because there was no art teacher or art room. Extra-curricular activities suffered most—boxing, fencing, scouting and riding were abandoned completely, and as we had no games-master, no coaching in soccer or cricket was provided. The annual Sports Day with its array of athletic activities had to be abandoned for reasons of economy and lack of facilities. I don't want to leave you with the impression that the war years were sterile, but rather to stress the difficulties that Lias and Reed had to face. That they succeeded in keeping the school operating in the face of these great odds is testimony to their ability as educators and pioneers. On the credit side, the war years saw the birth of the Prefect system, the Debating Society, the School Journal and for the first time the Captain of games chose the members of his team as well as led them on the field. As the school building was too small to house all the boarders, a flat was rented. It was on the top (5th) floor of a building overlooking the tram station, the govt. hospital and the school. This became Reed's House and he was aided by Winn, Bolton and Treen (the carpenter). Mrs. Bolton became the Matron and supervised the cleaning staff. In the school building there were two other dormitories—one for juniors and the other for seniors. This was Lias's House and he was assisted by Shiber and Miss Burgess. Mrs. Lias took over as Matron.

Edward Atiyah had a sunnier tale to tell of the war years at Victoria College. He came from a Christian Syrian family that was living in Omdurman. Sudan had been occupied by Britain in 1896 after the Mahdi Revolt had been quelled, and although the Anglo-Egyptian Condominium of 1899 allowed Egypt and Britain to rule Sudan jointly, in reality it was Britain that ruled. Many Christian Syrians worked under the British administration in Khartoum and Omdurman but, rather than send their children to be educated in Beirut, especially when the war broke out, they chose Victoria College. One of these Syrians was Kfoury, who was a friend of Edward's father and whose boys were at Victoria College. He showed Edward a prospectus of the school. On seeing the photograph of Mr. Reed and reading his name, Edward felt that he and Mr. Reed would like each other. When he did arrive at the school, it was lodged in its old buildings in Mazarita, and all he heard from the boys was praise for the school's own buildings and the expectation of returning there when the war was over. Intimidated though he was at first by the multi-ethnicity of the boys, especially by the Muslims and Egyptians, he soon grew to make friends with them all, to forsake the prejudices that the outside world had imposed upon him before his arrival, and to glory in the fact that the prevailing atmosphere was one of equality and friendship. As mentioned, two factors helped to create this atmosphere. The first was the influence of games and the consequent loyalty of the boys to the VC badge, which they placed above loyalty to nationality or creed. The second was the House system. Edward was in Reed House in the flats rented next to the school, and with him were two Copts from Upper Egypt, Kfoury and a Maltese. At bedtime Mr. Reed would make his rounds of the dormitories, and the boys would crowd round him, delighting in telling him stories, but even more fascinated to listen to him as he talked about Oxford in particular. Mr. Lias, being a Cantabrigian, had recruited masters from Cambridge, and most

Chapter 1

of the very early Old Victorians had gone on to Cambridge. When he became headmaster in 1922, Mr. Reed, an Oxonian, tended to hire masters from Oxford. However, his influence on the boys began earlier than that, when he was still housemaster. All his talk of Oxford dazzled the boys, and more of them started going there rather than to Cambridge. Among the early ones were Amin Osman, Malek Hanna, and Edward Atiyah. Edward's premonition, while he was still in Omdurman, that he and Mr. Reed would like each other turned out to be true. Since Edward's father could not afford to send him to Oxford, and since both Edward and Mr. Reed wanted that very much, Mr. Reed managed to get a scholarship for Edward from an Old Victorian for £150 a year for three years. He also secured a recommendation letter from Lord Allenby, the High Commissioner, and got Amin Osman to use his influence at Brasenose College where he was already studying. As a result, Edward did make it to Oxford.

Mr. Reed's influence on these two boys was profound. Both remained in touch with him throughout their lives. Both were anglophiles. During his school years Edward Atiyah allowed his character to be formed entirely by Mr. Reed and even his political sympathies were determined by Mr. Reed's opinions. When the Egyptian nation rose against the British in 1919, the boarders had to wait every morning for the day boys to bring them news of what was happening in the outside world, but the school itself took no sides nor did its boys get involved in any way with the revolution. It was only when Mr. Reed, who was antirevolutionary and politically conservative, showed his disapproval of the revolution that Edward, too, condemned it. His allegiance during his school years was to Mr. Reed and therefore to Britain.

Amin Osman was a good scholar like Michael Antonius, and like him, too, was head boy. In *The Victorian*, all his articles were descriptions of England: the snow, English high teas, green pastures, and the like, showing his fascination with the country that was forming his mind and imagination, but that he had not seen yet. He became an influential politician and one of the architects of the Anglo-Egyptian treaty of 1936, for which he was knighted by King George V. Before the treaty was signed, Amin Osman was to deny that an education at Victoria College detracted from a boy's love for his motherland. At an Old Victorian dinner in Zagazig in 1933, he said that the two main aims of Victoria College were "character building and the teaching of true patriotism. It had been said that those who went to Victoria College were taught to love England. It was true that Old Victorians came to love England, because they came in contact with all that was best in the English, but they did not love their own country any the less for that. You could not be a true Victorian without being a true patriot." Nevertheless, his connection with the British led to his assassination in 1946.

An even more ironic situation involving Egyptian nationalism and the British occupation had to do with the national hero Mahmoud Sami al-Baroudi. Prime Minister of Egypt in the critical year of 1882, he and Urabi Pasha, Minister of War, were exiled by the British to the island of Ceylon after the revolution had been finally stamped out in Tell al-Kebir and the British occupation of Egypt began. However, it was to a British school that his sons were sent. In 1905 and 1906 the names Ashraf Sami Baroudi and Kamal Baroudi were entered in the school ledger. Their parent was noted as Madame Baroudi Pasha, and their address was Gianaclis, Ramleh. The two boys left in 1909 to go to Nasrieh School in Cairo, but came back to Victoria College a month later, and graduated in 1911. Why did a national hero, who had led the revolution against the British, choose a British school for his sons? The answer, according to Mrs. Zizi Baroudi, the daughter of Kamal Baroudi, is that he did not. When in exile he had married the daughter of another exile, Yacoub Pasha Sami, and had refused to register the birth of his sons in Ceylon to ensure that they would not have a British passport. On his death his widow came to Alexandria and entered the sons in Victoria College, simply because it was the best school available. That was in 1905, when Victoria College was only three years old. Kamal Baroudi went on to Massachusetts Institute of Technology, and was one of the first Egyptians to graduate from that prestigious college. A similar story involved another national figure, Ismail Pasha Sidky. In 1918 he joined the Wafd, the Egyptian delegation under Saad Zaghloul that sought to present Egypt's demands for independence to Britain and the High Commissioner. He was exiled to Malta with Saad Zaghloul in 1919, but in the very same year his son Aziz Sidky joined Victoria College and remained there until 1926.

The end of the First World War marked the end of the Mazarita days.

CHAPTER 1

At the signing of the armistice, the boys cheered and demanded a full day's holiday. Mr. Lias complied and they rewarded him with three cheers. The move back to Siouf took place in July. All the boys had gone home for the summer vacation, with the exception of those sitting for the Lower and Higher Certificate exams. Along with Mr. Lias and Mr. Reed, the candidates went to Siouf, where they lived in Mr. Lias's flat. The exams were held in the morning and afternoon in the art room; in the evening they all sat on Mr. Lias's balcony, from which the sea could be seen. Accompanying them were Percy Bolton and A. Treen. Bolton, the school steward, joined Victoria College in 1907 and remained until his death in 1946. His wife was matron of Reed House during the second Mazarita days, and his son was to become a Victorian. Treen, the school carpenter, came in 1909 and he, too, stayed until the 1940s. A famous aphorism of his was, "Life without a wife is like a kitchen without a knife." Treen's apprentice was a little boy of seven, called Abdel Moneim Abdel Aal, who was brought to Victoria College in 1925 by his father, a supplier of the school. Abdel Moneim became carpenter of the school and remained so until his death in 1996, but long before that he brought his own son Suleiman to train for the job. Suleiman has been working at the school since 1966 and he represents the third generation of an Egyptian family that earned its living from Victoria/Victory College. That was another Victoria College tradition: several of its headmasters, masters, and workers stayed for so long that they considered the school itself to be their home. Some of the best-remembered masters were M. Georges Dumont, Sheikh Mohamed Tewfiq, Mr. R.R. Parkhouse, Mr. H.B. Rider, Mr. W.J. Scovil, Mr. J.R.G. Price, Mr. R.G. Highwood, Mr. Douglas Haydon, Mr. Edward St. Leger-Hill, and Mr. Charles Hamdy. Their presence from one generation to another created a family atmosphere and a sense of continuity that encouraged Old Victorians to send their sons to their *alma mater*, because they knew that the people who had taken care of them when they were boys were still there to extend the same care to their sons.

Now that the war had ended, the number of boys started rising once more. Numbers had dropped because of the war conditions and also because of casualties. However, the war was not the only thing that claimed the lives of Victoria College people. George Antonius was not alone in losing a more brilliant brother; Amin Osman's older brother Munir (VC 1909–16), who was reputed to have been more gifted than Amin, drowned at Aboukir while rescuing Amin. Miss Lias died in 1908, and Mr. W.J. Tookey (VC 1905–6), the drill instructor, died at the Greek hospital in 1906 after a short and painful illness. In 1913 Hussein Ghaleb (VC 1911–13), born in Constantinople in 1901, died of typhoid fever. Some time before 1912 Farid Saba (VC 1902–8), Mahmoud Moursy (VC 1903–7), and Omar Fadl had also died. By 1920 John Laskaridis (VC 1903–11), the second Cromer Scholar; Oscar Klat (VC 1907–15), the Cromer Scholar of 1914; Antoine Anhoury (VC 1915–16); and Zahir Sharara (VC 1909–20) had all passed away. These deaths were caused by disease, primarily typhoid and cholera, which in the first decades of the century were rife and not easily treated. In 1902 Victoria College failed to open on the scheduled day because of cholera, and in recalling that event on the first Old Victorian annual dinner in 1912, Mr. Lias said: "Thanks to a certain gentleman not unconnected with Victoria College—indeed he was one of the first promoters of the school—not unconnected with the Board of Quarantine, thanks to him I say, cholera years are rarer now. But just ten years ago cholera was still stalking through the land." The gentleman he was referring to was probably Dr. Ruffer.

Boys dropped out of the school for reasons other than death. A few left to go to other schools, mainly those run by the French Frères or the French Lycée, though there were not many of them and some even returned to Victoria College. Others were expelled. Between 1915 and 1919 four boys were expelled, among them Maurice D. Aghion, who was expelled for stealing a pair of boots as well as general bad behavior. Emile Diab left for a very different reason: next to his name in the school ledger is written, "Swore never to come again to VC owing to his failure in the School Certificate."

With the end of the war and the fundraising that Mr. Lias was managing in 1920 with Lord Milner and Lord Allenby, Victoria College stood on grounds firmer than it had previously known. During the next decade, the number of boys and masters would continue to grow and the traditions that Mr. Lias laid down struck deep roots that were to be further cultivated by Mr. Reed. One aspect of the school, which was started

CHAPTER 1

in 1907 and was to be developed, was the scholarship system. On Lord Cromer's resignation in 1907 as Consul-General of Egypt, it was decided to set up the Lord Cromer Testimonial Fund. In 1908 it was agreed that the fund should take the form of a scholarship to be awarded to pupils of Victoria College, and in particular to "the boy who, being under sixteen years of age, passes the best Examination of the Oxford and Cambridge Schools Examination." Judgment of who was the best boy was not passed by the school but by the examiners in Britain. The first holder of the Cromer Scholarship was Emile Cordahi (1908), followed by: J. Laskaridis (1909), M. Klat (1910), F. Cordahi (1911), A. Mires (1912), J. Michaelidis (1913), O. Klat (1914), and C. Vlasto (1915). The first English boy to hold it was A.R.D. Sergeant (1916), whose brother, Jack Prosper Sergeant (VC 1909–12), designed the Goar gymnasium of the school. Occasionally scholarships would be informally offered by Old Boys to Victorians, such as the one granted by Nicholas Sursock (VC 1910–16) to enable Edward Atiyah to proceed to Oxford. These generous gestures were prompted by Mr. Lias and, more specifically, by Mr. Reed, whose intimate knowledge of the boys and concern with their welfare distinguished Victoria College from other schools where the pupils were mere names. Gradually, public figures of the Alexandrian community began to donate scholarships to the school.

Not all scholars fulfilled the academic dreams of the school, though. Despite being the first Cromer Scholar, Emile Cordahi turned out to be an academic disappointment, for he did not go on to university as was expected of him. Mr. Lias was to say of him in 1910:

> This year we have to regret the loss of our first Cromer Scholar. It was proposed at first that he should stay with us another year as head of the school in order to prepare for an entrance examination at an Engineering College in Switzerland. At the last moment, however, it was decided that he should enter upon a business career at Alexandria. We may hope that his exceptional abilities as a draughtsman and mathematician, which would have been so useful to him as an engineer, will stand him in equally good stead as a man of business.

His cousin, George Cordahi, certainly made such a large fortune in business at the Stock Exchange that he was known as "Le roi de la bourse": his sons, Nicola (VC 1903–11), Joseph (VC 1903–12), and Pierre (1913–22) went to Victoria College, as did Emile's son (George Emile Cordahi) later. Emile Cordahi worked with his cousin and remained the manager of the Daira Cordahi for the rest of his life. He is remembered by Jean Chamas, a relative by marriage, as having been brilliant at figures and academically outstanding.

There certainly existed a fruitful relationship between the school and the world of business, one that exceeded the plans of the early promoters and the founders. Sydney Carver, one of the great cotton merchants in Alexandria, sent his son Felix to Victoria in 1905. Later, in 1924, the Salvagos—another of the giant cotton families—sent Pandely Michel Salvago. However, the school also produced an Egyptian alumnus who unseated these non-Egyptians from their position of undisputed leadership in the field of cotton export, which was one of the main sources of wealth in Alexandria and Egypt: Mohamed Farghaly Pasha.[28]

His father, Ahmed Effendi Farghaly, was a grain and cotton merchant whose cotton trade was confined to the internal market, since export was monopolized by the foreigners. After giving his son a preliminary education in the Jesuit school, he enrolled Mohamed in Victoria College in 1914. Farghaly Pasha recalls in his memoirs that he spent the most enjoyable time of his life at Victoria College and that he was a distinguished pupil who received especial care and attention from Mr. Reed. At school he got to know Amin Osman, who was a few years older, and their friendship lasted until 1946, when Amin Osman was assassinated.

Whereas Amin Pasha Osman had no hesitation in choosing a political career, Farghaly Pasha was adamant about avoiding politics altogether, although he had business and social relationships of varying degrees with successive kings, presidents, prime ministers, and ministers of Egypt. His burning ambition was to conquer the field of cotton export. The role of Egyptians at this time was limited to selling cotton at set prices to the foreign merchants who would then export it at astronomical prices and amass fortunes. In Minet el Bassal, the cotton exchange in Alexandria, Egyptians worked as laborers. At the outset of his career in 1927, Mohamed Farghaly exported 0.25 percent of the gross national

Chapter 1

product; by 1938 he was exporting 15 percent of it. By then other Egyptians had started exporting cotton, but he remained the largest single exporter, whether Egyptian or foreign. In 1935 he was elected to the post of Vice-President of Minet el Bassal—one of the three most important cotton exchanges in the world, the other two being those of Liverpool and New York. In the same year King Fouad conferred upon him the title of bey. It was only a few years later that he nominated himself in the elections for the presidency of the Cotton Exchange against Amin Pasha Yehia. His chances against this formidable opponent were slim: not only was Amin Pasha Yehia much older, but he was the brother of Abdel Fattah Pasha Yehia, who had recently been Prime Minister. Nevertheless, Mohamed Farghaly won the elections to become the youngest person and the first Egyptian to preside over Minet el Bassal Cotton Exchange, the oldest in the world, according to his memoirs.

The 1930s and 1940s were his most challenging and successful years. He was an investor in a number of companies and member of several councils and boards of directors, among them the Victoria College Council, the Municipality of Alexandria (whose members were mostly foreigners), the National Bank of Egypt, the Egyptian Senate, and several of the companies of the Bank Misr Group. He was also president of the Alexandria Produce Company, and his own company, Farghaly Co., made an annual profit of a million Egyptian pounds. Twice he was offered the post of Minister of Finance: once by Hassan Pasha Sabry in 1940 and a second time by Hussein Pasha Sirry in 1952. In keeping with his decision to avoid political positions, despite his close relationship with many leading politicians and policy-makers, he turned down both offers. He was granted the title of pasha in 1941 for the services he rendered in promoting the finances of Egypt.

In the year 1935 he acquired the habit that he retained until his death. He was a member of the Egyptian delegation that went to Britain to strengthen economic ties between the two countries. On the practical level the result was the establishment of the Misr Insurance Company and the Beida Company. However, for all those who knew Farghaly Pasha, something else stuck in the memory. The delegation was invited to an audience with King George V, and Farghaly was struck by the carnation in the King's buttonhole. Though protocol forbade visitors from asking the sovereign any questions, Farghaly asked the King why he was wearing it. The King answered that it was for the sake of optimism. From that day onwards Farghaly Pasha took to wearing a carnation buttonhole and this little affectation remained as firmly associated with him as was the title by which he was known to the foreign and Egyptian press: the Cotton King.

Farghaly Pasha was also famous throughout Alexandria for his Rolls Royce. But his love of beautiful vehicles goes back to a much earlier time. As early as January 1917, *The Victorian* reports that he joined his brother, Ahmed Farghaly (VC 1903–14), in their father's firm, "which is reported to have benefited by their industry and business acumen." More important, the magazine goes on to say that in "his leisure moments [Farghaly] may be seen riding or driving a phaeton, the envy of charioteers and the terror of pedestrians."

Ambassador Mahmoud el Falaky (VC 1912–18) is another Egyptian alumnus who played a major role in the financial life of Egypt. To begin with, he came from a family that had made contributions to science in both Egypt and the West. His grandfather, Mahmoud Hamdy, had been educated in France, worked there as an astronomer, and had been decorated by the Académie des Sciences for his cartographic work. Because of his work in astronomy he became known as El Falaky—the astronomer. Back in Egypt, Khedive Ismail, at the request of Napoleon III, commissioned El Falaky to draw a map of ancient Alexandria. After working for four years with engineers in Alexandria and discovering the ancient city beneath the modern city, he drew a map—which remains the authoritative map of the classical city—and published his *Mémoire sur l'antique Alexandrie* in 1872. He also drew the first topographical map of Egypt. The other book he wrote was *L'âge et le but des pyramides*, in which he asserted that the pyramid was a tomb. Despite the French education of Mahmoud Hamdy el Falaky Bey, his grandson, Ambassador Mahmoud Saleh el Falaky, was sent to Victoria College because his parents wanted to give him the benefit of a liberal, secular education rather than a Jesuit one, and from there to send him to a British university. From Victoria College he went on to Cambridge, which he could join only through the personal connections of his father, the personal doctor of Adly Pasha Yeken, Prime Minister of Egypt. Adly Pasha Yeken was then head of the Egyptian delegation which had gone to Britain in 1921 (instead of the nationalist Wafd Party under Saad Pasha Zaghloul) to negotiate the terms for Egypt's independence. Postwar conditions were such that it was difficult for foreigners to gain entrance to Cambridge University, and so Adly Pasha Yeken had to exert his influence with the Foreign Office to gain Mahmoud el Falaky a place at Pembroke College, Cambridge, where he studied economics. On his return to Egypt in 1928, he started on the lowest rung in the Ministry of Finance as a technical assistant under Mr. James Baxter, the Financial Adviser to the Ministry of Finance. From there he worked his way up until he reached the post of Under-Secretary of State for Finance, a position he retained even after the 1952 revolution. He introduced economic reforms in the 1930s when Ismail Pasha Sidky, then Prime Minister, abolished pensions in an attempt to adjust the budget of Egypt at a time of worldwide economic depression. Mahmoud el Falaky instituted the Pension and Social Security Fund for permanent government staff, whereby a part of their salaries was paid into the fund, which would be returned to them in the form of a pension. In this way the staff were guaranteed a pension, while the government benefitted by borrowing money from the fund to use for development.

At the outset of the Second World War, Britain held Egypt in debt for £150 million; by the end of the war, Egypt held British Treasury Bills amounting to £450 million, a debt Britain had accumulated as a result of the services and goods that Egypt supplied during the war. To reconstruct its economy and settle these sterling balances which it owed to other countries, including India, Iraq, and Syria, Britain needed ten years. In 1944 the Great Powers met at Bretton Woods in New Hampshire, USA, to discuss the reconstruction of Europe. Mahmoud el Falaky represented Egypt at the conference and secured from John Maynard Keynes, head of the British delegation, a commitment that after the war Britian would meet bilaterally with all the debtor countries and settle its sterling balances with them. The theme of his negotiations at the conference was that the terms of trade between the rich and poor countries were against the poor, raw-material-producing countries. It was in the interest of the rich industrial countries to redress these distorted terms: if they helped the poor countries by means of loans and fairer trade terms, this was not charity but a promotion of world trade, and prosperity, and would in turn decrease the need for wars. After Bretton Woods, Mahmoud el Falaky was seconded from the Ministry of Finance to the International Monetary Fund in Washington to be the executive director representing nine Middle East countries. After holding that post for six years, he became Egypt's ambassador to Paris, and finally became a member of the National Council for Production and Economic Affairs, an institution that is personally responsible to the president of Egypt.

Mahmoud el Falaky asserts that Victoria College prepared him well for Cambridge and his subsequent career. The fact that he was a boarder living away from his family also taught him discipline and self-reliance. Of his teachers, it is M. Dumont and Mr. Lias that he remembers with fondness and admiration—especially Mr. Lias, whose overwhelming personality he describes as unforgettable.

In 1922 Mr. Lias resigned on account of his eczema, which often made him irritable and was aggravated by Alexandria's humidity. When he lost his temper he was capable of furious canings. He occasionally had to retire to the drier climate of Helwan, south of Cairo, to calm his condition, but he eventually had to leave Alexandria altogether. He went to Damascus to continue with his studies of Arabic, then to Italy, Germany, and finally retirement in England.

He had been the first headmaster of the school, recruited its teachers from Britain and Alexandria, steered it through its most difficult days, helped it to grow, and determined its character and traditions. Doubtless his successors would have their difficult days too, but he had laid such solid foundations for the school that its reputation could only increase. He not only had provided his boys with a sound education but had also given them the kind of character that would qualify them to be leaders in whatever field they chose to pursue.

The man who had done so much for Victoria College and who ran it for twenty years was often gentle with the boys and cared for each person's welfare, yet there was a strong streak in him as well. In addition to exercising power over the boys, he could stand up to the obnoxious Mr. Dunlop and show him the door, and even defy the will of the Egyptian nation by receiving Lord Milner in style at Victoria College when the whole of Egypt had boycotted him. This was a person whose force of

Chapter 1

character, as well as his humane vision, allowed him to make of the school what it became (see Appendix G).

On Speech Day of 1929 Mr. Reed, as headmaster, was to pay tribute to him and acknowledge that it was his vision and spirit that formed the character of Victoria College and its boys:

> It was my predecessor, Mr. C.R. Lias, the first Headmaster of this School, who built up the character of the School and determined the direction which its development should take, and I believe that this character has been maintained and this direction pursued. His influence, I know, endures, not only in the hearts and minds of the Old Boys whom he taught, but also in the tone and spirit of the School to which he devoted twenty years of his life.

These words do reflect the moral and practical achievements of Mr. Lias. But a mysterious breach was to develop between him and Mr. Reed. In 1932, when Mr. Reed had to remain in England for around a year to be operated on and convalesce, Mr. Highwood assumed responsibility at Victoria College. It seems that Mr. Lias had wanted to depose Mr. Reed and return to Victoria College as a master, with Mr. Highwood as headmaster. The only reference to this conspiracy is a letter from Mr. Highwood to Mr. Reed in Britain in 1932, full of dark and mysterious allusions to Mr. Lias's intentions and lobbying efforts against him:

> The return of Lias in any capacity would of course be so dangerous an experiment that we feel with you that it ought never to be attempted. The reasons for this are quite obvious and although it may appear somewhat unkind of me to oppose his return so vigorously after so much kindness and in the face of so generous an offer, yet with Lias as he was, my attitude should be as it is, and how much more so should it be when you mention the hardened prejudices by name! I suppose the Committee would oppose any idea of his coming back

and I have no doubt at all that they would entertain no thoughts of allowing my salary to go off for the reason which would be given. Presumably some members of the Committee have heard of me but I think at present any idea of my succeeding you would horrify them . . . I am afraid I have not eased your burden for it still leaves you with the burden of dealing with C.R.L[ias]. And there is as you say no reason why he should not return to Egypt to offer his services, but perhaps you will be able to make up some material from this into a suitable obstacle and I will not presume to offer any help since you know how to deal with him so well.

What it was that Mr. Lias had done to turn Mr. Reed, Mr. Highwood, and the School Committee so strongly against him, or how Mr. Reed warded off the threat of Mr. Lias' return, is unknown. What is known is that when Mr. Reed took the torch of Victoria College from Mr. Lias in 1922, he continued to carry it, alone and unrivaled, until his death in 1945.

2
The Reed Phenomenon

Sahar Hamouda

I remember at the Old Victorians' dinner, when Amin [Pasha Osman] had said that there were only two people that count, or should count to old boys; those he said were Mr. Lias and Mr. Reed. I never knew Mr. Lias—and as I believe that Amin was right, you alone count to me—I shall never, never forget.
   Letter from Nicola Stamboulieh to Mr. Reed, 9 October 1935

Ralph Reed, MA, Oxon., later to be awarded the Order of the British Empire and made a Companion of the Order of St. Michael and St. George, was headmaster at Victoria College from 1922 to 1945. Along with Mr. Lias, he was responsible, more than any other individual, for the success of the school and the reputation it gained. When he became the school's second headmaster in 1922, he had already spent eleven years at the school as a housemaster, and was well acquainted with the country, the school, and the boys themselves. In fact, during his days as housemaster he had acquired lifelong disciples from among the boys, such as Amin Osman and Edward Atiyah. As headmaster, he continued with the practice of guiding his boys, forming their characters, looking after their welfare, and taking a personal interest in each and every pupil, even after graduation. In the address he gave on Speech Day 1938, he said:

> A School is not a mass of buildings or a series of lessons. It is an experiment in training. Its material is human

CHAPTER 2

beings, immaturely developed, and its aim is to develop the whole nature of man or rather to enable him to develop his whole nature. It is above all a human, organic process, the influence of mind upon mind, and it can only be accomplished in an atmosphere of reasonable liberty and reasonable security.

He therefore devoted his time as headmaster to establishing that sense of liberty and security for his boys and helping them to develop various aspects of their natures. In addition to that, he sought throughout his career to improve the standard of education at the school and raise its prestige in Egypt and the Middle East.

Mr. Reed suffered from ill health from the 1920s until his death in 1945. In 1928 his leg was amputated, and for two decades he was in and out of hospital and bed because of lung, chest, and, eventually, liver problems. However, indifferent health did not prevent him from taking a deep interest in the affairs of the school and in leading a very active social life that was partly an interaction with personal friends and partly a networking activity.

When Mr. Reed came to Alexandria in 1911, fresh out of Oxford, Britain was an anomaly in Egypt. The occupation, supposedly a temporary measure to maintain Khedive Tewfik in power, had prolonged into a presence that did not have a definite legal status. Virtual power remained in the hands of the British Agent and Consul-General, who became the High Commissioner after Egypt was declared a British protectorate in 1914. Lord Milner's failure to negotiate with Saad Pasha Zaghloul in Egypt, the deportation of the hero to the Seychelles, and the resignation of Adly Pasha Yeken from the premiership, led Britain to declare the end of the Protectorate in 1922 and Egypt's independence. Thus Mr. Reed's appointment as headmaster coincided with Egypt's new status, yet all these political changes did not affect the kind of pupils that were being drawn to Victoria College. The school was still attracting the sons of British subjects, of Egyptians, and of many other nationalities residing in Egypt and abroad (there was even a French boy who came from Algeria in 1926, Henri Jacques Louis Deschambeaux). Although there were good Greek and Armenian schools in Alexandria, many parents preferred Victoria College to their community schools. In a letter dated 6 July 1932 to Mr. Doble of Great Chesterfield College, a small but distinguished private establishment that prepared boys for British universities, Mr. Reed wrote:

> The first pupil I sent you was the son of a Pasha, the second the son of a Princess and this is the son of a King, so you will think that I deal exclusively with boys of very lofty connections. In fact, however, my school here is very mixed socially, as the East generally is.... The first boy [Kamel Wassef, son of Hussein Pasha Wassef] I sent you, however, was an Egyptian, the second [Ismail Chirine, son of Hussein Bey Chirine and Princess Emina Fazil] Turkish [Circassian] and this one [Emir Abdulillah, grandson of El Sharif Hussein of Hijaz] is an Iraqian of pure Arab blood descended from the Prophet.

This recommendation letter is just one example of many that Mr. Reed wrote for his boys, to recommend them for other schools, for universities, or for jobs.

He corresponded graciously with royalty, and although Her Sultanate Highness the Princess Nimatallah, grandmother of the Nabil Mohamed Tewfik Tousson, did not deign to write him letters, leaving that chore to the secretary of her Daira (see Appendix H), the Princess Emina Fazil consulted him about the future of her son Ismail Chirine. It was not above him to give a princess advice about where to shop or how to dress her son. He writes to her in 1932:

> With regard to Ismail's outfit, it is generally better (and cheaper) to get what is necessary in England than to buy it here and take it to England. He will, of course, need warm underclothes (either Jaeger or Aertex are the best), three pairs of strong shoes, a grey flannel suit and a Scotch or Irish tweed suit besides two or three ordinary suits, an extra pair of grey flannel trousers and two pairs of white flannel trousers, a pair of white tennis or crick-

Chapter 2

et shoes and three pairs of white socks, a white woollen jersey and a grey or brown pullover (or perhaps two, one with and one without sleeves), a warm overcoat and a light raincoat or waterproof.

Mr. Reed's concern was basically the welfare of his boys, and his tone to all parents was civil and sincere. Some of his staff were more amused than impressed by royalty and could not resist a joke or two at their expense. Mr. R.G. Highwood (master 1920–38) made the following remarks to Mr. Reed during the latter's sojourn in England in 1934:

> Owing to a temporary breakdown in Staff work, a very distinguished but considerably decayed old man and a vivacious looking female marched into the office the other day and announced themselves respectively as Midhat Yeghen Pasha and Princess Abbas Halim. It was very stupid of me but I could not remember whether the Prince was the one whose wives shot themselves from time to time, or the one who had escaped from a lunatic asylum prison and who had been so much in the limelight recently. However a sarcastic remark of the Pasha's indicated clearly that he was not to be a subject for discussion. The Princess, as I understand all Egyptian Princesses are, was charming and she is putting her son here (aged 14 and educated solely in England hitherto). The Pasha is the grandfather of the boy but the Prince is not the father (the Princess having been married before, a habit which I believe is common to all Egyptian Princesses).

Despite the names of royalty and notables that graced the school's register, Mr. Reed's words to Mr. Doble, that the "school here is very mixed socially, as the East generally is," rang true. Undoubtedly most of the boys came from families that could afford the high fees. Boarders came from Cairo and all the provinces: landed gentry and *omdahs* sent their sons from Asyut, Minya, Beheira, Menufiya, Mit Ghamr, Port Said, Ismailia, Simbillawayn, Samalut and Sallum. Some families sent their boys in droves, such as the Zanatis from Luxor and the Wissas from Asyut. In Alexandria most of the addresses were in the wealthier areas of Ramleh, such as rue Rosette and Moharrem Bey. Even in the 1920s Moharrem Bey and Manshieh were so distant from Victoria College that some families chose to send their boys as boarders rather than let them make the long trip daily.

Those who could not afford the fees, however, could find several means of financial help. British boys were allowed reductions of up to 50 percent, depending on the family's financial circumstances. Leslie Bolton (VC 1925–37), son of Percy Bolton the school steward, was educated at the school along with the sons of kings and ministers. His humble origins did not bar him from enjoying the privileges of equality the school boasted of, for he was a school prefect and games captain. He was also in the football and cricket First XIs (enviable positions in an establishment that set much store by sports), and was recommended by Mr. Scovil as being the best batsman in Egypt. Even lower down the social scale was another British boy, Arthur Colley (VC 1928–39). His initial address was Karmouz, a poor area in Alexandria; but a year after he joined the school his family moved to Mazarita. His father ran an electrical establishment in town, but failed and went back to England, leaving behind his wife to bring up the boy in straitened circumstances. Arthur spent eleven years at the school, during which time he got a reduction in fees of 30 percent. Leslie Fleming (VC 1933–40), who later became a teacher at the school, was another boy who benefitted from these reductions, though he was not, strictly speaking, British. He was born in Constantinople to a Russian father and a Turkish mother. It was his stepfather who was an Englishman of limited means living in Cyprus and who sought to provide a British education for his stepson. Mr. Reed offered him a reduction of 20 percent, which would bring the fees to LE 25 a term in 1933, not taking into account extras like books, pocket money, school cinema, bathing in the summer, school shop requisites (chiefly for football and cricket), and school uniform. Mr. Reed was willing to grant a further reduction if Mr. Fleming felt that the fees were still too high, on condition that Mr. Fleming not mention these reductions, which were given only to those "whose financial circumstances do not permit them to pay full fees," as Mr. Reed told Mr. Fleming in a letter.

However, Mr. Reed was for the most part willing to bypass certain regulations, especially in money matters, if it meant that a boy could have the benefit of a Victoria College education.

The school also offered a certain number of scholarships, for which boys under the ages of twelve and a half or fourteen and a half could sit and which were valid for two to six years. In addition to the Cromer Scholarship, which was started in 1908 and was still being awarded in the 1930s to the pupil who had in the opinion of the examiners performed best in the Lower Certificate examination, there were scholarships donated by the notables of Alexandria. The Smouha Scholarship, for LE 50, was donated by Joseph Smouha. The Smouhas were Iraqi Jews who had gone to Britain and made a fortune during the First World War manufacturing army clothing. After the war Joseph Smouha, now a British citizen, came to Alexandria with a cheque for a million pounds to set up a textile plant. Instead, he bought the marshes of Lake Hadara from Prince Omar Tousson, who had abandoned his plans for reclaiming the area. Joseph Smouha drained the marshes and created a new suburban garden city around Smouha Club along the lines of British garden cities. Smouha's sons became involved in the real estate business that their father had created. The other scholarships were: the Finney Scholarship (donor Mr. Oswald Finney) for LE 25; the Yehia Scholarship (donor Amin Pasha Yehia) for LE 25; the Choremi Scholarship (donor Mr. Constantine Choremi) for LE 25; the Rolo Scholarship (donor Messrs. J. Rolo and Co.) for LE 20, and the Swinglehurst Scholarship (donor the trustees of the late Mr. Henry Swinglehurst) for LE 20.[29] Then there were the Boarders' Exhibitions for boys not yet enrolled and unable to afford all the boarding fees.

Thus there were ways and means to get around the school fees. Yet it must not be overlooked that these ways were limited to two groups of boys: those who were British, and those who were intelligent enough to win scholarships and were consequently sure to be a credit to Victoria College. Reductions and scholarships did not cover all the fees or the expenses, and the high fees continued to be a headache to the school bursar, Mr. Ingham,[30] and the parents alike. The school files dealing with petty cash and accounts abound with threats from the bursar to turn pupils' files over to the school lawyers if arrears of a pound were not paid. Even well-to-do parents were not safe from the bursar's dreaded letters. They complained of the price of the laundry, the items in the school shop, and even of their children's extravagance. Headmasters and acting headmasters had to put up with all sorts of attempts on the parents' part to avoid full fees even if they could afford them, as Mr. Highwood remarked to Mr. Reed:

> Parents of course do ask funny questions but this year [1934] there have been several who have asked if there is any reduction if they pay the whole year at once; evidently this is the influence of American financial schemes and equally of course of the fact that they have sold their cotton. But this was quite a new one to me, when a man asked if the boys were divided into classes: doubtless you will think this is an easy one and the subject for a short speech but you would be wrong: the correct answer is "No, there are no classes, the School is not a train."

What about children who were neither British nor brilliant nor rich? Well, Victoria College was neither a charity organization nor a profit-making establishment. For Mr. Reed to put himself out for somebody, that somebody had to be the son of somebody, or show the promise of becoming somebody in the future, or, of course, have already been at the school for a number of years and then for some reason have become unable to continue paying the fees. One such example is Mustafa el Sakkaf. In the 1930s the fees for day boys were LE 18 a term, including lunch and bus,[31] and a boarder would cost his parents an average of LE 150 a year including expenses. That was such a large sum that Mr. Reed anticipated that many boys—whether day boys or boarders—would not be returning, and one of them, Mustafa, was about not to. He was the son of El Sharif Mohamed Said el Sakkaf, originally from Hadramaut. The Sakkafs were so plentiful in Asia that a local saying went that under every stone you turned you were sure to find a Sakkaf. Victoria College had several of them: Mohamed Said Omar el Sakkaf from Jeddah in 1905; Seyd Hadi Alsagaff, classified as a British Arab, in 1922; and Sayed Ali Alsagoff, a British subject in Singapore, in 1937. El Sharif

Chapter 2

Mohamed el Sakkaf had been the counterpart of the Minister of Finance to El Sharif Hussein of Hijaz (grandfather of Emir Abdulillah), who had led the Arab Revolt and had then been ousted by the Wahhabis. El Sharif Mohamed had gone into exile in Cyprus with El Sharif Hussein, then moved to Cairo, and then to Sanaa in Yemen, where he worked closely with Emir Badr, the son of Imam Yehia. He was placed under house arrest for some months for political reasons, and upon his release he married a relative of the Imam's. He later died mysteriously in Yemen. He also remained in close contact with the former King El Sharif Hussein and his three sons, Ali (briefly King of Hijaz after his father), Feisal (King of Iraq), and Abdullah (Emir of Transjordan), who were frequent visitors at his palatial residence in Cairo. He made numerous trips to Yemen, where he owned 4,000 acres of coffee plantations, and where he was probably working toward some form of Arab union, involving Yemen, Transjordan, Iraq, Egypt, Libya, and Ethiopia. When El Sakkaf decided to take a Yemeni wife for political reasons, his wife Aziza insisted on a divorce. He left her penniless with a son and two daughters to bring up.

The family moved to Alexandria, and the son, Mustafa, was sent to Victoria College in 1933. However, with the disappearance of his father in Yemen, Mustafa's education at the school became impossible. His sister, Abkar, presented the case to Mr. Reed in 1937, saying that it was imperative that Mustafa continue his education at Victoria College. Mr. Reed contacted Old Victorian Amin Pasha Osman, who wrote to Hassan Pasha Sabry, the Prime Minister, whose son Mounir Hassan Sabry was at the school. The Prime Minister referred the case to Sarwat Pasha, the Minister of Waqf (who also had a son at Victoria College), and the plea did not fall on deaf ears. The Waqf granted Mustafa an annual sum of LE 30 for two years. When Sarwat Pasha left the Waqf, Mr. Reed applied in 1938 to Hassan Sabry Shehayib Bey, the Under-Secretary of State for Waqfs, who also had a son at the school, to continue the grant. Consequently Mustafa managed to obtain his School Certificate in 1939, though his mother went on paying arrears (the Waqf grant had covered only part of the expenses) until 1945 at great personal sacrifice.

On Mustafa's graduation Mr. Reed tried to get him into the Military College, Barclay's Bank, the National Bank in Alexandria, and La

Compagnie du Canal de Suez in Ismailia, which in 1940 had advertised 200 vacancies to replace what had become the undesirable Italians and Germans. The procedure was in keeping with Mr. Reed's character, who always sought to help his boys in this way. However, Mustafa eventually worked for the National Bank of Egypt through his own family connections and at the age of thirty-four he became the director of the Bank of Import and Export in Alexandria, the youngest director of a bank in Egypt. Although he avoided politics, which his father had pursued with such energy, his financial acumen was a trait he inherited from his father and he employed it usefully. He became the Director of the National Bank in Alexandria, and from then on it was all the way to an international career in banking, culminating in the post of director of Dar el Mal in Geneva.

The story of Mustafa el Sakkaf illustrates the store that people set by a Victoria College education and the fact that it did pay off. Mustafa's success was due partly to the kind of education he had received, and partly to the benefits of the "school tie." Mustafa el Sakkaf narrates that in 1965 he was chosen by the International Monetary Fund to establish the Central Bank of Jordan, whose first general manager he also was. When the Jordanian authorities refused to grant him a visa, the Bank of England guaranteed him on the grounds that he was an Old Victorian. In 1969 his Old Victorian friend, Maamoun el Beheiry (former Minister of Finance of Sudan) asked him to become Director of the African Development Bank in Abidjan.

The story demonstrates, equally, Mr. Reed's energy in maintaining connections and networking on behalf of the school. He was most active in using his connections whenever he could help those who needed help. In 1937 he asked Amin Pasha Osman (addressing him as "My dear Amin") to pull some strings on behalf of the postman who had served the school for many years but who was now ill and required a lighter job. Also through Amin Osman (who obviously never refused his mentor anything) he managed to get free education at the Amira Faiza Secondary School for the daughter of the deceased Sheikh Mohamed Tewfik (Arabic master 1902–30). In 1940 he wrote to Gawdat Bey, director of the Passports Department at the Governorate of Alexandria, concerning "the two sons of Saida Nasr, who is the sister of one of our sewing maids at the School. These sons are at the present stranded in Palestine without any means of support and their aunt, who legally adopted them when they were babies is very anxious that they should come to Egypt to live with her, as she alone is responsible for their maintenance." If Mr. Reed was willing to do favors for humble people who were not in a position to further the British cause in Egypt, to what lengths would he not go to support his own boys?

Nicola Stamboulieh (VC 1927–32) was one of the boys toward whom Mr. Reed was especially caring. Nicola was the son of Gabriel Stamboulieh, a Christian Syrian who had formerly been in Sudan but was now a broker in Alexandria in financial trouble and struggling to educate his sons. In 1927 Nicola won the Finney Scholarship for boys under twelve and a half years old, and his brother the Karam Scholarship for boys under fourteen and a half. Despite this financial relief, the father still had difficulty in paying arrears and extras. Nicola, a gifted pianist, was enrolled at the Verdi Conservatoire after school hours; he qualified for the diploma recognized by the Italian government but could not afford the fees of LE 35. To raise the money, he thought of traveling to Khartoum to give a few concerts and, naturally, he applied to Mr. Reed for help. Mr. Reed wrote to Sir Wasey Sterry in Khartoum in December 1931, asking whether he could approach the Governor-General to be Nicola's patron. He also wrote to Mr. Morhig (whose sons were at the school) in Khartoum to take charge of the publicity and to introduce the boy to Englishmen and to Edward Atiyah. The result was that Nicola returned to Alexandria with a net profit of LE 50. The procedure was repeated, with huge success, in 1936, although by then Nicola had left the school and was working at the Municipality—most likely through the recommendation of Mr. Reed and Amin Osman. Mr. Reed did not forget to send Nicola a telegram on the day of the concert wishing him the best of luck. Nicola's financial problems increased with time, for his father's difficulties had increased and he had returned to Sudan, leaving Nicola to look after his mother and several younger brothers. Nicola had to bear the responsibility of the family, and life was hard. He poured out his woes to Mr. Reed, and in 1936 writes to him the following: "Ten pounds have dropped from Heaven; he who sent them did not like to mention his name. He did not want to lend me the money, nor did he wish me to know that he gave it. He only wanted to make me feel happy, because he knew I had troubles, and that man cannot be anyone else but you. God bless you." Nicola, whose name was eventually anglicized by Mr. Reed to Nicholas, became a teacher at Victoria College from 1943 to 1954.[32]

The more exotic cases had to do with pupils who came from outside Egypt and who were in some way connected with the activities of the British empire. Abyssinia (as Ethiopia was called by the school) regularly sent a couple of boys each year. Abyssinian boys were educated at Victoria College for political reasons. From the second half of the nineteenth century to the early part of the twentieth Ethiopia was a bone of contention between the British and the Italians, with the French occasionally taking part in the scramble. The "natives" who lost their lives in these contests had to be compensated.

Abyssinian boys first arrived at Victoria College in 1918, sent by Mr. Zaphiro in the British Legation at Addis Ababa. The first two were the grandsons of Blaten Gueta Heroui, but Mr. Reed chose to call them Michael and George because their names were "unpronounceable." George Heroui had another brother, Sirak Heroui, who was also an Old Victorian. When Addis Ababa fell to the Italians in 1936 and the Emperor Haile Selassie went into exile, Sirak went with him, but George was captured, tortured, and killed by the Italians. The wives and children of both brothers were also killed by the Italians, while the son of their sister managed to escape with other refugees to Palestine and enter St. George's School in Jerusalem. The grandfather, Blaten Gueta Heroui, who had been Minister of Finance in Abyssinia and was now in Britain, Sirak Heroui, and the Emperor himself all wrote to Victoria College requesting that the boy, Haillou Heroui, be admitted to the school, although all they could pay was the sum of LE 100, whereas the total cost of his education for four years would be LE 600. In memory of the boy's dead uncle George, and because of his own personal connections with the Emperor Haile Selassie, with whom he had struck up a friendship following his visit to the school in 1924 as Ras Tafari, Mr. Reed accepted the boy and promised to raise the funds for his education. Haillou was accordingly sent from Jerusalem in the company of a member of Barclay's Bank (Dominion Colonial and

Chapter 2

Overseas) in Jerusalem in 1938. In order to raise the funds, Mr. Reed had a meeting with two Egyptian Old Boys, Amin Osman (Muslim) and Kamel Boulos Hanna (Copt). Kamel Hanna volunteered to talk to a number of wealthy Coptic families and got them to donate the necessary LE 600 in the form of a scholarship in the memory of George Heroui. Haillou Heroui settled down happily at Victoria College and made friends with many boys, especially the Sudanese. He went to Sudan to spend the summer vacation with his Victorian friend, the son of Sir Sayed Abdel Rahman el Mahdi. Even the Mahdis had been placated by the British: they had been knighted and their sons were being educated at Victoria College.

The cousin of Haillou Heroui, Constantine Tegneh, also came to Victoria College for political reasons. In 1904 the British government set up a fund to educate the sons of an Abyssinian officer who had assisted them in their campaign against the "Mad Mullah" in Somaliland at the turn of the century. For some reason nothing was ever done about the sons. In 1933 Mr. Reed received a letter from the British Residency in Cairo notifying him that they now wanted to use that fund, which had by then increased, to educate the grandson. The trustees appointed were Sir Clifford Heathcote-Smith, the British Consul-General in Alexandria, and Mr. Barron, the chairman of the Alexandria Committee of the British Chamber of Commerce in Egypt.

Constantine Tegneh arrived at Victoria College in June 1934, and Mr. Reed reported to the Residency: "He speaks no word of English, French or Arabic; the poor boy was filthily dirty in clothes and person, and his sole luggage consists in a small attaché case. We have now, however, washed and dressed him and fitted him out." He was allegedly fourteen years old, but Mr. Reed guessed he was a good couple of years younger. Within two years he had "learned to speak English fluently and well"; the credit obviously goes to the school and not to his scholarly merits, for Mr. Reed describes him as "not a boy of outstanding intelligence and apt to be lazy." But since Victoria College developed all sides of its boys' characters, Mr. Reed happily noted that "we are very well pleased with the development of his character and personality; he has an excellent temper and good manners and a decided touch of leadership." By 1936 British concern over Constantine had begun to grow. The fund was quickly being depleted; his father was thought to have been killed in the Abyssinian war, and his mother, after getting remarried, disappeared into some remote village in Ethiopia. Mr. Reed, Mr. Barron, and Sir Clifford did not know what to do with the boy. He had been taken on at the school in gratitude to a soldier, but there was no longer any money to keep him at the school, and he showed no promise of ever distinguishing himself, having neither family nor brains. There was talk of applying to the British government for a grant, but Mr. Reed was against the idea. He wrote to Sir Clifford:

> On the general question as to whether it is worthwhile to keep Tegneh on at school here and to aim at completing his School course, if it were not a matter of application for special funds for this purpose I should say it was well worthwhile. I think that Tegneh has gained a great deal from the life and training that he is getting here and that in the ordinary way, even though he is not a clever and industrious boy, he ought to be given the opportunity of gaining a great deal more . . . In fact, I do not know why the British Government should be requested to give a grant at all. In a word, if there is any prospect of persuading the British Government that they owe more to the memory of Tegneh's grandfather than they have already paid, I think it would be an excellent thing to keep the boy on here; but if it is a matter of persuading them that he is a boy of exceptional merit I don't think we should be justified in doing so.

Mr. Reed, although he was as clear in his opinion as always, was torn between two good aspects of his self: his role as educator and his personal integrity, which refused to lie even in the interests of one of his boys. For the next two years the British Embassy tried in vain to find work for Constantine in Sudan, Palestine, Kenya, or Somaliland. Mr. Reed had maintained his close relations with the Emperor Haile Selassie, and in 1937 approached him: "At Bath, I had a long and interesting, though rather melancholy, talk with the Emperor of Abyssinia." The

Chapter 2

Emperor had just lost his empire and was too worried about his own fate to give much attention to the future of a schoolboy. Heathcote-Smith grew more anxious. He wrote to Mr. Reed, "The alternatives seem to be, (a) to send the boy back to Abyssinia—where he might be persecuted by the Italians on account of his British upbringing, (b) obtaining for him some post in Egypt: this would involve his becoming an Egyptian subject." Finally, in 1938, Mr. Reed, the fatherly educator, provided what help it was within his means to provide: he proposed that since for four years Constantine's fees had been paid in full to the school, Victoria College owed it to him to continue his education at its own expense. The proposal was accepted and Constantine remained at Victoria College until 1940, when, having finished school, he went to Sudan as a guest of one of his Sudanese school friends, and was heard of no more. He is remembered by his mates, Fouad Awad and Mustafa el Sakkaf, as a gentle and humorous boy.

The British role was certainly predominant in the Arab world. From the 1920s onward, Arab countries under British authority began sending their boys to Victoria College. Libya started late, when in gratitude to the Senoussi resistance to Italian occupation, the British undertook to educate some of the Senoussi sons at Victoria College. During the 1920s and 1930s it was mainly countries under British rule that sent their boys. Palestine sent Bahai' el Said, son of Assem Bey el Said, the mayor of Jaffa, in 1936, and Mohamed el Khalidi (VC 1932–34), son of Moustapha Bey el Khalidi, who became the mayor of Jerusalem in 1939. There were also other Muslim British Palestinians, such as Gad Abdallah, as well as Jewish Palestinians, such as the four Tenebaum brothers, who came in the 1920s. Rasheed el Nashashibi came from one of the best-known Muslim Palestinian families and was accepted at Victoria College as an exception. In 1930 he obtained a certificate from Bishop Gobat School in Jerusalem that qualified him to join the American University of Beirut. However, he wanted to join a British university, possibly Oxford or Cambridge, and so the principal of Bishop Gobat School applied to Victoria College to admit Rasheed so that he would eventually obtain the Higher Certificate. Mr. Parkhouse was the acting headmaster and turned down the application because the school did not accept boys over the age of fourteen. Mr. Bowman then wrote from Palestine and personally recommended the boy, upon which he was accepted. He turned out to be exceptionally weak and Mr. Reed refused to allow him to sit for the Higher Certificate, advising Mr. Bowman to get Rasheed to apply to the American University of Beirut instead. On the whole, however, Palestinian boys were few because the foreign and local schools in Palestine maintained a high standard of education, while the British school, St. George's School, offered the Matriculation Examination, which was an accepted qualification for entrance to British universities.

Sudan sent a more assorted collection: either Sudanese boys or the sons of Old Victorians working in Sudan, or the sons of Syrians and Armenians employed by Sudanese government under British administration.

Transjordan sent very few boys. In 1922 Heidar Ricaby joined the school—his father, Prime Minister of Transjordan from 1922 to 1924, was written down in the school ledger as "Ali Reda Pasha el Ricaby CBE, President of the Trans-Jordan Government. Nationality: Syrian Moslem." Heidar was a promising boy: he became joint head boy with Henri Farhi (a Jew), librarian, and vice-president of the Literary, Debating and Dramatic Society. After his graduation from the school he held a responsible position within the Alexandria Governorate, and in 1931–32 was a resident staff member at Victoria College teaching Arabic and Arabic translation. It seems that Mr. Bowman, as Director of Education in Palestine, followed with keen interest the progress of Arab boys studying at Victoria College. Writing to him in 1932, Mr. Reed reported: "The best boy we have ever had from your part of the world is Haidar el-Ricaby, the son of Rida Pasha el-Ricaby, who, after spending a year here as junior Arabic and Arabic Translation Master, has just returned to join his father in Damascus, where he will be helping to run with his father a newspaper and at the same time studying Law at the School of Law in Damascus." The Emir Zeid Shaker, who became Prime Minister of Jordan, joined the school in 1944.

Mr. Reed was heavily involved in networking in Iraq, which sent quite a number of boys. His contacts in the Iraqi Ministry of Education were Mr. Lionel Smith, until he left in 1932 and was succeeded by Mr. Edmonds, and Sir Kinahan Cornwallis, the adviser (and ambassador 1941–45); in the Ministry of the Interior it was Mr. Grice, the adviser. He had a copious correspondence with all four of them over the education of some of the Iraqi boys studying at Victoria College as well as setting up schools in Iraq.

In 1928 Mr. Smith sent Baba Ali (VC 1928–32), whose school fees the Iraqi government paid, to study at Victoria College. The boy's father was Sheikh Mohamed Suleiman, a Kurd, close to the royal court, who went into open rebellion against the government. In 1929, only a year after Baba Ali had joined the school, Mr. Smith was conferring with Mr. Reed about sending the boy on to Britain, and a year later, about entering him into the Royal Air Force College at Cranwell, saying, "The Englishmen who know Baba Ali best want him to go into the Iraqi Air Force, just about to be formed. This we hope will mean 2 years at Cranwell after he leaves you. It will also find him a career in this country, which is a most important thing. So far his father has not agreed to the air force plan, but I think his father has rather put himself out of court." Mr. Reed approved of the idea but doubted that Baba Ali would get his School Certificate. "When he came to Victoria College at the age of 15," Mr. Reed wrote to Mr. Grice, "he knew literally nothing . . . it is hardly to be expected that a boy of 15 who knows no English or French, very little Arabic and almost nothing else should after 4 years be able to obtain a Certificate of Matriculation standard." He advised Mr. Grice to seek help from the High Commissioner in Egypt and in Iraq, and from the Foreign Office. In 1932 he wrote to Mr. Smith (who had by then resigned from Iraq and become Rector of Edinburgh Academy, but was still interested in Baba Ali's future) that Baba Ali could be admitted to Cranwell only by a side entrance and that some strings needed to be pulled. Consequently, Mr. Smith wrote to Sir Robert Brooke-Popham, former Commander of the Air Force in Iraq, but by then the Ministry of Interior had decided against sending Baba Ali to Cranwell, since his parents were set against the idea. It was a pleasant surprise to all the Britons involved when Baba Ali succeeded in the School Certificate in 1932 and obtained credits in Arabic and science. Mr. Smith in Edinburgh and Sir Kinahan Cornwallis in Iraq gave Victoria College the credit for Baba Ali's success, though Mr. Reed and Mr. Smith were disappointed that Baba Ali would not be following a career in the Air Force as they had planned for him. Nevertheless, he did well at the Royal College of

Baghdad, where he studied medicine, and where the standard was high, the curriculum being that of Edinburgh University. After his first term there, Baba Ali wrote to Mr. Reed, "I shall never forget your kindness to me for having endeavoured so much to get the question of my career adjusted, and I shall be thankful also for the education I received at Victoria College under your guardianship."

A contemporary of Baba Ali's was Emir Abdulillah (VC 1928–32), son of Ali, former king of Hijaz, the brother of King Feisal of Iraq and Emir Abdullah of Transjordan. In his correspondence with King Ali in 1932, Mr. Reed did not hesitate to give his frank opinion concerning the pupil's progress: "He has lately made very satisfactory progress in his general studies, and is now able to speak and write English with some distinction. As I have remarked before, however, he has made a late start and he is not by nature industrious; in spite of good abilities, therefore, he is backward as compared with other boys of his own age educated from their early years on English Public Schools lines." The King responds with a letter of gratitude: "I am sure that most of the credit goes to you for the remarkable improvement he has made and for which I heartily thank you." Like Leslie Fleming, Abdulillah became a school prefect, though he was neither distinguished in his studies nor possessed of leadership qualities. Victoria College did not choose prefects on account of their academic merits or their pedigree, but in order to develop whatever positive qualities they might have had. Being a prefect obviously gave confidence to the Emir, who was shy and gentle like his father (English colonialists who had witnessed King Ali's brief reign in the Hijaz had remarked on these traits in his character). Mr. Reed commented with pleasure to King Ali on the way his son was turning out: "He is far less diffident and shy than he used to be and he is now able to mingle on friendly terms with others and to gain the respect of his fellows, a result for which his training as Prefect has been largely responsible. In fact I think his character has developed very favourably indeed."

A certain Kadry Bey—most probably an Iraqi official in the Ministry of Education—was also involved in the negotiations concerning the future of Abdulillah. When he asked Mr. Reed's advice about whether the Emir should proceed to England, Mr. Reed mapped out for him a plan for the Emir's general education:

CHAPTER 2

> I believe the best course for Abdulillah would be, after spending a month and a half in Baghdad . . . to proceed to England towards the end of August and to stay for a year in the family of a private tutor in the country, where he will have all the advantages of special tuition together with the amenities of English country life and good surroundings. . . . After one year spent in this way, I should like him to proceed to the London School of Economics and Political Science (which is a part of the University of London), where he would take the Diplomatic Course, intended to prepare students for the Diplomatic and consular services and for public life in general. This would take him two years, after which he would proceed to France for further studies in French over a period of another two years. In the meanwhile, during his three years in England he could spend a part of his vacations in France, so that he would already have acquired a good knowledge of the French language.

This is how Mr. Reed thought that Arab princes should be educated and prepared for public life. His carefully thought-out plan won the approval of the ex-King, who wrote back to him saying, "I come hereby authorising you to make the necessary arrangements requesting you to inform me of the steps you take in due course." Mr. Reed then contacted Mr. Doble, the Principal of Great Chesterfield College, to whom he had already sent Kamel Wassef and Ismail Chirine, and recommended the Emir as "a boy of very gentle and amiable character, and you will probably find him shy at first." However, Mr. Reed's plans were not carried out: in 1933 King Feisal died and the British Ambassador in Iraq decided to prepare Abdulillah for Cambridge. Obviously the words of the Ambassador carried more weight than those of Mr. Reed or King Ali, for Abdulillah wrote to Mr. Reed, "I must obey." (See Appendix I for his letter to Mr. Reed.) It seems that Abdulillah still retained confidence in his headmaster; when he needed a gardener for the royal palaces in 1941 (he was by then Regent), or a governess for the young princesses, it was to Mr. Reed that he applied. Mr. Reed, resourceful as ever, supplied him with a gardener from the Directeur du Service des Parcs et Plantations, Municipalité d'Alexandrie, and with a governess from Scotland.

Mr. Reed had more success with another Iraqi contemporary, Ahmed el Awa (VC 1928–32), son of Safwat Pasha el Awa, Chamberlain to His Majesty the King of Iraq. As Ahmed was about to obtain his School Certificate, his father wrote to Mr. Reed in some consternation, complaining that Mr. Reed had been encouraging Ahmed in his desire to study law. This was contrary to his wish, for although "the lawyer profession is very in vogue in England," it would not earn Ahmed a living in Iraq. Mr. Reed was required to make Ahmed understand that it was his father's wish—who had a lot of experience—that he become an engineer. Mr. Reed wrote back to justify his position:

> The reason why I am inclined to prefer subsequent training in either Law or Economics for Ahmed rather than Engineering is that he is relatively weak in Mathematics and Science (which are essential for Engineering), and relatively strong on the literary side. It is always well to consider a boy's aptitudes before deciding on his profession. Moreover, I did not suppose that Ahmed would in any case take up Law as a profession, but I rather looked to Law or Economics (with Constitutional History and Law) as the best training for government service, the diplomatic and consular services or political life, for any of which Ahmed is probably by nature better fitted than for the career of an engineer.

Maybe because Ahmed was not the son of a king or a rebel, Mr. Reed managed to have his way in Iraq at last. Safwat el Awa gave in and in the same year (1932) Ahmed wrote to Mr. Reed that he had been accepted at the London School of Economics and that he found the studies interesting.

Mr. Reed's experience was called on by the British in Iraq when they sought to establish a secondary boarding school in Baghdad. He responded enthusiastically to Mr. Smith's inquiries in 1930 and provided notes on the subject, but Mr. Smith left the service in 1932 and no evidence remains of whether Mr. Reed gave any further assistance to the plan. He did, however, maintain contact with Iraq, sending postcards of Victoria College to Mr. Edmonds (Mr. Smith's successor) who distributed them "to a number of leading Iraqis," among them former ministers. One was so interested that he asked whether there was a similar school for girls, or whether there was a girls' side at Victoria College. Despite that obstacle, Mr. Reed's publicity tactics in Iraq must have worked, as Mr. Highwood reports to him in 1934: "The market in new boys is only fairly brisk at the moment, Palestine is very active in large failures and Baghdad is moving slightly." Ja'far Pasha el Askari, who served as Prime Minister and held portfolios of Foreign Affairs and War at different times between 1920 and 1935, sent his two sons Ziad and Nazar in the mid-1930s, and Brigadier General Siam el Askari Bey (nephew of Ja'far Pasha and also in the Ministry of Defence) sent his brother Hussein el Askari in 1933. At one point there were four Askaris in Victoria College and the joke that circulated was that there was an "Askari" (guard) in each corner of the school.

By the 1940s more Englishmen in Egypt were involved in Iraq, among them Mr. Highwood, who had in 1938 left Victoria College for Cairo to become the first director of the British Evening Institute (later called the British Council). It seems his connections had become as powerful as Mr. Reed's, for here he is promising to help Mr. Reed in the mysterious question of the "absentee Iraqis." "I will do my best to get them back," he assured Mr. Reed in 1939. "I don't know whether it is the Russians or the Grand Mufti which will prove to be the cause." In the following year there was more mysterious correspondence between them over Iraq and the Englishmen there, with references to the "Council" and the importance of getting the British community interested in the scheme. They were possibly discussing the establishment of a British Council in Baghdad, since by then Mr. Reed was becoming involved in British Council work. He received orders from Lord Lloyd, now director of the British Council in London, to go to Baghdad "in an exploratory capacity without committing the Council to anything." He must have gone sometime in April or May, and on his return wrote frantically to Mr. Highwood that he had borne the expenses of the trip. The mystery deepened and it was revealed that some Iraqis, most of them Old Boys, might have been involved in the scheme. Mr. Highwood's letter read as follows:

> The news in your second letter about the expenses for the Baghdad trip is a great shock as I saw Safwat [el Awa] and Haidar on the last morning of my stay in Baghdad and they assured me that the matter had been taken up. I have an uncomfortable feeling that what the Manager of Cooks told me is true, namely: that Abdulilla is not very good at paying his debts or was in the past when he could not afford to.... I am writing by the next bag to Morray asking him to present the bill to Safwat. The original suggestion that you should go at the Old Boys' expense arose from a dinner party I had with Safwat, Baba Ali, Jack Abudy and Haidar, and they all agreed to foot the bill.... The Regent made the suggestion that he should pay the bill afterwards.

It is not clear whether this was the exploratory trip ordered by the British Council or an invitation from the Iraqi Old Boys, or some form of networking between the British Council and Mr. Reed's Old Boys. What is definitely clear is that Mr. Reed was not making any money out of his activities; on the contrary, he paid for them.

If Mr. Reed was engaged in extra-educational activities, no archival material has remained to prove it. The only reference to intelligence work found was in 1940, when he recommended Charles Issawi to Colonel Clayton of the Intelligence Department. By June 1940 Mr. Reed had secured for Issawi the post of secretary to Sir Edward Cook in the National Bank, but he had also put Colonel Clayton in touch with Issawi. Issawi reports to Mr. Reed a meeting between him and Clayton, saying that Clayton had asked him whether he was an Arabist, and that he had kept Issawi's name in mind in case he could be called on to "do odd jobs." In a letter dated 21 June 1940, Mr. Reed tells Issawi the following: "I think ... that you might do definitely useful intelligence work and I am glad to note that Col. Clayton proposes to keep in touch with you."

Chapter 2

Colonel Clayton would probably be the same Gilbert Clayton who in the 1920s had headed the British mission charged with determining the map and borders of the post-Ottoman Arabian Peninsula. In those negotiations the mediator on King Ibn Saud's side had been Harry St. John Philby; the negotiator on the British side with Clayton had been the Old Boy George Antonius. Now, in the 1940s, another Old Boy was possibly being recruited for intelligence work with the British. The nature and extent of Issawi's involvement is unknown, since no further communication between Mr. Reed and Issawi survives in the Old Victorian Association archives.

Whether Mr. Reed was so highly connected because he worked for British Intelligence, or because he was headmaster of the best school in the region, or because all who came into contact with him loved and admired him for his kindness, intelligence, and integrity, is a moot point. The fact is that until his death he remained a man of simple means. Many was the time when he helped pupils with money out of his own pocket. In the 1930s he traveled to England second class and sometimes third class. He spent his summer vacations in simple country places; if he went to London he did not stay at any of the well-known expensive hotels. The fact that he never had a permanent address in England indicates that he did not own a house there. Nor did he have children for whom he might be hoarding up money. Occasionally he would linger in Italy or France on his way to or from Egypt and England; the most exotic holiday he had was in the Dolomites in the early 1930s. He sometimes went to Aswan or for a few days to the Mena House hotel next to the pyramids of Giza, and frequently to Burg el Arab, outside Alexandria. There was mention one summer of a cabin in Sidi Bishr, the prestigious beach to the east of Alexandria, but that could have been the school's cabin. He also had to go once to Switzerland for medical treatment, and once to Palestine for the same reason—that was in 1944 when he was dying. And in all the years he spent in Alexandria he did not have a car. It was his boys who collected money among themselves to buy him a car for the disabled—a token of the love and appreciation they bore him.

What all the pupils of this period agree on is that during their school years they did not feel that the establishment was a colonial presence. Antoine Bassili (VC 1942–52), whose father and uncles were Old Boys and had donated the swimming pool to the school, Fouad Awad (VC 1929–40), who later sent his two sons to his *alma mater*, and Hafez Bassoumi (VC 1943–51) who returned to the school after his graduation from Alexandria University to work as an English teacher, are only a few of the Old Boys who remember that the school was a large family in which no differences of creed or nationality were ever felt. Antoine Bassili said in 1996, "At the time Alexandria was such a cosmopolitan city that we did not consider the non-Egyptians to be foreigners." Indeed, no institution can be a better reflection of the cosmopolitan nature of Alexandria. There were Brazilian, Chilean, Iraqi, Moroccan, Spanish, Italian, Russian, Polish, Hungarian, British, French, Turkish, Austrian, and Greek Jews all living in Alexandria. There were Muslim, Christian, and Jewish Egyptians and Palestinians. There were British Presbyterians, Catholics, and Anglicans as well as Irish Catholics. German, Dutch, Swiss, and Czechoslovakian Protestants were represented in the student body, but there were also Dutch and German Roman Catholics, as well as Italian, Maltese, Hungarian, and Russian Roman Catholics. Then there was an assortment of Cypriot, Afghanistani, Indian, Saudi Arabian, Bahraini, Libyan, Jordanian, Syrian, Turkish, and Iraqi Muslims. There were Abyssinian, Russian, Albanian, and Georgian Orthodox Christians. All these different nationalities and creeds coexisted peacefully inside the school. Most of the Old Boys grew to appreciate the cosmopolitan atmosphere of the school when they grew up. Again, Antoine Bassili says that Victoria College provided him with an "open mind and a facility to mix with people of different backgrounds and different social standards. This has helped me subsequently in my twenty-nine years with the United Nations in Geneva and Vienna, and in the numerous countries I have visited for them."

What happened outside the school walls might have been a different matter. Boys who lived in an ivory tower and saw what was happening in the "real" world outside the school wrote pieces in *The Victorian* that sounded like Lawrence Durrell writing a draft of his *Alexandria Quartet*: "But first, do you know what an Egyptian village is? It is a heap of dried mud with a lot of beautiful yellow straw on top of it. And do you know what an Egyptian house is in such a village? Two rooms, or three, awful, dark, dirty, with a little court in front where hens, cows, children and sheep are all in a muddle. Add to this the most evil smells, beautiful palm-trees and a blue sky, and you have the Magic Orient." This was an article written by A.P.W. in 1934. Clement Shama (VC 1931–36), a Jew with British nationality, applied in 1937 to the Anglo-African Trading Co. for a vacancy in trading posts in Africa. In his application letter he wrote that he had been working for a year as a supervisor in a cotton press, where cotton is cleaned, mixed, processed and pressed for shipping. "As a result," he claimed, "I possess some knowledge of handling and organising large numbers of natives, which I think should prove a valuable asset if I should be eventually appointed." The imperialist outlook is very clear, the message being "natives are all the same and if I can handle the Egyptians I can handle the Africans." He did not get the job, but did get himself killed defending the British empire in Tripolitania during the Second World War. He would not have appreciated Mr. Highwood's acidic sense of humor, who had gone to the funeral of a pupil in 1933 and reported the event in a letter to Mr. Reed:

> I was not impressed by the funeral, it being the first Jewish funeral I have attended: perhaps my mind was not attuned to pious thoughts as after careful enquiries I wore a top hat and with some reluctance walked from Nabi Daniel to Mazarita among a very moth-eaten crowd of mourners, although one Israelite on my right and one on my left quoted platitudes in English and French respectively.

Mr. Reed himself was not above racism. An anonymous contemporary teacher at Victoria College wrote of him as being "intellectually, if not politically, a Liberal." Mr. Reed confided to Charles Issawi (VC 1927–33) in 1932 that Egypt was on the way to becoming a truly independent country, "the real obstacle to her being so now, whatever people on one side or the other may say, is the deplorable lack of real brains and ability among the native Egyptians, even of the younger generation in this country." These private sentiments, however, remained precisely that and never spilled over into public action or discrimination between the boys, and this was the spirit of equality his boys were imbued with.

If the boys generally felt at home with each other within the school, they formed an elite group outside. Fouad Awad admits that they did not mix with boys from other schools, not even foreign schools or other British schools such as the British Boys School, which was established in 1929 to provide a British education for those who could not afford Victoria College. Adham el Nakeeb (VC 1930–43) and Chairman of the Old Victorian Association (1978–89) went so far as to claim, in his address to the International Reunion of 1988, that Victoria College schooled "the future rulers of state" while the British Boys School "trained the clerks of the future . . . to serve the state."

There are some cases of boys who felt that their superior education at Victoria College had alienated them from their surroundings in Egypt. When Nicola Stamboulieh went to work at the Municipality in Alexandria, he was dissatisfied with his colleagues. "The Municipality is an ideal institution to those lazy creatures whose only happiness and object in life is to be able to eat bread and onions for lunch, and olives and garlic for dinner, go about the town in the evenings, make love to the first cheap woman they meet, and spare enough money for some cigarettes," he wrote to Mr. Reed in 1939. "I have not been brought up at Victoria College to lead that life." Charles Issawi, whom Mr. Reed had recommended for Oxford in 1933 as being one of the ablest three or four boys he had taught in the past forty years, suffered even more from alienation. Charles enjoyed Oxford life at Magdalen College, which had broadened his outlook considerably and encouraged his appreciation of music, but he thought there was more to education. "I don't think that it is the sole function of education to increase the hedonistic faculties. I still think that education ought to increase one's capacity to serve, one's social function," he wrote to his headmaster from Oxford in 1937. He graduated with honors in the same year and returned to Egypt, where he worked first in the Ministry of Finance in Amin Pasha Osman's office (who had by then left the Municipality and was Under-Secretary of Finance in the Sidky Pasha government), then in the Central Bank. Although he had studied Philosophy, Politics and Economics at Oxford, he found his work distasteful. He wrote to Mr. Reed in 1938 of his job:

Chapter 2

> It's a very dreary job thinking of cheques and drafts and inflations and reserves; it's inhuman. There's only one job fit for a man: University or (second best) school teacher. One deals with human material, one influences human lives. When I think how much I owe to three persons: Edward [most likely Atiyah, whom he knew], yourself, and my philosophy don, I feel that teaching is the only possible job . . . But why do I tell you all this? Because I felt that you were somewhat surprised, perhaps even a little annoyed, at my settling down so prosaically to serve Mammon. I am more, I am indignant.

In the following year he was more dissatisfied with "improving Means to unimproved Ends." He could not reconcile himself to banking, especially as his eyes were giving him trouble and to rest them he had to avoid reading after work hours. Again he complained to Mr. Reed:

> With an effort I could accommodate myself to this sort of life. I am well paid and could presumably lead what people presume to be a very pleasant life. From the office to the Club; Tennis, Bridge, Dancing; an occasional play or picture . . . wife and children—what more can a man desire? But, I ask you, is this the kind of life you would like me to lead? . . . You may call it conceit but to me it seems evident that I am of an elite (only comparatively speaking) and must behave as such . . . I want help and advice . . . I can speak to you in a language you can understand—because it is from you that I have learned most of its elements.

Charles' sense of being a member of the elite had nothing to do with snobbery. It was more akin to the original meaning of the word "cosmopolis," which was coined in Greece in the fourth century BC to refer to a wise man's allegiance to other wise men in the community of mankind rather than to his own *polis* or city. Such an association of like-minded people would explain Charles' friendship with a certain Hourani, about whom he wrote to Mr. Reed in 1939: "A friend about whom I believe I have talked to you, Hourani, a Syrian who was up at Magdalen and who has the acutest mind among my generation—as well as discussing asceticism is spending Easter with me and I am hoping to indulge in orgies of Mosque and Coptic Church crawling." This friend would be the nameless person he had mentioned the year before to Mr. Reed:

> I spent a few days in the Lebanon where I met a prophet who urged me to repent. He's a double Ph.D. (Harvard—where he was Whitehead's favorite pupil and Fribourg where he was with Heidegger), a Syrian Christian, an amazingly fine chap, the only Oriental I've met who will, I think, enrich world thought . . . I am, of course, not thinking of specialists in e.g. Egyptology, Arab history and literature etc. who are of course adding to the knowledge of the world. He has an interesting scheme concerning the creation of an Everyman's library in Arabic, to consist mainly of translations from Greek, Latin, English, etc., which I would like to explain to you if I may, some day.

Hourani, the mysterious "prophet," can only be Albert Hourani, for there is an acknowledgment to C. Issawi in Albert Hourani's *The History of the Arab Peoples*.

Charles Issawi was a boy who had aroused Mr. Reed's special interest. His father, Elie Bey Issawi, a Syrian Greek Orthodox, worked in the finance department in Khartoum, then acquired Egyptian nationality in 1932 and within a year had moved to Cairo. He seems to have been a friend of Mr. Reed's. Like some other parents he could not afford the school's full fees, so it was a relief to him when Charles won the Smouha Scholarship in 1929. Charles showed considerable promise from the day he arrived at the school in 1927. Within a fortnight Mr. Reed was writing to Issawi Bey, "We are very well pleased with his intelligence and industry and his conduct is all that could be desired." However, the boy seemed to be having trouble with stretching out his pocket money, and started devising impractical theories about how to handle his finances.

Chapter 2

First he approached his father with a scheme for increasing his pocket money to cover items that were added to the bill at the end of each term. Before consenting, Issawi Bey, who handled the government budget in Sudan, consulted with Mr. Reed: "Charlie does not seem to appreciate the value of money. Do you think that if I increased his pocket money allowance from PT10 to PT15 a week he would be able to meet such extras as are now included in the two items of 'Trams, amusements, etc.' and 'Sundries' out of that allowance?" Mr. Reed flatly refused. Undeterred, Charles dreamed up another scheme, of being given LE 6 at the beginning of the term, out of which he would pay all expenses apart from fees. Again Issawi Bey consulted with Mr. Reed, who responded with a lengthy analysis that tore apart the budding economist's proposal:

> His proposal (and I suppose yours also) was that the School should hand him at the beginning of the term 6 pounds, out of which he was to pay in cash for all his extras incurred in the course of the term, so that you should have bills only for the actual School fees .... If anything remained over at the end of the term he was to pocket the balance, and if the extras came to more than six pounds, a matter which it would be impossible for him to judge beforehand, he was, I suppose, to apply to you for the balance. Now none of the extras are payable at all until the end of the term, so that for 3 months Charles would have 6 pounds (the property of the School) lying idle in his pockets, and knowing Charles's extraordinary carelessness as I do, I feel sure that in the course of a term a part or all of this money would be lost. What Charles actually proposed to do was to spend the whole of this 6 pounds at once upon a gramophone for the Captain's Study and in the course of the term to get back by weekly installments from the other Captains all but his own share of the expense, so that at the end of the term he might hope to have collected about 540, with which he hoped to pay the extras of the term. This is hardly a good way of teaching Charles the value of

money, of which he simply has no idea at present . . . I
am, as you know, very fond of Charles who is in all
essentials a very good boy indeed as well as a boy of
exceptional promise; but he is at present deplorably irresponsible, though I trust to his training as a captain and
a prefect to develop his sense of responsibility enor-
mously in the course of the next two years. I am not
however, of the opinion that the best way to teach a boy
the value of money is to give him a large sum of money
to do what he likes with it and then to find yourself in a
position of paying his debts at the end of the period: he
will only economise on all the wrong things and be
extravagant on all the wrong things.

With these minor financial crises settled, Charles continued to do bril-
liantly at his studies. He obtained his School Certificate when he was sixteen and a half, in 1932, with credits in scripture, English, history,
French, elementary mathematics, and science, and gained full marks in
the Chaucer paper. Charles was a rather whimsical boy who changed his
mind about his career three times a year. After gaining the School
Certificate, he decided he wanted to study medicine at Qasr al-Aini, so
Issawi Bey accordingly asked Mr. Reed to write the recommendation letter and make the necessary contacts. Mr. Reed responded with what must
have been the harshest letter in his voluminous correspondence, saying
that it would be criminal to take Charles away before he got the Higher
Certificate and deprive him of the opportunity of

developing his very unusual intellectual powers at a time
when they are ripe for development by means of studies,
which would prepare him to take his proper place among
the intellectual elite of any University to which he proceeds. As a doctor practising in Egypt, Charles will have
no possibility for distinction and will earn a humdrum
living for the rest of his life. Moreover, he is particularly unsuited, in my opinion, to become a doctor . . . I
regard it as so utterly wrong to place him in a fifth rate

institution such as the University of Cairo that I certainly do not feel disposed to assist you in ruining his career.

After this diatribe, Issawi Bey had no option but to return Charles to Victoria College to prepare for the Higher School Certificate and eventually Oxford, for Mr. Reed would not settle for any less than that for his protégé. What he had set his heart on was Balliol, to secure for Charles "when he comes out to Egypt again the great prestige of being a Balliol man like Mohamed Pasha Mahmoud, Ahmed Hassanein Bey and other prominent Egyptians." He therefore started corresponding with the Master of Balliol College about a scholarship for Charles, and with his friend Kenneth Bell, a Fellow of Balliol, about accommodation and tutors for Charles to prepare him for the scholarship exam. Bell was rather apprehensive and cautioned Mr. Reed, "You must not forget that you are going in for a race against the best trained horses of the best stables and that in cases of doubt they would select an Etonian or Harrovian." Mr. Reed remained undaunted and dispatched Charles to Oxford, writing him letters of encouragement and advice about which books to study, which questions to answer and which to avoid, what were his strong points and what the weak ones were. Charles returned to Cairo in January 1934, having sat for two exams, to await the results. One wonders who was the happier, Charles or Mr. Reed, when the good news arrived that Charles had won a demyship (open scholarship of £100 a year) to Magdalen College. Mr. Reed definitely celebrated in style in Alexandria. He popped the champagne and gave the school a whole day off in honor of its scholar.

Charles showed that the faith Mr. Reed had in him was not misplaced. He agitated for years to leave his jobs in the Ministry of Finance and then in the Central Bank, confessing to Mr. Reed that his dream was to find a teaching job, where "one feels that one is spending one's time developing minds, not increasing shareholders' profits. I can't forget the effect your influence had on me." However, he did not want to resign and then find himself jobless with a war on—this was in June 1939. In 1943 he left Egypt to take up a teaching post at the American University of Beirut. Eventually Mr. Reed's promise to Issawi Bey that Charles would distinguish himself was fulfilled, though Mr. Reed was dead by then.

Charles worked in the Arab Office in Washington DC and in the United Nations. The schoolboy who had wreaked such havoc with his pocket money became a professor of economics at Columbia University, Princeton University, and New York University, and the author and editor of numerous books listed in *Who's Who 1996* that remain standard references on Egypt and the Middle East.

From Sudan, too, came yet another amazing little boy. Edward Atiyah had ended up in Sudan like his father, and had sent his sons Michael and Patrick to Victoria College (1941–44 in Shubra under Mr. Reed; 1944–45 in Alexandria under Mr. Scovil). Like his father, too, Edward could not afford the school fees, and he suggested to Mr. Reed that Michael sit for the Smouha Scholarship exam, saying, "I feel sure, making full allowance for parental vanity—that they will both be a credit to the School. Michael reminds me a lot of Charles Is[s]awi at his age." Most likely Edward Atiyah had known Issawi Bey when the latter was in Khartoum, and used to see young Charles when he went there during the summer vacations. Michael indeed showed promise as soon as he arrived at Victoria College, with Mr. Reed noting, within a few weeks of his arrival, that he was very well advanced in mathematics and English. In 1945 Mr. Rider, the mathematics master, wrote in the confidential report: "Very Good. He has worked well and is not often in difficulties. Some of his results show intelligent application of principles. He ought to pass easily." Needless to say, the school was not mistaken in its assessment of its boys: Sir Michael Atiyah's success in the field of mathematics has to be looked up in *Who's Who 1996*, where it occupies a whole page. He has held many academically prestigious posts, among them President of the Royal Society (1990–95) and Master of Trinity College, Cambridge (1990–97).

Mr. Reed does not seem to have had much of a role in guiding Michael, possibly because Mr. Reed was continually ill by then. One interesting incident that took place occurred, rather, under the tutelage of Mr. Price (acting headmaster in Shubra 1944–45) while Michael was still at the Shubra branch. This took the form of an ideological difference between Edward and Mr. Price. Edward had wanted Michael to take scripture as a subject for the School Certificate, but Mr. Price had objected because Michael held unorthodox views on the Bible. Edward discussed the matter with Mr. Price:

Chapter 2

> Actually it was I who suggested that he should take it. He has not read the Bible yet and I very much want him to do so. After all there are other legitimate approaches to the Bible than that of pure orthodoxy, and what indeed is orthodoxy today? Of course, if the subject is taught by a clergyman who expects all the pupils to be orthodox believers and to approach it as such, then I understand your objection, but I think it a pity all the same that a boy should be denied the literary and moral benefits of a study of the Bible merely because he is not a believer in dogma.

Edward presented a convincing case, but so did Mr. Price. In response he wrote:

> I agree that there are other approaches to the scriptures than that of strict orthodoxy or else I should be ruled out myself, but to approach them in the mood of a militant atheist seems to me to be going outside the limits of legitimate approaches. For the Old Testament there is not really any valid objection, but the School Certificate Examination includes a paper on the New Testament for which a clergyman takes the boys. I have discussed the matter with Reed and he thinks it is not fair for the clergyman to have in his class people who are not professed Christians.

Both sides of the argument were valid, but the point to consider is that although Victoria College did not impose religious instruction on its boys, it expected them to treat the subject with respect if they chose to study it.

There was a more serious issue than ideological differences during Michael's stay at the school. In March 1942 Michael fell dangerously ill. Mrs. Reed stayed up with him and upon observing the acuteness of his case, did not wait until daybreak to call the school doctor, but contacted him immediately. Michael was promptly dispatched to hospital, where meningitis was diagnosed. For a few agonizing days telegrams were exchanged between Khartoum and Victoria College, until Michael pulled through and Edward was able to write to Mr. Reed a month later, "I have always known that my boys will be in safe hands at Victoria; now I feel sure that it was yours and Mrs. Reed's anxiousness and promptness that saved Michael's life."

Edward Atiyah had admired Mr. Reed ever since, as a young boy in Omdurman, he had seen the name and photograph of Mr. Reed in the school prospectus. He continued to correspond with him until Mr. Reed's death in 1945, exchanging ideas and asking for advice and help. In 1943 he wrote to Mr. Reed that he had nearly finished his book and was hoping to show it to him when they met in the summer. The book must have been *An Arab Tells His Story*, published by John Murray in 1946 and dedicated to Mr. Lias and Mr. Reed. His second book was *The Arabs*, published by Penguin in 1955. In 1943, too, Edward was beginning to want to leave Sudan and asked Mr. Reed to help him find a post in Egypt or Syria. Edward trusted that Mr. Reed's many connections, or his position as Representative of the British Council in Egypt (which he had taken up in June 1943), would help transfer him out of Sudan, where he felt his job was done:

> I am very anxious to be at the centre of things during the present important period when the future political and cultural relations of Britain with the Arab world are being shaped. I am, as you know, a great believer in the cause of the Anglo-Egyptian friendship, and I am sure that I have something to contribute to it in a wider field than Sudan. I feel that my job here is done . . . I have now reached the end of a phase in Sudan, and there is little for me to do in the new era into which the country is moving; little, that is to say, of any real value. On the other hand, I feel that I could be very useful in the new scheme of things which I can see taking shape in the Middle East . . . There cannot be many persons in the Middle East who have my peculiar dual qualifications for serving the cause of Anglo-Egyptian friendship—my Syrian back-

Chapter 2

ground, my English education, my political and psychological experience in Sudan where for 18 years it has been my job to effect adjustments and promote understanding and co-operation between Englishmen and educated Arabs, and between both and myself.

Edward was especially interested in British Council work, since he had helped to found and run a similar institution in Khartoum, Sudan Cultural Center. He felt that he would be most useful in Syria, and though the British were staying out of the country for the moment on account of the French, he hoped that things might change after the war and there would be an opening for him there. Failing that, he hoped to be fitted into a place like the Arab Bureau or in the Minister of State's office. Mr. Reed did not respond this time to a call for help. He was seriously ill in hospital, and Edward must have got into the Arab Office in London through other channels.

In the case of another Old Boy, Gaston Zananiri (VC 1914–21), Mr Reed was unable to help—for different reasons. Gaston's father, George Pasha Zananiri, was Secretary-General of the Board of Quarantine and Sanitation. His family was established in Alexandria at the beginning of the eighteenth century, and the Sublime Porte had conferred upon George Zananiri the title of pasha in 1910 for his services on the Board, which was, in some sort, an ancestor of the World Health Organization in the region. In the 1930s Gaston, too, was working for the Board of Quarantine and Sanitation, and often sent Mr. Reed outlines of lectures he might be delivering in Italy about Italo-Egyptian cultural relations in Egypt, or proposals, complete with lists of names and possible premises, for the establishment of an Anglo-Egyptian Union in Alexandria, or a copy of the "statute" of the Workers' Association along with a project and a résumé of a similar project realized in Mexico with great success. What did Mr. Reed want with the Workers' Association anyway? But he had been discussing something of the sort with Gaston. In 1937 Gaston read in the papers of changes within the Egyptian Ministry of Foreign Affairs. He wrote to Mr. Reed, asking him to secure for him the post of Secretary-General, since he saw that his work at the Quarantine Board qualified him for it. Mr. Reed forwarded his request to Amin Pasha Osman (who had only the year before played a central role in the Anglo-Egyptian treaty), and told Gaston that he did not think there was a possibility of getting the post of Secretary-General of Foreign Affairs, but that he had a chance of securing a diplomatic post, which he had mentioned to Amin. What Mr. Reed did not tell Gaston was that he had already decidedly advised Amin *against* considering Gaston for the post, instead suggesting a diplomatic post:

> It is true that he has done a great deal and had experience of foreign affairs of a sort at the Quarantine Board where he has for long held a pretty responsible post and has in fact done a good deal of work attributed to the Secretary-General. Moreover, he is of the opinion that one of his most notable characteristics is tact. Long ago, and now for some time, I have advised Gaston to give up his political ambitions, partly because he is a Syrian Christian, and partly because, although I have known him for a long time and like him very much I am afraid I cannot consider him in any way as first rate. He has a passion for bureaucratic organisation, the main object of which is always to create a good many expensive posts for figureheads (who are always Moslem Egyptians), while he himself in a sheltered post does all the work and rules Egypt. I cannot think this is the way things should be done or that he could do it . . . I do think that a Diplomatic post is one suited to Gaston's particular talents and abilities, which in their second rate way are very considerable. In other words he would be better, and definitely useful, out of the country; but in a responsible Government post in Egypt I think you would find his fussiness, excitability and fundamental incompetence quite intolerable.

As usual, it was Mr. Reed's integrity that won the day in the end. He could not recommend somebody—not even someone he liked—for a post he felt he could not fulfill. He also had a vision of how the government should be run, and maybe because his vision was clear and

Chapter 2

unbiased, Amin Pasha Osman allowed himself to be guided by his master in matters of politics. The extent of Mr. Reed's influence on Amin Pasha Osman in politics is unfathomable, but if it was considerable, then Reed was no better than Gaston Zananiri, whom he accused of using Egyptian Muslims as puppets while he stayed in the shadows and did all the work.

An important point Mr. Reed raised in his letter to the Pasha was the position of Christian Syrians in Egypt. Charles Issawi believed that he had no chances in Egypt because he was a Syrian, although he had acquired Egyptian nationality. In his first year at Oxford he wrote to Mr. Reed about the thought he had given to his career:

> In the course of this year I have come more and more to realise the absurdity of my, and my likes,' position in Egypt. I think, sir, you were fundamentally mistaken when you said that the Egyptians, wishing to do without European aid, would be compelled to fall back on Syrian assistance. I think they would sooner seek help from their dearest European foes than from us. And perhaps they are not wholly to blame. The first batch of Syrians who came over was anything but desirable and fully deserved the name of "intruders" which has clung to us ever since.

Despairing of a government job in Egypt, Charles decided, with his customary whimsy, to study law, which he found dull, instead of studying Modern Greats. The reason was that he had an uncle living in Palestine (Charles was half Syrian, half Palestinian) who assured him that lawyers had very good opportunities in Palestine—making it in Charles' opinion "the only country that suffers from a dearth of that most prolific of breeds." Charles was further encouraged by the idea of Palestine because he felt that there he would not have to blush at his Syrian accent. Mr. Reed of course knew what was better for his pupils than they knew themselves. He persuaded Charles to study philosophy and economics and found him a government job in Amin Pasha Osman's office in 1937, with a salary of LE 15 a month.

The schoolboys were generally unaware of what was going on in the upper circles of the school. They saw the Prime Minister, various ministers, the British Ambassador, the British Consul-General in Alexandria, and various other dignitaries at Speech Day and Sports Day. Sports Day was almost as important as Speech Day; it, too, was reported in the *Egyptian Gazette*, and in 1930 Prince Omar Tousson gave away the prizes. But the boys busied themselves mainly with school life. Political discussions were not looked upon with a favorable eye by the masters. Activities were encouraged. The Scouts had grown up and even had Cubs. A hut was built for them on the grounds, and lectures on various subjects were given to them: Mr. Reed lectured on the British Constitution, and Mr. Ingham, the school bursar, on economy. Antoine Bassili says that scouting, especially sea scouting, taught him discipline, it being no joke to find yourself in a boat in a rough open sea. Their jamborees were important events that they would remember with pleasure years after they had graduated. The jamboree of 1933 was held in Hungary and was graced with the presence of Lord Baden-Powell, the Chief Scout. The weather was so hot that the *Magyar Cserkész*, the jamboree daily paper, called the event the "Sunboree" and reported that even the Egyptians were feeling the heat. Nevertheless, the weather did not stop the 50,000 Scouts gathered from all over the world from enjoying themselves. The *Magyar Cserkész* published photographs of them having fun as they bent over the camp fire, waving flags and dressed up in their national costumes. The caption read: "Gay Camp Life."

Sports were compulsory. The poor mother of Arthur Colley received a severe letter from the school notifying her that her son had not been playing football for a whole term because he did not have football boots. If he did not manage to borrow some within a few days, he would be punished for "cutting compulsory organised games." The first time the young Fouad Awad went on the football pitch, he was surprised to find Mr. Parkhouse pulling at his clothes. To his embarrassment, Fouad discovered that the flannel his conscientious mother had dressed him in was forbidden during games. In addition to football and cricket (the greatest honor was to belong to the First XI of either sport or both, and was a fact to be mentioned in recommendation letters), hockey, sailing, boxing, fencing, tennis, ping-pong, cross-country runs, and bathing were on

Chapter 2

offer, for the purpose of which last the school had a hut on the prestigious beach of Sidi Bishr and buses to transport the boys there. In 1929 Mr. H.B. Carver provided the school with an experimental grass playing field, and through the generosity of Lady Barker trees were planted in the grounds. There were five football pitches and four tennis courts.

Matches against other teams, such as the RAF, the Hellenic Club, the Tram Club, or the Olympic Union Recreation Club, or involving the school itself—such as the school against the Old Boys, or the pupils against the staff—were taken very seriously, but those played against the English Girls' College were undertaken in a different spirit. Between the EGC and Victoria College there has been what Mohamed Awad (VC 1954–68 and chairman of the Old Victorians' Association from 1995 to date) jokingly called "a historic antipathy." The girls said that VC stood for "Vipers' Club" and the boys said that EGC stood for "English Gorilla Company." But if they got the chance, the boys were willing to go to any lengths to come closer to the girls. Just before setting off for a cricket match on the girls' home-ground, Mr. Reed gave the boys a lecture on how to behave as gentlemen. The boys dutifully set off, and after the match was played, the mistress said they could have a swim in the pool. When she blew the whistle the first time, she said, the girls would jump in. At the second whistle, the girls would get out of the pool and the boys would jump in. She then blew her whistle and the girls jumped in. In one body, the boys jumped in with them. Mr. Reed, hearing of the miscreant behavior of his boys, gathered them in his office and witheringly told them, "I didn't think you were savages."

The boys were capable of all sorts of naughtiness, finding no harm in confounding Miss Miller, who helped Mrs. Malloy (wife of S.E. Malloy the School Sergeant) in the tuck shop. Like the rest of his chums, Fouad Awad would give Miss Miller a piastre and ask for a sausage sandwich. With the sandwich safely in his hand he would claim that he had given her five piastres and demand the change. The poor woman must have shed tears of frustration at the constant deficits she had to work out. Parents often sent Mr. Reed presents from their farms for him to sample and share with the boys. Zikry Bey, who had four sons at the school, sent in 1932 some fish roes as a sample of the products of Lake Bardawil; in 1935 and 1936 baskets of watermelons, and in December 1935 a turkey for

Christmas. In earlier years, it was Mrs. Sadek, the mother of Ahmed (VC 1923) and Mahmoud Sadek (VC 1924), who regularly sent Mr. Reed a Christmas turkey. Their nephew, Ibrahim Sadek (VC Cairo 1943–56) remembers his uncles telling him the following story involving their cousin Saleh Sadek (VC 1926–36) and their friends Mustafa Zohdi (VC 1928–39), and Mohamed Moghazi (VC 1927). They conspired to steal the annual turkey, which was kept in the coal room to be fatted. After climbing into the coal room through the gymnasium window and carrying it away, they had a day boy cook it for them and bring it to the school. The group made a public meal of it in the dining room. Mr. Reed eyed the turkey and recognized it as his Christmas dinner, but since he had no proof, he could do nothing about it. Another of their friends, Mounir Hassan Sabry (son of Hassan Pasha Sabry), had what seemed to be fascist leanings. He crept down to the quadrangle at night and emptied a revolver into the air. When he went to Oxford during the war years, he again crept down to the quadrangle at night, this time with a gramophone on which he played the Horst Wessel, a most fascist song. "His father, Prime Minister or no Prime Minister," says Ibrahim Sadek, "Mounir Hassan Sabry was summarily sent down from Oxford." Galal Atif (VC 1938–45), who had stolen the sacred dinner song, did not fare much better. His brother and guardian, Ezz Eldin Atif, Captain of HMY *Mahroussa*, received a letter from Victoria College asking him not to send Galal back to school the following year since he was so hopeless at studies. Ali Ridha (VC 1934–40), however, did not create too many disturbances. His father was a deceased wealthy merchant and had been the governor of Jeddah from King Hussein's time until he died. On the boy's arrival at the school, Mr. Reed wrote to Mr. Calvert of the British Legation in Jeddah stating that although the boy knew no English or French, he was "evidently intelligent and well brought up." Ali Ridha studied petroleum engineering at the University of California at Berkeley, and became the Ambassador of Saudi Arabia to the USA and Representative of Saudi Arabia to the United Nations.

Victor Bassili (VC 1920–23) went on to study at the University of Lausanne and later became one of the school's governors, but he must have been an exceptionally naughty schoolboy. His friends were Edward Heneikati and Robert Khoury, and his son Antoine relates:

CHAPTER 2

This trio must have been particularly mischievous, because I remember Mohamed Hamada coming to see my father, some thirty years after they had left school to enquire "were we really so terrible?" He had gone to see Mr. Barritt [the headmaster] to ask him to be more strict with his son Hussein, and Barritt told him "from what I understand, Sir, he is a chip off the old block." . . . I recall a story he told me of a teacher they had who had lost an arm in the war and whom they used to carry their "cheating papers" from desk to desk by putting them in the pocket of his jacket, of course on the side that had no arm!

Another case of cheating is recounted by Fouad Awad. He took all the wrong steps to solve a problem, then copied the correct answer. Mr. Rider told him to come to his flat the following day at noon, which was unusual. The following day the guilty boy appeared and Mr. Rider asked, "Awad, have you had any assistance?" "Yes," the trembling boy answered in a sweat. "Don't do it again." Fouad Awad was grateful that he was spared the humiliation of an outright accusation and of punishment, and that he had learned his lesson without any loss of dignity.

Not everyone got away so lightly, however, punishment and discipline being bywords of the school. Punishment ranged from detention after school that did not exceed two hours, to punishment drills during break, to that most dreaded of all punishments: caning. It was reserved for the most serious offense (there were three sizes of canes, depending on the magnitude of the crime) and was so solemn an affair that only the headmaster could administer it. The offenders would be lined up in the headmaster's office to watch with terror while he flexed the cane and applied it to one buttock after the other. If a boy tried to lessen the pain by padding himself with extra underclothes, the expert wrist would immediately detect the ploy and expose the folly to the others. No boy was safe from the cane (Fouad Awad cannot remember a name that escaped it), not even the sons of ministers. Mohamed, the son of Ali Pasha Maher, was especially prone to punishments, and with Mr. Reed away in England for health reasons, it was left to Mr. Scovil to write the following letter to Ali Pasha Maher in 1933:

> While Mohamed has been rather troublesome this term I do not want you to take too much notice of it. Please remember that School life takes some getting used to for a boy who has been made a fuss of at home. I think that the best thing that you could do for Mohamed's development is to show him that both you and his mother approve of the School discipline and that he cannot expect sympathy when he is punished. This term I have had to give him a few light taps with the stick on two occasions, and I think it has had a very good effect. Of course the knowledge that his father is a very important person is apt to make a small boy very conceited, which is not very good for him.

Not even Charles Issawi, the apple of Mr. Reed's eye, was exempt from punishment. He came into the hall ten minutes late for lunch one day and was accordingly given an essay to write on "libraries" by Mr. Rider, who was in charge of the hall. Charles wrote an impertinent essay, thinking it would not be read, so he was punished again. He absented himself from lunch again as a protest against Mr. Rider's methods of discipline and told him as much, and was again punished. On Saturdays and Sundays the masters did not go in to lunch, but on Monday Charles once more absented himself, having decided to go on protesting until either he was removed from Mr. Rider's table or Mr. Rider from his. Mr. Reed could not tolerate this behavior and wrote to Issawi Bey, "This is an attitude I could not possibly permit particularly in a School Captain, and unless Charles is given a sharp lesson for his behaviour, I am afraid that his character will suffer very seriously and that he will be encouraged to indulge in this sort of childish and irresponsible wilfulness, which it is one of the main objects of public school education (especially through the system of prefects and captains) to overcome." Charles was too old to be caned, so he was deprived of his captaincy for the few days remaining before the vacation.

Discipline also involved keeping a close eye on all the boys' movements, because the school considered itself their guardian and therefore responsible for their safety. When Leslie Fleming broke bounds to buy sandwiches from a nearby store, his stepfather received the following letter from Mr. Reed: "This is a serious offence which, if repeated, will lead to his being sent away from the School. It must be understood that the Housemasters and I, as Headmaster, are responsible for the conduct, health and safety of the Boarders while they are at School and stand *in loco parentis* towards them. No boy is allowed to go outside the School grounds without previous permission from his Housemaster." At the same time the school insisted that boarders should have the opportunity to go out on Sundays and on vacations with guardians. Saleh Zikry had no guardian and so Mr. Reed wrote to his father, Mohamed Zikry Bey, "Entrepreneur and Concessionaire du Lac Bardawili, Port-Said and Ismailia," asking him to find a guardian for Saleh, for "it is rather hard, considering his age and position in the School [as prefect], that he is prevented from going out." When Mohamed Abdel Salam Bey, "Conseilleur à la Haute Court d'Appel" in Asyut, asked for permission for his son Shadi to be excused from school on 22 and 23 December, two days before the school holidays, to have enough time to visit his family now living in Upper Egypt, he was told that special leave was allowed only "in the case of the marriage or death of a near relation."

In return for the obedience it exacted, the school provided care and support in every aspect. There was a dancing master to teach the boys how to waltz, tango, and foxtrot, and a school doctor to look after their health. In a report written in 1926–27 Dr. Forrest said that the health of the boys had always been good because the school "has free exposure to the north air, not too near the sea to be damp, but sufficiently inland to be impregnated with healthy desert air." He also attributed their good health to the presence of a fully trained matron and day-to-day care, and to the tuck shop, which he said was well looked after and that "its moderate tariff inclines the boys to frequent it for their extra comestibles rather than to buy fly-blown beastliness from the hawkers' barrows." Lunch and dinner were three-course meals. Food was surveyed and comments were made on its quality and quantity. In 1942 Mr. St. Leger-Hill (master 1930–52) suspected that the boys were not getting large enough second helpings. He noted down the exact size of the second helpings the boys at his table were receiving over a period of three weeks, and convinced that it was insufficient for growing boys, he submitted the list he had made to the headmaster, with a copy to the bursar. He conceded that the quality was good.

The boys viewed the matter of food from a different perspective. They were not allowed to leave any food on their plates, so any meat considered inedible, recalls Fouad Awad, was promptly thrown under the table. He also remembers that when Percy Bolton mowed the grass, they would joke that they would be having *mulukhiya* for lunch that day. *The Victorian* reported in 1938: "It is suggested that the recent improvement in the school Molokhia is to be attributed to the fact that the Main Quadrangle has been newly planted with Uganda grass." The first Mrs. Haydon, who taught in the prep school, asked for lockers for the boys, a playroom for the boarders, and a cupboard. When none was forthcoming, she realized that the school had to economize and she gave up on the lockers and the cupboard, but not on the playroom: "The playroom, though, is very much on my mind . . . It would make such an enormous difference to the little boarders in the winter." She had by then left Victoria College and was in England for good, but she still worried about her little boys. Percy Bolton, the school steward (see Appendix J), and A. Treen, the school carpenter, were around for so long that they were "family" to the boys. In 1930 a tea party was held in their honor in the library; both men were presented with gold watches, Mrs. Bolton with a gold brooch, and Amin Osman gave a speech on behalf of the Old Boys. This sense of belonging seemed to be contagious and also extended to neighbors: Bandas, the fat Greek who had a small shop on the corner of Victoria College tram station and who gave the boys biscuits and "gazooza" on credit (the forerunners of Seven-Up were Saad Mustapha and Panero), survives in the memory of generations of Old Boys as "an institution in his own right." Ali Ridha was such a frequent client that he was nicknamed Bandas.

To give the boys the opportunity to be all-rounders, there was carpentry, gardening, a chess club, a school cinematograph, a photography club, a drama group (the annual school play was an important event), and a debating society. From 1932 till 1933 Mr. Reed was kept in England to have an operation and convalesce. During his absence Mr. Douglas Haydon (master 1929–48) and Charles Issawi, by then the head boy, kept him informed about what was happening at the school. The debating

Chapter 2

society, after an apparent demise, was restarted, and Charles was elected president. Mr. Haydon reported that the first debate, on the topic of cinemas, was not a success, though Charles made a spirited and excellent speech in its defense. What he deplored was the absence of open debate, and guessed that the reason was either that the boys had nothing to say or that they were too shy to talk in front of their teachers. *The Victorian* confirmed that "this debate was remarkable for its lack of speakers." Charles wrote about another debate, on "Town and Country," "a hackneyed subject it is true but one which none of us has spoken on in the Society. Only 16 members attended (none of whom was a member of the Staff) but we had 14 speeches . . . I was quite surprised to see the order we maintained in the absence of masters." Obviously Mr. Haydon's guess about the boys' shyness was right. The last session of the term had three debates and thirty speeches. Many boys got a training for public life through the debating society, and those who gave a speech for the first time felt apprehensive about delivering what *The Victorian* referred to as their "maiden speeches."

Another exciting activity must have been *The Victorian* magazine, which was still going strong at this time. As noted, it was published by Whitehead Morris, publishers to E.M. Forster, but Charles does not seem to have had much faith in them. Writing to Mr. Reed in 1933 he said that the magazine was at the printers, "but one never knows what will happen with people like Whitehead Morris." Mr. Highwood gave his side of the story: "You will be pleased to know that *The Victorian* is at the printers . . . it has done and for the next number is doing much to draw waverers to the side of the angels. Issawi, Cripps and Serroussi have been very keen and it is practically the result of their work with the assistance of two or three others and on the whole I think it is quite good." By then its price had risen to five piastres, and the annual subscription to fifteen piastres.

The fact that most of the staff were resident—encouraging, supporting, and monitoring the day boys during school hours and the boarders until they went to bed—gave the boys the incentive to be active in many fields. Mario Colucci, in 1996, still remembered with bitterness that his mother had sent him to the Lycée in the 1940s and resented the attitude of the French teachers:

As schoolchildren of eight we were treated as if we were at university. Though the system itself was efficient, there was no individual supervision of our work or of our education. Nobody cared if we were weak in one subject or the other. If you were good at Maths you were the teachers' pet; that was the only subject that mattered. We were overloaded with homework; all the teachers gave us daily homework with no co-ordination between them, so we ended up doing homework until 10 p.m., unlike the boys at the English schools, who were having so much fun. The only class I enjoyed was English, which was given by an English master, who taught us through fun. Arabic was not compulsory and we had no religious instruction, not even if the parents asked for it. There was no moral guidance of any sort either—we were left entirely on our own, both in education and moral guidance.

The Lycée contrasted sharply with the other famous French school in Alexandria, the Collège Saint-Marc, where the boys chafed under the priests' authoritarian discipline. Before joining Victoria College in 1941, Armand Kahil went to the Collège Saint-Marc—it was a family tradition, for his father had spent his primary years with the Frères before going to St. Andrew's School, in order to gain the benefits of both a French and an English education. Armand was to follow the same tradition, only his father quarreled with one of the Frères and Armand left the Collège after only three months. He does remember, however, some of the basic differences between the French religious and the English liberal institutions. While the Collège Saint-Marc was better at studies, Victoria College had a better spirit. The Frères scared the boys, who felt they were living in a police state. They were not allowed to fight and settle differences among themselves; rather, they were encouraged to spy on each other and report the misbehavior of others. A boy with a complaint went to the school authorities, who saw to it that the offender was punished. At Victoria College the boy who carried tales was himself punished, for to "tell" on somebody was considered most ungentlemanly in English public schools.

CHAPTER 2

Boys sorted out their problems in public, in the form of fights during breaks. These were important events in their schooldays and lent color to the breaks, when sides were taken, and cheering and clapping either applauded one fighter or commiserated with the other.

So Victoria College remained an example of the happy medium that is struck between liberal education and authority regulated by the care and discipline of the English masters. The contrast between English and French education may best be expressed by an Old Boy, who signed his article as E.A. in *The Victorian* of 1930:

> Education should be considered as an end in itself; its aim being to realise, within the limits of healthy discipline, the potentialities of every individual. Its aim should not be to put something in, but to bring something out, to help and stimulate the process of individual development. French schools may be divided into two main categories: the "mission laïque" schools, which are mere centres of instruction, and the schools of religious orders, which are rigid moulds in which everybody is given the same sharply drawn intellectual and moral outline. At the first, there is no personal contact between the masters and the boys; at the latter, the personal contact that there is is of a highly undesirable sort—both are pernicious. French religious schools are doubly guilty in that they propound a religious faith and a national faith; they try to make their boys French Roman Catholics. It may be a very good thing to be a Roman Catholic, and it may be a very good thing to be a Frenchman. But it certainly is not the task of education (and it certainly should never be the aim of education) to effect such conversions, however salutary they may be . . . Victoria College presents a wholesome and refreshing contrast to propaganda-schools. It is an English school, and its aim is to give pure education on English lines to boys of all nationalities. It neither preaches a religious faith, nor tries to propagate a national one.

Nevertheless, Victoria College did "convert" its boys to the English way of life, using more subtle ways. Jacques Deschambeaux may have started out as a French boy when he came from Algeria to Victoria College in 1926. By the time he left the school in 1933 his name had become Jack, he had been a prefect and a Smouha Scholar and had done those most British of things: he had won First XI football colors and was the captain of the team, and had won First XI cricket colors and was also the captain of the team.

Colucci was not mistaken in saying that the boys at English schools had fun, for Victoria College boys never felt that education was a strain. They acquired knowledge from classes and activities rather than had it forced down their throats. They also worked after school hours at their homework—though not until they dropped. The day boys arrived home in the afternoon, and since they had already had lunch at school and played a match or two, they could study for two more hours. The boarders, too, had an hour of homework, which was supervised by the head boy and prefects.

Colucci's remark about the importance of maths would have raised eyebrows at Victoria College. Nobody denied the importance of mathematics, and Mr. Rider lives as one of the school's memorable teachers; similarly, science masters had a lasting effect on the boys. Antoine Bassili remembers Mr. Fayez, and Mr. Charles Hamdy was another of the school's pillars. But Hafez Bassoumi's remark that the school devoted special care to the selection of its English and history masters is significant. How else can a man's character be formed if he is not properly grounded in the humanities? Mr. Highwood lamented in 1934 that he read in *Al Ahram* newspaper that in future only the top candidates in the Egyptian *baccalauréat* would be admitted to the medical, engineering, and science higher schools of Cairo University, and the rest, he concluded

> may go into the Schools of Commerce, etc. and of course the Faculty of Arts. The idea seems to be to raise the Scientific world of Egypt to a higher standard and the rest who go in for Arts and Commerce will become part of an educated populace who will not necessarily

seek Govt. Posts as the aim of their education. There is no doubt a lot in this but it is a pity that Arts rather takes a back seat and it will probably turn out an odd set of intellectuals.

Thus the Lycée may have been the more farsighted in its emphasis on mathematics, though it was not until the second half of the twentieth century that Mr. Highwood's fears were really justified. Among the boys who made the humanities their profession is Mahmoud el Manzaloui (VC Alex/Cairo, 1930–41). After leaving the school he joined the Department of English Language and Literature, Faculty of Arts, Alexandria University. From there he went on to Oxford, to start again at the undergraduate level and go on to obtain a D.Phil. in English literature. On his return to Alexandria University, he taught "British Life and Thought" and "Classical Heritage" in the English Department to generations of grateful students who until today cannot get over the magic of his lectures. "We were eternally spellbound," says Heba Tadros, one of his students. "The hours flew by as if they were seconds. And even though we never wrote down a single word, his voice rang in our ears while we were answering the exam questions—we could remember every word he had said in class." Dr. Manzaloui devoted all his time to academia and to his students. In 1968 he edited two volumes of *Arabic Writing Today*, published by the American Research Center in Egypt and also in Cambridge, Massachusetts. Even though he left for Vancouver in the late 1960s to teach at the university there, his name in Alexandria University still has the aura of legend surrounding it.

Victoria College appointed its English staff through the two famous scholastic agents that supplied much of Britain with its masters and tutors, Gabbitas and Thring, and Truman and Knightly. Its exams were still the Lower Certificate, the School Certificate, and the Higher Certificate. In 1927 arrangements were made by which the school became a center for holding the Matriculation, External Intermediate, and Final Examinations of the University of London. Mr. Reed looked down on the Matriculation, confessing that although pupils wishing to sit for that "depraved" exam could do so at Victoria College, he did not allow his own boys to sit for it. Nevertheless, he thought it a better exam than that of the Egyptian government schools. The Cambridge and Oxford Joint Board exam questions came sealed in a special pouch from England and were opened in the hall, and the answers were returned in the same manner. The breaking of the seals was a dignified procedure, though Mr. Highwood recounts an incident concerning the legendary French master M. Georges Dumont, who taught at the school from its founding in 1902 until his death in 1946: "One minor pantomime took place when Dumont came in to give the Lower Certificate Dictation as, of course, there were only five of his boys there and he gave a characteristic sarcastic laugh in which the class joined with great glee. It was not a very dignified opening to an exam but at the time it was very funny." The examination results were published in *The Times* and the masters followed them anxiously—whether they were in England or still in Egypt—and commented on how well or badly each boy had done. Occasionally, Victoria College could boast of results better than those of institutions in Britain. In 1932 it achieved a record number of forty-one certificates and aroused the envy of Mr. Lionel Smith, who admitted that this was more than Edinburgh Academy had managed. Naturally some boys left the school without gaining certificates, but the majority did obtain them, and in many cases with credits.

To achieve these results Victoria College carefully followed the syllabus in England; in 1937, for example the history masters noted that "the Higher Certificate special subject this year is the Chartist Movement, with the special books being Carlyle's *Past and Present*, Disraeli's *Sybil*, with Davis's *Age of Grey and Peel* and Hovell's *Chartist Movement*." The masters, in consultation with each other and the headmaster, also decided on extra books related to each subject, and ordered them from Messrs. Bowes and Bowes, Trinity Street, Cambridge. Even then, they thought the boys needed supplementary material, which they provided in the form of notes (though boys who wrote their masters' words in their essays lost marks because they were considered lacking in creativity). Some masters did not approve of their colleagues' choice of teaching material; Mr. Highwood, for example, thought M. Dumont conservative and would have liked him to teach Racine's *Mithridate*, which he had seen in the Hachette bookstore in Alexandria, in spite of the fact that it was printed on "lavatory paper." Masters took such great care over

CHAPTER 2

library acquisitions, following the book reviews in English papers and ordering any recent publications. Toynbee's *A Study of History* and Cromer's *Modern Egypt* were considered suitable reading material for schoolboys and valuable additions to the school library, though Arthur Conan Doyle and Agatha Christie were more popular authors with the boys. With so much devotion on the masters' part, the school reached such a high level that Prince Farouk's English tutors came to Victoria College for advice on what books to teach the Prince. Mr. Highwood received the visitors in 1934 (Mr. Reed was then in England) and could not avoid treating the matter with sarcasm:

> I understand that [Sir Miles] Lampson is anxious for Prince Farouk to go to Eton or if not, to Oxford or Cambridge, as I have had several visits from [Mr.] Rye who teaches the lad [indecipherable word] enquiring about the books on Medieval History which are not anti-Islam. I told him we usually started on European History after the Middle Ages . . . Yesterday his Maths teacher showed up and saw the books used in the school and was duly impressed, not to say a little depressed, as he started looking at the books with a pompous and critical eye and ended by telling very funny stories. Perhaps when they have settled among themselves, i.e. the various tutors, you [Mr. Reed] will be able to give them a little serious advice, as I did not feel particularly competent to advise Princes in Medieval History.

Despite the standard of education that the school maintained, some boys were capable of such howlers in their exams that they deserved to be quoted in *The Victorian*:

–St. Simeon Stylites sat for eighty-two years on the pillow of St. Patrick.
–Monasticism was the period when people thought they would go to heaven quicker if they led a holy life.
–St. Columba was the first man to discover America.
–Wolsey died on his way to New York.

Moreover, in contrast to the Lycée, all the masters followed the boys' progress in every subject and encouraged each boy to develop certain points that they thought were worth developing. When he was in Lower VI 2, the Michaelmas term report of 1946 of Shadi Abdel Salam (VC 1935–48) said that at drawing he was "Good but without personality." In the Easter term of 1947 it was "Could do better," but by the summer Term of 1947 it had become "Quite Good." In the same year he passed the Lower Certificate for drawing and in 1948 the Higher Certificate. It was Mr. Edward St. Leger-Hill who taught English, history, and drawing (which he had previously taught at Canford School in England). He was a gifted painter, and in 1938 Mr. Reed applied to the Ministry of National Defence, Coast Guards Administration, Alexandria, for permission for Mr. St. Leger-Hill to "go up Rue Fort Kait Bey as far as the fort for the purpose of making some colour sketches." Mr. St. Leger-Hill also designed the scenery and costumes for the school plays. It may have been an accident, but those were the activities that interested Shadi Abdel Salam until the end of his life (in addition to a great love of literature, history, and music). The recommendation letter that Mr. Barritt wrote for him in 1948 read:

> Throughout his career at the School, S. Abdel Salam was a quiet, well-mannered boy and during the last few years he took a great interest in Dramatics. He was Assistant Stage Manager for the Arabic plays in 1947, Assistant Stage Manager for the French Play "Le médecin malgré lui" in 1948, and Stage Manager for the Arabic plays in 1948. He made a very good King in the "Shoemakers' Holiday" given in 1948. Besides his ability as an actor and Stage Manager, Abdel Salam is a very talented artist and I feel quite certain that he will be very successful if he takes up a career connected with the Film industry or the theater.

Needless to say, it was indeed in this field that Shadi Abdel Salam excelled. After leaving Victoria College, he studied drama in England for a year, then returned to Cairo, where he studied architecture at the Faculty of Fine Arts. On his graduation he worked briefly with the renowned artist and architect Ramsis Wissa Wassef, then turned to the cinema. From 1956 to 1967 he was involved with designing costumes and sets (works of art in themselves) for Egyptian and foreign (particularly historical) films, with distinguished directors like Salah Abu Seif, Barakat, Helmi Halim, Jerzy Kawalerowicz, and Roberto Rossellini, who encouraged Shadi to direct his own film. The result was *al-Mumya* (The Night of Counting the Years), for which Shadi wrote the script and designed the costumes and the sets and which he directed in 1969. It received glowing reports in the foreign press as well as the 1970 George Saddoul Prize. It was chosen with ninety-nine other international films (and was the only one chosen from the Middle East) to be shown at the Centennial of the International Film in 1996. He also directed several other films, which received a variety of national and international prizes. He died in 1986 without having directed the film *Akhenaton*. He had spent the last fifteen years of his life writing its poetical script, completing in detail all the necessary designs, writing down the movements of the characters and cameras, and even considering the choice of actors. His disciples are still trying to raise funds to realize Shadi's dream and present the film to the public.

Shadi Abdel Salam was a Victoria College alumnus who refused to take his expertise abroad, but chose to devote his talents to the service of his country. His profound belief that Egypt's future and renaissance lay in drawing inspiration from its glorious Pharaonic past was a vision he sought to transmit to the Egyptian public through serious films. His aim was to penetrate the veil of time and discover the secrets that had made Egypt great, and make these accessible to the public so that they could be a source of inspiration for Egypt to rise once again to its former greatness. The following words from *The Book of the Dead*: "Ye that goeth shall return/Ye that sleepeth shall rise/Ye that passeth shall be resurrected" struck such a deep chord in him that he made it his lifelong mission to educate Egyptians in the history of their land, so that both the country and its people would be resurrected. He remains, as the French newspaper *Le Figaro* described him, "le cinéaste des pharaons. Le pharaon des cinéastes" (22 March 1986).

Victoria College kept the interests of its boys in mind even if their parents had withdrawn them from the school, as Hussein Bey Chirine had done with his son Ismail. In 1931 Mr. Reed sent the following letter to Hussein Bey:

> I saw your boy Ismail the other day outside your house and stopping to talk to him, I was very much distressed to hear that since you have withdrawn him from Victoria College he had not been to any school... It is a great pity that a boy of his age and intelligence should miss regular school instruction, the loss of which he will find difficult to make up for later, when he will have acquired habits of indolence which it will be difficult to overcome. I am very fond of your boy and shall be greatly disappointed if you do not send him back to Victoria College.

Hussein Bey gave in to Mr. Reed, and Ismail stayed at the school until 1934, when his mother officially authorized Mr. Reed (her husband having died soon after Ismail's return to school) to enter her son in a British school to prepare him for Cambridge (see Appendix K for the letter of authorization). Mr. Reed sent him to Great Chesterfield College, and from there Ismail proceeded to Trinity College, Cambridge, and eventually became Egypt's Minister of Defence in 1952. An interesting matter for speculation is whether Ismail Bey Chirine would have acquired enough discipline to qualify him for a military career if he had stayed at home and "acquired habits of indolence." A newspaper of 14 April 1949 wrote about him: "Ismaïl bey Cherine, l'époux de S.A.R. la princesse Fawzia, a fait ses études au Victoria College d'Alexandrie. Il étudiait, chez lui, l'arabe et la religion."

The fact that Ismail studied Arabic at home does not mean it was not offered at school. Mr. Reed certainly exerted himself to improve the standard of Arabic teaching at the College. The Oxford and Cambridge Joint Board Examination offered a Lower and a Higher Certificate in Arabic, for which Victoria College boys sat. This exam, however, was designed for foreigners, and was therefore not really equivalent to the Arabic studied at Egyptian schools. As early as 1930 Issawi Bey was discussing Arabic teaching at the school with Mr. Reed. The occasion was the death of Sheikh Tewfik. Issawi Bey comments:

CHAPTER 2

> As an Arabic scholar may I be allowed to suggest a change in the policy which is being followed by Victoria College, the Jesuits, the Frères and several other schools, of employing Sheikhs as Masters of Arabic. Conversant as they may be in that language, they generally lack the modern methods of teaching which teachers graduating from the Normal College possess.

Mr. Reed seems to have followed this advice; by 1931 he had reorganized the teaching of Arabic at the school in consultation with the Ministry of Education. The agreement reached was that the Ministry itself would recommend as Arabic masters two or three graduates of Dar al-Ulum who had obtained the Ministry's teaching diploma. This was an arrangement that suited both parties, providing the Ministry with the opportunity of finding jobs for its men, and guaranteeing for Mr. Reed that his Arabic masters would be fully qualified teachers approved by the Ministry. The arrangement applied only to the senior school, which required three masters to teach Arabic to Egyptians and to the Arabic-speaking classes. The junior Arabic staff, two masters and a mistress, who taught Arabic to European and non-Arabic-speaking boys and who therefore required different qualifications, especially a knowledge of English, were employed at Mr. Reed's sole discretion. However, Mr. Reed wrote to the school lawyers:

> The arrangement made by Victoria College with the Ministry of Education regarding the appointment of Arabic Masters to the Staff is a purely private arrangement and is not in any way binding upon Victoria College. In other words I have still, as I have always had, the right to appoint any Arabic Master without consulting the Ministry of Education.

In spite of Reed's efforts to improve the teaching of Arabic at the school, the Old Boys occasionally came up against bureaucratic difficulties regarding their appointments to government positions. The Egyptian government had been trying for decades, though in a half-hearted manner, to impose some form of control over foreign schools. The decree of 1897 concerning foreign certificates was interpreted by Sidky Pasha in 1931—when he was Minister of Finance—as an acceptance of the Joint Board Examination as being equivalent to the Egyptian *baccalauréat* for the admission to government positions. However, he added a proviso that the holder of the School Certificate, or any other foreign certificate, had to pass an equivalent examination in Arabic (which made Mr. Reed refer to him as "the brute"). This proviso held up Charles Issawi's appointment in 1937, and was bypassed when Mr. Reed asked Amin Pasha Osman to get the appointment approved by the Council of Ministers. The procedure of resorting to the council to get appointments for those who had foreign certificates was a legitimate step and not a violation of the law, as other Old Victorians and graduates of other foreign schools were appointed in the same way. It is unlikely that the teaching of Arabic by graduates of Dar el Ulum raised the standard of Arabic to the level attained by Egyptian schools, though it must have improved. Peter Lewin, an English boy born in Jerusalem, remembers that he once won a prize in Arabic; this, however, does not indicate much, since many of his classmates were not Egyptians or Arabs. Some boys spent the year between leaving school and joining university studying Arabic because they considered their command of the language weak. Charles Issawi was one; another was Adly Yeghen (VC 1925–33), who may have been the grandson of Adly Yeken Pasha (Egypt's first head of government in 1921, and again in 1926 and 1929, as well as holding the portfolios of Foreign Affairs and the Interior from 1914 to 1929). Adly's mother was British, and, in his recommendation letters of 1934 to the Cambridge colleges of Sidney Sussex, Corpus Christi, and St. John's, Mr. Reed wrote of Adly, "He has been very carefully brought up at home, English rather than Arabic is his language and his up-bringing has been definitely English rather than Egyptian." Although he was accepted at Sidney Sussex, Adly studied Arabic at home from 1934 until 1936, when he joined the Faculty of Engineering of Cairo University.

Government intervention was a ghost that always haunted Victoria College and that Mr. Reed tried to keep at bay by remaining on good terms with the Ministry of Education and with Ali Pasha Maher. (In fact, from 1936 to 1938 he was conferring with both Ali Pasha and with

CHAPTER 2

Heikal Pasha about the establishment of Farouk College and even offered to train the new English staff of Farouk College at Victoria.) In 1940 the government tried to increase control over foreign schools by proposing that Egyptian history and geography had to be taught in Arabic. The announcement stung Mr. Highwood, who was by then in Cairo, into writing to Mr. Reed:

> This sounds very like Iraq. I imagine that as far as Victoria College is concerned you can work out some friendly arrangement with the Ministry. Jamali is coming to Egypt sometime next month I think, at the invitation of the Egyptian Government to study educational methods; it would be a wonderful feather in his cap if he found that Egypt was following his lead in controlling all education! It seems to me therefore important that he should not go away with the impression that Victoria College is also controlled, and to do this it would be very helpful if an important education official could tell him what the position is as an Egyptian.

As with the question of the appointment of Arabic masters, the final word had to be that of the headmaster, or else British authority was in danger of being threatened by the Egyptians. The intent of Mr. Highwood's letter had nothing to do with education but everything to do with the maintenance of British dominance in the Arab world—with the sanction of the ruled people, as his insistence on the presence of an Egyptian official indicates.

Not all the teachers at Victoria College had such a chauvinistic attitude toward politics. Mr. Haydon had hopes for genuine democracy in Egypt. He wrote to Mr. Reed (in England) in January 1933:

> The political situation has suddenly become interesting. I expect you have heard of the expulsion of Aly Maher from the cabinet. A pity, I think. It seems to show that the government is unprepared to modify its somewhat terrorist methods. Sidky might take a hint from

Mussolini and realise that clemency is sometimes a virtue in a dictator. The divisions in the Wafd, and now this split in the Cabinet, provide an opening for the formation of an intelligent opposition under Mohamed Mahmoud, although it is impossible to say whether this will happen.

Even though Mr. Haydon regarded the Anglo-Egyptian treaty as "a precious piece of humbug," he thought some good might come out of it for the Egyptians:

> I gather that it has alarmed and horrified the die-hard element among the British community in Egypt, but there would be far more reason for disgust among the Egyptians. It may be a necessity of the immediate situation that they should be bound to the British Empire, but I should have thought they would have objected to paying for the chains that bind them . . . I imagine with the Treaty out of the way, the Wafd may break up, and a genuine parliamentary [indecipherable word] become at last a possibility.

Mr. Reed may himself have had some sort of role to play in the Anglo-Egyptian treaty of 1936, for a letter from Mr. Haydon in September 1936 mentions Mr. Reed being "very busy seeing the different members of the Egyptian delegation." One of them, of course, was Amin Osman. After the treaty the title High Commissioner was changed to Ambassador. The British Ambassador dominating Egyptian politics during that period was Sir Miles Lampson, elevated to the peerage as Lord Killearn. He was a personal friend of Mr. Reed and of Amin Pasha Osman.[33] After the assassination of Amin Osman in 1946, Lord Killearn wrote a report to Ernest Bevin, the British Foreign Secretary, saying that in the negotiations for the treaty, Amin Osman, as Secretary-General of the Egyptian delegation, "contributed most powerfully to the successful conclusion of the treaty. Indeed, it is doubtful whether without him it would have been possible to overcome the innate suspiciousness and the

Chapter 2

traditional intransigent tendencies of the Wafd. All through the negotiations he played a moderating role, and helped both sides to find compromises in the frequent difficulties which inevitably arose during the negotiations."[34] In the same report, dated 8 January 1946, Lord Killearn describes at length how important Amin Pasha Osman had become to the Embassy, for he "consistently exercised a moderating influence on Nahas Pasha, who had grown to trust him to quite a remarkable degree, and he had now become the recognised liaison between the Wafd Government and the Embassy. In this role he was able to smooth out innumerable difficulties which arose between the Wafd Government and ourselves during the first delicate period of the execution of the Anglo-Egyptian Treaty."

In 1942 Amin Osman was again called on by the Embassy to resolve a crisis, when Lord Killearn lost patience with "the boy," as he insisted on referring to King Farouk. Germany was by then advancing along the Libyan desert toward Egypt, many Egyptians were hoping fervently that Germany would win the war and liberate them from the British yoke and were demonstrating in the streets against the British, while Lord Killearn grew increasingly suspicious that Ali Pasha Maher, the King, and his mentor Ahmed Hassanein Pasha (Chief of the Royal Cabinet and a man whom Lord Killearn disliked) were pro-Axis. He approached Amin Pasha Osman and insisted that to bring stability to the country, a Wafd government had to be formed under Mustafa Pasha Nahas. Amin Pasha Osman relayed the message, which Nahas Pasha agreed to. On 2 February 1942 the Hussein Pasha Sirry government resigned, and Lord Killearn immediately insisted on a Wafd government. For two days Amin Pasha Osman acted as liaison between the Palace, the Ambassador, and Nahas Pasha, until the fateful day of Wednesday, 4 February, when Lord Killearn summoned Hassanein Pasha and delivered the ultimatum to be conveyed to King Farouk: either form a Wafd government under Nahas Pasha or abdicate. Lord Killearn then got in touch with Amin Pasha Osman:

> I finally got him soon after 1 p.m., when I told him what I had said to Hassanein and that it was vital that Nahas should be on hand. He would please tell Nahas the exact words that I had used to Hassanein. I hoped there was no

question of Nahas wriggling out? Amin said none whatever. Nahas had been asking the same question about us and Amin had assured him we were in grim earnest. Amin added that Makram [Ebeid] was being summoned to the Palace. I said I hoped there was no question of Makram doing a wriggle either for our zero hour stood at 6 p.m. and there must be no mistake about it. Amin went off promising to keep in touch with Nahas the whole afternoon.[35]

Soon after lunch Lord Killearn writes in his diary that he had decided to push zero hour to 9 p.m. and "that if the boy [King Farouk] caved in we should be putting ourselves in a false position if we pushed him out."[36] He also sent for Amin Pasha Osman to make sure that Nahas Pasha was still in agreement with their plans; "Amin said he would bet his bottom dollar on Nahas being firm."[37] Next, he proceeded to Abdin Palace with "an impressive array of specially picked stalwart military officers armed to the teeth,"[38] followed by British armored cars, which surrounded the palace. The King caved in and Nahas Pasha formed his Wafd government. Nevertheless, in his 1946 report to Ernest Bevin, Lord Killearn denies that Amin Osman had been negotiating between the Embassy and Nahas Pasha:

> King Farouk *was under the impression* [italics added] that Amin Osman had been the intermediary between the Embassy and Nahas Pasha to secure the previous consent of Nahas Pasha to take office after the action which we were forced to take against King Farouk, owing to his encouragement of anti-British elements and discouragement of those Egyptians co-operating with us during a particularly delicate phase of the military operations in the Western Desert. This belief was responsible for a still more violent prejudice on the part of King Farouk against Amin Osman. During the Wafd regime of 1942–44 Amin Osman Pasha again played the invaluable role of intermediary between Nahas and the

CHAPTER 2

Embassy, and by his influence with Nahas Pasha was able to iron out the many difficulties which occurred between the Wafd Government and ourselves, and to assist us powerfully in our war effort during one of the most critical phases of the war, including our retreat to Alamein. When the Wafd fell from power in October 1944 Amin Osman again played the rôle of a moderator of the Wafd in opposition. If, almost to the moment of his death, the Wafd refrained from going all out against us, this was largely due to Amin Osman Pasha's immense influence over Nahas Pasha.

The deep involvement of Amin Osman in the 1942 affair was to have serious repercussions later, as some Egyptians saw that, along with the British Ambassador, he had forced the King to appoint Nahas Pasha.

In October 1945 an Egyptian delegation, among whose members were the two Old Victorian friends Amin Pasha Osman and Farghaly Pasha, went to England to commemorate the El Alamein victory. In his speech Amin Osman asserted that political, cultural, and economic ties between England and Egypt must be consolidated, and that the relationship between them was like a Catholic marriage. Farghaly Pasha, in his memoirs, explains this sentence as meaning that Amin Osman hoped that Egypt would benefit from a country as developed and culturally advanced as England, and not that Amin Osman wanted England to go on occupying Egypt, as some Egyptian papers claimed. This sentence, however, led to his assassination—or so the late President Anwar Sadat maintained in his memoirs, *al-Bahth 'an al-dhat* (The Search for Identity). According to his memoirs, Sadat had belonged to a secret organization that sought to end British occupation not by killing English soldiers and high-ranking officers, but by liquidating those Egyptians who intrigued with the British. On top of the list of traitors was Nahas Pasha and Amin Osman— both condemned for supporting Lord Killearn in 1942, when he humiliated the Egyptian monarch and surrounded Abdin Palace with British tanks, and Amin Osman in particular for likening Anglo-Egyptian relations to a Catholic marriage. Sadat recruited a certain Hussein Tewfik to carry out both assassinations. The attempt on the life of Nahas Pasha failed, but

Amin Pasha died of bullet wounds on 6 October 1946. Sadat was imprisoned and tried, but was acquitted in 1948.

Mohamed Hassanein Heikal provides a different interpretation of Sadat's involvement with the assassination in his book *Kharif al-ghadab* (Autumn of Fury). Both Amin Osman and Mustafa Nahas had won the unrelenting hatred of Ahmed Hassanein Pasha, who, in revenge, plotted with Sadat to have them murdered, supported Sadat when he was imprisoned, and secured his acquittal.

Sadat also mentions the precise spot where Amin Osman was shot. It was in a building on Adly Pasha Street, which was the headquarters of a political party called Rabitat al Nahda. He himself had attended some of its meetings, since, he says in his memoirs, he made it a point to attend meetings of every single political party in Egypt. However, Farghaly Pasha, in his memoirs, records that Amin Osman was shot as he was about to climb up to the Old Victorian Club, where the two of them had an appointment. The Old Victorian Club was on Adly Pasha Street.

After he was shot, Amin Osman was immediately carried to hospital, where he was visited by Farghaly Pasha, Nahas Pasha and his wife, and Lord Killearn and his wife. Lord Killearn was very moved by the condition of "poor little Amin"[39] and asked for his own personal doctor to be sent for. Amin Osman revived for a short while and commended his daughter Ayesha (who had been at Victoria College in kindergarten in 1927) to Farghaly Pasha, after which he passed away. As for the controversy of whether Amin Pasha Osman was a British agent or not, Farghaly Pasha insists that though Amin Osman greatly admired English culture and civilization, he never thought of himself as anything but an Egyptian, and tried to use the trust that the English had placed in him for the good of his country.[40] This belief is also evident in Lord Killearn's 1946 note to Mr. Bevin, where he analyzes Amin Osman's Anglo-Egyptian sympathies and the blow that his death dealt to both countries, though it is necessary to underline the fact that, for Mr. Bevin, Egyptian patriotism meant an understanding with Britain:

> This persistent determination of Amin Osman to play the honest broker between Egypt and Great Britain was due not only to a sentimental sympathy toward Great Britain

CHAPTER 2

but also to an enlightened patriotism which saw in loyal Anglo-Egyptian co-operation the only salvation of his own country. His death is, therefore, not only a personally tragic event, but little short of political disaster for the future. The Wafd, though out of power and not so strong as in the past, still remains the largest party, with the most popular backing, in the land. Before Amin Osman's death it had become evident that the Wafd, getting impatient, was beginning an anti-British campaign. His death means the disappearance of the only man who was in a position consistently to influence Nahas Pasha in the same sense of moderation as regards Great Britain. The Wafd in opposition are henceforth under no such enlightened restraint. Sooner or later it is likely that the Wafd will again participate in the government of the country, and maybe also in the negotiations for treaty revision. The absence of Amin Osman in those events will be severely felt by us. The Wafdist leaders are of a suspicious nature and do not establish easy relations with foreigners. There is no personality like Amin Osman who can act as an intermediary between the Wafd and ourselves in order to promote mutual comprehension and mutual compromise. Relations with the Wafd either in opposition or in the Government will, therefore, be much more difficult than in the past. It is no exaggeration to say that, with the death of Amin Osman, Egypt has lost a patriotic and younger politician, whose influence was always exercised on rational lines in the interest of his own country and of Anglo-Egyptian understanding, which to him was the corner-stone of enlightened Egyptian nationalism. His disappearance is, therefore, a major misfortune for both countries . . . We have lost a most loyal friend: and Egypt a great and true patriot.

The question that needs to be raised once more is the measure of Mr. Reed's involvement in politics during this period. There is no firm evidence at hand, and so this question must remain in the realm of conjecture until any proof is found. However, there is no doubt that Mr. Reed did have considerable influence over Amin Osman, who in turn, according to Lord Killearn's repeated affirmations, had "immense influence" over Nahas Pasha. Moreover, the sentiments of Mr. Reed and Amin Osman regarding the Anglo-Egyptian relationship are similar. When Mr. Reed was appointed in 1943 as chairman of the Egyptian side of the British Council's work (at the recommendation of Amin Osman), he outlined his philosophy concerning the political aspect of British Council work:

> We must have something of the missionary spirit and realise that we are working here for the social, moral and intellectual benefit of the Egyptians. The political value of this work is indirect, but enormous. I have often said that I believe that the better type of Egyptian to be more readily in sympathy with and more easily influenced by educated and disinterested Englishmen than by any other foreigners. When Egyptians increasingly speak and read and think in our language, depend upon British advice, help and models in all their work and activities, establish more friendly personal relations with greater numbers of Englishmen and a growing commercial relationship with them, then political ties have been so firmly woven that it becomes increasingly difficult for intrigue, jealousy, rebellion or war to pull them asunder.[41]

When B. Ifor Evans was in the Cairo office of the British Council as Educational Adviser and was considering appointing Mr. Reed, he felt that Mr. Reed's contribution to Council work would be invaluable, but he also expressed the fear "that Reed since he came to Cairo from Alexandria has been more interested in politics, or at least in the political figures who have been associated with his school."[42] One can only speculate what form Mr. Reed's interest in politics took, and what the outcome was.

CHAPTER 2

Regardless of all the tensions between the English and the Egyptians, the Anglo-Egyptian understanding made a very impressive show on public events like Speech Day and, on a smaller scale, in Old Victorian dinners. Speech Day and prize-giving were held in December and hosted no less than a thousand people. English and Egyptian public figures received, in addition to the formal invitation card, a personal letter from Mr. Reed. The High Commissioner (after 1936 known as the British Ambassador) and his wife usually presented the certificates and prizes, which were ordered specially from Britain,[43] and the High Commissioner, the British Consul-General in Alexandria, and several ministers were asked to make speeches. Mr. Reed's personal invitation to Ali Pasha Maher in 1935 read: "Your speech last year made so wide an impression that I hope very much you will be able to come again this year. I am also inviting Hilali Bey. If he can come he will no doubt speak in French, but I hope you will speak, as you did so excellently last year, in English." Who wrote the ministers' speeches in English is an interesting question, to which Edward Atiyah had an answer. He wrote to Mr. Reed from Khartoum in 1942:

> I was delighted to see in the Egyptian papers a full account of the ceremony with a photo showing you presiding triumphantly and smilingly while [Mustafa Pasha] Nahas delivered his generous tribute to you and the School. As soon as I began reading that noble oration I had a feeling that although the voice was of Nahas the words were presumably those of Amin—a suspicion which turned into final certainty when I found the Venerable Leader quoting Dr. Johnson. I could see you and Amin exchanging swift and mischievous smiles at this point, and I joined you from here with a hearty chuckle.

The speeches delivered by the Britons were also given due consideration and served to outline the policy of British education and Anglo-Egyptian relations in Egypt. One speech, given by Sir Henry Barker, KCMG, on Speech Day of 1926, required much preparation and coordination over a period of several weeks, and meant that he had copies of the speeches of the High Commissioner and the Prime Minister before he drafted his own. (see Appendix L for the texts of speeches delivered on Speech Day, 1926). After the speeches were over it was customary for the head boy to ask the High Commissioner or Ambassador for a holiday and the whole school would respond with three cheers. The request for a holiday differed from one head boy to the next and demanded great subtlety. On Speech Day 1938, M. Harari, after thanking Sir Miles Lampson for his speech and Lady Lampson for the prizes, said, "It would add greatly to the worth of those prizes if [the boys]were granted time in which to enjoy them, and left the solution of this problem to Sir Miles," as *The Victorian* reported.

With the British diplomats, Mr. Reed was capable of a certain kind of humor in his personal invitations which he possibly felt would be either lost on the Egyptians or too forward of him. In his invitation in 1938 to Sir Clifford Heathcote-Smith, the British Consul-General in Alexandria, Mr. Reed wrote:

> There will be four speeches, mine and Amin's, then Mohamed Bey Farghaly proposing "The Guests" and you, I hope, responding. Who exactly the Guests are is rather a moot point seeing that everyone is a guest. (The cost of the dinner is being put up by Farghaly, but this is supposed to be a secret). However, the actual burden of the speech would be to say a few nice things about Amin Osman and, on behalf of all those who had been invited, to say what an excellent dinner we have given you. I am sure you could do this extremely well.

Speech Day was definitely the most important event that took place in the school, but other events and activities were also given special attention by Mr. Reed in order to raise the prestige of the school and secure connections for his boys. In 1933 the Rotary Club awarded a prize of LE 30 to Charles Issawi, and assured Mr. Reed that the rewarded pupils would always receive the moral support of the club when they grew up, "provided they remain good citizens and honourable men." Mr. Reed

Chapter 2

was invited to be the guest of honor at their lunch, where he spoke at length of Charles' virtues and received offers of jobs for Charles from several Rotarians. The presentation of the cheque to Charles was postponed till Speech Day March 1934, when Mr. Reed wrote to Issawi Bey in Cairo warning that Charles had to attend because "the whole Rotarian Club is going to be present en bloc, and the presentation of the medal and diploma will be made with ultra-masonic solemnity, Mr. H.B. Carver [Director and past President of the Rotary Club, and member of the Victoria College Council and Executive Committee] making a long speech on behalf of the Rotary Club."

The Old Victorian dinner was also an occasion for Old Boys to meet and perhaps make contacts with either other Old Boys or important people that Mr. Reed chose to invite, such as Amin Pasha Osman and Nahas Pasha (See Appendix M for an invitation to one such dinner). The Old Victorian Club generally offered opportunities for Old Boys to relax, socialize, play matches, and join cultural activities such as poetry reading. In 1929 serious steps were taken to form a club in Cairo, but in 1934 the Old Boys were still struggling. Dr. Mahmoud Abaza offered financial help, and Charles Issawi offered to look after the subscriptions. He had trouble with the Old Boys, who were too lazy or too careless to pay, and it was in 1938 that he made his complaint, "Like Ysolde I have waited patiently and like her I have waited in vain." He had received only two subscriptions of fifty piastres each, one from the Sadek family and one from Raouf Kahil. By 1944 the club had become a flourishing establishment, although Mr. Haydon had to check heavy gambling and forbid the members from playing American poker.

In Sudan the Old Boys had no premises in which to meet, so the Cultural Centre, which Edward Atiyah helped to found and run, served in some capacity to promote Victoria College. In 1941 Old Victorian Henri Farhi (winner of the 1927 Speech Day prize for English, Arabic, and Science, as well as of the 1928 O.V. Lias Memorial Prize in Reading; also joint head boy with Heidar el Ricaby, and honorary secretary of the Literary, Debating, and Dramatic Society) gave a lecture on the school, and elicited from a British member in Edward Atiyah's office the comment that "Victoria College must have all the virtues and none of the vices of the public schools of England"—which, Edward said, was what he had always thought. Even during the war years Mr. Reed continued uninterrupted with the school rituals and with extra activities, though the elaborate ceremony of Speech Day was discontinued from 1939 until 1945. Fouad Awad remembers that Mr. Reed once gave a cocktail party to which he invited schoolboys and important public figures. When the boys asked what the purpose of the party was, he replied, "In the years to come you have to know the important people who were attending."

The Second World War did, however, make some fundamental changes in the school. As early as 1933 the situation had seemed serious to some of the British masters, with Mr. Haydon finding things going from bad to worse in the Far East and predicting that if Japan was allowed to follow her course unchecked, they would have to deal with a "formidable power later on." In the summer of 1936, Mr. St. Leger-Hill went to Italy and France and commented, "Italy was dirt cheap and the people most pleasant. The trouble is that they are so pleased with themselves for getting the better of an uncivilised nation [Ethiopia] with all the modern weapons of warfare that they think they can tackle anybody now. There seemed no sign of poverty or unemployment anywhere. France was a very different story. Grim and dismal and everything as dear as could be." In 1934 the murder of the Austrian Chancellor, Englebert Dolfuss, caused such an outcry that a Jewish British pupil, Nouri Elie Harari, spat on the car of the German Consul-General and was reported to the school by the police. By 1938 the first Mrs. Haydon was beginning to feel sorry for the Jewish refugees in England and criticized the Nazis for suppressing and persecuting a large number of Germany's "ablest and most morally responsible citizens." Sympathy for Jewish refugees was widespread among people who were connected with Victoria College, culminating in Edward Atiyah's suggestion in 1941 that the exhibition [scholarship] of LE 40 that was to be given to his son Patrick go to a family of Austrian refugees in Khartoum who wanted to educate their son at a good English school but could not afford to.

When the war actually broke out in 1939, most of the British staff were away on vacation, as the resident staff usually left Egypt from the end of July to mid-September. Mr. Haydon was in Alexandria, and on 23 August 1939 he wrote to Mr. Reed that he was considering the question of evacuating the school premises, which were to be requisitioned as a

Chapter 2

military hospital. The Royal Air Force at Aboukir promised to lend the school a number of packing cases, in which he hoped to pack the contents of the bookroom, the office, and the laboratory, keeping the library until the end. The British Embassy had suggested the Hotel San Stefano as alternative premises but remained noncommittal about help with packing and transportation and about the date on which to move. When on 3 September Mr. Haydon heard that fighting had begun, he went to the Embassy and suggested the Italian School as alternative premises, but the Embassy had to check with the military first. San Stefano was finally decided upon, and the move was made without a hitch. Most of the English staff returned to Egypt, and Mr. Reed could write in November that they were "comfortably installed" in San Stefano. They had managed to bring over all they needed, including the library, and they even had an art room. Noel Dawson, the architect who had designed the school cricket pavilion in 1930, made the alterations that would transform a hotel and casino into a school.

Oswald Weisz (VC 1938–45) recalls, "San Stefano was pleasant with its gardens and the beach. There was a dining hall with a stage for school plays and an impressive wood-panelled room which served as a library where we had a chess tournament under the eagle eye of Mr. Rider."

Football and cricket were played at Victoria, which the boys went to either by the school buses or by tram. Once Oswald Weisz tried to get a lift from Mr. Parkhouse as he passed by in his old car. "Please, Sir, can you bring me till Victoria?" asked the boy. "When will you learn some English?" sighed Mr. Parkhouse, but gave him a lift anyway. Mr. St. Leger-Hill began to agitate for permission to use the San Stefano beach for bathing. His excuse was that the two buses previously used to transport the boys to the bathing hut in Sidi Bishr were engaged in transporting them to cricket, so there were no means of transportation to Sidi Bishr. He must have succeeded in getting his permission, for Fouad Awad recounts that the boys would go into the Arabic class and put their towels and bathing suits on their desks instead of their Arabic books. Aggan Effendi would get the hint and send them off for a swim. The boys seem to have been unaffected by the war and resumed their naughtiness with gusto. They flirted outrageously with the beautiful daughter of Philippe, who sold sandwiches in the canteen at the nearby tram station. The offended father ran after the boys brandishing a knife in the air; the boys ran up and down the Corniche until the father gave up the chase and they could return to the safety of the school. However, the next morning he collected an officer from the San Stefano police station next door and marched into Mr. Reed's office in search of justice. Mr. Reed replied that his boys were not to blame if the girl was a flirt. Naturally, he gave them a good talking-to in private and reminded them that they had to consider the school's reputation, but in front of the stranger he had to demonstrate the school's solidarity.

The school year 1939–40 passed safely. As if Mr. Reed could never be wrong, he predicted in June 1940 to Charles Issawi that the war would end in October 1941. "When, by November 15th, Hitler finds that he still has not starved or bombed or invaded England into submission," Mr. Reed thought, "he will be faced with famine and disease all over Europe. In the spring of 1941 one hopes that the United States will come in and become really effective in the summer, when we shall have to make a blitzkrieg invasion of Germany and Berlin—October 15th." Until July he still felt that Egypt was safe because it was not at war with Italy. There was no indiscriminate bombing in Alexandria and at the sound of the siren the boys went into well-protected shelters. Soon, however, Mr. Reed's predictions for once proved wrong and it was decided that the situation had become rather critical and that the safety of the boarders had to be considered. Mr. Reed went to Cairo and became headmaster of a branch of Victoria College that was established in the grounds of the Italian school in Shubra (now that Italy had joined the war, its property was taken over). Seventy boarders and ninety day boys were transferred to Cairo, while Mr. Scovil became acting headmaster of 360 day boys at San Stefano.

In Alexandria parents grew anxious. Nine of them sent a letter to Mr. Scovil requesting that the school finish at 1 p.m., since the long tram journeys filled them with anxiety over their boys. After consulting with Mr. Reed in Cairo, Mr. Scovil assured them that unless daylight raids began, the boys were safe. Parents who were worried about their children arriving home after dark could arrange for them to leave school at 3.45 p.m. If the alarm sounded at night, school would begin the following morning at 9 a.m. In fact, the air raid shelters were safe enough, having

Chapter 2

been supervised by Mr. St. Leger-Hill, who, during the First World War had been in charge of the Officer Training Corps at the Royal Grammar School in Worcester and had conducted his duties well. This training stood him in good stead in Alexandria when, in 1940, he decided to set up a voluntary fire brigade with the help of the Old Victorian Club and get the Old Boys to "take the lead in . . . something of considerable importance in the safeguarding of the city." He did not succeed in interesting Old Victorians in his scheme, but finally, in cooperation with the Municipality of Alexandria, he created the nucleus of a force based in the district of Kom el Dikka. Over 90 percent of his volunteers were Egyptians, mostly working-class boys. It was all his work: the establishment of the force, and the organisation, supervision, and training of the volunteers in dealing with incendiary bombs. Soon he had ten posts, each manned by four volunteers, who worked from 8.30 p.m. to 6.30 a.m. He would stay with them until 3.30 a.m. and continued to supervise and train them even during termtime, when he had his classes to teach. In 1941 he managed to procure from the YMCA a van that would serve as a canteen truck to go round the ten posts providing refreshments to the volunteers. To stock it, he got Mr. Reed to ask Old Victorian Mohamed Pasha Farghaly (who, along with other Egyptians, had just contributed in presenting the British forces in Egypt with the *SS Arabia*) to start a fund of one pound a night (totaling LE 400) by the wealthier Egyptians in Alexandria to provide the refreshments. Farghaly declined.

By February 1942 Mr. St. Leger-Hill was doing such valuable work that Colonel Thornton in the Alexandria Municipality requested Mr. Reed to relieve Mr. St. Leger-Hill of his teaching duties in Cairo, which took up two days a week, so that he could devote more time to the auxiliary fire service. Mr. Reed could not spare him either. In August of the same year the *Lewa* (General) F.D. Baker Pasha, Commandant of the Alexandria City Police, recommended Colonel Thornton for the Third Nile Medal and Mr. St. Leger-Hill for the Fourth. The Governor of Alexandria signed the recommendations and the letter was forwarded to the Egyptian ministry, where the minister's signature was held up for no acknowledged reason. In a series of confidential letters between Mr. Reed and Baker Pasha in March 1943, Mr. Reed thought that the decorations were being deliberately delayed because of Colonel Thornton's unpopularity with the Egyptians, and if they did not want to decorate him, they would not be able to decorate Mr. St. Leger-Hill either. Baker Pasha agreed with Mr. Reed and since the matter was not discussed any further, it seems that Mr. St. Leger-Hill did not get his medal. Nevertheless, he continued to serve at the school until his death in 1952, when he was buried in the British cemetery in Chatby.

Victoria College, too, turned some of its activities into war efforts. In 1942 the performance of *The Merchant of Venice*, directed by Mr. Haydon, was reported in the *Egyptian Gazette* to be a success, though, as Mr. Haydon remarked, they had to economize on the costumes: "As far as I was able to judge people did genuinely enjoy it, and some of the acting was definitely good. . . . The costumes were mostly very fine, though there was some criticism of Portia's. We adapted a dress already in the wardrobe, as we were cutting down expenses as far as possible, and the result was considered by some people to be rather meagre." Mr. Reed was in Cairo then, but as usual, he did not fail to send a telegram wishing Mr. Haydon and the cast good luck. The cost of the play was LE 23.165, the whole amount being borne by the school. Forty pounds were handed over to the British War Fund, and a pound to the Malta Relief Fund.

Dramatic activities launched budding artists on their careers. It was as a pupil that Joe Chahine, known to the Egyptian public and the world as the film director Youssef Chahine, started his career. He acted in the school play *Carmen Miranda* in 1942, directed his own play in the Alhambra Theatre, and immortalized his schooldays at Victoria College in his film *Iskandareya leh?* (Alexandria, why?) in 1978. At the Cannes Film Festival of 1997 Chahine's film *al-Masir* (Destiny) received a special award to coincide with the fiftieth anniversary of the festival.

As in the Balkan and First World Wars, Victorians found themselves fighting on opposite sides. Hans Perkunder (VC 1928–38) was the son of the Chancellor of the German Consulate in Alexandria. Hans was called for service, fought at El Alamein (who knows, he might even have come face to face with Clement Shama, who fell in Tripolitania), and then fought in Europe, where he was taken prisoner of war by the Allies. His knowledge of English served him well during his capture as well as after the war, when he became a diplomat. The hostilities, however, did not affect the strong ties that had been forged during his

CHAPTER 2

Victoria College days. In the 1990s he returned to Alexandria and rang the doorbell of one of the houses in Bulkeley. It was the house of his old friend Fouad Awad.

Although the story of Hans Perkunder ended happily, the war was not without its tragedies. Selim Paul de Bustros (VC 1926–33), a British subject of Syrian extraction, had got a job at Barclay's Bank in Alexandria when he was chosen for a commission from among 200 applicants on the strength of Mr. Reed's recommendation. In January 1941 he applied to the Army General Headquarters for a commission, and his father, Alexander de Bustros, asked Mr. Reed to help, saying, "Now I know very well that the only chance to success is to be backed by some influential person, and no better man than you could do it." Mr. Reed complied and Selim got his commission, only to die in action six months later. His father wrote to Mr. Reed: "He was a fine boy, physically and morally healthy, and I have long since attributed to Victoria College, to its splendid staff and to its headmaster the merits of these fine results." Not all Mr. Reed's recommendations to the military ended so tragically. In 1942 he wrote to the Commandant of the Royal Military College in Cairo to recommend Fouad Zikry (VC 1930–42), a brother of Saleh Zikry. The recommendation letter read as follows:

> I hereby certify that Fouad Zikry has gained the School Certificate (Matriculation Standard) of the Oxford and Cambridge Joint Board with credits in Elementary Mathematics and Additional Mathematics, and passes in English Language, English Literature, Arabic, French and History.
>
> I have much pleasure in recommending F. Zikry as eminently suitable for training as an officer in the Egyptian Army. He has been a boarder at Victoria College for twelve years and he has always borne a good character. During the last two years he has been a School Prefect; he was joint Captain of the First Eleven Football Team and a member of the First Eleven Cricket Team and a good all-round athlete: he has rowed for the Royal Rowing Club and is a very good swimmer.

Fouad Zikry went on to become a great sportsman, winning several national and international yachting championships and earning over twenty silver cups and trophies. But it was as Commander-in-Chief of the Egyptian Naval Forces (1967–69) that he became famous. It was under his command that in October 1967 an Egyptian Navy unit sank the pride of the Israeli Navy, the destroyer *Elath*. He "ordered the rescue of the survivors—but [his] offer was stubbornly rejected by the Israeli authorities, thus denying him the obligations he strongly believed in as proclaimed under international law"—thus wrote his widow Nadia el Shazly in a letter to the *Independent* on 22 October 1995. He also wrote *al-Bahariya al-misriya: al-tariq ila Uktubir*, (The Egyptian Navy: The Road to October), published by the Egyptian Navy Press in 1986. Like many others recommended by Mr. Reed, Fouad Zikry proved that he was worthy of the Headmaster's recommendation: he became Admiral of the Egyptian Fleet.

Under the guidance of Mr. Reed the school had been a safe haven for many boys during the war, and its numbers increased rather than decreased during the 1930s and 1940s. Twenty-seven new entries, including thirteen boarders, had been considered "not bad" by Mr. Reed in September 1931, what with an expected decrease plus "a great number of disappointments in boys not returning or returning only for a short time through inability to pay fees." Those had been the lean years at Victoria College, when the Great Depression had affected the landowning classes, from which a large proportion of the boarders was drawn. Consequently, the number of boarders fell, though the number of the day boys rose. By October 1944 Mr. Reed was reporting roughly 600 day boys and 130 boarders in Alexandria, and 400 day boys and thirty to forty boarders in Cairo.

In the spring of 1944 the military authorities began to evacuate the school buildings, to which Victoria College returned in October. It was the end of the war but also the end of an era in Victoria College, for by then Mr. Reed was seriously ill. In March his right lung had collapsed and had to be operated on. Before going into hospital for the operation, he displayed his usual courage, kindness, and concern for the welfare of the school in the following letter to Mr. Price, who was headmaster in Cairo:

Chapter 2

A word of "au revoir," as I hope, but possibly of goodbye. A word, if I may say so without sounding unduly sentimental, of affection and gratitude. Please give warm personal messages (which I would like to write, but that would be too exhausting) to my friends in the Staff and among the Senior boys. You will remember, will you not, if necessary, that my will is with you in the safe? I have spoken to Lord Killearn and written to Teddy Peel [Sir Edward Peel KBE, DSO, MC, Chairman of the College Council since 1942] about my ideas for the future of V.C. in Alex and Cairo—and you are well acquainted with these ideas. The best of luck to you. Zero hour for me is 2 p.m. tomorrow. I am feeling in good heart about it.

He survived the operation but did not realize how ill he was. He sat up in his dressing gown and did an hour's work in the morning and in the evening. In July he had a recurrence of liver complications that made him feel extremely ill, and in September he went to Palestine for medical treatment. In August 1945 he died, aged fifty-four years. The school had returned to its original buildings in Siouf, but the headmaster was now Mr. Scovil. The Reed years had ended.

3

From War to War

Colin Clement

On enviait presque les élèves de la Victoria School, avec leur uniforme de collégiens anglais; avaient-ils tiré le bon numéro pour l'avenir?
Ilios Yannakakis, Alexandrie 1860–1960

When writing about Alexandria during the Second World War, Ilios Yannakakis, an Egyptian Greek, conjures up the milling of troops, the bustle of newly opened bars, and the swift spread of English as the essential language of exchange. Within the classrooms of their French Lycée, Yannakakis and his schoolmates suddenly became "more attentive in English lessons." As Britain once again placed its hand firmly upon the Egyptian state, there seemed every reason to envy the pupils of Victoria College in their British-style uniforms. Perhaps they had indeed picked the right ticket for the future, and yet the very nature of that future was in question. Yannakakis writes, "Did we sense that the end of an era was approaching with the end of the war? But what kind of end? An end to cosmopolitan Alexandria or an end to cosmopolitanism as a civilisation, a way of life, of social being?" While such rhetorical questions are obviously posed in retrospect, the school, the Egypt, and the world at large that emerged from the Second World War were considerably different from those that had entered it. The changes were sometimes not immediately evident, but the seeds had been firmly planted.

Even before 1939, while the school was steaming full speed ahead under the energetic and influential captaincy of Mr. Reed, the situation in

CHAPTER 3

Egypt had been shifting. Although the Anglo-Egyptian treaty of 1936 was largely a conciliatory gesture on behalf of the British, Egypt's formal independence was extended. As noted, the British High Commissioner now became simply known as His Majesty's Ambassador, Egypt was free to conduct her own diplomatic affairs, the national army would henceforth be headed by an Egyptian commander-in-chief, and the Military Academy accepted a wider range of Egyptians, one of whom was the young Gamal Abdel Nasser. The following year the Montreaux Convention abolished the system of Capitulations under which foreign nationals had been effectively exempt from Egyptian judicial control.

Earlier still, certain movements—inimical to the liberal, secular atmosphere in which Victoria College had flourished—had made their appearance. In 1928 Hassan el Banna had founded the Muslim Brotherhood. "They presented themselves as an alternative to the rule of so-called secular politicians, and thus to the total imported European model of society and government."[44] In 1933 and in a similar vein, though with a different agenda, Misr el Fatat (Young Egypt) began as an association, religiously conservative and essentially xenophobic. By 1938 it had become a political party with a paramilitary youth organisation known as the Green Shirts. Its motto was "God, Fatherland, and King."

All these developments, underpinned as they were by the "national question"—how to get rid of the British—could not but affect the apparently independent existence of Victoria College. Whether or not the school was seen in itself as a good thing, its fate was to be tied to greater issues outside its control. As a mirror of the laissez-faire, cosmopolitan city in which it had been founded, it was destined to share the same history.

When war broke out in 1939, martial law was established and the Prime Minister became lieutenant of the realm. All railways and aerodromes were placed at the disposal of the British, all communications and press were censored. These actions were in keeping with the terms of the 1936 treaty and would have seemed obvious and necessary to the British authorities; however, to the growing Egyptian nationalist movement they were signs of a reoccupation. Victoria College was also reoccupied but without a similar resentment. As we have seen, the school buildings—as in The First World War—were requisitioned to be used as a military hospital, and the masters, boys, and their paraphernalia decamped to the San Stefano Hotel. *The Victorian* describes the move:

> On the 6th [September] the Royal Engineers arrived, and politely but firmly demanded an office and explained to us some of their plans for making a school into a hospital. The following morning an army of workmen appeared and began to brick in the pelote courts, to remove celotex partitions, to explore our drainage system, and in general make us feel strangers in our own land. Meanwhile we were busy packing books, files, school Shop material, linen, kitchen equipment, personal belongings, test tubes and Bunsen burners, and a hundred other things . . . Three days later, the move started, and people at the Hotel end of things began to feel uncomfortable. Hotel guests were still living in the building, and as they descended for their meals they were confronted with the rather unusual sight of school desks being piled up at the end of the Casino normally reserved for the dance band. . . . The clearance at Victoria had no parallel at San Stefano. Passages were gradually cleared, but only that the grounds might take on the appearance of the Caledonian market after an air raid. . . . We derived a good deal of incidental amusement from deciding to what purposes we should convert the various rooms of the Hotel and Casino. The harem became the Junior Prep Room, the Casino bar was turned into boys' common rooms, the American Bar was fitted out as the Headmaster's Study, and the gambling tables in the Casino Club gave way to Prep School desks. A large advertisement for Stella Beer was removed only at the last moment from its place of honour over the School Entrance. And so on the morning of the 10th things opened at the Casino with a different kind of swing from that previously associated with it.

Chapter 3

And so the daily round continued. The "School Notes" of *The Victorian*, 1940, state that "apart from the great upheaval of the move," the war had had "little effect on the life of the school so far." That, however, was to change when, on 10 June 1940, Italy declared war on the Allies. Shortly thereafter Alexandria suffered its first air raid, and it was the realization that, come the new school year, parents of boarders would be less than keen to send their sons to a town under bombardment that caused Mr. Reed to make arrangements through the British Council for setting up the Cairo branch. Victoria College, Cairo (though not at that time accorded its full title), opened its doors on 8 October 1940 in the confiscated premises of the Italian commercial school in the Shubra district. There were seventy boarders and ninety day boys under the watchful eye of Mr. Reed, who took with him some of the longer-serving teaching staff—Messrs. Price, Wollaston, Howell Griffiths, Gately, and Wightman—in support.

Marcel Behar (VC 1933–43) remembers the school in Shubra as being "very well-equipped when I arrived there as the first student boarding in the school. There were glass cases full of all sorts of equipment, typewriters and a fine chemistry lab." Indeed the school possessed a small theater, four and a half feddans[45] of sportsfield, a good gymnasium, and an indoor swimming pool, yet in 1949 Mr. E. Burney, member of a team of His Majesty's School Inspectors claimed that "the premises . . . might be briefly described as damnable."[46] It was, however, situated in a rather populous part of town, unlike the splendid isolation of Victoria College, Alexandria, in those days, and the clamor and dust of the surrounding Cairo streets are common to the memories of Old Boys. Some years later when it appeared that new and permanent premises for Victoria College, Cairo, were to be built, the editorial of *The Victorian*, Cairo (1947) would read, "Perhaps we shall regret a little our dear Shubra, with its trams and loud speakers and think longingly of its donkey tied to the school railings, interrupting with morning song even a History Master's solemn discourse. We may remember how, as the problems approached solution, the sound of our eager heart beats was drowned by the carpet beats of the bint [servant girl] on the balcony."

Meanwhile back in Alexandria Mr. Scovil became acting headmaster, air raid shelters were dug on either side of the San Stefano Hotel, and school life continued with little real disruption. As most of the bombing raids were at night, the shelters were rarely used and it was only punctuality in the mornings that was occasionally upset by the troubles of the night before. "Willy" Alexanian (VC Alex, 1941–49) admits to there being a sense of danger and fear but, "School was during the daytime and so everything was normal. We'd catch the school bus in the morning; go to Siouf for football and cricket; compare the chunks of shrapnel we'd picked up in the street." San Stefano was not, however, like the real school. "The classes were not so nice there," he recalls. "There were often broken panes of glass and with the cold wind off the sea we'd have to sit on our hands to keep them warm." Nevertheless, some of the privileges of being a Victoria boy had followed the students to San Stefano. The school shop still stocked woollen blazers and socks, football boots, and good-quality copybooks, all of British manufacture and unavailable in town. By summer 1942, however, a threat greater than the air raids presented itself. The Afrika Korps under General Erwin von Rommel had pushed to within 100 miles of Alexandria, and the British forces had dug in around El Alamein for what looked to be a last stand. The Royal Navy steamed out of Alexandria harbor, there were mass civilian evacuations into Palestine, and in Cairo a pall of smoke from burning documents in the British Embassy compound spread ash over the city. The future looked bleak. Mr. Rider, the mathematics master, notes in his unpublished memoirs that as he was holding an end-of-term meeting with fifth-form boys to discuss their final exam subjects for the following year, one pupil politely asked him, "Isn't all this just wishful thinking, Sir?" As it turned out, General Montgomery and the Eighth Army held the line and then pushed the Axis army back westward out of Egypt and into Libya. By the time the October term was due to start, the state of emergency had passed. The school, it would seem, was impervious.

If the school was not actually flourishing, it was definitely swelling. By the end of the academic year 1942–43 Victoria College, Alexandria, held 450 day boys, up by ninety since the split, and Cairo had some 300 day boys and about 100 boarders. The Shubra buildings had become so overcrowded that in November 1942 a separate preparatory school and kindergarten department had to be opened in a rented villa in Giza. Scovil states in his report for that year, "In spite of the wide demand for

Chapter 3

English education, it will be impossible to raise the number of pupils at the School any further." The problem for both branches was not just one of space but of resources. While blazers and socks could still be found, there was a shortage of those eager, committed young British men who made up the resident staff. Scovil writes, "the teaching of Science is a difficult problem; before the war there were four English Science Masters; since 1940 there have been none." Recruitment of those deemed suitable—British university graduates—was to remain a constant problem up until the nationalization of the school in 1956, and yet the numbers kept growing. At the end of the year 1944–45, by which time the Alexandria school had returned to its home in Siouf, there was a total of 673 pupils, of whom 169 were boarders. The Cairo school, initially viewed as a temporary measure, had begun the year with 429 boys, including fifty boarders. Scovil would once again write, "the School has reached the limits of its capacity for expansion."

This continual growth in the student body was not occasioned simply by the school's disinterested desire to bestow the benefits of a British education upon all those who wished for it, although there was certainly no lack of parents wanting such an education for their sons; the increasingly successful prosecution of the war had seen to that. The acceptance of more and more pupils had a financial side. The war was having a distorting effect on the Egyptian economy. Although local industry was booming, since imports had been cut to a minimum, the massive expenditure of the Allies in Egypt—some £2,400,000 sterling per month[47]—caused prices to rise, with resultant speculation, hoarding, and shortages. The worst hit were, as always, the already poor, who were rallied by the populist, nationalist movements to demonstrate and riot occasionally, but life for everybody was becoming expensive. If Victoria College was to increase its revenues it had only two choices: raise school fees, which it did regularly but always with an eye on the prices of its competitors in the foreign school market, or accept more students and risk falling educational standards by stretching its teaching resources. By the end of the war, the school was suffering just such a fall, and its finances were in a mess.

Of course, there were other reasons for accepting certain pupils into the school that were not tainted by the filth of lucre. In its short history,

Victoria had never shied away from finding room for boys who seemed to be the "right" sort for social or political reasons. In fairness, this elitism was balanced by acceptance of poorer boys from the wrong side of the tracks who could be "bettered" by a Victoria education. This policy, if it was such, did not change during the war; indeed what better moment to anglicize the surrounding notables.

In January 1940, Scovil sent a note to Reed asking, "Would it be possible to take the son of Kayed Seif el Din El Senoussi?" He explained, "Some years ago the Kayed spoke to me about it, but I knew that he could not afford it; then about a month ago a Major Thompson again reopened the subject, and I understand from [Major Jennings] Bramley that they will be able to raise the necessary fees. The Kayed was the Senoussi General fighting against the Italians in the last war and he is a very agreeable person. It is quite possible that his son may eventually become the head of the Senoussi sect." Shortly thereafter, Reed received a brief letter dated 28 January 1940 from Headquarters, British Troops in Egypt, Cairo. It was marked "SECRET" and signed simply "Wilson." This Wilson was, in fact, Lieutenant-General Sir Henry Maitland Wilson, General Officer Commanding British Troops in Egypt, known as "Jumbo." The text reads, "It is thought that it might be a good thing to give education to the son of the Sayed Safi ed-Din [sic]. I rather think that either Major Jennings Bramley or Major Thompson have been in consultation with you on this matter." Reed, who was perfectly aware of just why it might be a good thing, nevertheless rejected the proposed boy as "altogether unsuitable for admission here; he is a very big fellow, knowing hardly any English, and has apparently already been dismissed from two schools." Fortunately for the Grand Design there was a younger brother, Kamal, who was granted a school exhibition worth LE 40, the other LE 60 necessary being provided by the War Office.

And so Kamal, at seven and a half years of age, became a boarder at Victoria College in February 1940. It was not to be a glittering career and was made even less bright by the fact that the school had to badger the War Office for the money promised. On 12 October 1945, with the war safely over, a certain Captain Florence, Civil Affairs Branch, wrote to Douglas Haydon, who was then standing in as headmaster of Victoria College, Alexandria, "Our Administration is revising all Bursaries grant-

CHAPTER 3

ed to Pupils in various schools in Egypt. We would be most grateful [for a] confidential report on the progress [of] Kamal Safi el Din el Senoussi." Mr. Haydon was blunt in his reply, "Very weak and doubts have been expressed as to his ability to make any effort," but Mr. Scovil, writing to Brigadier Cumming CBE of the Civil Affairs Administration, was even blunter. After casting doubts upon the legitimacy of Kamal's birth he proceeds, "this boy does not appear to have any brains whatsoever." Such a judgment is all the more damning when it is realized that the school files are full of glowing recommendations for boys elsewhere described as average, lazy, difficult, etc. Poor Kamal, so clearly the object of some cynical political conniving between the War Office and the school, was not to last much longer, though it was his own actions that finished his Victoria days. The theft of some money, a watch, and a gold fountain pen were reported from his dormitory. The boy confessed to having taken the money but not the other objects. It did not matter; the school wanted him out, though it remained ever sensitive to the political ramifications. The Civil Affairs Administration replied, "extremely obliged if you will not permit this to leak out, as the disgrace if it were known in Libya will be very hard on the old man." The last piece of correspondence relating to the case is dated 10 November 1945. Brigadier Cumming writes to Mr. Scovil, "Thank you for your letter. . . . I agree with you that it would be most unfortunate if the reason for his expulsion became known and I have taken steps to ensure that the papers are destroyed." Nobody thought to do so at Victoria.

The War Office tried to push a further five Senoussi boys into the school during the war though it appears that only one of them was accepted. In this case the letter from the Civil Affairs Administration to Mr. Price, acting headmaster in Cairo (April 1944), has none of the discreet style of "Jumbo" Wilson's note to Reed. "Sayed Saddik el Senoussi is not only one of the leading members of the Senoussi family, but also one of the most reliable, and it is strongly desired to help give his son an English education. This might be of considerable benefit in the future of Cyrenaica." Young Mohamed proved to be a "keen" and "industrious" student and by October 1954 is making plans to go to Peterhouse, Cambridge, but politics will not leave him alone. In December 1955, his father writes to the school asking that Mohamed should not be allowed off the grounds except as part of an organized excursion. No reason is given, but a handwritten addendum to the English translation by his housemaster says that Mohamed is suspected of plotting against his great-uncle, King Idris! The following year Mohamed has still not made it to Cambridge, moving Mr. Rider, then acting headmaster of Victoria College, Alexandria, to write to S.L. O'Rafferty of the Department of Education, Provincial Government of Cyrenaica, "I am sorry that Peterhouse has turned him down for I feel that it is important that Senoussi should go to Oxford or Cambridge and someone in authority ought to push him in on political grounds."

It would, of course, be simplistic and unjust to suggest that the school had merely become a robotic tool of British foreign policy, and yet it would be equally naive to deny the political significance of a large British-style public school that brought together the sons of Egypt's and the surrounding countries' elites. When Victoria College was established in 1902, Alexandria was an almost independent zone, a city-state, managed and financed by a coterie of grandees who headed the various and sizable foreign community organisations. While the Governor of the town was Egyptian, the members of the Municipal Council were these very same community leaders and cotton barons. The founding of Victoria College at that time was not a political act and indeed it initially received no official support from the British government—Lord Cromer's policy on education was one of deliberate neglect. It was more of a response to the need of a fast-growing city, and its secular and cosmopolitan nature was the inevitable result of its situation in Alexandria. To propose, as the school did, or accept as the pupils did, a British-style education, was not to make a political choice or statement about national belonging or support. In any case, the concept of nationality in turn-of-the-century Egypt was still very fluid. There was, for example, no such thing as formal Egyptian nationality, the country being still a province of the Ottoman Empire and a British protectorate. The Greeks, Italians, Jews, and Syro-Lebanese who made up the bulk of Alexandria's "foreign" population often had only the vaguest notion of their "homeland" and saw the city as their "nation." By the 1940s, however, the geopolitical environment had changed radically. Egypt had been nominally independent since 1922, the Ottoman empire had broken up in the wake of the First World War, bor-

Chapter 3

ders, even if colonially imposed, were solidifying in the Near East, the Zionist movement was causing increased tension in Palestine, and the aggressive nationalism of Italy and Germany presented a new political model for certain groups. The abolition of Capitulations in 1937 implicitly meant that all activities on Egyptian soil—commercial, cultural, and political—would now come under Egyptian jurisdiction, and there is nothing like a war for drawing lines around people. Like Alexandria itself, the school was now subject to external forces beyond its control, and like it or not, the school was no longer just another facet of a multicultural society. It would now be identified, if only abstractly for the moment, with the nation whose cultural values it purported to express.

Naturally, such analyses were generally far from the minds of those involved at that moment, and today when Old Boys state their pride in having been part of Victoria or the esteem in which they held the dedication and fairness of the teachers, one should not draw convoluted political conclusions. Nevertheless, the tensions within the surrounding Egyptian society were there and were inevitably to affect the school.

On 4 February 1942, just two days after the demonstrations in Cairo when the crowd had chanted, "Forward Rommel; long live Rommel,"[48] came the notorious confrontation between King Farouk and the British Ambassador, Sir Miles Lampson. The events that followed have been touched on in Chapter 2. The Egyptian government had just been dissolved after the resignation of Prime Minister Hussein Sirry, and the British Embassy had informed the King via the Chief of the Royal Cabinet, Sir Ahmed Hassanein Pasha, that the new government should be led by Mustafa Nahas Pasha, leader of the Wafd Party, who was viewed as more amenable to Britain's wartime interest. This proposal was swiftly followed by an ultimatum which read: "Unless I [Sir Miles Lampson] hear by 6 p.m. that Nahas Pasha has been asked to form a cabinet, His Majesty King Farouk must accept the consequences." A hurried protest by the Royal Cabinet at this attack upon the independence of Egypt was ignored by the Embassy and Sir Miles advised Hassanein Pasha that he would be calling on the King. By 9 p.m. some 600 British troops and a number of armored cars had sealed off Abdin Palace. The King was faced with abdication or acceptance of the British demands. Nahas Pasha became Prime Minister.

Laying the foundation stone of Victoria College,
Mazarita, 25 April 1901;
from left to right: Sir Charles Cookson,
E.W.P. Foster, J.A. Tarrel, Lord Cromer,
Sir G.B. Alderson, R.J. Moss

Victoria College at Mazarita, 1904

The school staff 1905; front row: Sheikh Hamid, C.R. Lias, G. Dumont; back row: F.G. Lowick (1st year), A.E. Aubrey (3rd year), Ambrose Mustard (1st year), Alfred Morrison (2nd year)

The boarders in the dormitory, 1904

Returning from school by the Alexandria & Ramleh Railway

The school carriage, 1904

Preparatory school, 1905

Football team, 1904–05; front row: M.S. Yaghen, T. Checri, A. Verni, R. Frangi; back row: Y. Sirry, A. Psaltis, F. Saba, N. Suter, S. Checri, G. Valassopoulo, A. Nimr

School boys, 1905; from left to right: H. Elmasri, Abd El Sattar, J. El Masri

Boys at picnic with Mrs. Lias; back row: A. Psaltis, M.S. Yaghen, N. Suter, B. Nimr, Mrs Lias; middle row: F. Stent, M.I. Khalifa, E. Harle, M. Delanay, G. Darmalli, F. Khouri; front row: A. Khayatt, F. Khouri, M. Bolton, I. Barda

The school buildings at Siouf under construction, c.1906

The new school at Siouf, c. 1910

The Duke of Connaught's visit to Victoria College, 1909

The new school at Siouf, c.1910

The new school at Siouf, c.1910

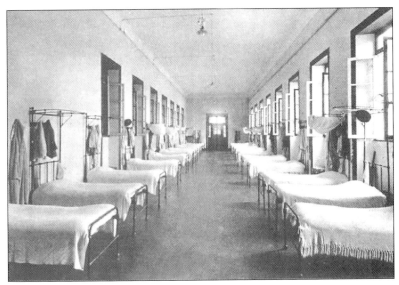

The dormitory

The dining room

The library

The laboratory

A view of the garden

The V. Bassili swimming pool, 1950

The Headmaster, Mr. Reed, shows Haile Selassie of Ethiopia around Victoria College, 1924

Football team, 1922–23; back row: M. Chervet, W.B. Mattar, G. Coutsouridis, A. Fakhry, A. Itriby; middle row: M. Hamada, Mr. R.R. Parkhouse, Mr. A. Dale, A. Gazieh (captain), Mr. H.B. Rider, E. Heniekati; front row: I. Labib, A. Hamdy, H. Bodourian

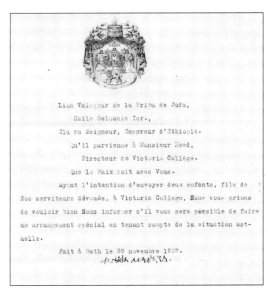

Letter from Haile Selassie to Mr. Reed, 1937

Victoria College scout troop, 1921–22; back row: E. Amzalak, M. Haile,
L. Arteen, B. Bassili, A. Shoucair, T. Kyriacopoulo, M. Bedrossian;
middle row: V. Bassili, Mr. L.A.S. Watson, Mr. R.R. Parkhouse,
Mr. R.G. Highwood, E. Heniekati; front row: A. Khattab, E. Paris,
A. Bassili, C. Polity, H. Attal, R. Zananiri

Visit of H.H. Prince Abdulillah to
Victoria College, 1948;
back row: H.B. Rider, A.J. Wollaston,
D.D. Haydon, R.R. Parkhouse;
front row: St. Leger Hill, H.E. Barritt,
H.H. Prince Abdulillah,
H.H. Prince Raad Hussein

His Majesty King Feisal of Iraq (right) and H.R.H. Prince Abdulillah, Regent of Iraq (left) having tea with Mr. St. Leger Hill (center) after attending Speech Day, February 1951

A party of scouts, 1930s

The school Sidi Bishr cabin, c.1932

The Alexandria VC Drama Society, 1930s

The boys' Motor Bus Service, c.1930

Mr. Reed, some Old Victorians, and Upper School boys enjoying dinner, early 1930s

Mr. Reed and Amin Pasha Osman, late 1930s

Victoria College buildings, 1930s

Victoria College at San Stefano Hotel, 1939–44

1st XI cricket colors, 1932–33;
back row:
K. Fahmy, V. Cripps, S. Simbul, D. Munir, R. Molloy, O. Bartolo;
front row:
S. Ghaleb, A. Fahmy, J. Deschambeaux, Y. Klidjian, M. Rifaat

The Alexandria community at the annual Sports Day, 1930s

Football match,
1930s

Cricket match, 1930s

Cricket 1st XI, c.1939–40; back row: N. Loutfi, K. Nassif, F. Awad, S. Zikri, J. Knopp; front row: S. Safwat, M. Masri, J. Kayarian (capt.), Mr. R.R. Parkhouse, S. Hosni, A. Andropoulos

Victoria College, Cairo, cricket 1st XI, c.1946–47; back row: S. Hakim, A. Bolaui, A. Tat, M. Chalhoub (Omar Sharif),

P. Carmena, M. Sobhi, S. Koutry; front row: D. Many,
M. Hinds, H.M. Hussein, I. Kehale, A.A. Alaily

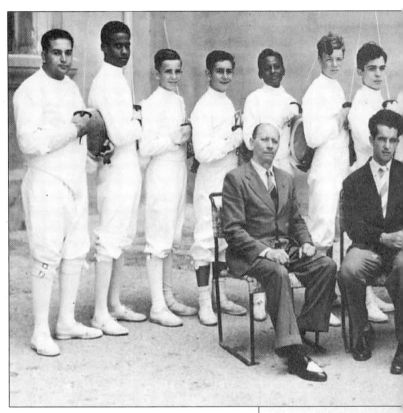

Victoria College, Alexandria, fencing team, 1948–49. The young man in the center of back row is the future King Hussein of Jordan

Victoria College, Cairo, new buildings at Maadi, 1950s

Victoria College, Cairo, new buildings at Maadi, 1950s

Maadi preparatory school classrooms, 1950s

The school play, Alexandria, 1958; W. Mehelmi (girl with dog), Mr. J. Abaza, T. Khalifa, M. Shindidi, M. Fawzan

Reading the morning papers, Maadi, 1950s

The school play, Alexandria, 1962; M. Kerdani as Julius Caesar

Musical performance, school band, Alexandria, 1962

Prize distribution by Mr. A. Koreish (headmaster), Speech Day, Alexandria, 1963

S. Siglabi, M. Nofal,
and others in Fat
Boys Race,
Sports Day,
Alexandria, 1962

A. El Ikyabi performing gymnastics,
Sports Day, Alexandria, 1962

Left: Art exhibition with Mr. A. Koreish (headmaster), center, Alexandria, 1964

Work from an art class, Alexandria, 1964; this drawing by Tarek Abdel Moneim El Wakil records an official visit to Egypt by President Tito of Yugoslavia; the writing at top left reads: Tito, Nasser, men of peace.

OV get-together at G. Shaker's residence, London, 1996; back row: N. Anagnostaris, L. Naudi, S. Khedr, H.M. King Hussein of Jordan, H.E. Mansour Hassan,

H.M. King Simeon of Bulgaria, Dr. M. Sika, F. Loutfi,
K. Shaalan, E. Khedr, M. Basta; front row: E. Arida,
G. Shaker, H.H. Prince Zeid Shaker, G. Shaker.

OV reunion, Palestine Hotel, Alexandria, 1998

A. Farghali Pasha (wearing tarboosh) among Old Victorian (OV) boys at monthly dinner at Alexandria Club, 1978

Mr. Rider at Grosvenor House OV reunion, London, 1982

The effect of this intervention on Egyptian public opinion was to strengthen the nationalists' hand and Sir Miles even noted, "our action has also caused much resentment among the princes and princesses, and among the upper classes, more especially in Cairo and Alexandria. There has been a tendency to a social boycott."[49]

One member of the upper classes caught right in the middle of this sorry affair was Sir Ahmed Hassanein Pasha. A sophisticated and urbane man, Hassanein had made a name for himself as a desert explorer and had been awarded the Gold Medal of the [British] Royal Geographical Society. He had been the young King's tutor, mentor, and general confidant, and he also had two sons at Victoria College.

Tarek and Hisham were born within a year of each other, and before they were even old enough to enter Victoria Mr. Scovil was writing to their father asking if they were to be placed in the school. When they did begin their studies at Victoria in 1937 Reed wrote, rather unctuously, to their mother, "I have been looking forward for a long time to getting your boys here as boarders." Their school career was, at first, uneventful. They were both average students, Tarek being the quieter of the pair, and they eventually followed the boarding house move to Cairo in 1940, only to return to Alexandria in 1944. Then in January 1945 Tarek made a request to study engineering in the United States. While this is none too strange in itself, it is not the predictable path of a Victorian who is the son of a Balliol man. By the end of the month an incident is reported whereby brother Hisham had got into a serious quarrel with "older boys" and questioned the authority of the prefects. This was apparently part of a running feud that had begun in Cairo and moved with the boys back to Alexandria. His punishment—to give up his studyroom and do his class preparation work in the evening with the other upper school boys—proved to be too humiliating, and Hisham broke grounds and disappeared for a couple of days.

The exact nature of this quarrel is not clear, but subsequent developments may shed some light. In March Tarek is still wanting to study in America against the wishes of the school and, in fact, of his father, and a letter from Reed to Abdel Fatah Amr Pasha, a civil servant in the Foreign Affairs Ministry responsible for boys studying overseas, hints at the crux of the matter. "I believe he [Tarek] felt very acutely his father's

CHAPTER 3

position during the early years of the war, and I believe he is devoted to His Majesty the King. All this has tended to colour his opinion." In the end father and school prevailed; Tarek was to be sent to Cambridge to study engineering and Hisham to a crammer, but at the last minute there was a series of bureaucratic blunders and no college would accept Tarek. When Hassanein *père* heard that it had all fallen through, Scovil reported to R.A. Furness of the British Council, "he flared up," and "he did appear to think that 'you English' were prejudiced against him for political reasons. He said—what is true—that Harvard or Yale would accept his son with open arms." There was then much hurried correspondence and kid gloves were employed until a place was found at Corpus Christi for Tarek and one at Balliol for Hisham, but there is no happy ending. In February 1946 Hassanein Pasha was killed in a road accident involving a British army truck, and by the end of the year both boys had left Oxbridge, Tarek to enter the Engineering Faculty of Cairo University and Hisham to go into the army. In October 1946, Mr. Scovil wrote to H.D. Lee at Corpus Christi:

> As I think I told you before, neither of these boys wanted to go to England having become bitterly anglophobe on account of the attitude Lord Killearn took up with the King. Naturally, they heard a great deal about this from their father who was very bitter about it. . . . Hassanein Pasha's death and particularly the circumstances of it was most unfortunate . . . the boys feel that their father's death was directly due to the action of the British soldier.

Throughout the whole affair, the school, as personified by the headmaster and his staff, genuinely and in good faith tried to do what they thought best for the boys, but the cards were being dealt at a different table. If two such pupils, from the upper ranks of the upper class, with a Balliol-educated father and a mother with royal connections, two boys more at home in English than in Arabic (Hisham had to resit the Arabic exam of the School Certificate), if such boys could be "bitterly anglophobe" after eight years at Victoria, albeit in particular circumstances, then a change was in the air.

From War to War

The immediate postwar years saw other changes and problems of a more internal nature that had likewise to be faced. The death of Mr. Reed in 1945 was obviously a great blow to the school and, as if to underline the fact that an era was ending, a number of other long-serving members of staff disappeared. Miss Ethel Millar, for twenty years the school matron, resigned for reasons of ill-health in 1945, Percy Bolton, the steward for nearly forty years, died in 1946. Sir Henry Barker, Chairman of the School Council for thirty years had died in 1942, and in 1947 M. Georges Dumont, French teacher since the founding of the school, retired. In that same year Mr. Scovil, who had been on the staff since 1920, acting as Headmaster, Alexandria, since 1940 taking the post proper in 1945, finally retired. But the greatest obvious change was the fact that the school had now become two schools.

The Annual Report of 1944–45, by which time the return to Alexandria had been effected, actually holds two reports. In the "Cairo" section a passage explains:

> The year 1944–45 brought considerable changes to the School. The Military Authorities returned our Alexandria building and a complete reorganisation became necessary. The Cairo Branch had been opened originally to maintain the boarder connection, but the improvement in the local military situation and the return of the School buildings in Alexandria made this function no longer needed. It was therefore decided to transfer to Alexandria those boys whose homes were abroad or outside Cairo. As a result 88 boarders were transferred to Victoria College, Alexandria. This number is sufficient indication that the Cairo Branch had fulfilled the purpose for which it had originally been intended. The success of the Cairo School, however, showed that there was a strong demand for such a school and a further decision of the Victoria College Council laid it down that the School should continue mainly as a day school with restricted boarding accommodation for boys whose homes were in Cairo.

CHAPTER 3

The section ends, "The general spirit of the School and the increasing demand indicated by the steady flow of applications show how great is the need for Victoria College, Cairo, to be permanently established."

A careful reading of this passage is instructive. There is an initial reference to a "Branch," which becomes "the Cairo School," which grows into "the School"—with the passage ending with a plea for "Victoria College, Cairo." The fact of the matter is that at the end of the war there was a new school in Cairo, whatever one might wish to call it, and its position had to be regularized, something that old Alexandria hands found somewhat difficult to swallow. Of course, this being a British-style institution, any wrangles were couched in diplomatic and gentlemanly language. Thus, in the School Council minutes of 27 October 1947—there was still only one Council—item 6 is titled "Relationship between Cairo and Alexandria Schools." It begins, "The Chairman [Sir Edward Peel] said that it appeared that Sir Ronald Adam [director of the British Council] was under the misapprehension that there was rivalry between the Alexandria and Cairo Schools." Such a suggestion was roundly denied in a mass of circumlocution about the Cairo committee being a "sub-committee for administrative purposes, responsible to the Alexandria Council" and yet quite independent "as regards the project for a new school."

The main issue that was at the root of this perceived, and in fact real, rivalry was not openly discussed, and that issue was money—and not just the money Alexandria had invested in setting up the Cairo "branch" but also the money that would be gained in the future from fees, most particularly boarders' fees. While the two schools would have their own catchment areas for day boys, they were bound to be in competition when it came to attracting the more lucrative boarders. Back in 1944, when it was decided that the Cairo school should continue its activities, it was noted that it would be "a dayschool with restricted accommodation for boys whose homes were in Cairo." This proviso was quite clearly designed to protect the Alexandria school. Several years down the road, with the Cairo school a given, and indeed now having to refuse applications, this restriction was not likely to last.

Also in the balance, and related to the question of boarders, was the very name of the new school. In December 1947, Harry Rofé, a long time member of the School Council, wrote to Sir Edward Peel on a number of matters and ended his letter with, "I would like to say that, if the name of the Cairo College comes up for consideration during my absence, I am distinctly adverse to it continuing to use the name Victoria College." In the same month, Herbert Barritt, the newly appointed headmaster of Victoria College, Alexandria, had written to Sir Edward, "I think that when we [VC Alexandria and Cairo] separate there should be only one Victoria College in Egypt. Given the necessary financial support we must carry on the great tradition." It might be suggested that Barritt, having arrived from a school in India, would not be subject to any sentimental attachment to the name. His reference to tradition is more likely in terms of what the name will signify in the future as a means to attracting new students. Why should a new school in Cairo benefit from a reputation forged in Alexandria? However, the important word here is not "tradition" but "continuing," as written in the letter of Rofé. The school in Cairo had already been called Victoria College, Cairo. The school existed, it had a name, and that effectively was that. The wrangling would continue over its name and status into 1948, but by then the arguments were academic as moves were already afoot to build permanent premises for the Cairo school, which brings the discussion back to money.

In September 1947, the *Times Educational Supplement* published a two-part article entitled "British education in Egypt." The first part under the subheading "A financial problem," begins with a sadly predictable imperialist slant:

> Britain has great opportunities in the Middle East today and in no direction are these opportunities greater than in that of education. For seven years the whole area has been thronged with British troops; English, perhaps for the first time in history, has effectively replaced French as the second language of the average Arab; everywhere the demand for British education is immense.

It then goes on to bemoan the cutting back of British Council grants and the lack of a central authority to oversee British education, and the education of the British, abroad. The second part of the article is effectively a rallying call to support Victoria College, Cairo:

> All the necessary steps have been taken to build a new school outside Cairo to carry on Victoria College's great tradition. There still remains the crucial problem of securing the money required, and in view of the current rising prices it is expected that a total sum of not less than £225,000 will be needed. For the site a generous option has been granted by the Delta Land Company on 20 feddans of land in the garden-suburb of Maadi; plans for the buildings are largely complete and £50,000 has been promised from the Victory Thanksgiving Fund.[50]

It is perhaps telling that these two articles carried no byline. The initial presumption of authorhood, given the exact details quoted, would be someone within the organization of the nascent Cairo school; however, information gleaned from other sources shows that there were bigger fish with bigger ideas who were keen on establishing a VC Cairo. Indeed, the germ of the idea can be traced back to 1933. In November of that year Sir Percy Lorraine, British High Commissioner in Egypt, sent a long dispatch to Sir John Simon, the Foreign Secretary in London, in which he stated that "the question of maintaining and developing English education and culture in Egypt is becoming of such gravity that if our political and commercial futures in these parts are not to be irremediably compromised, His Majesty's Government must re-examine the whole problem." Sir Percy was seriously concerned by the clear dominance of the French in cultural fields—schools, institutes, cinema—and by the growing activities of the Italians. Although Egypt was nominally an independent country, it was still perceived as Britain's fiefdom and Sir Percy rightly remarks, "The failure of England to make use of the forty years from 1882 to 1922 [the date of Egyptian independence] to create for herself a strong cultural position in Egypt is one of the most extraordinary phenomena in our illogical imperial story."[51] And as the 1930s progressed there was another competitor for the hearts and minds of the Egyptian and other peoples: Nazi Germany.

The ultimate result of Sir Percy's dispatch was the foundation of the British Council—and, whatever the great and good works it has done over the years, it was initially established as a cultural propaganda wing of the Foreign Office, set up to counter the growing influence of continental European powers at a time of considerable international tension, and to push what was seen as the best of British culture. With such a remit, it is hardly surprising that all eyes should turn to Victoria College. Here was an independent institution catering to the very clientele that the British Council were looking for, and almost inevitably it was taken as a model to be copied. In a letter from a certain R.W.A. Leeper of the Foreign Office to Sir Miles Lampson, then British Ambassador to Egypt, dated 30 November 1937,[52] Mr. Leeper writes at length on proposed British Council grants to existing British schools (those only for British nationals) in Egypt before going on to consider "British schools for Egyptians." He states:

> if any attempt is to be made to provide an education for Egyptians on British lines, it must be a separate system of schools. At Alexandria this need is amply supplied by Victoria College and the new English College for Girls [sic]. . . . At Cairo, there is only the English Mission College, which . . . does not offer the 'public school' education for which Victoria College has become celebrated. What appears to be required at Cairo *from the point of view of the Council's work* [italics added] and what, I understand, the Egyptians themselves would be glad to see, is a counterpart to Victoria College.

Leeper realizes that it "would of course be highly undesirable to set up such a school in rivalry to the older foundation," and suggests that "perhaps, therefore, any school of this kind started at Cairo should be a branch of Victoria College, subject in name at any rate, to the Headmaster at Alexandria, if Mr. Reed is willing and able to take on this fresh responsibility."

While there are no surviving papers to suggest that an attempt was made to set up Victoria College, Cairo, at this early stage, the clear interest in such a project expressed within the highest British political circles surely helps to explain the alacrity with which the British Council assisted Mr. Reed in establishing the Shubra branch in 1940. Indeed, Leeper foresaw that eventually "the Cairo school would require extensive buildings of its own, if the demand for the kind of education which it would give is as great as has been suggested."[53] Some two years after the Shubra branch was opened, B. Ifor Evans wrote in a report on British Council work in Egypt destined for the London headquarters, "The outstanding educational achievement under British direction in Egypt is Victoria College . . . it is obvious that the Council must do all in its power to assist in the development of the College. I recommend that we should find the funds for a site in Cairo on which a permanent Cairo branch of the College could be constructed."[54] And this type of message was to be restated time and time again.

The British Council had, rightly, recognized the worth of Victoria College, but not merely on the purely disinterested level of spreading education in the Middle East. It is noteworthy that these documents are held within folders entitled "British Cultural Propaganda," and a memo prepared by one C.A.F. Dundas, British Council representative for the Near East, on the reorganization of the Cairo office, dated 14 February 1943, displays the somewhat calculating nature of the Council's approach.

> Mr. Reed's appointment [as British Council representative for Egypt] should be of a temporary nature, say for one year with an extension up to three as a maximum. It would be, I think, a pity for the Council to find itself in the position of being unable to replace Mr. Reed after the war with a younger and fitter person should they wish to do so. There might be the danger of getting stuck with "an old man of the sea." It will be, I feel, in the next year or two when the Council's work in Egypt is being placed on a firmer basis that Mr. Reed's qualities and experience will be of the greatest value to us.

Of course, Mr. Reed himself might not have been so surprised by these lines. Edward Atiyah described his old headmaster as a

"Conservative. . . . He believed in slow progress, and aristocracy, and expediency,"[55] and Reed himself undertook for the British Council "to draw up . . . a short-term and a long-term plan for the spread of English cultural and educational influence in Egypt."[56] While in no way wishing to impugn Mr. Reed's integrity, it could perhaps be suggested that partisan politics, which were officially taboo among the pupils of Victoria, were beginning to worm their way into the administration of the college. Whether this was merely an unfortunate effect of the war does not ultimately matter; Victoria was becoming a victim of its own success and others wanted a part of that success for their own reasons. In a document entitled "Establishment of English Public Schools in the Middle East"[57] dated 28 January 1945, a copy of which was sent to Professor Bose of the British Council, Cairo, the first item under the heading of "Suggested Priority" was titled "The continuance and permanent establishment of Victoria College, Cairo." Items two and three referred to the setting up of "an independent school on English Public School lines" in Baghdad and in Damascus. Victoria was becoming a matter of policy.

Given the parlous state of the Alexandrian school's buildings, finances, and staffing at the end of the war, it was perhaps necessary for an outside hand to come in to push the new school. The demand for a permanent Cairo college by parents of potential pupils was real enough, but the momentum built up during the war years was a necessary but insufficient condition for the continuance of Victoria College, Cairo. There had to be a forceful and determined will and there had to be money. In this it is interesting to note a letter from Sir Walter Smart of the British Embassy, Cairo, sent to Sir Edward Peel, Chairman of Victoria College Council and dated 7 September 1946.[58] Sir Walter states in a preamble that "His Excellency [Sir Ronald Campbell, British Ambassador] is of course convinced that Victoria College, Cairo, is an institution worthy of every support and he hopes that the necessary financial support will be forthcoming." He then continues, "His Excellency notes, however, that no detailed and concrete proposals regarding the future prospects and needs of Victoria College, Cairo, have ever been presented either to the British Council or to the Victory Thanksgiving Fund Allocating Committee." Sir Walter then suggests that the College Council should establish a body to formulate such "concrete proposals"

CHAPTER 3

and he goes as far as to list the matters that should be covered: "the number of pupils, the number of boarders, the location of the site, the cost of the site, the cost of the building, the cost of furnishing, and no doubt an architect would have to be consulted."

Whether or not it can be suspected from this letter that Victoria College, Alexandria, was dragging its feet with regard to the future of the Cairo school, what is once again evident is the active interest of British political representatives, and this was to remain the case over the next few years as the moneys required were collected and squeezed from a sometimes reluctant Treasury in London. Sir Ronald Campbell did not mince his words in the several letters he wrote to the Foreign Office. In a dispatch dated 9 April 1947,[59] which included a copy of the proposals listed above, he writes "I am more than ever convinced of the value of Victoria College, Cairo, and of the importance of its continuing [existence]. . . . Conversely, if Victoria College, Cairo, were to close down next year this would be a great blow to our prestige in Egypt and in the Middle East. . . . I must repeat that this is a test case for the future of British influence in Egypt and the Middle East as a whole." Some two months later, after the initial British Council grant of £120,000 has been whittled down to £25,000, Sir Ronald writes directly to Sir Neville Butler of the Foreign Office reiterating his concerns:

> Victoria College, Cairo, occupies a position whose importance is really vital in Anglo-Egyptian relations . . . the military aspect of our influence is now less immediate and may well diminish both for 'geo-strategic' reasons and as a result of the trend of world opinion. Relatively our position has become less pre-dominating than it was. We must surely buttress and strengthen it with every legitimate support that lies ready to our hand. . . . One of the surest and the simplest and, with little doubt the cheapest, of these is to inculcate British ideas and British standards into those who are most likely, in the present order of things, to be called upon to direct the government and the commerce of their countries. . . . The alternative, the drawing-room communism which

has already gained a strong foothold among the more intelligent students at the Universities, has potentialities whose dangers are only too apparent.

Sir Ronald finishes his letter on an equally combative note. "Either the Treasury agree to provide the British Council with an extra £95,000 . . . [or] some 450 boys, many of them the sons of men whose friendship we can ill afford to neglect, will be thrown out, with little or no hope of acquiring a British education elsewhere."[60]

What is perhaps most important in these revelations is not so much the fact that powerful British political interests were behind the establishment of the Cairo school, but rather what this meant in the longer run of things. The independence of Victoria College, in both cities, was being gnawed away from two separate sides. On the one hand, the Egyptian government was trying to impose a certain measure of control on academic institutions established on Egyptian soil and catering to its citizens, while, on the other, the British government, through its educational proxy—the British Council—was gradually inserting itself ever more firmly into the management of Victoria. It should be remembered that until 1945 Victoria College, Alexandria, had been completely self-financing, having weathered various crises through the benevolence and generosity of former pupils. In that year, however, the school received an unsolicited grant of £1,500 from the British Council. While this may have been a welcome injection of funds, it was also clear that, at some time or another, he who pays the piper calls the tune. If the school governors had been attempting to sidestep the various decrees issued by the Egyptian Ministry of Education in their apparently honest belief that they were incompatible with their educational aims, they should also have seen that closer ties with official British representatives were ultimately incompatible with the school's existence in Egypt. The immediate postwar years saw riots, demonstrations, and assassinations regularly directed against the British presence and those people and institutions associated with it. Victoria College would, in any case, have fallen into this latter category; however, the shift from an independent British-style public school to a school that was directly funded by a foreign power was more than significant.

CHAPTER 3

So, by September 1947 the Cairo school had a site, building plans, and money. A deputation of Old Boys (Fares Sarofeem, Mahmoud Abaza, and Edward Atiyah), who traveled to the Foreign Office in London seeking direct Treasury support, had come away with £25,000 of British Council money, considerably less than they and the Foreign Office had hoped for or even required, but money nonetheless. John Poltock, the architect of the Maadi buildings, was forced to scale down his proposal from his original quotation of £400,000 to £175,000, but not without complaints, which he addressed to the British Council in London. From there, he received a rather mealy-mouthed response written by E.R.J. Hussey, Director, Middle East Department, who stated, "The British Council is not directly involved in this project. . . . The fact that our Schools Officer, Mr. Brandon Laight, has been assisting the Chairman and Council of the Victoria College in this matter does not, in fact, imply any responsibility on our part for this new project."[61] While this may have been strictly true, it has already been shown just how concerned the British Council was about the success of the project, official British interest stretching to the extent that Mr. Poltock was able to send his architectural drawings back and forth between Britain and Egypt by means of the diplomatic bag.

In any case, building commenced, and on 30 September 1948 the Council of Victoria College, Alexandria, ceased to be responsible for the Cairo school, which now officially became "an independent college administered by its own constitutionally appointed governing body."[62] The British Council, however, remained closely involved. It continued to provide an annual subvention of £3,000, to be reviewed in the year 1950–51, at which time it was expected that the school would be occupying its new premises in Maadi and therefore would be justified in raising school fees. Subsequently, in March 1950, a further £25,000 was granted to continue the building program.

There are two documents from this period that bear citing if only to illustrate once more the behind-the-scenes calculations that were so fundamental to the foundation of Victoria College, Cairo. The first is an extract from an appendix to a report on education in the Middle East, dated July 1949. Point 4 reads, "With regard to the two Victoria Colleges and the English Girls' College . . . HM Inspectors remarked in their report: 'We hope that these schools . . . will before long be able to stand on their own financial feet. . . . It may, however, be thought desirable for political reasons and in order that the British Council may still have a hand in their affairs, that these schools should continue to receive subventions from the Council.'"[63] The second is a memo from the British Council overseas accountant to the auditors of the Middle East Department, 2 September 1949. It reads, "The amounts of the [British] Council grants showing in the income and expenditure accounts [of VC] agree . . . with our accounts for the same period." However, it then continues, "We also provided £19,935.17s.11d for purchase of the new site and building for the Cairo College in March 1948. This does not appear in the accounts, but neither does ownership of the building appear among the assets for Cairo. The College apparently acknowledges thereby that the site and buildings belong to the Council."[64] It is not clear how this matter was settled, although surviving papers would suggest that the British Council did not ultimately claim ownership. Nevertheless, such thinking would seem to undermine the notion of Victoria College, Cairo, being a completely "independent" college.

When the new school was finally ready for occupation in 1950, it was deemed that political conditions in Egypt militated against a grand gala opening, and it was only in March 1951 that a modest tree-planting ceremony was held to mark the occasion. The following month, by happy coincidence, Mrs. Reed, widow of the late headmaster, was in Cairo to visit old friends and was duly invited to present the prizes at Sports Day. Thus Victoria College, Cairo, in all its shining modernity, was launched, and its novelty did not rest only upon its pentagonal classrooms. In February 1951, Mr. J.R.G. Price, who had been with Victoria since 1934, and had followed the move to Cairo in 1940 eventually to become acting and then full headmaster, had been compelled to resign for health reasons. His place was taken by Alan Guy Elliot-Smith, a graduate of Oriel College, Oxford, and former head of Cheltenham College, Gloucester, and around him was a bevy of new masters: Messrs. Lowe, Humphreys, Lennox Cooke, Doyle, David, and Hill.

Cairo, it might seem, had stolen a march on Alexandria and, in a way, it appeared better set to meet the new future. It had a good name and reputation, borrowed, of course, from the "mother" school; it had a plentiful demand; and it was to be installed in brand new premises equipped with up-to-date facilities. The Cairo school, starting with a clean slate, could simply plan its future and then begin its work; the Alexandria school, somewhat a captive of its past, would have to plan, change, and begin again. Mr. Scovil had been aware of this problem when he wrote in the annual report of 1944–45: "To comply with modern requirements it has become necessary to enlarge the curriculum. Many subjects formerly treated as optional extras are now regarded as integral parts of a British education." Furthermore, he added, "The war interrupted the regular expenditure on repairs and improvements. A large sum of money is needed to repair and modernise the buildings." Indeed, some four years later, the report prepared by HM Inspectors wrote of Victoria College, Alexandria, "The buildings are generally dingy and 'institutional,' and require extensive redecoration and brightening."[65] The moneys needed for renovation would not be earned simply from more boarders; capital investment was necessary.

If there were two single elements fundamental to the Alexandria school's ability to pick itself up and get going again, they would have to be the Victory Thanksgiving Fund (VTF) and the new headmaster, Herbert Barritt, OBE.

The VTF appeal was launched in 1945 by Lord Killearn with the object of improving and endowing British schools and hospitals in Egypt. Two years later it had amassed some £545,000, almost entirely contributed by Egyptians, and the sum was to grow to around £700,000. Victoria College, Cairo, was ultimately to benefit to the tune of £80,000 and Alexandria was to receive around £62,000. J.S. Blake-Reed, jurist, School Council member and on the VTF Central Committee, who prepared a detailed and rather wordy memorandum on the allocation of the VTF, pointed out that claims from such already well-endowed schools aimed at a well-to-do clientele such as Victoria, "are supported by the argument that the employment of grants in the form of capital expenditure will justify an increase in fees and result in larger income." The implication being that this "larger income" would allow the institutions to be self-supporting and less likely to require hand-outs in the future. He also pointed out the inequitable nature of such grants in that poorer schools for poorer students were unlikely ever to break even, and building extensions would simply result in increased maintenance costs. Such schools, he believed, would be better served by an annual subvention and, in fact, his final proposals were for the establishment of a trust fund to disburse moneys as and when necessary rather than splash out on large capital grants, since, as he noted somewhat prophetically:

> It may be wondered, in view of existing political conditions, what is likely to be the position of English education . . . in the course of a few years. Such will largely depend on the future policy of the British government with regard to Egypt. It is not beyond possibility that a general allocation . . . might simply result in the wasting and ultimate loss of a handsome sum of money, which could have been more profitably employed if handled . . . with an eye to its *permanent* [his stress] utility in the cause of British education in Egypt.

The "existing political conditions" that Blake-Reed mentions involved mass strikes, demonstrations, rioting, and political assassinations—most notably, in the case of Victoria College, that of Amin Osman in January 1946—all of which were in one way or another related to the British government's reluctance to renegotiate the 1936 treaty. In 1946, various student and workers' organizations assigned 21 February as "Evacuation [of the British] Day." This led to a clash between thousands of protesters and British army personnel in central Cairo, resulting in several Egyptian deaths. The demonstrations spread to other cities, including Alexandria, and no sooner had they ended than March 4 was designated "Martyrs' Day," which occasioned more violent confrontations. In Alexandria, some twenty-eight students died in clashes with the police and in an exchange of fire with British troops on the seafront.[66]

It cannot have been a particularly propitious moment to arrive in Egypt as the new headmaster of a British-style public school, and one may wonder how Mr. Barritt felt, especially as he was coming from India, a country that had just gained its independence from Britain against a backdrop of Partition and considerable bloodletting. Herbert W. Barritt was a fifty-year old Yorkshireman, a graduate of Peterhouse,

Cambridge, and an accomplished cricketer. After spells as a science master at Wellingborough and Maidstone Grammar School in England, he then moved to India, where he spent two years at the prestigious Doon School before being appointed principal of the Rajkamar School in Rajkot. He had the credentials and experience for the job as headmaster of Victoria College and was clearly not afraid of speaking his mind. Within eight weeks of being at the school he wrote a hard-hitting memorandum to be presented to the School Council. "I must state frankly," it read, "that the College in its present state is not providing an education on modern lines. . . . I am afraid that we are not giving value for the fees we are charging for tuition." His particular concern was with the teaching of science. "The state of science is not, unfortunately, due to our present inability to obtain science masters . . . but to the total inadequacy of the laboratories and the equipment . . . our laboratories are at least thirty years behind the times. . . . It is obvious to me. . . that scant regard has been paid in the past to science teaching in Victoria College . . . we must give very early consideration to the construction of new laboratories and the purchase of new equipment," and he envisioned providing more time for science lessons "by cutting down the overweighted French," a very un-Alexandrian thing to do. He was also "very shocked to find that the boys in the Upper VI are actually trying to cram in the work of all Groups for a Higher School Certificate into one year, when the examination is definitely based on a two years' course. I cannot of course be party to this."

From the Council meeting of 10 December 1946 when this memorandum was presented, the minutes record that "He [Barritt] did not consider the reconstruction of the Preparatory school and the provision of a Gymnasium to be of first priority." The problem was that the allocation of moneys from the VTF had supposedly been decided and provided for both of these projects, while ignoring the needs of the science department. Indeed, according to the terms of the VTF, money was not to be spent on equipment but on fixed capital. It is clear, however, that Barritt managed to modify the application, and an itemized report from December 1948 shows that laboratory equipment was being bought. The school was to get its gymnasium and a swimming pool in 1950, thanks to the generosity of, respectively, Edwin Goar and the Bassili brothers

Victor, Albert, and Jack, all Old Boys. The poor preparatory school, however, was placed on the back burner, or, in fact, removed from the hob altogether. In 1950 Sir Edward Peel was writing to the allocating committee of the VTF requesting a further £15,000 to "cover the cost of a new building to accommodate the Preparatory school and Kindergarten now so badly needed to replace the temporary Army huts." These huts had been built during the recent war and Sir Edward points out that they "have a limited life and are quite unsuitable for the purpose." Five years later and despite a grant of some £10,000, construction had not begun for want of a further estimated £11,000, and the headmaster and Sir Edward were demanding action. It was once again deemed "necessary to find alternative accommodation for the Preparatory School Classrooms, as it was becoming increasingly obvious that the present ex-Army hutments, owing to dilapidations, were inadequate, insanitary, unsightly and quite out of keeping with the standards and requirements of the College." These huts are, nevertheless, still in use today.

Barritt's drive to modernize the school was not targeted simply at the academic side of life. As a keen cricketer—he had played for the Yorkshire Second XI in his youth—he was unlikely to drop Victoria's long-standing attachment to the playing field, and what rivalry there may initially have been between the Cairo and the Alexandria schools over money and boarders was swiftly translated into sporting encounters. In these a certain Michel Chalhoub, better known in later life as Omar Sharif, and then a pupil of Victoria College, Cairo, "showed promise of developing into a very useful batsman," as *The Victorian*, Cairo, 1947, reported. (It might also be added that Edward Said [VC Cairo 1949–51] has referred to Sharif as a "chief tormentor when I was a relatively junior boy"![67]) But Barritt also saw the benefits in other forms of extracurricular activities. As part of an address to the British Institute of Alexandria on 22 March 1948 entitled "A full education," he emphasized what he called "training for leisure." When he took over as headmaster, he was "surprised to see that the boys were attending thirty-four lessons per week—between Monday morning and Saturday midday. I looked around for the leisure hours and found that the cupboard was very bare." Thereafter, Wednesday afternoon was set aside for leisure activities, not all of the bat-and-ball variety. A scientific society came into being, a model club was started, Cubs, Scouts, and Sea Scouts took advantage of the time, a 16-mm cinema projector came into use, debates were debated, and actors rehearsed plays in English, French, and Arabic. In fact, drama at the two Victorias gave that first whiff of grease paint to such luminaries of the Egyptian stage and screen as the previously mentioned Michel Chalhoub, Ahmed Ramzi, and Samir Sabry (described in one school report as having "more wit than wisdom").

Overall, Barritt took to the school wholeheartedly, whether in the classroom, where he taught a good deal more than was generally expected of a headmaster, on the cricket pitch, or even in the musical society, where he was not averse to giving solo recitals. His pride in the school is quite evident from this letter to the master of Balliol, from November 1949:

> Victoria College, as you know, is the oldest school in the Middle East and is run on the English Public School system. As a result of an inspection by His [Britannic] Majesty's Inspectors, last February, the School has been recognised as efficient by the Ministry of Education and this does not just mean recognition of the standard of scholarship. I think very few educationalists realise how well this School compares with the average Public School at home or that we play a large part in promoting good relations between the countries of the Middle East and the mother country.

It was these "relations," good or otherwise, that were to take up a considerable part of the headmaster's time from now on as the process of change accelerated.

The most immediately remarkable aspect of change inside the school during the postwar years was within the make-up of the student body itself. Although the gathering and analysis of fully reliable statistics is difficult, given the incomplete state of the school files and the rather uncaring storage of such for some time, certain patterns are discernible. First and foremost, there was a growing number of pupils coming from surrounding Arab countries. Prior to 1945, for example, only four Saudi boys had entered the school; in 1947 nine new boys arrived with a similar number the following year, twelve in 1949, thirteen in 1951, and twenty-three in 1952. Before 1945 there had only ever been seven Sudanese pupils in the school; five new boys entered in 1949, with seven the following year and a further five in 1953. The available figures for Iraqi students do not show such leaps, but there was a steady six to eight entries per year from 1945 to 1956. The first Kuwaiti pupil arrived in 1947, to be followed by eleven in 1949, nine in both of the next two years, and eleven again in 1954. Prior to 1948 a total of nineteen Palestinian students had entered the school, whereas sixteen arrived in that year alone. On the other hand, the entries of Greek boys did not seriously fluctuate between 1945 and 1954, with an average of five per year. The present database of students compiled by the Old Victorians' Association, Alexandria, is unfortunately not dextrous enough to calculate general figures for Christian entries, there being too many separate rites marked on the individual student files (Coptic, Roman, and Greek Catholic; Coptic, Armenian, and Greek Orthodox; Protestant, Methodist, Presbyterian, etc.). Nevertheless, a brief sample of those designated as simply "Orthodox" shows an average entry of nine pupils per year, with a flow from fifteen in 1945 to four in 1952 to thirteen in 1955. Those listed simply as "Christians" are limited to between one and three entries for the postwar years. As for the number of Jews, there is a marked decline. For the years 1939 to 1941 there are ten entries per year, jumping to twenty in both 1942 and 1943 and then twenty-one in 1944. This high drops to four in 1946, picks up again to ten in 1948, and then for the next six years (1949 to 1955) there are one, five, three, five, three, and none. The statistics for the number of pupils entering the school and designated as "Muslim" show the opposite pattern. Starting with a random sample from the years 1920, 1925, and 1930, there were one, one, and eleven entries. The growth really begins in 1943 with twenty-eight entries. Thereafter the figures are: 1944: 44; 1945: 32; 1946: 39; 1947: 52; 1948: 52; 1949: 77; 1950: 55; 1951: no figure available; 1952: 70; 1953: 67; 1954: no figure available; 1955: 65; 1956: 50.

As mentioned above, and this should be stressed, these statistics cannot be viewed as 100 percent accurate, but only as a rough tool; the information they present is nonetheless interesting and indicative of a changing environment within, and perhaps without, the school. The cosmopolitanism of Alexandria was beginning to crack. During the war, the Greek community had been violently split between "progressivists" (often communists) and royalists, foreshadowing the civil war that would break out in 1946; the Italian community had been dislocated by Mussolini's anti-Semitic race laws and then interned by the British as enemy aliens; the British community, never particularly large and mostly Maltese in origin, gradually withdrew with the troops; and the Jewish community of all different nationalities, Egyptian included, became the object of threats and attacks as a result of the 1948 Arab–Israeli war. Although there may not have been any mass departures as yet, the vitality of this ethnic mix was going if it had not already gone. In any case, the numbers of these "foreigners" had been falling since the 1930s and, as the school grew, it was inevitable that the new intakes of pupils would include more genuinely indigenous Egyptians. Thus there may have been just as many different nationalities represented within the student body as before, but the proportions were shifting and a certain "arabization" had begun. Georges Balit (VC, Alexandria, 1946–55) has clear memories of this:

> I must emphasise that Victoria was two very separate schools: (a) the day school which was an Alexandrine school for "Qawagas" [sic] the name used for upper crust Egyptians, who spoke French at home and very often were of Turkish stock, and Greek, Italian, Maltese, Jewish and a limited number of British boys, who spoke a multitude of languages but Arabic was not one of them. . . . Whereas (b) the boarding school was a different kettle of fish altogether as at least 95 percent of the boys were either Egyptians from the Delta or Upper Egypt . . . who were all Arabic speaking and the great majority Muslim, or from other countries in the Middle East, all Arabic speaking except for the odd Indian, Afghani or Ethiopian. The standard of Arabic amongst the boarders was very high, especially with the Saudi, Kuwaiti, Sudanese, Iraqi and Syrian boys. The majority had finished primary school in their own countries. . . . This made an enormous

difference in the behaviour and attitude of these boys as compared to the Qawagas of the day school.

Balit also remembers that "Politics was a favourite subject in school, as we had so many ex-kings and princes of reigning monarchies, although none of the royalty really got involved in these discussions but their friends were very militant and argued for them." And the arguments, as often as not, centered on Arab nationalism and anticolonialism, ideas which, according to Balit, "cut through the boarding house like a hot knife through butter."

The split that Balit perceived inside the school was in some way a reflection of a split that was occurring in the surrounding country. The British had eventually evacuated their bases and withdrawn to the Canal Zone, where trouble would follow them. The old Egyptian political set of bickering parties, led by a landowning elite, was proving itself incapable of dealing with the mass unrest that swept up and down the country. Governments swiftly came and went, with the podgy finger of King Farouk often found to be stirring the soup. The debacle of 1948, when the Egyptian army was roundly trounced by that of the newly declared state of Israel, effectively discredited the ruling establishment. On all fronts, the old order was in retreat and yet, however fiery the discussions after lights out in the dormitories and whatever the carnage on the streets, Victoria appeared to be sailing on through the waves. Lessons were taught and cricket matches were played. Peter Lewin (VC 1940–1953) recalls that there "was never any attempt whatsoever from the local population to attack Victoria so that the school was a kind of safe haven from the surrounding turmoil." However, he also says, "At Victoria College there must have been a very close relationship with the local police, because on numerous occasions from 1947 till 1953 we had whole detachments of police in riot gear to protect us." Nevertheless, for Lewin, "Victoria College during that period was a model of co-operative multiculturalism. National and religious bigotry was not tolerated, in contrast to what was going on nationally."

It is remarkable just how often this sentiment is repeated by Old Victorians of the period. Whatever Georges Balit may have felt, this idea of harmonious multiculturalism is what is most often expressed.

Chapter 3

The school clearly viewed itself collectively as an elite institution engendering a specific pride within the individual pupils. When asked why their parents chose Victoria, the vast majority of Old Boys will simply reply that it was the best, the implication being that once you joined the school you became one of the best. As Mahar Youssef (VC Alex 1941–53) put it, "There were no political tensions in the school. We were one body. We were proud of being Victorians." Or Alexander Ghorayeb (VC Alex, 1941–52), "We were all the same, regardless of sex, race, religion. Of course, we didn't realise at the time that this was all so important, that the way we were all brought up together would make a difference in our mentality."

According to most, this homogenizing effect extended itself to the newly arrived boarders. Abdel Fatah Loutfy, who spent his whole school career from kindergarten in 1936 through to graduation in 1951 at Victoria, Alexandria, remarks, "There was no real difference between day boys and boarders. When the Saudis or Sudanese or whoever came to VC, they integrated and made friends quickly. They became VC boys and thus equal." Ismail el Mahdi (VC Cairo/Alex 1948–53), who was one of these Sudanese boarders, has a slightly different recollection. "In Shubra the boarders were small in number and so it was easy to integrate. There was no real split between dayboys and boarders. But in Alex you felt it. It is perhaps because the boarders in Alex were mostly from countries outside Egypt, or perhaps the foreign communities of Alexandria may have influenced this split. Maybe dayboys tended to stay in their groups." Other Old Victorians might hesitantly suggest that the day boys were more "sophisticated," but this would hardly be a surprise given the contemporary differences between Alexandria and, say, Khartoum or Riyadh. In any case, according to Mansour Hassan (VC Alex/Cairo 1944–54), "The boarders considered themselves the real VC boys—the dayboys were just visitors. Also the ties between boarders were much stronger; you lived with each other!" Once you were in, however, you belonged, and as Abdel Fatah Loutfy insists, "Everyone was treated alike, whether king or low-income pupil. You never felt the differences between the boys." While low-income pupils were never that numerous, there certainly were more crowned, or ex-crowned, heads than the average school could boast. Romanovs, Saxe-Coburgs, Hohenzollerns,

Glucksburgs and Zogs all passed through the school, primarily the result of having been displaced by the Second World War. And there was also an Arab nobility within the halls of Victoria, which was not fleeing anything. Saudi Arabia sent, among others, Hisham Nazer, head boy in 1953 and later Minister for Petroleum, Adnan Khashoggi, subsequently famous for being rich, and Kamal Adham, brother-in-law and confidant of King Feisal. From Sudan came boys from the Merghani, al-Mahdi, and Abu al-Ela families, all of which were at the heart of the country's political life. Sons of the Sabbah and Ghanem clans came from Kuwait, Mohamed Uzdi, brother of the Sultan of Zanzibar, came, and Victoria educated two future Prime Ministers of Jordan, Zeid bin Shaker and Zeid el Rifaai, as well as the Jordanian Prince Raad bin Zeid. And, of course, there was the late Hussein Ibn Tallal of Jordan, perhaps Victoria's most famous Old Boy. Ismail el Mahdi shared a dormitory with Hussein and remembers him as a "very sweet chap, very kind. You didn't think of him as a prince, just one of the boys, nothing too royal about him." The late King himself wrote in his autobiography:

> I was enrolled at Victoria College in Alexandria, a school with an excellent combination of Arabic and English lessons. Immediately a whole new world opened up for me—football, cricket, books, companionship. I can see in my mind's eye to this day the long spartan dormitory which I shared with about thirty other boys, the cold showers every morning, the uniform of grey flannels and college blazer. . . . My two years at Victoria were among the happiest in my life.[68]

Abdel Fatah Loutfy can even claim to have put the future king in detention for some petty misdemeanor, and he duly did what he was told. Loutfy, who was captain of cricket and vice-captain of the football XI, recalls that at an Old Victorian reunion, King Hussein called him "Captain Loutfy." He remonstrated, saying, "But you are a king," to which Hussein replied, "But you were my captain." And so, as Lewin puts it "life within the school grounds went on with a surrealistic state of 'British Fair Play.'"

CHAPTER 3

One aspect of this sense of fair play was admirably demonstrated by the school's reaction to the results of the Arab–Israeli war of 1948. While there is no direct mention of the war in any surviving documents, it is clear that a number of Palestinian pupils were suddenly unable to pay their fees. Without exception these boys were permitted to stay on and to run up arrears that would, in other instances, have provoked sternly worded letters threatening recourse to legal action. In at least one case, the debts continued to mount well into the 1950s, but the school stood by its boys. Indeed, throughout the troubles, the school never seemed to lose sight of its mission: to turn out well-educated, well-rounded young men, whether this involved arranging for crammer courses in Britain, sending the Scout Troop to an international jamboree in Austria, or advising on dress codes. Alexander Ghorayeb remembers Mr. Parkhouse telling the boys "not to wear rings or jewellery or scent or Brylcream. And he taught us what we should need as clothing when travelling." The essential, apparently, was a white shirt, blue blazer, grey flannel trousers, a grey suit, black shoes, and a striped tie. "This was all you'd ever need to meet royalty or on any other occasion." Such advice was so solidly driven home that Ghorayeb claims, "I was always correctly dressed. For years I couldn't go out without a tie!" Correct table manners were similarly a matter for the school's attention, as is noted in the minutes of the Executive Committee meeting of 4 July 1951. The headmaster declared that he was "very concerned about the state of the Dining Hall and the conditions under which the boys had to take their meals. He pointed out that the cultural side there was badly lacking and that only the best conditions would enable the College to carry out this important part of its education in a proper manner." The Committee roundly backed Mr. Barritt in this and likewise expressed their "very strong views on the Dining Hall and the importance of its cultural side," to the extent of voting a salary of LE 200 per annum for a new resident Lady Superintendent to oversee such matters. It is undoubtedly this sort of attention to detail and imperturbable Britishness that made Victoria great. But was there not also a Nelson-like tendency to hold the telescope to the blind eye?

During the winter of 1951–52 Egypt was more or less at war. In October 1951, Egypt had unilaterally abrogated the 1936 Anglo-Egyptian treaty and the 1899 Sudan Condominium Agreement. The

British responded by reinforcing their garrison in the Canal Zone and were unhesitant in their use of force against guerrilla operations and sabotage. Armed clashes continued from November through to January 1952 and occasionally escalated into pitched battles. The public mood was ugly. In the Annual Report of 1951–52, Barritt wrote:

> On October 23rd, I was informed that it would be advisable to close the College. The College was accordingly closed on the afternoon of the 23rd and for the whole of the 24th. We carried on until November 13th but had to close on that day and on the two successive days. About this time we began to sense a feeling of tension owing to the strained political situation. The situation gradually became worse and many incidents took place. . . . I do not think that any School staff has ever had to face such a trying time. Suffice it to say that the situation was met in a grand spirit by one and all and we came through the term knowing that better times lay ahead.

Having said this, Barritt goes on to write, "Then came the events in Cairo on January 26th."

On 25 January 1952 the British commander in the Ismailia area demanded that the Egyptian police and gendarmeries lay down their weapons and leave the city. They refused and were blasted out by artillery and armor, leaving over fifty dead and many more wounded. The following day a well-organized mob burned central Cairo, specifically targeting foreign businesses. Some thirty people were killed and hundreds injured, many being deliberately attacked by the rioters. Barritt continued in his report, "These [events] were bound to cause alarm amongst parents and boys and, sure enough, all the Kuwaiti boys were taken away to their hostel in Cairo on the 27th. About eight Saudi boys were removed during the following week and there was a general feeling of uncertainty. We were compelled to close the College on January 26th." The closure lasted for no more than ten days, but it was an inauspicious start to what should have been a big year for the school. For 9 November 1952 was to have marked the fiftieth anniversary of

CHAPTER 3

Victoria's foundation, but since the school decided to forgo the annual Speech Day and take out riot insurance on the school buses, the moment did not lend itself to planning lavish, high-profile celebrations. Instead, a subcommittee was formed that would meet during the summer holidays to look into the matter. That summer, however, saw other ructions in the Egyptian body politic. On 23 July the clandestine Free Officers movement within the Egyptian army launched a coup. Peter Lewin writes, "Tanks were out at strategic points in the town in support of the coup, and I remember the protected motorcade of the king passing us on the Corniche on his way to his palace at Ras el Tin where he was to board his yacht for Italy, never to return again. There was genuine happiness in all of Egypt at the time, at the departure of this most inept, fat and disliked monarch." Barritt's comments from the Annual Report of 1951–52 were, "The political upheaval in July gave me much food for thought and, in particular, I wondered whether I should hear of many cancellations from parents and boarders. Much to my surprise I received news of normal entries, and when I returned at the end of September the College was as full as ever. The fiftieth year had undoubtedly been the most colourful in the history of the College but we started the next half-century with justifiable enthusiasm."

Once again Victoria seemed to be bobbing along on the surface, unswamped by the troubled waters of history, and the plans for a jubilee celebration were quickly dusted off and scheduled for May 1953. With typical Victorian confidence an invitation to attend was sent to General Mohamed Neguib, nominal head of the military junta. Unfortunately, General Neguib was obliged to send his regrets citing a prior engagement, but passed on a message wishing the school "every success." The British Ambassador was also unable to be present for reasons of ill-health, but despite the absences of these big guns, who might have been shy of sharing the same stage, the festivities took place from 1 to 7 May. They included a Speech Day, a cricket match, athletics, theatrical plays, an Old Boys dinner, which was the occasion for much ribald reminiscing, and an open day for parents and guests. This last event was a first in the history of the school and behind it one might see the modernizing hand of Mr. Barritt. The school was effectively thrown open in the morning and afternoon of 6 May and visitors were allowed to watch lessons in progress, see the dormitories, and observe various sporting displays and experiments in the science laboratories. The school was putting its best foot forward as it stepped into the new era, but there must surely have been some reservations as to what the future might hold.

The new military leaders had quickly made it evident that they had not kicked out the king simply to leave the country in the hands of the old political parties. While the government remained essentially civilian in the first instance, it was the Revolutionary Command Council, with Gamal Abdel Nasser as its chairman, that held the real power, and it wanted change. The nationalist ideas that Georges Balit had heard bouncing around the boarding house were soon to be official policy.

As early as February 1953, Mr. Barritt had received a letter from Mr. Brandon Laight, then headmaster of the English School, Cairo, which merits being cited in full:

> Dear Herbert,
> I have a circular No. 198, dated the 27th of December 1952, from the Northern Cairo Zone, quoting instructions issued from the Under-Secretary to the effect that "The Ministry instructs schools of all types to teach their pupils the two songs 'Sowt el Watan' (Voice of the Fatherland) and 'Alittihad, Wannizam Wal'amal' (Unity, Discipline and Work)."
>
> It adds that "measures should be taken by the schools to encourage their pupils to recite these two songs in school parties and excursions."
>
> I shall be grateful to know whether you have received this circular, and, if so, what you propose to do.
> Yours,

It is unknown whether Mr. Barritt had received a similar notice or what he would have done if he had; however, it is clearly difficult to imagine a school such as Victoria, proud of its liberal, multicultural tradition, encouraging the boys to chant such jingoisms. But while this request might easily be swept under the carpet, other seemingly incongruous notions could not be so simply ignored. Later that same year, in

CHAPTER 3

November, a delegation of Saudi gentlemen, accompanied by the controller of foreign schools at the Egyptian Ministry of Education, paid a visit to Victoria. Saudi Arabia was now sending a fair number of boys as boarders and it was to be expected that the home country should take an interest in the institution. It was also in the interests of the school that the delegation should be satisfied and it is noted that they "expressed themselves pleased with all they saw and the explanations given by the Headmaster but certain points regarding Moslem religious observances were raised. The delegation asked that Moslem boys should be given facilities to pray a minimum of 5 times per day, collectively, if possible."

What would appear to be a perfectly reasonable request from the Saudi point of view could hardly have seemed appropriate to a multi-confessional, and therefore secular, British-style public school. When the headmaster tactfully explained that there was unfortunately no available room that could be turned over exclusively for prayers, the visitors expressed their willingness to build a mosque in the grounds. It is noted that the council meeting to which this was reported "considered these remarks and decided that no further action could be taken at present." A Nelsonian application of the telescope was once more the order of the day, but it is hard to imagine just how the school might otherwise have reacted. A straightforward refusal to countenance such an addition to the school buildings would have been an affront to the new and important clientele and yet to accept would have been to go directly against the very ethos of the school. And if there were a mosque, there would need to be a synagogue, and if a synagogue then a church, and if a church, to what rite would it be consecrated and so on? Victoria had been founded in a multiconfessional city where religious observance was a personal matter and it had recognized that state of affairs from the very beginning. Had the school tied itself to any particular creed, it is highly unlikely that it would have succeeded to anything like the same extent. None of the many contemporaneous mission or foreign community schools ever boasted quite such an elite student body, or produced such a breadth of eminent alumni. The school's secularism and therefore its non-exclusiveness were fundamental to its nature, but for the city in which it stood, times were changing.

Other aspects of the general arabization of both the country and the surrounding area simply could not be disregarded. The school was subject to the laws of Egypt and wriggle and jink as it might, its independence of action was destined to be gradually curtailed.

The Egyptian government had, in fact, been trying to gain a measure of control over foreign schools since the 1930s, but without any marked success. In March 1940, however, a law was passed requiring the teaching of Arabic, Islamic history and religion to all Muslim students, and Victoria was obliged to comply. The school in any case had had provisions for teaching Arabic from its foundation but the language was viewed as optional and on a similar level to Latin. Although Latin was still considered a serious course of study in the first half of the twentieth century, it is hard to equate a dead language of purely academic interest with the living language of the host country. Law 38 of 1948 was to be a stiffer affair, at least on paper. All foreign schools were henceforth to be under official government supervision, whether preparing their students for general government exams or not. It is worth remembering that Victoria boys were prepared for Oxford and Cambridge Certificate exams that were both set and marked in Britain. The tenth item of the new law stipulated that foreign schools were obliged to give their students of different nationalities a level of Arabic equivalent to that of their counterparts in government schools. Victoria thus had to increase the number of Arabic classes and introduce lessons on Egyptian geography and history. Barritt could casually remark in the Annual Report of 1948–49, "Fortunately, our house had been put in order and we did not find any great difficulty in complying."

In any case, outside intervention could come in other forms. In 1950 the Egyptian government introduced several acts of legislation designed to deal with the socioeconomic problems of the country, one of which was the High Cost of Living Allowance Law, by which employers would be obliged to significantly increase the salaries of their Egyptian employees. The school immediately sought legal advice as to whether the law would apply to it and after various, sometimes contradictory, communications with the Ministry of Education it was decided that foreign schools, if not actually exempt, could at least ignore the law. But the matter did not rest there. In early 1953, probably as a response to the new "revolutionary" atmosphere, a Union of College Servants was formed

CHAPTER 3

and Victoria was quickly asked to grant the High Cost of Living Allowance to the school servants according to the government rate and to abandon the system whereby certain servants were given two months' leave in summer but were paid only one month's wages. One Executive Committee member suggested that the College servants should be regarded as domestic servants and therefore excluded from the terms of the existing labor law. Fortunately, such a cynical move was rejected, but the general notion of simply shifting the goal posts was adhered to, and a system of seasonal contracts was proposed to overcome the two months' leave/one month's wages problem. The servants effectively got little more than they already had, the school insisting that although it did not grant the High Cost of Living Allowance, the wages they paid were of a sufficiently high level. The dispute dragged on into the courts, and according to Hassan Ahmed Hassan, known as Abou Khebir, who joined the servants' staff in the 1940s, the school won the case, expelled thirty-five workers, gave the rest of them an end-of-service payoff and then instituted the seasonal contracts so that there was no pay at all during the summer months. Abou Khebir never joined the Union, his attitude being, "We had everything we wanted already."[69]

Although the school was able to repel the servants' initiative and win its case in court, when the attack on its independence came from the lawmakers of the country themselves, there would not be such freedom of movement. In the autumn of 1953 a group of inspectors from the Ministry of Education visited the school and submitted a report concerning the teaching of Arabic. While it would appear that the report was complimentary as regards the standard of Arabic taught, it proposed an increase of three periods per week in both the preparatory and the lower schools. The Council minutes note the headmaster's response: "To comply with this demand would entail a major re-adjustment of the Time Table and would in fact, make it very difficult to continue the work of the school on the present lines." Given the good report on the standard of Arabic, the Headmaster "felt that it would be unfair to force these additional periods upon the School." At this point, Mr. C.D. Howell of the British Council, who sat on a government committee to regulate the teaching of Arabic in foreign schools, suggested that "there might have been some misunderstanding in the present case and he would be glad to approach the Ministry of Education on the subject." Barely one month later the minutes of the Executive Committee record that "Mr. Howell was of the opinion that the Ministry of Education might eventually insist on an increase of periods for the teaching of Arabic," and "the Meeting was in agreement that every effort should be made to resist any pressure to increase Arabic periods."

The objection was not necessarily to the teaching of Arabic per se, but to what this would imply: first, less time for the traditional subjects of a British curriculum and, second, "such a situation might affect the proportion of Staff required as between those recruited from the United Kingdom and those locally appointed." This point was important. If Victoria College was to retain its unique status, it had to maintain its large overseas teaching body. It was not simply an English-language school but a British-style public school and to continue as such would need at least British-style, if not purely British, masters. To compound the problem, these British masters were becoming ever more difficult to find. There was a shortage of teaching staff in the United Kingdom, and Victoria was compelled to raise salaries and perks in order to attract the well-qualified young men that had hitherto been a notable feature of the school. Given the upheavals of the recent past, Egypt was not always viewed as a safe destination and as Victor Bassili, Old Boy, benefactor, and School Council member, remarked, "It was not only a question of obtaining good masters in the first place but of making prospects attractive enough to encourage them to remain at the School beyond their initial contract." He also noted that "the number of the present staff with long service was very small." To provide for these attractive prospects, fees had to go up. The school was beginning to feel the squeeze on all sides.

In April 1954 Mr. Barritt, ever the innovator, set off on a two-week visit to Iraq, Kuwait, and Bahrain. Given the growing number of boarders from this general area, the headmaster "thought that it would be in the mutual interests of boys, parents, Old Boys and the College if [he] were to tour these countries," and it was in keeping with his conviction as to the importance of "personal contact." The trip could also be viewed as a clever realization by Barritt that a changing game required changing tactics. Victoria could no longer rest on laurels that were being seen as less valuable or relevant. It needed to attract its new customers

CHAPTER 3

and to understand what they might wish aside from what Victoria already offered. In this he may well have remembered the request of the Saudi delegation of the previous year. It is interesting to note that Barritt did not just meet with parents, Old Boys, and officials from the various ministries of education but also visited a number of schools in the area and, perhaps most important, port installations and oil fields, where he "stored as much knowledge as possible for future use in the College." The newly wealthy countries of the Persian Gulf provided an obvious catchment area for an elite school and, as mentioned above, Victoria had already received pupils from this region. Barritt's voyage was recognition of this fact and an appreciation that Victoria College, if it were to have a future, had to know the market. Furthermore, if the school was slowly being regarded as less indispensable and unassailable within Egypt, it would do no harm to find supporters in Egypt's rich and potentially influential neighbours.

The gambit, if it can be considered as such, ultimately failed. The catastrophic attack on Suez by British and French troops in October 1956 made sure of that, but even without this act of aggression, events of 1955 and early 1956 would suggest that Victoria was simply not to be allowed "to continue the work of the School on the present lines," as Barritt wished.

Gamal Abdel Nasser had gradually been consolidating his power over the government and country. Leftists and Islamists were purged from the junta and others arrested and tried by a "People's Court" presided over by military officers. In November 1954 President Neguib, as he had become, was dismissed from office by the Revolutionary Command Council for alleged contacts with the Muslim Brotherhood and other so-called subversive elements. Earlier that same year an artillery major had been appointed as Minister of Education and other Free Officers were brought into the government. By 1955 there were over 3,000 political prisoners in the country.[70] The *coup d'état* of 1952 was developing into a real revolution as the state became ever more intrusive in civil affairs. The long arm of the law, and not the friendly police who had guarded Victoria in riot gear, began to grab at the school in earnest.

In November 1954, the school was informed that it would be liable to taxation under Law No. 56 of that year. The following March the

School Council heard to its relief that "the Alexandria Municipality had decided to request the Government to amend the Law to enable all Schools to be exempt from taxation as in the past." This, however, was not to be. On 26 May the bursar received an estimate of the tax at LE 1,275.680 per annum with effect from 1 January 1954. The notice was dated 1 December 1954 and the last date for protesting the assessment was 31 May 1955. The demand for payment of LE 1,955.924, being the tax for 1954 and six months of 1955, was received on 30 May. The school had to pay up.

In October of 1955 the Executive Committee met to discuss the provisions of Law No. 419 of that year, whereby every employer of over fifty workers was required to join the Government Providence Scheme and Insurance Fund. Exception could be granted by a governmental committee if the employer had a valid contract with an insurance company for an equal or a better scheme. To receive such an exemption it was estimated that the school would need to increase the value of its insurance payments from LE 1,216 to LE 2,196 per annum. Inevitably, "the Meeting then discussed . . . the question as to whether the School as a whole could be exempted from the provisions of the new law." It could not.

In May 1956, the Municipality, formerly the very hub of cosmopolitan and autonomous Alexandria, announced the expropriation of some 1,638 square pics of College land in order to widen Iqbal Street at the main gate of the school. An independent estimate of the value of this land suggested LE 5 per square pic. The Municipality offered LE 2.

While these three measures in effect touched only the finances of the school—a tender point in any case—they were nevertheless indications that the net was tightening. As the Executive Committee and School Council huffed and puffed about the injustice of it all and set the lawyers to work on all three briefs, the net was about to close. On 6 February 1956, at the end of a Council meeting that had gone over the details of Law No. 419 and discussed salaries, travel, and baggage allowances for various teachers, Mr. Barritt dropped a bombshell. He recounted a conversation he had recently had with a senior inspector from the Ministry of Education about a proposed law dealing with foreign schools that would come into force as from October 1956. The minutes of the meeting record, "The Headmaster was given to understand that the Executive Regulations to the Law, which would be published shortly, contained a clause to the effect that 80 percent of the teaching would have to be carried out in the Arabic language." It was not until May that the actual text of the law was available, and the School Council reported, "From a preliminary study it seems doubtful if full compliance with the Law is compatible with proper fulfilment of the objects for which the School was founded." This initial reaction was possibly somewhat alarmist, but over the next few months correspondence shuttled back and forth between the several British schools in Egypt and the British Embassy in Cairo. Deputations were sent to the Ministry, and delegations were received from the Ministry. Informal conversations over lunch with officials were carefully and diplomatically resumed in letters that were circulated to the interested parties. By August the school had thrashed out some sort of agreement whereby the number of periods for Arabic, religion, and Islamic history would be increased and Egyptian history and geography would henceforth be taught in Arabic. More worryingly perhaps, the government would have the theoretical right to "interfere" in examinations, the movement of boys from class to class, and the composition and duties of the governing body of the school. All of this, however, need not have spelled disaster. According to a memo written by a British Council legal adviser, the new law was "so badly drafted that it is often difficult to follow its provisions" and, in any case, the schools "will be able, if only by dint of a little judicious evasion, to carry on much as ever."[71]

In the end, of course, none of this mattered. The previous July, during a public speech delivered in Alexandria, President Gamal Abdel Nasser had announced the nationalization of the Suez Canal. The response of the some 250,000-strong crowd that crammed into Muhammad Ali Square was ecstatic. The response from London and Paris was less so. After a summer and autumn of pronounced saber-rattling and just as the academic year was beginning, Israeli armor rolled into the Sinai and, under the pretense of separating two belligerent armies, the British and French invaded the Canal Zone. This time the external forces were simply too great for Victoria. While certain French schools, run by religious brotherhoods and sisterhoods, could raise the Vatican flag and pretend to have nothing to do with the home country, the two Victorias, for all their much vaunted independence, were simply too British to escape unscathed.

It is perhaps surprising that so few Old Victorians of this period appear to have been aware of the contradictions in being an Egyptian, or indeed an Arab of any nationality, attending a British-style school at a time when the British government was so busy meddling in the region's affairs. There is a general insistence that whatever may have been going on in the country around, the school was a sanctuary where politics never interfered. The desire to get rid of the British was almost an abstract concept and, where it became concrete, it was always the army that was targeted. Kamel Sid Ahmed (VC Alex 1943–50) reckons that during "the war years the [political] tensions didn't touch the students. There was never an attack on the school. Perhaps there was a differentiation between the political and education. The riots went against the occupation of the British army. The school wasn't identified as being colonial, that is, as part of the British army." Nevertheless, this was a time of growing nationalism, both within individual countries and on the pan-Arab level, and while the physical structure of the school may not have been touched, the minds of its occupants cannot have been closed to these ideas.

The evidence is contradictory. Georges Balit (VC Alex 1946–55) has stated, "Politics was a favourite subject in school," and Mansour Hassan (VC Alex/Cairo 1944–54) agrees, "Yes, there were political discussions. When you're a boarder there is a communal feeling and when there is a big subject [to argue about] you have all this time to talk about it." On the other hand, Marcel Behar (VC Alex/Cairo 1933–43) claims, "In those days we were apolitical. The only political ruckus that I can remember was when we were asked to contribute to a fund to build a swimming pool for the British soldiers and one student from Upper Egypt objected very strongly." And Said Zulfiqar (VC Cairo 1944–47) specifies, "Our friends were a mix of nationalities and religions so our tolerant attitude was not just a function of the school. In any case, the anti-British element was usually the rabble in the street being egged on by the Wafd. Nationalist notions did not really percolate into the school." Ismail el Mahdi (VC Cairo/Alex 1948–53), who as a Sudanese might well have been concerned by politics given that both Egypt and

Britain were wrestling for control of his country, is disarmingly frank. "I wasn't very keen on politics but some of us were very much aware and followed the newspapers. However, we didn't have the same youthful awareness of political ideologies as you'd find in any secondary school in Egypt or Sudan. There, you'd have groups of communists or Muslim Brothers, but not in VC." Alexander Ghorayeb (VC Alex 1941–52), an Egyptian, would have it that, "There was no Arab nationalism because we didn't feel like the rest of the Arab world." He has also said, "Pro-British? Absolutely. I presume we were brainwashed." And yet it is not at all clear how the school achieved this brainwashing. El Mahdi is adamant that, "In school, the masters gave us a free hand in debating and discussing literature. We never found the staff trying to stop this. I remember one famous occasion in the Arabic debating society when the subject was Palestine and the Balfour Declaration." It is obvious that any discussion of those topics was bound to break the unwritten taboo on religion and politics.

  Abdel Fatah Loutfy (VC Alex 1936–51), who thought of himself as pro-Victoria rather than pro-British, certainly noticed a difference in mentality between Victoria boys and other schoolboys once he had left and entered the engineering faculty of Alexandria (then Farouk I) University. "It was a big change. There was no discipline and a lot of nationalism. People talking politics and demonstrating. It was not that we [VC boys] weren't nationalist; we just didn't indulge in politics. They [non-VC boys] were into politics in secondary school and would say, 'You are the product of an imperialistic upbringing,' but we didn't bother. In any case, the faculty courses were taught in English which we knew well, so we ended up helping them."

  It is difficult to discern at this remove just what, if any, were the political currents that ran through the student body. It is entirely possible that since the pupils were, in the vast majority, pulled from the upper classes of their societies, they were inherently conservative and accepting of the way things were. And yet those "things" were palpably in a state of flux. Edward Said (VC Cairo 1949–51), who might be expected to be an enlightening critic given his subsequent career in analyzing East–West relations and discourse, has remarked, "British imperial power was nearing its end immediately after World War Two, and this fact was not lost on us, although I cannot recall any student of my generation who would have been able to put anything as definite as that into words."[72] Elsewhere he has written, "The students were seen as paying members of some putative colonial elite that was being schooled in the ways of a British imperialism that had already expired, though we did not fully know it."[73] It is quite clear from his autobiography that Said disliked his time at Victoria. He claims that, "Most of the staff were celibate and rumoured among the students to be depraved pederasts."[74] He continues, "To the imported English staff we were viewed as either a distasteful job or as a group of delinquents to be punished anew each day."[75] Those of the masters that Said remembers by name, he portrays as cripples or sadists, as weakened and corrupt as the empire that they represented. Sadek el Mahdi (VC Alex 1949–52), former Prime Minister of Sudan, reckons that the school's reaction to the changing environment and anti-British demonstrations "was to launch a more explicit process of acculturation and the first manifestation of this was the requirement of all boys to sing the school anthem before classes." Despite the fact that El Mahdi can still remember the song, he states, "It was too much. I for one rebelled against this and simply refused to come back to school." But he qualifies his personal rebellion, "I was not that politically conscious but I rebelled culturally."

There were, however, incidents that reflected the pressures of the time. During the period of armed clashes between British forces and Egyptian irregulars in the Canal Zone, graffiti appeared on the school walls and some (unnamed) students wished to display their solidarity with the Egyptian cause. Certain leaflets appeared within the school grounds, one of which found its way into the headmaster's study. Another tale is recounted, again involving unknown pupils, wherein the case of an empty hand grenade was left in Mr. Parkhouse's room. The most celebrated instance of a pupil clashing with the school authorities involved Mansour Hassan (VC Alex/Cairo 1944–54), who subsequently became Egyptian Minister of Culture and a successful businessman, when he managed to get himself expelled for waving the Islamic and nationalist flags a little too vigorously.

Hassan's reasoning, recounted more than forty years after the event, is interesting. As a boy of seven he moved from the rather distant

CHAPTER 3

province of Sharqiya in the eastern Delta, where his family of modest means lived in the village of Abu Kebir, to become a boarder at Alexandria. Come the events of 1948 with the nationalist movement, tension with the British, and the Arab–Israeli war. "Given my personal background and finding myself in a 'foreign environment' plus the surrounding events, something ignited. This took the form of reaching for roots. I couldn't understand [why] I was supposed to cut myself off from everything Arabic. I remember going out of school to the kiosk at the tram station just to buy an Egyptian newspaper. You became religious. You wanted to read the Koran and pray." Hassan became the leader of a group of boys who, for want of a proper mosque within the school grounds, took to praying on the sportsfield. As the numbers grew, the school was confronted with the problem of accepting or rejecting this all too open display of religious appurtenance. As Hassan relates, "Mr. Barritt [the headmaster] was a tough man but, in hindsight, I see that he was wise and diplomatic. He said 'If you want to pray, go to the gymnasium.' And so the gym was opened for prayers every day, noon, afternoon and evening." Not satisfied with this, the boys then pushed to be allowed out to the mosque on Friday, which was a normal school day. Eventually Barritt laid on school buses, and more and more boys began to take advantage of the opportunity.

At this point, Hassan reckons the school decided that things had gone far enough, but was at a loss as to how to deal with him. "I was an A class student and a fairly good sportsman and yet I was part of the 'Movement.' This posed a problem for the school; I wasn't just a troublemaker." Slowly he began to feel as if the masters were deliberately giving him the cold shoulder. The situation finally became so uncomfortable that he transferred to Victoria College, Cairo, but not without some difficulty, which he puts down to connivance between the two schools. There, once again, he became involved in what he calls the "Movement." He and a group of pupils had some anti-British posters printed and then, one night, stuck them up around the school. Nobody was actually caught for this, but Hassan suspects that the school authorities knew who was responsible. He also talks of "skirmishes" with the staff and of graffiti, but the *coup de théâtre* involved, once again, religion. The headmaster, Mr. Elliot-Smith, proved less accommodating than Barritt over the question of prayers so, one Friday, Hassan and about forty other boys simply cut classes. "At 11 o'clock, after the third class, we dropped our books and walked over to the mosque in Maadi. This was very daring—breaking grounds was a serious offense. We also caused quite a shock when all these VC blazers turned up to pray!" The boys involved were eventually called in to see the headmaster and there was much scolding, but no direct action was taken at that time. It was only later, when Hassan was in his last year at school and preparing for his final exams, that he was suddenly expelled for, in his view, no just cause. His father, who was apparently aware and supportive of Hassan's activities, took the school to court, the case being to prove that Hassan was, in fact, a model student, guilty merely of wishing to practice his religion and express support for the legitimate national aspirations of his country, and that the school had no right to expel a pupil for these reasons. Hassan relates that he won the case and was supposed to be reinstated in the school; however, Elliot-Smith refused to have him back and was supported not only by his own staff but also by British teachers throughout Egypt, who threatened to strike. According to Hassan, his case became the subject of negotiations between the British Embassy and the Egyptian Ministry of Education, with even the Revolutionary Command Council following the affair. Ultimately Hassan did not rejoin the school but was helped to finish his studies and allowed to sit his final exams.

The actions and reactions were just more signs of the times. As Hassan puts it, "The demise of Victoria College was not due to itself but because it [the school] represented an empire on the fall. As Britain fell, so everything connected to it fell as well." One perhaps comes back to the dichotomy of vision as regards the British presence in Egypt. For all that Georges Balit is firm in his memories of political consciousness within the school, he too says, "I must emphasise that the feeling at school was anti-colonialist—getting rid of the British as the colonising authority—not getting rid of the British *per se*."

It may be interesting at this point to quote a passage from *Beer in the Snooker Club*, one of the greatest English-language novels ever written by an Egyptian. This is a semi-autobiographical work by Waguih Ghali[76] (VC Alex/Cairo 1944–47), set before and after the Suez invasion.

Chapter 3

Without mentioning the name Victoria, Ghali has his central character, Ram, talk of his school as being "run for rich Arabs and Egyptians who, it was hoped, would rule in their parents' place. The school was there to see that they ruled in Britain's favour." Nevertheless, Ram is profoundly anglophile while still capable of expressing his reservations:

> I wrote a letter from England once, some years later, to someone in Egypt telling him not to send his son to an English school. If his son was one of those who swallowed what they were told, he would one day be disgusted. At school . . . I had been among the very few who "swallowed." We said "this isn't cricket," and didn't smoke with our school blazers on because we had "promised" not to do so. We had been implanted with an expectation of "fair play" from the English. This stupid thing of expecting "fair play" from the English, alongside their far from "fair play" behaviour, was a strange phenomenon in us. Perhaps in our subsequent outcries against the English, there was the belief that if they *knew* that what they were doing wasn't fair play, they would stop it. In spite of all the books we had read demonstrating the slyness and cruelty of England's foreign policy, it took the Suez war to make us believe it.[77]

4
Victoria into Victory

Hala Halim

Sooner or later they will leave our country, just as many people throughout history left many countries. The railways, ships, hospitals, factories and schools will be ours and we'll speak their language without either a sense of guilt or a sense of gratitude. Once again we shall be as we were—ordinary people—and if we are lies we shall be lies of our own making.
   Tayeb Salih, Season of Migration to the North

Alexandria, summer 1956. On 20 June, the governors of Victoria College meet at the exclusive Union Club at 11 a.m. The academic year over, the headmaster's Annual Report is reviewed and pronounced "excellent." Indeed, on the agenda of the meeting is the announcement of the resignation of Mr. H.W. Barritt, Victoria College's headmaster since 1947, whose "efforts ha[ve] been crowned with the success he deserve[s], throughout the last nine very difficult years." Invited to attend the meeting is Mr. H.B. Rider, now appointed acting headmaster. Time and again, the headmastership had eluded Rider, Victoria College's legendary senior mathematics master for over three decades; now the chance must have seemed within reach.

Before the meeting is adjourned, the chairman, Mr. H. Alwyn Barker, broaches the subject of one of the school's *bêtes noires* of the past year: the new Law No. 583 of 1955 concerning private schools. Barker remarks gravely that "the implications of this Law [are] being very carefully studied by the council with a view to ascertaining what effect the

CHAPTER 4

Law might have in relation to the Articles of Constitution of the College." But, unbeknownst to the governors as they leave the Union Club, this is to be the last meeting of the council. It is only one month away from Nasser's announcement of the nationalization of the Suez Canal, an announcement that will trigger the Suez War, of which Victoria College will be one of the casualties.

The egyptianization of Victoria College, dimly presaged in the preceding years, is usually dated to the departure of all its British staff and the sequestration of the school by the Egyptian government in the wake of the Suez War. November 1956 was to herald a metamorphosis of Victoria College from an independent, British-style public school into a semi-English-language, fee-paying Egyptian government school, operating according to the guidelines of the Ministry of Education and Public Instruction. However, rather than the abrupt transformation it is thought to have been, the egyptianization of this institution was a subtle, complex process effected over a whole decade, from 1957 to 1968. Although the name of the school was to change to Victory College only a few months after Suez, the intricate relationship between the old school and the emerging one makes Victoria College an ideal case study of the cultural, ethnic, economic, and political permutations in Egypt at this critical juncture.

The school year 1956–57 started quietly enough. In late September, the decision was made to postpone the opening date from 3 to 8 October. While some parents responded to the postponement huffily, the vast majority were relieved. Indeed, that October the classrooms and the lines at the morning roll-taking were quite depleted. Many parents of day boys thought it wise to keep their children at home. A number of Saudi Arabian and Kuwaiti boarders, including Ali Abdullah al Jaber al Sabbah, from the royal family, never showed up again.

Most noticeable by their absence, though, were the few remaining British pupils, whose parents, already in September (probably acting according to instructions from the British Consulate), had notified the school by letter of their withdrawal. In these letters, sent by cotton-exporting fathers from addresses like "Norfolk House, Domaine de Siouf," there is a certain note of regret mingled with a recognition of the high caliber of the instruction their boys had received at Victoria

College. "May I take this opportunity to thank you for all you have done for my son and also to convey my thanks to your staff which has prepared him for further efforts in his scholastic education," wrote Anthony Rye's mother to Mr. Rider, who back in 1952 had admitted the boy to school at short notice because his father, Sydney Rye, was an Old Victorian. Mr. Rider himself had in mid-September prevailed on his wife to listen to "strongly worded advice" and take their young son James, then at Victoria College, back to England.

Amid the general atmosphere of euphoria about the nationalization of the Canal, mingled with trepidation about Britain's response, explains Mr. Charles Ahmed Hamdy, who had just replaced Mr. Barritt as senior science master, "we observed very strictly the rules of comportment, in other words the taboos of VC, namely no discussion of religion, no discussion of the family, no discussion of politics. These were absolute taboos." But there was a minor incident that indicated that the pupils could not be kept down. One day, a group of boys dropped a bag of firecrackers from a building opposite the dining hall. "There was a big bang," recalls Mr. Hamdy, "and Mr. Rider, on one of his usual rounds, just missed the bomb." The following day, continues Mr. Hamdy, "there was a big splash in the media: 'Bomb Thrown at VC.'" Whether this was a mere boyish prank or whether Mr. Rider was deliberately targeted as the nearest symbol of "perfidious Albion" cannot now be known. Nevertheless, such an incident would have been inconceivable on the campus of Victoria College a decade or two earlier. But one should perhaps not read too much into it, as the somewhat conservative attitude of the pupils to a number of later changes in the school would demonstrate.

Soon after the "bomb" incident, the enforced semblance of normality became untenable. On 31 October, the sound of an explosion sent the boys running out of the classrooms, and then, about midday, instructions arrived from the local branch of the Ministry of Education and Public Instruction to the effect that the school should be closed, much to the jubilation of the pupils. Meanwhile, the British staff of Victoria College, Cairo, was being shipped to the mother school in Alexandria, "though as guests or lodgers was not clear but we did lodge them, of course," recalls Rider. Early in November, too, half the school buildings were taken over by the Egyptian army ("well disciplined and friendly," according to

Chapter 4

Rider). The process of mutual readjustment was not without mishaps, as Rider records:

> There were one or two bits of trouble caused by our guests [from Victoria College Cairo] who did not always quite understand the position. From time to time there was an air raid warning then a blackout was enforced. This they were often careless about and the armed patrol, which tramped round the school, tended to fire warning shots. So the officer commanding agreed that I should join the patrol and be allowed first a shout or two.

As the war wore on in the Canal Zone, the British members of staff at Victoria College were instructed "to stay within school bounds, a sort of house arrest," in Rider's words. There are two scenarios as to what happened next at Victoria College; the widely propagated and, as it were, canonical version, current among Egyptians and British alike, and another, hitherto unrecorded narrative. That British and French nationals, as well as stateless Jews, had their property sequestrated and were deported at very short notice is history. That British schools, including Victoria College and the English Girls' College, changed hands from British to Egyptian administration at this stage is a fact. "Then towards the end of November we were asked to leave Egypt," writes Rider, the verb "asked" reconfirming the canonical narrative of instructions from above, of the die being cast and the old order ruthlessly smashed to smithereens.

Yet there is an alternative narrative that indicates that at least for Victoria College, and as far as the Egyptian government was concerned, the option of a middle course was open during those days of November 1956. The protagonists of this other version of history are Rider (who makes no mention of the episode in his notes for a memoir, which his widow generously provided access to), Charles Hamdy, and Mr. Roha, director-general of education in Alexandria who, in his dealings with Rider the preceding year over ministerial interventions, had shown a sympathetic stance toward Victoria College. Charles Hamdy's account, later corroborated by Nicholas Stamboulieh, another old-timer with a very different profile and affiliations, goes as follows:

The English headmaster and resident staff at Victoria College were not expelled. On the contrary, they were requested, urged even, to stay and carry on, with Mr. Rider as headmaster with an Egyptian co-headmaster. They were offered by me, on instructions from Mr. Roha, director-general of education in Alexandria, on behalf of the Egyptian government. I remember well Mr. Rider's reaction. He looked at me with his enigmatic smile and said: "No, Charles. Two heads make a monster."

To recast the drama of Victoria College in November 1956 as a miniature re-enactment of the wider drama of the Suez Canal would be to oversimplify the complex relationship between the two chains of events, a relationship at times of cause and effect, and at others of rule and exception. True, it was the nationalization of the Canal and the subsequent tripartite aggression against Egypt that precipitated the crisis at Victoria College; however, whereas the Canal was to be fully egyptianized, the school was being offered a British say in its affairs. Yet the punning idiom in which Rider couches his refusal is charged with political significance. This is no mere "too many cooks spoil the broth"; what was on offer was not merely a dual headmastership but a binational one. With Suez marking the last gasp of a dying empire, terms such as "monster" are in keeping with the now exacerbated colonial discourse which demonized the once subject race, a discourse most memorably articulated by Anthony Eden, then Prime Minister of Britain. But if Rider echoed that discourse, it was only when speaking in his official capacity. Years later, in his notes toward a memoir, he would remember with a regret not entirely free of political guilt that when "they [the governors of Victoria College] asked me to take charge . . . I agreed to [do so] with pleasure. As it turned out I succeeded to a *damnosa benedictes* for Sad Suez intervened."

More alarming, perhaps, for Rider than the prospect of two heads with conflicting visions and decisions would have been the apprehension that he, as the British co-headmaster, would have found himself reduced to token status. Whatever interpretation he had placed on it, Rider would

Chapter 4

certainly have remembered the *cas célèbre* of St. Andrew's Mission Scottish School a few months earlier. When the headmaster of St. Andrew's, Mr. Waights, refused to comply with government instructions to teach religion, the school was sequestrated. "The following day, Waights was amazed to find his desk occupied by the new co-headmaster, whose name was Mr. Guindi, while he was allotted a small table as his desk," recounts Mr. Hamdy, who was serving as senior science instructor at St. Andrew's at the time.

On the Egyptian side, the offer is no less indicative. It is not known whether such a proposal was also made to heads of other British schools, and the fact remains that after Suez, all these institutions acquired Egyptian headmasters and headmistresses. Yet, Victoria College, as Gamal Abdel Nasser, who spent part of his childhood in Alexandria, would have known, was among the oldest and most established of these schools. It need not have been solely Victoria's reputation as the *alma mater* of Arab royalty that occasioned this princely Egyptian gesture. A small number of British nationals remained in Egypt throughout the Suez disaster, among them English women married to Egyptian men as well as British men performing jobs in which they could not have been easily replaced.

Such was the experience of John Heath-Stubbs, the English poet, who in 1955 had taken up a post as lecturer in the Department of English Literature, Faculty of Arts, Alexandria University. As Heath-Stubbs recounts in *Hindsights: An Autobiography*,[78] he did not heed the warning that a friend in the British Foreign Office gave him during his 1956 summer vacation in England, to the effect that "something might be brewing."[79] Back in Egypt, when the Suez crisis broke out and the expulsions of British and French subjects began, not only was Heath-Stubbs allowed to remain in the country on account of his employment in an Egyptian institution, but his British personal secretary was granted the same privilege. Although Heath-Stubbs was temporarily placed under house arrest, so perfunctory was the order that he learned of it only by chance on a visit to Professor Mahmoud el Manzalaoui, a colleague in the English Department and an Old Victorian. When the University reopened after the war, Heath-Stubbs took up his teaching duties again, finally deciding to leave Egypt, for personal reasons, at the end of the academic year 1957–58. Heath-Stubbs' verdict on his post-Suez years is that "[t]here was very little hostility from the local population or from the students. The general opinion seemed to be that if this man has been allowed to stay by our authorities he must be all right."[80] In Heath-Stubbs' and similar accounts, there is every indication that those who stayed on were seen as being on the right side of history, as it were, and consequently accorded deferential treatment.[81]

At least two British Victoria College pupils, both of whom had enrolled in 1953, continued their studies at the school until graduation. Alfred Edward Griffin's father worked for the Khedivial Mail Line, and whatever became of his occupation, the entire family remained in Alexandria, at least until their son graduated from Victory College in 1964, and the Headmaster sent a glowing recommendation on his behalf to St. Mary's Hospital Medical School in London. More intriguing, perhaps, is the case of John Glover. When the boy enrolled in Victoria College, the headmaster, Mr. Barritt, granted him a 50 percent reduction in tuition fees on account of his father being "a storekeeper with the British Army in the Canal Zone." While school correspondence continued to be addressed to John's father into the 1960s, it is not clear what occupation Mr. Glover now held. Indeed, it may well have been his decision to remain in Egypt, despite his close association with Suez, that further commended the family's bid for residency renewal.

But for the British teachers of Victoria College to have remained in Nasser's Egypt of 1956, cooperating with the Egyptian Ministry of Education and Public Instruction, would have been construed by Eden's government as almost tantamount to defection.[82] "Rider," explains Hamdy, "gave me to understand that they were under instructions from the British Consulate, representing the Foreign Office, to leave."

Word got around that the British staff would soon be leaving, and some of the older boys trekked in to pay their respects. One Old Victorian, who was a senior at the time, remembers going "to see the lot" and being "stopped at the door by an armed policeman." When the policeman learned about the reason for the visit, "he said: 'Oh, are you going to miss them terribly?' He made me feel I was doing something I shouldn't be doing—I was siding with the enemy." On the actual day of the departure of the British, though, the only people from the school to

CHAPTER 4

see them off were the Nubian *farrashin* (school servants), who stood in line, recounts Amm Abdou Bahr, and waved good-bye.

Later, the *farrashin* were to watch listlessly as government inspectors meticulously inventoried all the school furniture and the contents of the British housemasters' and headmaster's flats, before sealing all the doors with red wax. To Judge by Rider's account, the inventory would have been lengthy:

> When we prepared to leave Victoria we were told that the maximum amount of luggage was 2 suitcases, which meant saying good-bye to many clothes. In any case we had to leave behind carpets & rugs, pictures, glass and silver and saddest of all, perhaps, over 1000 books, some quite valuable. After a decent interval some compensation was given. . . . We [left] on an Egyptian steamer first to Beirut where we spent 2 days & where some Old Victorians took Parkhouse and me out to lunch, then to Piraeus where we dashed to Athens where we drank cold beer sitting outside in the warm air, then to Naples where some took the plane to London others, including me, by train to Rome where we spent the day and after a night at an hotel by plane to London. Then a new life started.

In more than name, it was still Victoria College when the boys were back, just before Christmas, for a much shortened academic year, bound to be full of catching up and cramming. The most visible change was a new headmaster—an Egyptian headmaster. But then, Ahmed Helmy Ali's first statement to the teachers was that he was there "to keep the school just as it was"—a somewhat tall order, given the fact that the school had just lost all its British teachers, housemasters, and heads of departments. At this early stage after Suez, though, the Egyptian government was anxious that all property and institutions hitherto administered by the British should be seen to run smoothly and competently. As with the Canal, so with the school: shipwreck was to be avoided at all costs.

A quick salvage operation, the school year 1956–57 saw an upheaval in the school's hierarchy. The job descriptions of the remaining staff—both Egyptians and members of foreign communities—were redrawn, with plenty of promotions all round. It helped that there were a number of Old Victorians on board—John Abaza, Charles Hamdy, Nicholas Stamboulieh, among others—whose knowledge of the system, the traditions, and the boys was never more in demand. (Years later, their students would invariably refer to these teachers, both individually and collectively, as being "more British than the British.") Whether Old Boys or simply old-timers—and whether motivated by the nationalist discourse of the day or driven by personal agendas—the teachers now had every reason to give the school all they had got.

"These guys [the non-British teachers] were not too happy with Rider or with Barritt. They were not British, and this was the old school of Britishers," observes Fouad Ghubril (VC Alex 1950–61), whose impression may owe more to hindsight than to memory. That Egyptian teachers, teaching subjects other than Arabic, had been considered substandard at Victoria College was the opinion firmly held by Mr. Scovil, for one. Back in 1947, Scovil wrote to Barritt (who was to replace him as headmaster), asking him to try and recruit Poles, Austrians, and Germans as science teachers. Barritt was still in England at the time, and Scovil, anticipating the inevitable question, outlined his position on the recruitment of Egyptian teachers: "We may be asked why we do not employ Egyptians, but it is quite impossible to find men who know English well enough. . . . During the war we had to employ some Egyptian School Masters to teach Science and the result was quite deplorable. Their English was not good enough and one and all were quite incapable of keeping their classes in order."

It would appear that in his reply, Barritt, drawing on his experiences in India, had begged to differ, for Scovil then wrote back elaborating on his argument: "I note that you have found Indian teachers very successful, but the difference here is that with such a cosmopolitan lot of boys, there is a tendency to despise Egyptian teachers—even among Egyptian boys."

Charles Hamdy, on the other hand, reflects that "the Egyptian staff in the Science Department were as academically qualified as the British before October 1956. . . . We were as good if not better." And, indeed, the school had on board two very competent Faculty of Science Ph.D.s, Dr. Mohamed Aglan and Dr. Hussein Kamaleddin. Both had been sent to the United Kingdom on Egyptian university scholarships and had upon their return found their academic careers cut short by the 1954 purge against alleged communist elements in the universities. Later, Dr. Aglan would find his ambition to enter parliament thwarted, while Dr. Kamaleddin ended up in the Oasis Prison where alleged communists were interned from 1959 until 1964.[83]

Socially, too, the division between British and non-British teachers pre-1956 was visible both on and off the school campus. "The English had a very different social life. . . . They formed a very closed group. They wouldn't mix with us and we couldn't have afforded it. . . . Our salaries were much smaller," recalls Mr. Hamdy. If the lower salaries of Egyptian teachers, and those of the local foreign communities, could be explained by the fact that the British teachers were expatriates and thus entitled to more remuneration, the social segregation on the school grounds cannot be so easily dismissed. "They [the English] were aloof with other teachers. They had marvellous common rooms that were out of bounds to non-British staff. Meanwhile, we had one room with benches," continues Mr. Hamdy.

Liberating and exhilarating as the move from the back benches to the front seats would have been, it allowed some teachers to set their sights on even greater promotions. Things were in a state of flux: the school was now under sequestration, and Ahmed Helmy Ali was both headmaster and the sequestration authorities' guardian of Victoria College. It was understood that this was a transitional status for the school, after which, it was speculated, Victoria College would come under the aegis of the Ministry of Education and Public Instruction. When this finally happened, would there not be an opportunity for an Old Victorian as headmaster? One man who seems to have mulled over this question that year was Nicholas Stamboulieh. It had been an auspicious year for him: in addition to heading the Mathematics Department after Rider's departure, he had been promoted to deputy headmaster, post-Suez.

But promotions and reshuffling of cadres notwithstanding, there remained gaps left by the British teachers, notably in the General Certificate of Education (GCE) history and geography syllabi. For this purpose, a number of young lecturers from Alexandria University who had obtained their Ph.D.s in Britain were delegated to teach at Victoria College. Their recruitment came under the rubric of a national duty: "The Dean of the Faculty of Arts called us in and said the university requests you to help the state by teaching these subjects in English at Victoria College," recalls professor of geography Abdel Fatah Weheiba, then fresh from England and thoroughly anglophile. By way of compensation for what they may have regarded as a demotion (and some like Weheiba certainly did: "I was the wrong man in the wrong place") these young scholars were generously remunerated. At LE 2 per hour, Victoria College did better by them than Alexandria University, where the pay, says Weheiba, was LE 1.25 per hour.

But how did the boys react to all these upheavals? With short memory spans, the younger boys seem to have taken things in stride. Mohamed Awad (VC Alex 1954–68) was not too sorry to see the back of his form teacher: "Mrs. Emby was a rather tough lady. Strict and tough. She hardly ever smiled. And I was a small child and was smiling all the time. I think she didn't appreciate that very much." Among the older pupils, however, the picture was different. One Egyptian graduate, a senior during the academic year 1956–57, describes Victoria's first Egyptian headmaster, Ahmed Helmy Ali, in tones of utter contempt, inflected perhaps by internalized racism: "His accent was all wrong, his clothes were wrong; he would do ridiculous things like lean out of his office window and yell: 'I want dee-scee-pleen!'" Similarly, while the older pupils adapted smoothly to the familiar faces of Victoria College teachers now coaching them in the upper forms, they were quite restless, at times even rebellious, during classes taught by the university delegates. After all, who were these new Egyptian arrivals who had replaced their British teachers? Abdel Fatah Weheiba recounts:

> The pupils were not happy about the change. They didn't seem to understand why they suddenly had strangers coming in to teach them. They would go to the window and look at the playground during lessons, and there were fights. We were not allowed to beat them. I could only give extra homework as punishment. My friend Dr.

CHAPTER 4

> Mohamed Hassan [from the Geography Department, Faculty of Arts] was also fed up with the students. I'd overhear him saying: "Please keep quiet, otherwise...!" But the boys just laughed.

Now that all diplomatic relations with Britain were severed, how were the boys expected to sit for their GCE exams? The older pupils at Victoria College and other erstwhile English schools had already been grounded in the British education system leading up to the GCE and thus could not be tutored according to any other system. Early in 1957, therefore, an "Egyptian Board of Examiners for the Examination Equivalent to the Secondary Education Certificate" was formed. Based in Cairo, the board was composed of senior Ministry of Education and Public Instruction inspectors and professors from Cairo University, who both set and corrected the exams, which were modeled along the lines of the various boards of the British GCE. In effect, then, this was an Egyptian surrogate body conferring a quasi-British GCE—a most accommodating scheme.

The GCE syllabus, for the academic year 1956–57 at least, remained the same. Thus Professor Loutfy Abdel Wahab, a delegate from the History Department of the Faculty of Arts, Alexandria University, taught *A Text Book of Modern European History, 1830–1919*, a tome engraved in the memories of generations of Victoria College graduates. This was a history of the continent, written from the point of view of Great Britain, where the only direct reference to the British occupation of Egypt is one that explains that it "had caused dissatisfaction in France."[84] No wonder Professor Abdel Wahab, who had returned from Britain with an English wife and had just lost a brother in the Suez War, asserts that "it never crossed my mind that we were putting an end to one culture and replacing it by another culture, but rather that we were maintaining the culture that was there through Egyptian hands."

As a part-timer teaching the upper forms, Professor Abdel Wahab could not have known that already in 1957, all but imperceptibly, a process of egyptianization of syllabi had begun, moving from the base upward. Post-1956, explains Mr. Hamdy, "Primary, elementary, middle and upper school were squeezed into ten years," and in 1957 the Egyptian syllabus leading up to Thanawiya Aamma (the Egyptian high school certificate) was introduced—first in Class 1, then in 1958 to Class 2, in 1959 to Class 3, and so on. For an entire decade, the two educational systems, the British and the Egyptian, ran parallel, the latter finally overtaking and replacing the former in 1968, when the first batch of Victory College students sat for the Thanawiya Aamma exams.

Old Victorians who were in the lower forms during this period remember a sense of uncertainty, of things being adrift. In the upper forms there was considerable consternation among parents that an eleventh-hour decision would be made, and that their sons would find themselves sitting for Egyptian-system exams in Arabic, for which they were ill-equipped. Hany Yassa, whose class followed the British syllabus, remembers the agony of having to take private lessons in the syllabus of the Idadia, the Egyptian middle school certificate, in the evening—"just in case," as his father put it.

Later the two systems would intersect, although modifications were handled in a mild manner in contrast to the somewhat inquisitorial post-Suez expurgation of school texts witnessed by Radwa Ashour when she was a pupil at a secular French school in Cairo, most probably the Lycée Français although she does not name it. In her autobiographical novel *Atyaf* (Specters and Shadows), Ashour, a professor of English Literature and an activist on behalf of Palestinian causes, recounts:

> One day, three employees from the Ministry of Education and Public Instruction came to school. Each with a red pen and a pair of scissors in hand, they passed by every pupil in class. (The teacher had given us instructions the day before to bring with us Molière's play *L'Avare* and a book on the history of ancient civilisations, both of which were part of the syllabus.) . . . One of the men leaned toward me and crossed out a sentence from the play—crossed it out completely. Then he took hold of the section containing the chapter on the history of the Hebrew civilisation and cut it out. To this day I do not know if the French author had linked the ancient Hebrew civilisation to the contemporary state of Israel or not.[85]

CHAPTER 4

As for the ex-British schools, there would be no scissor-wielding show: the GCE history and geography O-level syllabi were modified here and there, "to treat the subject matter in a more objective manner," as one memo put it. Furthermore, Arabic language and Arab history and geography lessons were introduced in classes later to sit for the GCE. The intention, obviously, was to ensure that these anglophone boys would not also turn out anglophile.

When interviewed in Cairo in 1997 about the government's policy vis-à-vis the ex-foreign schools, Kamaleddin Hussein, who was Minister of Education and Instruction in the 1950s, explained: "We had the public welfare in mind: we wanted pupils to benefit from the high level of foreign-language teaching in these schools, but we also wanted to ensure that they receive religious instruction and study the history and geography of their country." A Free Officer, Kamaleddin Hussein resorted to political terminology in summing up the educational policy: "It was no longer possible to allow these states-within-the-state to continue."

Back at Victoria College, there seems to have been no announcement about the gradual egyptianization of the syllabus. The change may have been announced in the newspapers, but in any case the pupils' files contain no circular regarding the matter. However, one event that took place in spring of 1957 should have spelled out, unequivocally, the direction in which the school was going.

Sports Day, by definition an occasion for fanfare and pageantry, was that year the setting for a most dramatic announcement: that Victoria College was now Victory College. The choreography of the scene in which the announcement was made, together with the cast of characters who "performed" the scene, is revealing. The setting was one of the sportsfields, in the center of which a mast with the Egyptian flag had been erected. The *dramatis personae* were the Director of the Educational Zone, an officer, the headmaster, and the deputy headmaster. The officer stepped forward, raised the flag, and declaimed: "Tahya gumhuriyat Misr al-'arabiya!" (Long live the Arab Republic of Egypt!) "It was most impressive," recalls Mr. Hamdy, who had himself recommended Sports Day as "the best public show for the declaration."

There is a widespread legend among Old Victorians which has it that although the name of the school changed, the tram station named after it still goes by the name Victoria. But the fact is that poetic justice did not tarry for long at Victoria tram station. Although it is still popularly referred to as Victoria, it was, in the early 1960s, likewise rebaptized El-Nasr—meaning victory, the new name of the school in Arabic.[86] The renaming of the school was part of a far-reaching post-Suez policy of arabization of nomenclature, a policy which had its parallels in many decolonized countries. The intention here was to erase colonial and monarchist names, but in the process names that were not reducible to either register, and which encapsulated much social history, were likewise obliterated. The new appellations of erstwhile foreign institutions, tram stations, streets, and public squares in Egypt reflected the approved lexicon of the regime, which drew on notions of "victory" and "pan-Arabism," as well as ancient Egyptian symbols.

Now that the sun had finally set on the empire, surely it would not do at all for Egyptian and Arab boys to receive tuition at a school named after a British queen. Because the change from Victoria to Victory was phonetically minimal the school song was easily expurgated. In any case, it was only the opening stanza of the lyric that called for doctoring:

> VICTORIA!
> Proudly acclaimed by the sons who adore thee,
> Thy fame shall be honoured in lands far apart.
> Victoria. Name that once swayed a great Empire,
> Shall now reign forever as queen of our heart.

Instead, at Speech Day the boys now sang:

> VICTORY!
> Proudly acclaimed by the sons who adore thee,
> Thy fame shall be honoured in lands far apart.
> Victory. Name of our famed and great college,
> Shall now reign forever as part of our heart.

Admittedly an acute case of colonial nomenclature, Victoria College was not the only school to be renamed. Victoria's sister school, the English Girls' College, was to become El-Nasr Girls' College, an attempt having been made here too to preserve at least the acronym of the institution embroidered on the badges of uniforms: VC was still VC and the EGC remained the EGC. Only in the case of the British Boys' School were the initials beyond salvage: the BBS became El-Nasr Boys' School (EBS). However, the exercise backfired somewhat: because there were too many "El-Nasrs," it became necessary, in Arabic correspondence at least, to cite the old names in order to avoid confusion—thus, "El-Nasr, formerly Victoria." Meanwhile French schools run by nuns and friars—among them Collège Saint-Marc and Collège Notre Dame de Sion—retained their original names, not to mention a great deal of their autonomy, partly in deference to religious sensibilities, and in part because these francophone schools allegedly functioned under the aegis of the Vatican and not the French Republic. ("You've got no idea what a headache the Vatican schools gave me," recalled Kamaleddin Hussein, in his then capacity of Minister of Education and Instruction.) Secular French schools, by contrast, acquired alliterative, double-barreled names, as with the Lycée La Liberté.

Iconographically, too, the new regime wrought its symbols and emblems onto the campuses. The morning roll-taking by prefects at Victoria College was replaced by the saluting of the Egyptian flag at Victory College. Neither students nor teachers recall when the portrait of Queen Victoria disappeared from the dining hall, but it would be safe to assume that it went at about the same time that Nasser's portrait came to adorn the walls. At the El-Nasr Girls' College, the new Egyptian headmistress, Mrs. Aziza Rashed, was less accepting of similar impositions because, she argued, this was an educational institution in which there was no room for political indoctrination. Although she got her way, her tenure was short and she was replaced in 1959 by Mrs. Ann Khalafallah.

An English mathematics mistress at the EGC since 1945, Mrs. Khalafallah was married to an Egyptian Azharite scholar who later became Vice-Rector of Ain Shams University, then Dean of the Center for Islamic Studies. Mrs. Khalafallah made the gesture of displaying Nasser's portrait at various strategic points on campus, in return for which, and also by dint of a charismatic personality, she remained headmistress for well over two decades and skillfully negotiated the transition by combining the character-building aspects of the British system with the emphasis on national awareness that marked the postrevolution Egyptian educational system. When Mrs. Khalafallah stepped down in 1982, for health reasons, it was only after she had ensured that her choice of successor—an EGC graduate, Mrs. Enam Defrawi—would go through.

At Victory College, the headmaster situation could not have been more different. As the school pulled out of that watershed year, Ahmed Helmy Ali was replaced by Mohamed Ezzat Nureddin—again, an outsider to the school, brought in by the Ministry. Nor did Nureddin last long: his appointment was terminated only one year later. In retrospect, both his appointment and his short tenure mark the emergence of a pattern that was subsequently to govern the entrances and exits of Victory College headmasters: invariably they were outsiders to the school and were there for short terms, the longest being five or six years. Mr. Hamdy explains the pattern of quick replacements as a by-product of the promotions system, but the fact remains that it did not apply in the case of El-Nasr Girls' College, which would indicate that there was a gender issue at work. Both schools traditionally catered to the upper class, the only difference being that Victoria College tutored the sons while EGC educated the daughters. There was, then, a conscious and concerted effort on the part of the Ministry to ensure that at Victory College, as a boys' school that once catered to the aristocracy, no one headmaster would sit too snugly and for too long on the throne. The headmasters at Victory College would have been selected by no other than El Sayed Youssef, a relative through marriage of President Nasser, who was Under-Secretary of the Ministry of Education and Public Instruction and head of the National Institutes, explains Hafez Bassoumi, an Old Victorian who joined the school staff in the late 1950s.

Without the benefit of hindsight, Nureddin's arrival may not, back in the autumn of 1957, have indicated such a policy was forthcoming. What would have already become obvious to the teachers, though, was that no Old Victorian, or even old-timer, would ever rise to the position of headmaster. In the eyes of the new regime, they were the Old Guard. Nicholas Stamboulieh resigned at the end of the academic year 1957–58 and left the country for good. It has been said by more than one contemporary of his, that Stamboulieh had hoped and even lobbied to become

Chapter 4

headmaster of Victory College. But the Old Victorian who had anglicized his first name was considered to be too pro-British to be granted such a post.

For his part, Stamboulieh has a different explanation for his resignation; the impression one gets from his account is of a man trying to swim against a strong tide but finally abandoning the struggle in exhaustion and despair. Now living in Houston, Texas, Stamboulieh says that he "fought hard to keep the school as it was, and left because it turned out to be impossible to keep things as they had been." His greatest grievance was his failed attempt to arrange for the Victory College boys to sit for the GCE as administered and corrected by the Oxford and Cambridge Board of Examiners in England and not the post-Suez replacement, the "Egyptian Board of Examiners for the Examination Equivalent to Secondary Education Certificate." Stamboulieh explains that he asked for permission from Kamaleddin Hussein, Minister of Education and Instruction, before writing to Rider in England to ask him to intercede on the school's behalf with the Oxford and Cambridge Board of Examiners. When Rider wrote back saying that he had successfully accomplished his mission, Stamboulieh took the news to the Minister. But the Minister, according to Stamboulieh, washed his hands of the matter. "He [Kamaleddin Hussein] said: 'Why did you do it? I never gave you permission to do it.' I said: 'This is education, not politics.' But it was no use. The boys who were hoping to obtain a British GCE to go to university in England were disappointed, but I couldn't help it."

For a while after Suez, Stamboulieh recounts, he kept up a correspondence with Rider in an effort to keep him interested in Victory, but Rider eventually lost interest. Stamboulieh's loyalty to the British was a bone of contention between him and that other Old Victorian, Charles Hamdy. While Hamdy describes Stamboulieh as "more British than the British," Stamboulieh describes Hamdy as "a devout Egyptian.... He didn't have a kind word to say about the British teachers. He often said: 'I'm glad they left. They shouldn't have stayed here for so long.' We used to argue about it." Stamboulieh's assessment of the Egyptian headmasters is that they were, if not given to certain excesses, at best "inefficient" token figures who paraded themselves on the grounds, while he "ran the school" himself. In any case, Stamboulieh's resignation deprived the school of a competent mathematics master and a commanding figure.

But Victory College could have had no greater boon than its new deputy headmaster, Charles Hamdy, whose love for the school can only be described as uxorious. Given that the headmasters were ill-acquainted with the traditions and ethos of the school, Hamdy played the mediator. It was a delicate role, and the axe of the "pro-British" charge, he says, always hovered over his head. "I was often accused of being very pro-British. I was not pro-British but pro the British educational system," he explains, before elaborating on the British system's emphasis on sports and character-building activities and the accent placed on rote learning in the Egyptian system.

Fortunately for Mr. Hamdy—and for the school—he brought to his role as mediator the skills of a cool-headed diplomat, skills honed perhaps during his tenure at the Alexandria Municipality in its multicultural, multiconfessional phase. Mr. Hamdy became the Mr. Chips of Victory College. At the annual Christmas party, the boys had no trouble correctly guessing the identity of the cotton-bearded man in the red costume, who went about distributing gifts to clever pupils and theatrically boxing the ears of lazy brats. At Mr. Hamdy's retirement party in 1975, there was so much insistence that he continue to teach that he returned after a two-month holiday, though only as a senior science teacher and no longer deputy headmaster. With characteristic modesty, Mr. Hamdy ascribes what he sees as "the successful transition of the school" to "the understanding and cooperation of the headmasters."

As for Nureddin, he is described as "an excellent headmaster" by virtually all who had any dealings with him, staff and students alike. Certainly, he did not see himself as a mere figurehead, there to enjoy the privileges of his status, but took a keen interest in every little detail of the school. Every morning at 7 a.m., while the boys were being dragged out of bed, Nureddin and Hamdy would take a stroll around the grounds and discuss school affairs. One area that concerned Nureddin in particular was extracurricular activities, which were lagging, as he observed in a circular to the teachers dated 5 November 1957: "I am sorry to note that only a few of the School Societies have started their activities.

Chapter 4

Would you please nominate your Presidents and Secretaries and establish a programme for the school year. Boys should be told that a final display of their work in the form of an exhibition, match or concert, etc. must be made before the end of the year." Nureddin also cut a very disinterested figure. The resident staff at Victory College, including the headmaster and housemasters, had food rations every week and each had a private servant. Nureddin, by contrast "never took the food rations, and every day we saw his private cook bring food from the market," maintains Hamdy.

Yet Nureddin's tenure witnessed further transformations in the school's status, transformations illustrated by some unfinished business left by the British—namely, the Victoria College versus the government lawsuit over the school wall overlooking Iqbal Street. Already in May 1956, as noted in Chapter 3, then headmaster H.W. Barritt had received a letter from the Alexandria Municipality informing him that the Municipality was going to expropriate the frontage of Victoria College for the purposes of widening Iqbal Street. The portion expropriated was a large one, including the wall, the fence and gate, flats for the resident staff, and trees, as well as part of the lawn and of the First XI football pitch.

A wall, particularly a frontage one, is important, since it defines territorial boundaries. In the ensuing panic and flurry of memos at the school, there would have been no time to think back wistfully to those days at the beginning of the Second World War when, on being informed that the British army was about to take over Victoria College buildings to be used as a military hospital, a bit of string-pulling at the Governorate procured the San Stefano Hotel and Casino as the venue of the school. What may have come to mind at Victoria College was the similar downsizing of the British Embassy and Residency in Cairo after the 1952 revolution. On instructions from the Revolutionary Command Council, the headquarters of which were right across the Nile from the British Embassy, the Embassy grounds (which ran all the way down to the Nile in Garden City) were encroached upon by the construction of that stretch of the Corniche. It was a loaded act of wing-clipping, signifying that despite the "symbolic" British force in the Canal Zone, Egypt was no longer ruled from the Residency.[87]

The British administration at Victoria College, headed at that time by the chairman of the School Council, H. Alwyn Barker, promptly charged the architectural bureau of Max and Claude Zolikofer to provide them with an estimate not only of the value of the property expropriated but of the entire school grounds. The plan was to accept the conservative reparation figure offered by the Municipality and then lodge an appeal against it, demanding a reassessment of the value of the lost property. Enter "Maître" Abdel Aziz Hassib Abbadi, indefatigable lawyer and future thorn in the side of generations of Victory College headmasters. When "in the process of legal proceedings and opposition the aforementioned college was put under sequestration," as one widely circulated memorandum by Maître Abbadi puts it, both the sequestrator and the Ministry renewed his power of attorney, instructed him to continue with the lawsuit, and supplied him with funds. (The ministry, it will be recalled, was represented by Nasser's in-law, Under Secretary El Sayed Youssef.) The indomitable Abbadi obtained indemnity for the school from the Municipality and a reassessment by a Municipality-endorsed engineer of damages incurred, which would have brought the school a tidy sum.

Suddenly, though, Abbadi was stopped in his tracks by a further twist in the fate of Victoria College. Law number 111 of 1957 transferred the ownership of ten English schools (including Victoria College) and nine French secular schools to the Ministry of Education and Public Instruction, through a transaction between the Minister (as buyer) and the General Sequestrator of British, French, and Australian properties.

What this meant, among other things, was that the lawsuit was now between two government bodies: the Ministry of Education and Public Instruction, which now owned Victory College, and the Alexandria Municipality. Meanwhile, the court hearings continued. Nureddin, who, in his capacity as headmaster and therefore as the prosecution, was scheduled to attend the proceedings, found himself caught in a double bind. His letters soliciting instructions from the Ministry and various governmental bodies were left unanswered. To make matters worse, the Ministry had neither finalized the paperwork of his appointment nor supplied him with a job description as headmaster, this last being a far-from-redundant request given that Egyptian headmasters of ex-British schools were a new breed, and that the status of these schools was in the process of being redefined.

For Nureddin the choice was agonizing: to attend the hearings would mean inserting himself into a politically dubious position, for which he could be penalized; to absent himself was to forfeit the school's interests, for which he could be held accountable. He opted for attending. But then, a number of court hearings and official letters later, he decided not to show up in court, and the lawsuit was dropped. Perhaps Nureddin did finally receive instructions to desist. That was certainly the suggestion Abbadi made in the many letters addressed to just about every involved party in an effort to obtain the remainder of his fees. The pending issue of the sizeable sum owed him, for which the school had no budget, was to trail through the tenures of two subsequent headmasters into the early 1960s. If Maître Abbadi did get remunerated, there is no archival evidence of it.

Thus, the issue of Victoria College's frontage, which began as one of the symbols of Egyptian curtailment of British sovereignty over the school, evolved, through the twists and turns of Suez and its aftermath, simply into a mark of Victory College's loss of autonomy and its annexation to the Egyptian government.

That the Ministry was, nevertheless, anxious that former foreign schools should have a semblance of independence, and retain something of their higher level of instruction, is evidenced by the creation in 1957 of the National Institutes. Formed by presidential decree (No. 70 of 1957), this surrogate nonprofit-making institution was entrusted with the task of administering the former foreign schools. Financed by public funds and theoretically independent of the Ministry of Education and Public Instruction, the National Institutes were nevertheless manned by inspectors and officials from the Ministry who were thoroughly grounded in its policies, which they were expected to apply in their dealings with the schools. Henceforth, recruitment of teachers would go through the National Institutes.

The fate of these schools was codified and sealed with Law 160 of 1958. This stipulated that headmasters and headmistresses of private schools (defined as fee-paying) would be Egyptian citizens; that, whatever other syllabus a private school followed, it was expected to teach the government-set syllabus in Arabic, history, geography, civics and religion, and that inspectors from the Ministry of Education and Public Instruction were entitled and authorized to examine all aspects of these schools. As P.J. Vatikiotis puts it, Law 160 of 1958 "abolished all foreign schools as such."[88]

From 1956 onward, fewer and fewer would be the European boys wielding the fencing swords, and the Macbeths and Othellos would soliloquize in recognizably Egyptian accents. When school reopened in December 1956, among the nationalities of pupils already enrolled and who stayed on were American, Armenian, British, Greek, Iraqi, Italian, Kuwaiti, Libyan, Palestinian, Saudi Arabian, Spanish, and Sudanese, not to mention Egyptian. Although the pupils' files are incomplete, a reading from sample years is nevertheless indicative of the ethnic changes in the student body of the school. New pupils enrolling for the academic year 1957–58 came from the following nationalities: Armenian-Egyptian (1), Egyptian (39), German (1), Greek (2), Italian (1), Kuwaiti (1), Palestinian (1) and Saudi Arabian (16). In 1960–61, new Egyptian pupils numbered 32, Saudi Arabians 17, Kuwaitis 9, Libyans 5, Sudanese 2, Transjordanians 2, Yemeni 1, Iraqi 1, Armenian-Egyptian 1, Greek-Egyptian 1, Yugoslav 1 and Bulgarian 1. On the other hand, in 1964–65, the new Egyptian pupils came to 122, Libyans 36, Saudi Arabians 4, Jordanians 3, Indians 2, and British 2, while Sudanese, Palestinians, Syrians, and Kuwaitis were represented by one each. More telling perhaps than the small and ever-declining ratio of Europeans to Arabs seen in these sample years is the fact that most of the European boys left Victory College before graduation.

Alexandria's once large foreign "colonies" had shrunk in the 1960s to mere pockets, which were further depleted by the sequestrations or the threat thereof. Unlike the post-Suez wave of sequestrations, these were not nationality-oriented, but rather part of a large-scale, socialist-inspired state policy of dissolving the private sector and private ownership in certain sectors of the economy, such as trade, industry, and banking. This policy was preceded and paralleled by the implementation of "agrarian reform laws." "They were very grim days, and there was a general atmosphere of gloom at VC," recalls Mohamed Awad. But the boys, it would appear, never swapped sequestration stories. Apart from

CHAPTER 4

the stigma of straitened financial circumstances, they had been warned at home not to blab at school about such politically delicate matters—this was a decade away from the change of political regime that would bring, among other things, the social quirk of whispering loudly that family property had been sequestrated under Nasser, leaving the listener to conjure up the desired image of impoverished aristocracy. For the moment, the Victory College boys watched the tell-tale signs of classmates who—once driven to school by uniformed chauffeurs—were now commuting by tram.

The fees, which had always been reasonable, were not jacked up after the takeover—but then neither were they subsidized by the government in keeping with the socialist principles of the day. Most Egyptian boys whose families had lost out in the sequestrations managed to scrape together the school fees. It was among the foreign residents that the impact of the sequestrations was felt most. Deprived of their businesses and unable to obtain work permits, they felt it was time for them to cross the Mediterranean in the opposite direction to that taken by their grandparents years before in search of the Alexandrian dream. Even among those Greeks and Italians whose professions lay outside the scope of sequestrations, it was understood that they were biding their time in Egypt, and that they would eventually pack up and go and had therefore to ensure that their sons' education was portable.

Granted, the school would continue for a while to offer the Egyptian GCE equivalency exam—as transferable an education as one could now get in Egypt—which drew a number of students from the old foreign communities. And as for quality of education, the constant chorus of parental complaints about the Egyptian GCE being far more difficult than the British one lent a certain kudos to the system. (Indeed, exam questions, set as they sometimes were by university professors, were often way above the level of school pupils, and Victory College teachers did not mince their words about it in their memoranda to the GCE equivalency headquarters in Cairo.)

European and American universities accepted the Egyptian GCE, but it would be several years before their British counterparts acknowledged this *ersatz* qualification. Then came the controversial decision from Cairo that A-levels would no longer be offered, O-levels being sufficient to qualify a student to join an Egyptian university. For foreign students who had set their sights on universities abroad, this was not good news. A case in point is Spiro Vafris (VC Alex 1952–61), a Greek-Egyptian with a golden scholastic record and the unswerving ambition to enter the London School of Economics and Political Science.

Having passed his O-levels at Victory College, Vafris arranged to sit for his A-levels at the British Council in Athens and applied for his exit visa from Egypt (this was 1962). After much loitering in corridors, awaiting an "OK" from the Missions Bureau, a governmental body responsible for overseas Egyptian students, his application was refused the day before the examination and an entire academic year was missed. In an eloquent letter that Vafris sent to the headmaster of Victory College, Mohamed Zaki Sidahmed, soliciting his intercession with the Missions Bureau for a new application, he states his case, which—give or take a few details—clinches the position of the now culturally and educationally dispossessed European resident: "Since my childhood I have been in English schools, i.e. Homecraft House and Victory College. Thus, all my middle education has been in English, with the only aim of continuing higher studies in an English university, in my case the London School of Economics and Political Science. This is unfortunately why I am unable to study in an Egyptian university."

The letter Sidahmed then wrote to the Missions Bureau not only evidences the sympathy that was there at Victory toward students from Vafris' background, but also provides, in its turns of phrase, a study in the niceties of Egyptian national sensibilities in the 1960s. Vafris, "one of our Old Boys, a UAR national of Greek origin," explained Sidahmed—rather than being desperate to get out and too ambitious for 1960s Egypt—"is very keen to continue his studies at a higher level but his poor knowledge of Arabic makes it impossible for him to join any of the local faculties. . . . I have no hesitation whatsoever in writing to you on his behalf and would personally be most grateful for anything you can do to help him leave the country."

Then there were the younger European boys at Victory who, unlike Vafris, had missed out on the tail end of the British syllabus and whose parents deemed that the progressively Egyptianized curricula of the school would not translate across national borders. The autonomous

CHAPTER 4

position of foreign community schools and those catering to the sons and daughters of diplomats was safeguarded by Law 167 of 1959. For the time being, therefore, the old community schools once spurned for education *à l'anglaise* became once more an attractive proposition. Hence another phase of missing faces. But what of the minority of European boys who remained at Victory College? Did they perceive themselves as ethnic and/or religious outsiders, now ill at ease among their classmates? Or were they integrated within the emerging order of the school?

Certainly, some aspects that made for the multiculturalism of Victoria College still remained in place. In the earlier years of Victory College, the staff, for example, continued to include quite a number of foreign teachers. There were, for a start, the Swiss M. J.G. DesMeules (the French language teacher with a "temper as short as a fuse"), Mr. A. Armaos (who ran the sports in school), and the two mathematician in-laws, Mr. Nicholas Stamboulieh and Mr. S. Mouzzouris (who always played records of Beethoven's music in the background during private lessons), in addition to Michael Constantinidis (the biology master), Mr. E.C. Penglis, Miss A. Annaniantz, Miss A. Joannides, Miss A. Moschovachi, and Mrs. G. Salvatore, later to be joined by Mrs. Gilbertson and a Greek national, Mrs. Litsa Florentis, as well as by two British members of staff, Miss Cook (who supervised the boarding house) and Mr. Green (a housemaster and history teacher). These and their Egyptian colleagues were dedicated to upholding Victoria College's trinity of taboos—namely, religion, politics, and social class.

However, the school was no longer impermeable to the outside world and within that no-longer-outside world a war had taken place in which Egypt had been the subject of a tripartite aggression by Britain, France, and Israel. As far as the boys were concerned, Suez firmly turned over the cards of nationality and religion and placed them face up. "Egypt before '56 was different from Egypt after '56. This was the turning point," says Fouad Ghubril; "I had friends in my class whom I didn't know anything about. We didn't know who was a Muslim, who was a Christian, who was a Jew, who was a Greek. . . . After '56 everybody knew. I had classmates who disappeared and I didn't know why they had disappeared and I realised they were Jews—I didn't even know they were Jews. We didn't care. Later we became very aware of religion."

While Suez may have sowed the seeds of awareness of differences, the locus in which ethnic, social, and religious tensions problematized themselves appears to have been the newly introduced government syllabus.

With the exception of community schools and those for the sons of diplomats, all schools in Egypt now followed the same government-set syllabus, which was taught in Arabic. As a special concession to the ex-British schools, the syllabus was distinguished by an additional course of "Higher Level" English and by the fact that science and mathematics were also taught in English. Under the collective rubric "social subjects," later renamed "Egyptian national subjects," came history, geography, and civics. The content of these subjects was informed by and intended to promote national pride, anti-imperialism, pan-Arabism, and, at a later stage, socialism. Geography was primarily that of Egypt and the Arab world. History began with a cursory glance at ancient Egypt, proceeded down the ages to Bonaparte's expedition, disposed of the Muhammad Ali dynasty with a few damning sentences, brought into focus the British occupation of Egypt, and strung the independence movements into a sequence of precursors to the 1952 revolution; the history of the Arab world was also covered in-depth. Civics was primarily a matter of instruction in the principles and achievements of the revolution.

It may well have been the Arabic classes that presented the boys with the greatest challenge, which was that of learning by heart huge chunks of poetry and classical Arabic prose texts. Needless to say, the rote learning involved in the new system marked the beginning of the fully fledged private-lesson phenomenon at Victory College. The hardest hit were the "cosmopolitan" boys, whose knowledge of the language, if it even went beyond the pidgin Nubian-Franco-Arabe spoken in their kitchens at home, would not have spanned more than the colloquial of everyday transactions. Hence such petitions to the headmaster as that written by Stefy Poriasi and signed by other non-Egyptian parents:

> Dear Sir,
> The present is being addressed to you by the undersigned, in agreement with Messrs. Poriasi, Agami, Khoury, Koridjian, Manganaris, Varvis, etc. for the purpose of informing you that our sons attending the "O"

class of Upper V in Arabic find it beyond their capacity to follow the courses of this class.

We would therefore kindly request you, in view of the difficulties presented to our sons, to re-establish the former "C" class for Arabic.

By doing so, you will be giving them a fair chance of succeeding, as well as aiding them in learning the language of our country.

Hoping that this petition will be favoured by your esteemed consideration.

Yours faithfully
Stefy Poriasi
(dated 27 October 1959)

The request was granted and a class "C" was established. Further segregation between the Arab and non-Arab boys would occur during religion lessons.

The ex-British schools witnessed, post-Suez, the introduction of religion as a mandatory course, though it was not until 1967 that it became a pass–fail subject, and to this day a student's score in religion does not affect his or her general average grade. At Victoria College, religious instruction cannot be said to have been neglected. According to the prospectus of the school as set by its first headmaster, Mr. Lias, "Religious instruction, which is not obligatory, will be given only to those pupils whose parents express a wish to that effect." Moreover, special arrangements were made for the boarders, whereby buses would take Muslims to the mosque on Friday, Jews to the synagogue on Saturday, and Christians to church on Sunday. After 1956, there was a partitioning of the class during religion lessons, with Christians, as the smaller group, going to a different classroom; those Jewish pupils who remained at school usually joined the Christians in this separate classroom.

As to how all the changes in the syllabus affected the students' perception of ethnicity and religion is a murky area, fraught with contradictory evidence. At one end of the spectrum of opinion is André Aciman, whose Victory College experience, as recounted in his memoir *Out of Egypt*,[89] would certainly indicate that he was discriminated against. An

Alexandrian Jew, and Italian by nationality, Aciman joined the school at the age of almost nine and remained at Victoria College for only two academic years (1959–61). According to Aciman's account, one flagrant instance of racism that he experienced was during a fistfight with an Egyptian classmate. In response to Aciman's mockery of his heavily accented English, the boy calls him *kalb el arab*, dog of the Arabs. The teacher, Miss Badawi, who then tears them apart, allegedly says, "But you are the dog of the Arabs."[90]

Yet the *coup de grâce*, Aciman continues, was precipitated during a religion lesson. On his father's instructions, Aciman had joined the Muslims during religion, to improve his Arabic. During one such lesson, the boy changed into gym clothes while the teacher was not looking and the rest of the boys copied him. Aciman recounts that as the perpetrator of the mutiny, he was dragged to the office of the head of the primary school and severely caned. After a confrontation between his mother and the primary school head, Aciman "never returned to VC again."[91] His last "report card was disastrous and [his] grade for Egyptian National Studies, a course taught entirely in Arabic, was—predictably enough—*zero*."[92]

Aciman's file does not entirely correspond to his narrative. One should, first of all, point out that Aciman's family name was originally Adjiman. The author of *Out of Egypt* does not mention the frenchification of his originally Middle-Eastern-sounding name; there is, however, no doubt that the file of the Victory College pupil André Adjiman is that of André Aciman. This is corroborated by his age (a few months over eight years old), his nationality (Italian), his father's address (Cleopatra) and occupation ("Industrial"), and the academic years the pupil spent at the school.

Although Aciman did get a "zero" in Egyptian national subjects (ENS), this was not noted in his last report, but rather in his first year at school, when the verdict is that, "with the exception of ENS, he has done well on the whole" and that his "behaviour is good." Nor was his last "report card . . . disastrous," his performance being judged "fair" in most subjects (including ENS), except for mathematics, which he was to retake. There is no reference to the religion class incident. Indeed the slot for religion is left empty in Aciman's reports for 1960–61, whereas his end-of-year report for 1959–60 describes his performance in religion as "F[airly] Good."

Nevertheless, if for the purpose of argument, we take Aciman's word despite the absence of archival corroboration, then the question should be asked whether he was discriminated against because he was a foreigner, or because he was a Jew, or both. While most Jewish pupils did not return after Suez—some, like Albert Chabrit, held French nationality—not all were expelled from the country. An Egyptian Jew, Albert Politi, for one, had dropped out of school in July 1956. In 1958, then headmaster Mohamed Ezzat Nureddin, on request, sent a reference letter to Politi's new school, Van Nuys High School in California. Having reviewed Politi's record, Nureddin vouched that, "[t]hroughout his stay at school Politi's conduct and behaviour were very good. Politi was a conscientious boy who worked very well and made creditable progress." In the upper echelons of the school administration, therefore, ethnic and religious factors did not provoke any biases.

There were at least three other Jewish boys at Victory College, Alexandria, while Aciman was there: Spanish national Alain Aslan Agami (VC 1950–61), Egyptian Eugene Roditi (VC 1950–61), and Iraqi Roddy Shashoua (VC 1951–62).[93] Possibly because all three were older than Aciman, he does not seem to have known them, for he casts himself as the only Jewish boy at Victory College. He suggests, however, that his religion was not known at school. Drawing on his boyhood recollections for the memoir, Aciman may not have been aware that in his application form sent to the school his parents had written "Jewish" under "religion," and that his school file also contained a copy of his birth certificate which gives his religion as "Israelite." That fact would have been known at least to the teachers.

In the wake of Suez, the textbooks were replete with rousing nationalist poems against the "tripartite aggression against Egypt," and the distinction between "Zionist" and "Jew" may not have always been clear in pupils' minds. Xenophobia, concedes Mohamed Awad, was in the air at the time. And, indeed, Henry Zaidan (VC Cairo 1953–61) remembers:

> My awareness of the world around me came with the
> 1956 invasion and the disgusting display my classmates

and I made towards an English boy, and a Jewish boy, who had been with us in class since kindergarten. Not that we really knew, at the age of nine or ten, what we were doing or why. But it was the thing to do. Very soon after that, Nasser became an "Arab" leader, and we lost our English teachers. . . . That was when I realised I was a Christian and was in trouble with my classmates because of it (though that problem didn't last too long).

Yet, the overwhelming consensus among graduates from this period is that the school was free of sectarianism of any form. "It was a sort of melting pot; no one felt this one was Armenian and that one was Greek; we all belonged to the same school and we visited each other at home," says Yusri Chehata (VC Alex 1953–65). "And," adds his friend Mohamed Ezzat (VC Alex 1953–65), "anyone who says otherwise has a chip on his shoulder." In complete agreement is Serge Tchidoukdjian, who left Victory College in 1963 when his family moved to Australia, but who continued to revisit Egypt to see his childhood friends and ex-classmates until he moved back to Alexandria in 1998. "There was absolutely no racial discrimination," says Usama Kassem from Libya (VC Alex 1960–67), who together with his three brothers was a boarder at Victory College; "it never crossed anyone's mind that this one was a Muslim and that one a Christian, this one was Saudi and that one Egyptian. . . . There were no barriers."

While Mr. Hamdy points out that "there were no Christian headmasters," he adds that "the new regime was biased, but it didn't show at school." On the question of social class, he explains that after the takeover of Victoria College, "admissions were made by the [Ministry of Education] zone . . . and the school was opened up. . . . Soon, you had sons of plumbers, taxi-drivers and tile-layers, mingling with the sons of the wealthy professional classes, but all united together," he says, and "the differences were all forgotten once you put on your uniform."

Nor did royalty absent itself from Victory College. While Arab princes were a bit more equal than other students at Victory, teachers could take the liberty of hammering out the jagged edges of inequality. To this day, Usama Kassem has not been able to forget that Saudi Prince Feisal al

Chapter 4

Saud received more substantial pocket money than any of the other boarders. "As boarders, our weekly allowance of pocket money was twenty-five piastres, which we received every Thursday from Miss Cook. She would penalise you if you were caught talking Arabic, and if you were a captain she cut off more. Faisal was the only one whose pocket money was bigger: he was given LE 1 per week, by special arrangement with the consul. But Miss Cook never regarded the fact that he was a royal and the son of a king." Kassem pauses, then continues gleefully, "He was very mischievous and spoke Arabic all the time. Miss Cook used to beat the life out of him, and he never got more than sixty piastres."

But what about pupils from the regime's new elite—the sons of naval and military men? The example of Mahmoud Tewfick Nashed is revealing in this respect. In 1950, when Nashed joined Victoria College, his father was a captain in the Royal Egyptian Navy. It may have been on account of the father's profession that Mr. Rider who admitted the boy to school, wrote in the letter of acceptance that the school was "prepared to stretch a point in your favour"—the privilege of a 50 percent reduction in fees that the boy would continue to enjoy until he left school in 1964. From a shy, academically middling boy, Nashed grew up into a rule-breaking teenager with a poor academic record. By this time, in the early 1960s, his father was an admiral in the navy. In January 1963, Nashed's father received a letter from the headmaster, Mohamed Zaki Sidahmed, to the effect that the boy had broken a cupboard in the common room, and would be made to pay the school carpenter for the repairs, and that, "in case of a repetition of such misbehaviour," he would "be dismissed for good." By December of the same year, Nashed gave a repeat performance, and although he was fined LE 5, the same headmaster wrote that if he was not "taking more drastic measures" this was "only because of the fact that [the pupil] is in L. VI. and in need of all the tuition he can get." In November 1964, however, Nashed was again "guilty of gross misbehaviour," and the new headmaster, Abdel Aziz Koreish, dismissed him for good from school. While it might seem that Nashed was treated with remarkable leniency on account of his father's position, it is worth bearing in mind that dismissing the son of an admiral was a decision that few other headmasters would have dared to take in 1960s Egypt.

If neither royalty nor the regime's new elite could get away with many privileges, then by the same token, boys from the Egyptian *haute bourgeoisie*—traditionally Victoria College's staple constituency—whose families had fallen on hard times as a result of the sequestrations, were treated with consideration. One such case is Taher el Masry, from a prerevolutionary upper-middle-class background. El Masry had joined the school in 1953, on the recommendation of Mr. K.P. Birley of Birley Hall fame. On Union Club stationery, Mr. Birley had written:

> This is to state that I have known Mr. Mohamed Ismail el Masry for a number of years & can vouch for his character. I believe him to be a wealthy man, who owns a ginning factory: he is also a landowner. I have always found him most friendly and honest. . . . He has a son, Taher Mohamed.

It was while Taher was in lower school that the sequestrations caught up with his family, so that when he graduated in 1965, he owed the school LE 119 and thus was not entitled to his School Certificate until the sum was paid in full; meanwhile, university was about to open. His father, therefore, wrote to the headmaster, reminding him that the reason for the nonpayment was that "all our money has been sequestrated and the sequestration authorities have not refunded us the sum [of LE 119], as has been their wont. . . . You can demand the sum from the sequestrator, and on my part I shall also ask them. . . . Had it not been for these circumstances I would not have been late in paying the fees. . . . Thus I ask you to help me build the future of this student [Taher] by giving him these documents before the chance is missed." A note scribbled on the bottom of this letter, obviously by someone in the administration at Victory, says that in the past the sequestrator has often referred such demands back to the parents. Nevertheless, the headmaster gave instructions that Taher's documents be released.

It must not have been a very pleasant task for these dispossessed sons of the Egyptian *haute bourgeoisie* to learn *al-Mithaq* (The Charter) by rote and then regurgitate it in class. Presented by President Nasser in May 1962, this was the manifesto of the revolution in its new-found socialist guise, the ten chapters of which modulated, in highly rhetorical language, such themes as "On the Necessity of the Socialist Solution," "Society and Production," and "The Application of Socialism and its Problems."[94] At every corner, it must have seemed, the students tripped over the *Mithaq*. During the morning assembly, choice morsels of the *Mithaq* and their explanation were broadcast. In class, a distillation of the principles of the *Mithaq* awaited the pupils in the civics course; in the Arabic class, throughout their school years, they were required to recite verbatim whole chunks of the text. In addition, a celebration was held annually on 21 May to commemorate the announcement of the *Mithaq*.

At the mention of the *Mithaq*, Mohamed Awad explodes:

> We could not swallow it. It was a most disagreeable experience. We had to learn passages by heart, which was most unpleasant because we couldn't understand the context or the language. It seemed to us quite irrational: blah-blah-blah, rather than anything meaningful. I enjoyed pre-Islamic poetry, which was also a different language, but then it had music and beauty. But the *Mithaq* seemed to be something we had to swallow and parrot without understanding its importance. Whenever there was the word *ishtirakiya* [socialism] we didn't understand, and whenever we used to ask the Arabic teachers they'd click their tongues dismissively. It was totally beyond our comprehension.

Students certainly reacted differently to the propagandist component of the syllabus. Of his Arabic and civics teacher at school, Serge Tchidoukdjian says, "He was always very much against the regime and I always got good marks writing propaganda essays. During private lessons at my place we used to listen to an Egyptian *ancien régime* underground radio station based . . . somewhere in Europe; the theme tune was the beginning of the opera *Aida*; neither of us was in favour of propaganda—it was just a game." Henry Zaidan, on the other hand, remembers:

> The students of the school (and the country) were brainwashed by the system. We were led to believe and think the way they wanted us to; and for the most part we fell for it. The Revolution, Socialism, Arabism, etc. I remember distinctly how upset I was when I travelled to London for the first time in 1963. It was the country of the colonial imperialist. I realised that I was expecting to see a city and people with no colour. I was so afraid. . . . You cannot imagine how beautiful a red Coca Cola sign looked to me!

The policy of mass mobilization took on other forms outside the classroom. Like all schools in Egypt, Victory College was expected to send its students to official rallies and demonstrations. Many were the occasions and destinations for which the boys were dispatched to exercise their cheering skills. The Russian premier, Nikita Khrushchev, was arriving by ship, so it was off to the harbor; the short-lived marriage between Egypt and Syria had come to grief, so off to a staged demonstration in the stadium; Nasser's motorcade was to pass somewhere in the vicinity of Victory College, so send in a busload of uniformed boys to line the road. These were fun occasions for the pupils—they got an approved break from their lessons and spent the morning outdoors. Some, like Mohamed Nofal and his friends, chanted nonsensical lyrics in tune with the rhythm of the cheering, much to the amusement of bystanders.

"It was the Educational Zone that suggested it [taking the boys to rallies]," explains Mr. Hamdy, "the Headmaster was in the direct line of fire—anything against the policy and he'd have been dismissed." Solemn and grand is how one such rally is depicted in the Annual Report for the academic year 1965–66, compiled by the Teachers' and Parents' Council:

> President Tito's visit to the Republic in April 1966 was a grand national occasion in which the College showed its spirit of patriotism towards the Leader Gamal Abdel Nasser and his honoured guest. All the pupils and the

staff turned out to receive the President and his important guest in the harbour. The pupils were in high spirits. Given that the school buses were insufficient, the supervisors had to rent extra buses so that everyone would enjoy participating in this event. The warmth of their [the pupils'] reception, the sincerity of their emotion and their earnestness aroused the admiration of the officials and security men one and all.

Then there were the military training lessons, which had become a condition for graduation from school. These were not yet the fully fledged drills designed to prepare the boys to literally take up arms to defend the nation (proper military training awaited them during their undergraduate years at university, as well as after graduation). Rather, the aim at this stage was to instill national pride and loyalty to the regime. Some pupils, like the Lebanese Fouad Ghubril, initially resented all activities presided over by the military, but later found sense in them. In October 1960, the headmaster wrote to Ghubril's parents informing them that the boy was temporarily suspended from school owing to his absence from the "Raising of the Flag," in spite of the "many warnings regarding attendance at the daily Raising of the Flag by the Military Contingent of the School," and that the boy had even cut detention for this misdemeanor. Interviewed in London in 1997, Ghubril merely recalled that "the officer tried to teach us patriotism and he succeeded—all of us became very patriotic." Although the officers assigned to Victory College are said to have been handpicked for their patience, the perceived "sissiness" of the boys did not always go down well with them. "There was one boy... who was very delicate and quiet, so the officer picked on him, especially since he didn't hit the ground hard. We told him just to bang his feet really hard. At the end, the officer was astonished at how manly we were," recounts Mohamed Nofal. It did not help that what Victoria College traditionally stood for was diametrically opposed to the principles of the revolution. Tchidoukdjian remembers an incident when an officer "told the students something like 'You know, you people from privileged backgrounds, you know you'll have to adapt . . .' and they took him and locked him up. He got changed very quickly."

It may not be surprising, then, that the boys whose families had lost all their property under Nasser would take out their anger on the school in acts of vandalism, mostly of an incendiary nature. What with the propagandist syllabus, the rallies, and the military training, Victory College had become identified, in the minds of such pupils, with the regime. It was Mr. Hamdy, as deputy headmaster, who took the brunt of these incidents. With characteristic discretion, he refrains from citing the names of the pupils in question.

Mentioning an *ancien régime* family, Mr. Hamdy explains that after their property was sequestrated, the father was given "a pittance ... 100 pounds a month, and he opened a tie shop. No one was too sympathetic, no one tried to provide them with subsistence. The boys at school were very bitter. There was a fire in the Birley Hall—the supposed burning of the flag. I was called in by state security and asked about the red and white tatters [of the flag]." In the 1960s being summoned to the state security offices, invariably timed for the wee hours of the morning, was, at the best of times, not something to look forward to; when the issue was the burning of the flag of the republic, it would take considerable ingenuity and sangfroid to emerge into the daylight. For the occasion Mr. Hamdy concocted a long-standing Victoria College tradition: "I explained that the students had burned theatrical costumes and that I knew nothing about the flag."

That was not the last of Mr. Hamdy's after-midnight errands on behalf of the boys. On another occasion, "the prefects burned their work studies to vent their venom against any symbol of authority. I was called in again by state security." This time, however, the officer was not going to allow himself to fall for Mr. Hamdy's mild-mannered charm. "Asked what I had done—as resident Housemaster—about the library incident, I said I had cut the boys' pocket money as well as other punishments. The officer asked me if I had presented a *procès verbal*. I said yes, but that I had the papers locked up in my office. The following day at 8 a.m. he was there to see them."

Other pupils, if they experienced a similar alienation from the school as a symbol of state authority, identified with Victory College as a physical body and, in a startling reversal of roles, took it upon themselves to safeguard the school against misguided changes. It was in the mid-

CHAPTER 4

1960s, remembers Yusri Chehata, that the then headmaster, Abdel Aziz Koreish, decided to have the trees in the quadrangle in front of the dining hall cut down. The quadrangle was a favorite meeting-place during break-time. "We took a petition to him, and he took us very seriously," says Chehata, "but nothing was done about it."

By 1963–64, it was obvious to all and sundry that the school was in a state of crisis and "many thought that this institution was on its way to its demise," notes the report for the academic year 1965–66, compiled by the Teachers' and Parents' Council. The long-term ramifications of Suez and the redrawn state policies in its aftermath had finally caught up with the school. The student body had dwindled to reach an all-time low of 390 in 1963–64. With the social order of the country in the throes of change, the school could no longer count upon its traditional clientele from the cosmopolitan upper and middle classes. Since Victory College was expected to be self-financing, and given that its main source of revenue was students' fees, the budget deficit was LE 13,800 in 1963–64. Consequently, "the school was obliged to abandon any maintenance or restoration of the old buildings until many of them fell into ruins." The school buses were too few and in such disrepair that they functioned as an anti-Victory advertisement, as they rattled through the city. The government policy of delegating teachers to the school meant that the new staff members, being there on a temporary basis, were unwilling to invest more than the minimum in their jobs.

That Victory College pulled through was the result as much of a well-orchestrated plan as of sheer luck. In the academic year 1964–65, Abdel Aziz Koreish became headmaster, having been transferred from the EBS. He brought with him as mistress of English Mrs. Litsa Florentis, who was later to become deputy headmistress. Such was the popularity of Koreish and Florentis at the EBS that a considerable number of EBS boys followed them to Victory College. On the financial front, when in 1965 the Islamic Conference proposed to rent the school grounds for its summer camp, Victory made its acceptance conditional on the conference restoring the buildings, a project which cost LE 3,500. Taking its cue from this experience, Victory College now rented out its facilities—the theater, the sportsfields, which could be used as camping grounds, etc.—during the summer vacations.

A number of the wealthier parents, too, "willingly subscribed to assist 'the revival of the College,'" as one headmaster put it in his Speech Day address. Most notable among these parents was Ahmed Abdel Rahman Kassem of Libya, who donated LE 300 for the refurbishment of the main gate of the school and offered Victory College a "superb magnetophone." At the school's behest, the new batch of teachers were appointees and not delegates. Headmasters capitalized on Speech Day to make public, albeit subtle, calls to the representative of the National Institutes present to provide financial assistance to the school. Foreign consuls were invited to this high-profile annual event in the hope that they would rope in boarders from among the sons of their compatriots. Boarders were now required to pay an annual sum of £150 sterling in hard currency. The boarding house, of course, had the added asset of bolstering the school's pan-Arab credentials and its "significant national message."

But where were the boarders themselves in all this? Did the avowed spirit of pan-Arabism lead to greater bonding between the Arab boarders and the Egyptian day boys? What effect, if any, did the "war of words" between Nasser and certain Arab monarchs in the 1960s have on them? There is no doubt that the increase in numbers of boarders from Saudi Arabia, Syria (during the union), Libya, and other Arab countries was owed in large measure to the pan-Arab spirit of the day and Egypt's leading position within the Arab world. Victory College's Egyptian curriculum, coupled with the character-building extra-curricular activities of the British system, presented a beneficial educational formula. However, in the classroom, on the playgrounds, off campus, the Egyptian and foreign day boys on the one hand, and the Arab boarders on the other, remained steadfastly two separate cultural and social groups. The division, which appears to have manifested itself more in the shape of a mutual aloofness than in an antipathy, came partly with the territory and the lifestyles of the two groups—as would have been the case in any other school.

However, in Victory, as opposed to Victoria, there was the added element that from the early 1960s onward, Arabic took precedence over English as the language spoken outside the classroom; accents and regionalisms marked out the cultural differences between the students. "We always regarded the Arab boarders as not being very sociable, and that somehow they belonged to a different culture," says Mohamed

CHAPTER 4

Awad, "also we spoke English all the time . . . whereas the boarders didn't speak English. They all spoke Arabic among themselves and with us." As for sports, the boarders could not take defeat with a sporting spirit. Whether it was a day boys against boarders match, or Victory College against another school, they invariably beat up the team that had lost. Chehata remembers the day the boarders "broke up the school shop and took out the hockey and cricket bats and beat up their team."

One aspect Victory retained from the old days, which marked it out from other schools, was the wide range of extracurricular activities on offer. These ensured that, even if they had now to learn by rote, the students also had a chance to develop their personalities and interests. Certainly the infrastructure of extracurricular activities—be it of playgrounds, laboratories, the house system, the long second break—lasted for several years. Minor mutations, though, occurred early on. Although the house uniforms remained, the house names were egyptianized soon after Victoria became Victory. It was out with the likes of Rider, Parkhouse, Reed, Alderson, Birley, and Barker and in with Ahmes, Urabi, Ramsis, Saladin, Archimedes, Plato and co. Most students, the main bulk of whose Victoria College education was under the British, find the new names impossible to recall: "My house was Alderson and it became—I can't even remember. I was brainwashed," says Fouad Ghubril, who admits that he was totally ill at ease after Suez and who eventually emigrated to England.

Certain traditions, particularly those of houses for boarders, were eroded. Usama Kassem, for example, speaks of "a tradition we [the boarders] inherited from our predecessors: at the end of each academic year . . . we would break something, we'd break a window, lamps. . . . This was usually the extent of it. It was an outlet, and it was accepted by the headmaster and teachers." (On one occasion, though, the Libyan boarders, led by the impish Ahmed Fawzi Ben Kato, sabotaged the pupils' art exhibition—leaving only Nasser's portrait intact—a day or two before the date of Arts Day, to get their own back on "a very arrogant new teacher who was organising the event," says Kassem. Although a full-scale police investigation took place, the identity of the culprits was never discovered, he adds.)

What Kassem is unaware of is that this allegedly approved "tradition" evolved in part out of the vacuum left when the end-of-year "house feast" was cancelled. Mr. Hafez Bassoumi, who was a boarder at Victoria College and graduated in 1951, was surprised to find that the "house feast" had ceased to exist by the time he returned to teach in 1958. "The house feast was a big party at the end of the year for the boarders. It was a very special occasion. Parents made donations or sent food; my father, because he was a farmer, always sent a sheep. We were served turkey and mutton, and afterwards a new film would be shown. . . . When I went to school as a teacher, I found that the house feast had disappeared," recounts Bassoumi.

Apart from sports—typically British sports like cricket, badminton, and fencing survived for a while alongside football and tennis—students could pick and choose from a number of societies for various hobbies: photography, carpentry, agriculture, arts, music, among others. Such was the popularity of these activities, that even when the long second break was cancelled in the late 1950s, the students continued to develop their hobbies at school. By far the most popular of these societies was the Science Society, the products of which ranged from the aerodynamic (model aeroplanes fitted with small motors) to the stodgy (a model of the High Dam).

The Dramatic Society, run by Mr. John Abaza, introduced some modern touches. Hitherto, boys played the female roles: Ibrahim el Kirdany, in female garb, is part of latter-day Victory College legend. El Kirdany, now a popular television personality, "used to prance around in a bra backstage and we wolf-whistled him. We really gave him a lot of stick about it," recalls Mohamed Ezzat. But by the mid-1960s, EGC girls were roped in to play the female roles. The first Victory College play in which EGC girls participated was *Macbeth*, where they were cast as the three witches, remembers Yusri Chehata with a chuckle. Perhaps Victory was letting its hair down—it could not have been that a temporary truce in the sibling rivalry between the two schools had been struck.

The EGC—with the commanding, no-nonsense figure of Mrs. Khalafallah at its helm, the fanfare of its public events, and its modern, flirtatious girls—exercised an ambivalent fascination over the Victory boys. They were forever trying to sabotage EGC events, such as Speech Day, with their stink bombs and their boos. "Hooligans," Mrs.

Khalafallah was often heard muttering as she watched the Victory College boys being evicted from her jealously guarded dominions. One familiar Victory College face at the EGC was Taher el Masry. Today a member of the Shura (Consultative) Council and married to an EGC Old Girl, Taher's dossier of "gross misbehaviour" includes trying to sneak into the swimming pool of the EGC. Such escapades, matched by wild antics on the home turf, caused not a little embarrassment to the Victory headmasters, who fretted over "the reputation of the school."

It was a grievance with Victory College teachers that all forms of corporal punishment were strictly forbidden under the Nasser regime, which viewed these practices as symbols of an age of servitude under the yoke of colonialism. Not that the ban was assiduously upheld at the school. Disquisitions by former pupils on the refinements of corporal punishment at Victory College ought to be set in context. "There were," as André Aciman was to recall, "gradations of corporal punishment, ranked by the severity of the crime or the whim of the teacher: first there was the teacher's palm, with blows striking wherever they fell; then there was the ruler; then the stick; then the cane, the frightful *kharazanah*."[95] Such practices, it should be said, were by no means a peculiarity of the egyptianized school; rather, it is that the teachers, particularly the old-timers and Old Victorians, found it hard indeed to relinquish *le vice anglais*. Victory College headmasters, aware that a complaint by a parent to the Ministry could put the school in a very awkward position, were constantly sending out memos reminding the teachers that "all forms of corporal punishment are strictly forbidden and must not be inflicted under any circumstances whatsoever." The scale of "approved" forms of punishment ranged from "the copying out of a piece of poetry," to detentions, suspensions, and expulsions.

Around 1965, parents started receiving printed misdemeanor forms, with the name of their son filled in by hand above the dotted line. This measure indicates that the school tacitly acknowledged that it was dealing with a phenomenon and not a series of isolated incidents. Whether the boys were temporarily suspended or expelled, there is no doubt that, beyond such punitive measures, day-to-day discipline at Victory College had slackened and that the students' culture was undergoing radical changes. Mohamed Awad remembers:

We really had a jolly good time. It was fun. Of course the strict atmosphere of the British had relaxed and we became naughty. There was this revolt against discipline, which was now a possibility. The motto was to break all the rules. And the British strictness and traditions had eased up. Especially for me, when I was a small child [at Victoria College] I felt that it was too strict. Even the continuity of the British strictness with Mrs. Hussein made me feel ill at ease. Then it all changed.

The country was not insulated from the pop culture of the West; Beatlemania was rife among the students, and teachers like Hafez Bassoumi were forever grumbling that Bugs Bunny meant more to the Victory College boys than the Mona Lisa, recalls Mohamed Ezzat.

So it was that in 1968, sporting Beatles hairstyles, the first batch of Victory College students sat for the Thanawiya Aamma exam. Now that the Thanawiya Aamma had replaced the Egyptian GCE equivalency, the egyptianization of the school was complete.

From the mid-1960s onward, a series of encroachments on the playgrounds wrought conspicuous changes in the physiognomy of the school. As the property of the Ministry of Education and Public Instruction, the school could make no objection when the tennis courts were sliced off from Victory College to become the Nasser Military Academy. As for the building of the college mosque, this was a proposal that came from within the Teachers' and Parents' Council. The mosque was the brainchild of Haj Nofal, who had three sons at Victory College and was a very active member of the Teachers' and Parents' Council, which body was officially entitled to approve or deny his proposal. The Teachers and Parents' Council, which replaced the Board of Governors post-1956, differs from its predecessor in both composition and scope. Although the parameters of its power were considerably narrower than those of the Board of Governors, the school being now under the administration of the National Institutes, the Teachers' and Parents' Council could nevertheless debate and vote on matters relating to the internal policy of the school, such as renovations, the allocation of the budget, and extracurricular activities.

Chapter 4

If there is any one parent that Victorians from this period remember vividly, it is Haj Nofal, who personally supervised the building of the mosque and thus was regularly present on the school grounds. A portion of the First XI football pitch had been chosen as the site of the mosque. Haj Nofal caused considerable resentment among his sons' classmates by his habit of "driving his car on the grass of the First XI and Second XI [pitches] as if it were his home—they let him," as one Old Boy put it. Haj Nofal's son Mohamed remembers being mercilessly taunted about the whole affair: "My classmates would say things like, 'What does your father think he's doing . . . this is not Al Azhar, this is Victoria College.' I found it very difficult," he recalls. "When the mosque was opened," adds Mohamed, "there were 5 to 10 percent of the students—the *fellahin* and Egyptians from Upper Egypt—who used to say how great it was to have a mosque. Also the boarders would go to pray and study in the mosque. They appreciated what my father did. But 90 percent of the students didn't. They would go on about my father driving his car on the First XI."

Theories about Haj Nofal's motives, politics, and religious inclinations abound. Some of his sons' contemporaries assert that Haj Nofal belonged to the Muslim Brotherhood. Banned under Nasser, who imprisoned its key figures, the Brotherhood operated much like an underground Free Masonry in the 1960s. Haj Nofal's son Mohamed maintains that his father had no connection with the Brotherhood and was simply a very pious man: "He was very religious. He used to go on the Haj every year. But he never had a beard in his life, and he didn't show off his piety." Mr. Hamdy, who had occasion to observe Haj Nofal's stance on school policy at close quarters, concludes with his characteristic circumspection: "He was very anti-anything-non-Muslim."

The trauma of the sequestration of Haj Nofal's sweets factory was, according to his son, compounded by the fact that he had shown a great deal of allegiance to the revolution: "My dad loved the revolution. The factory used to make banners whenever Nasser visited Alexandria, and he used to send sweets to be distributed during the rallies in Manshieh Square. Then they sequestrated our factory, and my father became very conservative."

After the loss of his factory, Haj Nofal threw himself more heavily into Victory College affairs. That was when he broached the idea of a school mosque at the Teachers' and Parents' Council. Mr. Hamdy who, as a member of the Council, witnessed the entire episode, suggests that "there couldn't have been any voiced objections about the mosque. But as for the location, yes [there were]." Perhaps Haj Nofal's zeal was overwhelming, for he also got the Council to approve the location. But, as for the funds, it is known that he ended up footing more or less the entire bill. "My father collected money, but the collection was so small it would have taken years to build the mosque, so he funded the whole thing," says Mohamed Nofal.

Most "foreign-language" schools did not have mosques at the time, any gesture in the direction of providing a place of worship being a simple prayer room (*musallah*). Indeed, the EGC did not acquire a prayer room until the mid-1970s, and its mosque was not built until the 1980s. True, Nasser's regime was keen to avoid the perceived taint of atheism associated with Egypt's allies in the Eastern bloc. However, there is no doubt that a separation between religion and public life and politics was upheld—as seen in the constitution itself. Under Nasser, the constitution stated that Islam is the religion of Egypt, while safeguarding freedom of religious belief, as was the case in the constitution before the revolution; however, it was not before Sadat, in an amendment to his 1971 constitution, that the Sharia (Islamic Law) became the source of legislation.[96]

And yet if any parents had wished to argue against the building of the mosque, it is unlikely that they would have had a strong case to make. A decade after Suez, there were barely any vestiges left of the Western liberal education offered by Victoria College, or indeed of the semi-colonial, multi-ethnic, multiconfessional society from which it had sprung and to which it had addressed itself. Victory College had emerged from under the shadow of Victoria and come into its own as an Egyptian school catering first and foremost to Muslim Arab students. Religion had been taught at Victory for several years by then. Furthermore, on the national scale, the 1967 defeat in the war with Israel brought a collective religious revival. The alleged visions of the Virgin Mary at the Coptic church dedicated to her in Zeitoun, Cairo, drew thousands of Muslim and Christian Egyptians for months on end in 1968.

On the governmental level, there was a marked pandering to religious feeling and an acknowledgment of the solace that religion could provide for the grief and humiliation of the 1967 defeat. On both radio and television, religious programs were given much bigger time slots. Tellingly, too, the Minister of Education at the time, Mohamed Helmy Mourad, decreed that religion would become a pass–fail subject in schools.

In his autobiography, *Awraq al-ʿumr: sanawat al-takwin* (Papers of a Lifetime: Formative Years), the late secular thinker, writer, and literary critic Dr. Louis Awad wrote a lengthy tirade on religious instruction in schools. He recalls how, at a primary state school in the 1920s, he felt ill at ease when, during religion lessons, he and his Christian classmates left the classroom to take their lesson elsewhere. In secondary school, he adds approvingly, religion was replaced by ethics. Despite his reservations about the teaching of religion at all, Awad nevertheless finds the state policy on the subject during his school years much sounder than it was later to become:

> Half a century later, things had so deteriorated in Egypt that the first decision made by Dr. Mohamed Helmy Mourad, when Nasser appointed him Minister of Education after the 1967 defeat . . . was to make Religion a pass–fail subject in schools. Whether his motive was to flatter the rabble, to apply the religious pecking-order scenario, or whether he was acting on his own convictions, I do not know.
>
> At the time, I wrote the minister a letter [protesting against the decision]. . . . Then I tore up the letter, because I felt it was pointless, now that the decision had been made.[97]

Looking back on Victory College's decade-long transitional period, Mr. Hamdy reflects that "the old order changed very gradually and gave way to the new Egyptian system and VC entered joyfully into the ranks of the leading Egyptian state schools in Alexandria." There is no doubt that a large portion of the 1960s graduates went on to distinguish themselves in various fields and careers in Egypt and abroad. This was also the generation of what Mohamed Awad describes as "the brain drain—the mass exodus of Victory College graduates."

Two of the most illustrious examples are the Elmasri brothers, Ramez and Maher. Ranking top of their year in their school-leaving certificates, Ramez and Maher continued to rank first as undergraduates at the Faculty of Engineering, Alexandria University. Ramez, who obtained his Ph.D. in computer science from Stanford University and is now a professor at the University of Texas, Arlington, is the author of *Fundamentals of Data Base Systems*, a textbook that has been translated into five languages. Maher, who studied mechanical engineering at Alexandria University, earned his Ph.D. in 1978 from Massachusetts Institute of Technology where he also taught for a decade. With at least one patent to his name, Maher has now set up his own company, Thermoflow Inc., for thermal engineering software for the power industry.

The moral of these and other success stories is that 1960s Victory College did produce all-rounders, equipped with the qualities of initiative and self-confidence, as well as the linguistic and cultural flexibility to fit in and succeed in foreign environments.

Not so, however, the Victory College of the postscript—a distorted, gargantuan mirror image of even its 1960s self, let alone of Victoria College. The figures speak for themselves: in a campus originally built for 500 students, the population of Victory College leapt from 750 in 1968 to approximately 2,500 by the mid-1970s to the current 6,000-odd figure. Needless to say, the phenomenon is a reflection of the demographic explosion in the country as a whole. Nor did it help Victory that until the early 1990s, it was the only "English-medium" school in that part of town. Appointed by the Ministry, Victory College's headmasters put up little or no resistance to the ministerial pressure to take in more pupils.

The impact of Victory's population boom on the quality of instruction, extra-curricular activities, and the school amenities requires little comment. Dormitories were scrapped and the boarding house consequently downsized; teachers' flats, of which there were about twenty, went next; then came the turn of some of the halls and corridors; the Second XI pitch became the new preparatory school building. Educationally, the mushrooming of the student body has taken a considerable toll on discipline in the classroom and also on the amount of individual attention teachers can give their pupils. By the early 1980s, too,

CHAPTER 4

most of the old Victoria College teachers had retired. It is no wonder then that, fee-paying though they are, Victory College pupils are as dependent on private lessons as their peers in free government schools.

If there was any positive side effect to the Ministry's policy of loading ever greater numbers of pupils on Victory, it was that the school became, for over a decade, coeducational. The EGC's self-motivated and very successful coeducational policy, begun in the early 1960s, coupled with its high academic standard, had run away with a portion of Victory College's clientele, including sons of Old Victorians. But the Ministry of Education's decision to admit girls into Victory College appears to have been prompted less by any pro-liberal line than by the down-to-earth concern of finding places for female pupils, especially in view of the EGC's less accommodating approach to expansionary ministerial requests.

Coeducation at Victory College was matched by another "first": a female deputy headmistress, Mrs. Litsa Florentis, who took the post on Mr. Hamdy's retirement in 1975. Indeed, when Mrs. Florentis joined the school back in 1964 as mistress of English, Mr. Hamdy had a few reservations about her suitability for the post on grounds of gender. "On my first day at VC," recounts Mrs. Florentis,

> I was interviewed by the Deputy Headmaster Mr. Charles Hamdy—who became a dear, sincere friend—and Mr. Shami, the Head of the secondary school. I remember they were quite opposed to having a woman, and a young one, the first woman . . . to teach in the secondary school, but [the then headmaster] Koreish, knowing very well my character and personality, insisted. . . . The boys tried all sorts of tricks to annoy me, but it seems that my way both in teaching and handling them with strictness, love and understanding won them over.

Apart from her competence as a teacher, Mrs. Florentis played a prominent role in school activities and social life until she left in 1988—occasionally lunching with the boarders, organizing school trips to Cairo for the pupils to watch football matches between the Ahli and Zamalek teams, introducing the daily broadcast in English, and organizing Speech Day. Thus she sailed successfully through school posts that had always been a male preserve, first as head of the secondary school, then as deputy headmistress of the school. Having established her capabilities and credentials at Victory College, Mrs. Florentis experienced no discrimination in any form: "I think there was no negative reaction to the idea of having a woman Deputy Head at VC—[in spite of my] being also Greek and a Christian! I think this was due to the fact that I had become a part of VC, a part of the pupils' lives."

In Mrs. Florentis' view, "co-education was successful at the beginning as the boys tried their best to behave well. But as the number of girls increased, problems started and stricter supervision was needed." In any case, coeducation meant that Victory College now had home grown female talent on which to draw for its Shakespeare plays—except that by the mid-1970s the tradition had died out completely and the costumes in the basement of what had come to be referred to as "The Theatre" (and not "Birley Hall") had long since been devoured by moths. It would take the intervention of a *deus ex machina*, in the form of the London-based Alexandria Schools Trust Charity, to revive Victory College's dramatic society, among much else.

The Alexandria Schools Trust Charity (ASTC), as it stands today, is yet another educational subplot that developed out of the Suez War. Having returned to live in England after the war, the "exiled governors" of Victoria College (Alexandria and Cairo), the EGC, and the BBS started working on compensation claims for the loss of the schools in 1957, recounted Michael Barker, the chairman of ASTC until his recent passing (Mr. Ralph Carver currently holds this post). The separate trusts set up for each of the schools received in 1960 "compensation [from Egyptian funds held in the UK] . . . paid to the exiled British Boards of Governors . . . form[ing] the capital of the Trusts." The compensation for Victoria College, Alexandria, was £659,898 sterling, the EGC £429,883 sterling, and the BBS, £93,899 sterling. The "Governors of each Trust included many of the same people who had known each other well for many years and continued to do so in their new status as refugees," explained Michael Barker, whose father, H. Alwyn Barker, was the chairman of Victoria College's Board of Governors at the time of the Suez War.

CHAPTER 4

Eventually and for the purpose of amalgamation, the trusts shared one aim: "to promote and maintain the teaching of the English language and culture in the Middle East and through such work to promote mutual interests between the United Kingdom and the countries concerned." While relations between Egypt and the UK in the early and mid-1960s did not allow for any such cooperation, it was in the late 1960s that the first batch of British teachers was dispatched to the EGC. As for Victory College, its turn came in the mid-1970s when David Thomas, later to be joined by Neil Connelly, came to teach English language and literature. The school had some excellent Egyptian teachers of English, such as Mr. Adel Shaarawi, but apart from one or two English women married to Egyptians, Thomas and Connelly were the only native speakers of English on the staff. But the two friends' efforts on behalf of the school went way beyond their teaching job descriptions in the twenty-odd years they taught at Victory College.

Realizing that, given the size of the classes, more native speakers of English were needed to teach at Victory College, Thomas and Connelly proposed to the trust the creation of a "volunteer" system whereby British university graduates with an interest in the Middle East would come to teach at Victory in return for a local salary, health insurance, and their airfare. "At one stage," explains Thomas, "we had four fully-paid contractees and three volunteers." One of the volunteers, Colin Clement, recalls that the students were "very noisy and rowdy, not malicious but not particularly well behaved.... The level of English was not bad, but you could not say you were working in a school where the medium was English. The girls were much more mature than the boys ... and had a calming influence. And quite a few of them were quite flirtatious." Thomas, who has since left Victory, remembers that "some of the students were exceptional. I stayed all this time because of the pupils.... The system was terrible, the buildings were in ruins but the pupils were excellent, a lot of them. You wanted to stay for their sakes."

One of the main contributions of Thomas and Connelly to Victory College was reinstating the annual Shakespeare play. With funds from the Trust, the school acquired a new wardrobe of costumes and new spotlights for the stage. As for the make-up, this was the contribution of the

English women teachers from the EGC. "I think it trained the pupils in the idea of team work—that people come and do something for nothing," says Thomas. For a few years, Victory College went through Shakespeare's tragedies—*Julius Caesar, Macbeth, Othello, Hamlet,* among others—with the Portias and Ophelias locally supplied, much to the muffled envy of the busloads of EGC girls who came to watch. Such was the success of these plays that a group of students put on a performance of George Bernard Shaw's *Arms and the Man*, with a great deal of support from Thomas and Connelly.

Indeed, these productions proved, in at least one case, a talent-spotting occasion. Usama Kamal's slick, consummately evil Iago, recalls Thomas, was his entrée to stardom. In the course of an interview on the radio about his performance, Kamal was invited to do a voice test. From then on, it was plain sailing. Today, Kamal has his own pop music program on the radio, and is a television news announcer and presidential interpreter.

Such was the contribution of the Alexandria Schools Trust to Victory College. A far less happy liaison has been that between Victory and the Egypt-based Old Victorian Association (OVA) and its various offshoots abroad. The OVA officially came into being in January 1978. Although Victoria College alumni clubs existed long before that date, they became inactive after Suez. "After '56," explains Armand Kahil, Honorary Secretary of the OVA Board, "the Old Victorians disbanded . . . because of the political situation inside the country. Nobody dared to gather. The OVs kept a low profile for a long time, because most graduates were from the elite—many of them were the sons of pashas. And the elite was not liked at the time."

While it was the change in the political climate brought on by Sadat's regime that allowed for the creation of the OVA, the initiative for the formation of the association came from a certain Victoria College graduate/teacher. "There is an Old Victorian who was a teacher at Victory College—Mr. Charles Hamdy. It was his idea, approved by then Headmaster, Abdel Kerim el Masri, to have the Old Victorians regroup and form a club, with a particular intention: to influence the graduates in Europe to help the school, because the school was in need of funds and support and they thought the wealthy Old Victorians would assist," adds

CHAPTER 4

Kahil. As it turned out, the course that the OVA and its various overseas offspring took was widely divergent from this "intention."

The OVA, under the initial dynamic chairmanship of the late Adham el Nakeeb, was to develop into a much more "serious" and cohesive body than any Old Boys' grouping before it, registered as it is at the Ministry of Social Affairs and run according to clear-cut statutes. After such a long lapse in regular gatherings, with Old Boys dispersed in far-flung countries, many were out of touch with each other, except perhaps for classmates, school friends and Old Boys living in the same city. Hence the inestimable value of the series of "Old Victorian World Directories," compiled, with hardly any funds at first, by Kahil, who has for the past twenty years donated his efforts and office facilities to the OVA. Arranged alphabetically, the entries are also cross-referenced by country, hobby, profession, and business establishment, thus enabling graduates to keep in contact. (A parallel effort, albeit one independent of the OVA, was recently undertaken by historian and Victory College, Cairo, graduate Samir Raafat, who has provided yet another "site" for alumni gatherings—this time in cyberspace.)

The success of the OVA's monthly dinners and annual reunion galas in Egypt in the late 1970s inspired the formation not so much of chapters but look-alikes. London was the first to follow suit with a Victoria College Association. Next came the Victoria College Association of North America and a number of groupings in Jordan, Kuwait, Saudi Arabia, Sudan, and Switzerland. The old spirit of competition between Houses soon transposed itself to the activities of these various bodies, centering on such issues as who managed to land the late King Hussein's patronage, whose newsletter is glossier, whose dinners more celebrity-studded, and which excursion destinations—Cannes, Marbella, you name it—more glamorous.

But to what extent has either Victory College, the Alexandria or the Cairo one, benefitted from this remarkable revival of the graduates' bond with Victoria College? Although the Alexandria school buildings were renovated, the swimming pool refurbished, and the fields regreened, these improvements were designed for the purpose of two reunion galas held at Victory College in 1983 and 1988. In recent years, too, the OVA has donated photocopiers and computers to the school. Annual bonuses are offered by the OVA to the old *farrashin* and school hands, but only those of them who predate 1956.

To date, however, no scholarship has been created by any of the Old Boys' associations for needy pupils to study at Victory College or, perhaps more pertinently, for Victory graduates to study at universities abroad. Nor has the Alexandria Schools Trust been financially aided in recruiting native speakers of English to teach at Victory College. No employment fair is held at the school in which established Old Victorians might recruit recent graduates. Some of these ideas, indeed, were put forward by certain Old Victorians, notably Kahil in Egypt and George Kardouche and André Sharon in London; however, none of these proposals was taken on board. This reluctance on the part of the Old Victorians to become involved in the affairs of the school would appear to stem from a sentiment that Victory College, and by extension its graduates, are dubious poor relations of Victoria College and its graduates.

"Definitely the spirit of Victoria College was destroyed, brutally and wilfully, in 1956. To my mind it perished for good," reflects Dr. Fawzi Abou Seif (VC Cairo 1939–46). "I am a strong advocate of severing relations with the present illegal offspring of our old VC except probably for accepting [in]to the OVA graduate sons of Old Boys, as a favour to their fathers and not because they deserve the [label] of Old Victorians, as they are not." Nor is Dr. Abou Seif's position such an idiosyncratic one; it is a position that can determine who is admitted to or excluded from alumni gatherings even on the other side of the Atlantic, as Hany Yassa (VC Alex 1949–60) discovered:

> I emigrated to Montreal, Canada, in 1986. Early in 1987 I learnt that there was a monthly Old Victorians' dinner gathering at a downtown restaurant and I decided to attend after convincing another Old Victorian, Dr. Ahmed Sobhi, to join me. We were greeted by the late Richard Nessier who immediately asked me of my graduation year—I was only 43 and looked too young to belong. I told him 1960. "We are not sure we can accept you—you are a borderline case," he said. I said: "Who

Chapter 4

are you to tell me if I'm an Old Victorian or not." "That is a typical Victorian answer. We will accept you," he condescended.

To be fair to the Old Boys' associations, the school itself, until quite recently, regarded their proposals with suspicion, as seen in the Ahmes Khalifa Fund episode. A Victoria College graduate and secretary-general of the VCA in London, Ahmes Khalifa was in charge of the London business of Saudi Arabian tycoon Sheikh Kamal Adham, according to Kahil. When Khalifa was brutally murdered in his own home in London in the late 1980s, various friends of his, mostly Old Victorians, raised "a fund of £150,000 to be offered as a reward for catching the assassins," recalls Kahil. When this mission failed, it was decided that the Ahmes Khalifa Fund, replenished by many donations, should be invested in a sports pavilion—to be built at Victory College, Alexandria—to commemorate his name. Thus at the 1988 reunion held at the Alexandria school King Hussein laid the foundation stone of the pavilion.

While the headmaster approved of the scheme, the school's Board of Directors eventually put forward a number of conditions relating to the design and running of the building that were incompatible with the donors' wishes. To the Old Victorians, it appeared that the Board of Directors wanted full control of the fund, and resented any "meddling" by the graduates in school affairs. This interpretation was substantiated by the fact that the only Old Victorian whom the OVA managed to get on the board, Abdel Maqsoud el Zorba, appointed by the Under-Secretary of the Ministry of Education, encountered so much resistance that he resigned after a year, according to Kahil. In any case, a stalemate was reached and the Ahmes Khalifa Fund was channeled elsewhere. "A sum of LE 100,000 was given to the Alexandria Sporting Club to help needy sportsmen, and the remaining amount was given to the Alexandria Rotary for the completion of a home for the elderly in Smouha district, La Residence in memory of Ahmes Khalifa," says Kahil.

The past few years, however, have witnessed a sea change in attitudes, both on the part of Victory College, Alexandria, toward the Old Victorians and vice versa. It is of no little significance that the current chairman of the OVA, professor of architecture Dr. Mohamed Awad, is a

Victory College graduate and from the class of 1968—the first year that a group of Victory College pupils sat for the Thanawiya Aamma. The trend to draw in more Victory graduates, explains Kahil, comes as part of the recognition that "we [Victoria College graduates] will disappear sooner or later, and for the association to continue, we have to accept new recruits." But it is not solely the need for "new blood" that has effected the change. In his obituary of Mounir Chalaby, the chairman of the London Association, since dissolved as a result of financial crises, George Kardouche fully articulates the argument:

> Because the VCA did not endow any educational activity, such as scholarships for Egyptians at the two successor schools, assistance with modern equipment, or teachers, there was little left after the reunions ended. Hankering after the past in a nostalgic and at times pathetic way, not forging any meaningful link to the present schools, the VCA carried on its decreasingly celebratory reunions that, looking back on it, were doomed to a slow oblivion.[98]

While Victory College, Cairo, has consistently closed its doors to the alumni, Victory College, Alexandria, has recently shown a more cooperative attitude. This came about with the Minister of Education's decision in the mid-1990s to dissolve the old Board of Directors and appoint the then Vice-Rector of Alexandria University, Professor Fathy Abou Ayana, as chairman of the new Board (1996–98). And as far as invitations go, none could have been more emphatic than the plea for the participation of the Old Victorians made by headmaster Mustafa el Medani in an undated letter, in Arabic, sent to Mohamed Awad on the occasion of the Greater Bairam Feast in spring 1998. Among other proposals, el Medani recommended that, "a committee of trustees drawn from . . . distinguished graduates be formed to work within the school alongside the Board of Directors." The task of the projected committee, once approved by the Ministry of Education, would be "to raise the profile of . . . this old and proud college, to preserve its cultural and historical distinction . . . and to rid the school of certain insinuated and opportunist elements that destroy rather than build." El Medani clinched his appeal with the following words: "All are now counting on you [Old Victorians] and expecting your prompt and enlightened action to take the initiative of modernising and correcting conditions, for the benefit of the sons of this college to which you belong and whose name you bear."

The gauntlet has been thrown down before the Old Victorians. Will they rise to the challenge? The scope for improvement is indeed vast and the amount of ministerial leeway now possible is greater than at any other time in the past four decades. Over forty years after the debacle of Suez, the educational policy of the country has, if not come full circle, then certainly considerably extended its range, in keeping with the policy of privatization and encouragement of foreign investment. A wide variety of schools and educational systems are now available. There are private, profit-making schools following the Egyptian syllabus but employing native speakers of English to teach the language, as in the case of the Kaumeya International School in Alexandria (run by Nasser's nieces) and Al-Alsun School in Cairo; there are the private foreign schools, independent of the Ministry of Education syllabus, as in the British International School in Cairo, the foundation of which was financed by a capital loan from the Alexandria Schools Trust.

Since the early 1990s, too, the Egyptian Ministry of Education has introduced the International General Certificate of Secondary Education (IGCSE) as an alternative to the Thanawiya Aamma. Given that the IGCSE is entirely in English and that the exam papers are marked in Cambridge, schools can obtain a licence to set up an IGCSE department only if they receive favorable reports from the University of Cambridge Local Examinations Syndicate (UCLES) inspectors. While the many schools offering IGCSE are now hard put to accommodate all the applicants, Victory College's application for a licence had been turned down twice, in 1991 and 1993. It was only in the late 1990s that new laboratories and restoration work made it eligible for a licence.

Despite the "also ran" status of Victory College in today's educational race, the Victoria College of legend continues to produce quasi-reincarnations. Among these are Victoria College, Jordan (which received the patronage of the late King Hussein), and two UK-based attempts, Victoria College, Surrey, and the Avicenna School. Significantly, these schools are hybrids of Victoria and Victory. Designed to provide Arab pupils with an anglophone education, they combine features of the British public school system of Victoria College with Victory College's emphasis on religious instruction as well as Arab identity and history. Although the clientele and the demand are there for such a formula, both the U.K.-based attempts flopped in the course of a few years for financial reasons, perhaps because they were located outside the Middle East.

Will the legacy of Victoria College, Alexandria—whatever portions of it are still viable—fall exclusively to Victoria College, Jordan? As the mother school in Alexandria enters the second century of its existence, the answer to that question lies with both the Ministry of Education and the Old Victorians. The issue is not whether the funds are there to restore the buildings, upgrade the facilities, and offer a scholarship or two. The issue is whether the Old Victorians and the Egyptian government possess the will and the vision needed to refashion the school to meet the present educational, cultural, and political imperatives of an entirely different Egypt and of a Middle East that bears little or no resemblance to either that of 1902 or that of 1956.

Appendix A

Middle East in Miniature

Douglas Haydon, former master, reflects on twenty years at Victoria College, undated (possibly mid-1970s.)

"Small wonder if we dreamed sometimes that the harmony we knew might spread through the Middle East. This vision was, of course, shattered by outside events."

"I wonder if, in the end, the school will have served the other Arab countries and the world at large (with its scattered Old Victorians) more than Egypt?"

As I try to squeeze out the essence from two decades of life at Victoria College in Alexandria, it seems appropriate to begin with these two quotations. The first is from an article I wrote for the December issue of *The Arab*—the London journal of the Arab League. The second is from a letter written last October by an Egyptian Old Victorian. Together they bring out the essential aspect of the school we both knew so well: its racial, national and religious diversity.

When I arrived at Victoria in the winter of 1928–29, one of the first people I met was the head boy, Sirak Heroui, a son of the Abyssinian Foreign Minister.[a] (The term Ethiopian was not then in use.) With him in the Sixth Form were among others, a Moslem Syrian, whose father had once been Prime Minister of a land under French mandate, and an Egyptian Jew.[b] These two were joint Head Boys next year of a school where Egyptian Moslems were the largest single group. The arrangement

APPENDIX A

worked well and the fact in itself illustrates the harm that has been done by Middle East developments outside Egypt in the last forty years. At that time and during the early thirties, parents sent their sons to us from places as distant as Kenya, Zanzibar, the Seychelles, Singapore and even Brunei. Our Iraqi boarders were an especially interesting group. Shortly before I got to Alexandria, there arrived the nephew of King Feisal I and a Kurdish boy whose father was causing the Baghdad Government a lot of trouble. The two got on very well and shared a study when they became prefects. Another friend of Baba Ali, the Kurd, was a Turkish day boy. They were often together, though each told horrific stories of the deeds committed by the other's people. There were the various sons of Jaafar Pasha,[c] one of the heroes of the Arab Revolt. Some were terribly disturbed by the political murder of their father, but there was a beaming, jolly younger boy who kept wicket with great resolution and the aid of plasticine in his gloves. Later on there were the sons of an Indian merchant in Baghdad. They travelled to Alexandria in separate planes, in case of accident. The main influx from Saudi Arabia did not come till after the war, and most of them went to the Cairo school, but I recall in this earlier period the son of a leading Jedda merchant, a cheerful young man who later represented his country in the United Nations.[d]

We benefitted in many ways from the variety in talent and outlook that came to us from other lands, but we were, above all, an Egyptian institution. Boarders came from all parts of Egypt, the sons of government officials, landowners, doctors, occasionally politicians. There was a time when Victoria College became something of a political institution, but it never had a political attitude—except that inscribed in its motto *Cuncti gens una sumus*. There were sons of senior Palace officials, of Wafdist ministers, and of two Independent prime ministers. In class and on the playing field they were indistinguishable from the boys springing from less publicised farming or professional families. The day boys reflected the cosmopolitan character of the Alexandria of those days, the Alexandria Lawrence Durrell knew, and another Alexandria, alive in quite a different way.

During most of my two decades, our community was presided over by one of the most remarkable headmasters any school can ever have known. My first meeting with Ralph Reed was in hospital, when he was recovering from the sixteenth operation he had in thirteen months. At the beginning of the series of operations, eminent medical opinion had given him twenty minutes to live; he survived for eighteen months after that, though afflicted with a variety of illnesses, many of them commonly regarded as fatal. No man without a most unusual vitality could have pulled through, and it was this vitality, combined with intellectual power and force of personality that made him a political figure in Egypt and beyond. It is less well-known that he had those essential qualities in a schoolmaster, great faith in the boys and in the importance of the individual. He was not speaking altogether in jest when he replied to a visitor who supposed that he had a lot of trouble with the boys: "Oh, no. The boys are never troublesome. The staff are sometimes, and the parents are always troublesome." One reason for his success was that a boy with whom he dealt knew that Reed regarded him as a person, and not one of a group who must if necessary be sacrificed in the group's interest. There was an occasion when all the masters he consulted advised him not to allow a particular boy to return, because of the mischief this boy would cause. The Headmaster did not dispute that damage might be done to the community, but he thought even greater damage would arise if we treated our society as more important than one of its members.

It may surprise those who knew of Reed as the confidant of ministers, a man who could gain the affection and admiration of leaders bitterly opposed to each other, that he gave as much thought to the welfare of one bad boy as he did to the fate of a political party. As to his standing in Egypt's public life, it is perhaps enough to recall that the Wafdist leader, Mustafa el Nahas, came unexpectedly to a memorial service for Reed in Alexandria, and that during an earlier illness, the stalwart enemy of the Wafd, Ismail Sidky Pasha, paid him a long and friendly visit. Such incidents meant more than ministerial attendance at Speech Days and dinners.

One must now ask why it should be that a predominantly Egyptian school whose headmaster held so unique a position in the country's public life, may yet have had no great lasting influence on the country. For the Egyptian Old Boy who wrote to me last autumn was probably right.

Appendix A

It would be easy to say that the school's connections were with the old, pre-revolutionary order, the Palace and the parties and the landowners. That is true, but it is not the real answer. Egypt was the scene of great educational activity by foreigners, except the British. The French had been busy there as elsewhere in the Eastern Mediterranean, and the Italians and Greeks also did a great deal. Until the British Council was set up, any form of English education overseas had to be a matter of private, and generally struggling, enterprise. Victoria College was founded at the beginning of the century by the comparatively small British community in Alexandria, and struggle it did for its first forty years. Apart from its finances, it was in any case just one school on its own in a developing country which already had a system of public education. So, whereas French education made a recognizable impression on the national and administrative life of Egypt, the British started too late and on too small a scale to affect more than a comparatively few individuals. That, of course, was very well worth doing, but more might have been achieved but for the mixture of meanness and indifference in England.

When all the reservations are made, however, it was a privilege to live and work in the community of Victoria College. To take pride in the success of a Lebanese boy winning an open scholarship to Oxford;[e] in a dashing hundred scored by one of our more temperamental Egyptian batsmen; in the dazzling forward play on the football field of an Armenian; in the performance of a Greek Shylock and a Jewish Portia, of an Egyptian Tony Lumpkin and a Syrian Mr. Hardcastle, a Russian Trinculo. . . . These were highlights, but year in year out we had the pleasure of watching the boys develop from their varied backgrounds into members of one society.

Douglas Haydon: a Biographical Note by his son, Mr. Christopher Haydon, 1996

Despite his never learning Arabic, he clearly threw himself into life in Egypt, culturally, politically, journalistically. At Victoria College he taught English and History, produced school plays (Shakespeare tragedies, largely, from stories I recall) and coached cricket. I think that Alexandria with its thriving multi-cultural and multi-lingual population was for him a paradise.

He did not begin formal education until the age of seven. He wrote of this unusual occurrence that it afforded him "a year or so longer without any formal discipline and therefore a better chance to develop my own oddities than most of my middle class contemporaries. That may have been a handicap, but I fancy it has also been an advantage."

In March 1924 a school reference—he attended Archbishop Tenison's Grammar School, founded in 1685—cited him as "straightforward and gentlemanly in conduct . . . with a particular aptitude for literary work" and applauds his moral and intellectual qualities. In July 1924 he received another letter, this time from the Chairman of the School Governors congratulating him on his scholarship to University College and awarding him a Tenison's Leaving Scholarship of £20 a year for three years.

At the end of 1928 he sailed for Egypt and Victoria College, aged twenty-three.

On New year's Eve 1942, Douglas Haydon 7921634 Sgt. Alexandria Battalion (Civil Defence Force) Royal Armoured Corps, having served for two years and risen to the rank of Sergeant ('Military Conduct'—'Very Good') was discharged. Such services were given voluntarily.

While teaching at Alexandria, Douglas filed regular book reviews, 'dramatic criticisms' and editorials for the *Egyptian Gazette*. Then in July 1948 he joined the editorial staff as literary editor. He became the paper's principal leader writer, was responsible for sub-editing local news involving translation from French to English (a talent he kept firmly hidden in later years) and also produced the weekly book page.

In April 1949 he married for the second time. He has a daughter by his first marriage, who was born in Alexandria in 1940; his son by his second marriage was born in Cairo in 1950.

APPENDIX A

Owing to the political climate of 1952 he and his young family left Egypt altogether for a life in the UK.

The editor of the *Egyptian Gazette* in a letter dated 29 July 1952 regretted his departure, noting his easy style of writing and sound judgement. (The *Gazette* letterhead boasts 1880 as a founding date and claims to have been the only English daily newspaper published in Egypt and covering the Middle East.)

As a sign of his deep love of Egypt and the Arab and his lifelong concern for Middle East affairs, he sat on the editorial board of a journal, the *Arab World*, of which the first issue was published in autumn 1968.

Notes

a. Later to be the Emperor Haile Selassie's companion in exile at Bath.
b. Heidar el Ricaby and Henri Farhi.
c. Jaafar Pasha el Askari.
d. Ali Ridha.
e. Charles Issawi.

Appendix B

Pupils' list, November 1902
In order of admission

Michael Antonius (Syrian)
George Antonius (Syrian)
Albert Antonius (Syrian)
Constantine Antonius (Syrian)
Edwin Harle (English)
Themistocles Checri (Syrian)
Scipio Checri (Syrian)
Hassan Sirry (Egyptian Moslem)
Yussef Sirry (Egyptian Moslem)
Farid Saba (Syrian)
George Valassoupolo (Greek)
James Barda (Israelite)
Clement Barda (Israelite)
George Straftis (Greek)
Moïse Bendeli (Syrian)
Stephen Lagonico (Greek)
Hassan Mansur (Egyptian Moslem)
Eliott Toriel (Israelite)
Hector Arbib (Israelite)
Joseph Arbib (Israelite)
Freddy Sachs (Israelite)
Elie Aghion (Israelite)
Fernard Aghion (Israelite)
Max Piha (Israelite)
Albert Messiqua (Israelite)
Réné Mires (Israelite)

APPENDIX B

School management, 1902

Trustees (ex officio)

HBM Plenipotentiary and Agent General (The Earl of Cromer, GCB)
HBM Consul General at Alexandria (E.B. Gould Esq. ISO)
The President of the British Chamber of Commerce (R.C. Abdy Esq.)

General Committee
(as constituted at meeting held 13 January 1900)

E.B. Gould, Esq.
A.D. Alban, Esq.
G.B. Alderson, Esq.
W.R.B. Briscoe, Esq.
Baron Jacques de Menasce
Dr. Ruffer
E.W.P. Foster, Esq.
J.A. Tarrell, Esq.
H.P. Kingham, Esq.

Judge Sandars
H. Barker, Esq.
A. Buchanan, Esq.
S.H. Carver, Esq.
R.J. Moss, Esq.
A. Ralli, Esq.
J. Rolo, Esq.
Saba Pasha
Sheikh Mohamed Suleiman Pasha

Cairo
E.C. Manuk, Esq.
Robert Rolo, Esq.
L. Carton de Wiat, Esq.

Executive Committee

E.B. Gould, Esq., *Chairman*
H.P. Kingham, Esq., *Hon. Treasurer*
A.S. Preston, Esq., *Hon. Secretary*
G.B. Alderson, Esq.
Baron Jacques de Menasce

Appendix C

Judge Sandars

*The laying of the foundation stone at Siouf,
24 May 1906
Lord Cromer's address*

Mr. Gould, Ladies and Gentlemen,

When the Victoria College was first instituted, some doubts were expressed as to its future. It was wisely decided to move tentatively. These doubts have now been removed. The institution may be said to have passed out of the experimental stage. We are assembled here to-day, on the anniversary of the birthday of our late revered Queen, to lay the foundation stone of a larger and more complete institution than that which formerly existed. This unquestionable success is, I think, mainly due to two causes. In the first place it is due to the persistent efforts of the committee, and notably to the generosity of a fellow-countryman who in many directions has conferred many benefits on the town of Alexandria; I need hardly say that I allude to Mr. Alderson. The second cause is that, under the impulse given by Mr. Lias, what is probably the best feature of the English public school system has been introduced. In a recent report, Mr. Lias, paraphrasing an expression of that great schoolmaster, Dr. Arnold, said that he wished to make this college "an epitome of the home." Perhaps it would have been more correct to say, "a reproduction of the home." This is what is being done. The masters are brought into close and constant contact with the pupils; and I understand that the committee has, very wisely, decided to introduce the system of housemasterships, thus giving the assistant masters

APPENDIX C

a direct and permanent interest in the institution. Two observations of a more general nature occur to me on the present occasion. One is, that I trust that everyone of influence in this country, in his own sphere of action, will do all in his power to prevent the evil spirit of religious dissension from blocking the path of educational progress. So far, I am happy to say, that spirit has not, in spite of the great diversity of creeds in this country, shown itself to any considerable extent. There are schools where the Koran is taught, and there are schools where instruction is given from the Bible by the various persuasions of Christians. Religious instruction in this particular college is, as you are aware, not obligatory. It is, however, given at the request of those parents who desire it, by teachers whom they themselves have chosen. Gentlemen, there is plenty of room in Egypt for schools of all these descriptions. I may add that, though I have been frequently urged to move the Egyptian Government to place its educational policy in the matter of religious teaching on a different, and perhaps somewhat more theoretically defensible basis than that which now exists, I have always held, and still hold, that this is a case where the homely proverb of "leaving well alone" applies with special force. The main consideration, to my mind, is to let education advance—and it is advancing with rapid strides—without spreading the fires of religious strife.

The other point which strikes me is that the composition of this college is a very good representation in miniature of the cosmopolitan society of Egypt. I am informed that, out of a total of 186 pupils, 90 are Christians, 67 are Israelites, 39 are Moslems; whilst as regards nationalities, there are Egyptian, Turkish, Syrian, Armenian, Maltese, Greek, English, French, Italian, Spanish, Dutch, Swiss and Belgian pupils. There are many such schools and colleges in this country. They cannot fail to do good. In the first place, as regards the relations between Europeans and native Egyptians, I would fain hope that this amalgamation of races may, in process of time, produce some effect in the direction of removing those misunderstandings which, even to a greater extent than any solid difference of opinion, do much to foster racial animosity: whilst, as regards the Europeans *inter se*, it may be hoped that the more the rising generation of various nationalities see of each other, the more they will appreciate a fact of which I have for several years been convinced. It is that the European residents in Egypt—on whom the progress, whether material or moral, of the country so much depends—are bound together by a common interest. I think I notice, during the last two or three years, distinct diminution of that petty international rivalry and acerbity which, in the past, has done infinite harm. It is my earnest hope that this healthy movement will grow apace, and that all the educated and influential Europeans in this country will realise that they stand together as the representatives and champions of western civilisation. For this, amongst other reasons, I welcome the establishment of the Victoria College, as an institution worthy of the great sovereign whose name it bears. It will, I trust, help in some degree towards the political and social fusion of the various nations who inhabit the valley of the Nile, and who, although they are not all Egyptians in the ordinary and technical sense of the term, deserve that title in its wider, and, as I think, truer sense, in that they are all dwellers in Egypt, and all equally interested in the welfare of the country. In my opinion, it is in the direction of facilitating this fusion that the efforts of all true Egyptian reformers should be turned.

Appendix D

Staff list, first year at Siouf, 1908–9

Headmaster
C.R. Lias, M.A., King's College, Cambridge

Second Master
A. Morrison, M.A., Late Scholar of King's College, Cambridge

Assistant Masters
A. Mustard
G. Dumont, Academy of Neuchâtel
Sheikh Mohamed Hamid, Al Azhar University, Cairo
A.E. Aubrey, B.A., Late Scholar of Emmanuel College, Cambridge
Sheikh Mohamed Tawfiq, Al Azhar University, Cairo
V.R. Mustard
J.J.P. Curnow, Art Teacher's Certificate
F.J. Page, B.Sc., London University
H.E. Wortham, B.A., King's College, Cambridge
Osman Effendi Murad

Staff list, first year at Siouf

Preparatory School
Miss D.G. Barwell, Froebel Certificate
Mlle. H. Staiger
Miss A.J. Harris
V. Fagan

Extra Master
H.C. Tookey

Matrons
Miss. S.A.E. Smith
Miss D. Grant

Appendix E

*Note on Victoria College, Alexandria,
submitted to the Special Mission to Egypt
by four former pupils of the school,
dated 24 February 1920
Courtesy of Professor William Cleveland*

In submitting this Note, the undersigned, who are all old pupils of Victoria College, wish to bring to the notice of the Special Mission to Egypt their own appreciation of the work done by their old School; and to lay before the Mission certain considerations, which, in their opinion, entitle Victoria College to a special measure of interest and of help. The signatories, who are taking this step entirely on their own initiative, have been unable, owing chiefly to exigencies of time and other material obstacles, to convene a General Meeting of Old Victorians for the purpose of appointing from among themselves a mandatory body with power to speak on behalf of all former pupils of the School. In that sense, the signatories do not come forward as an officially representative body. But on the other hand, from their constant intercourse with fellow Old Victorians, and from what they have recently ascertained in the course of informal discussions, they are confident that the views and the hopes which they have tried to express in this Note, are those of the majority of the former pupils of the School:

    A. Nahas, Doctor of Dental Surgery, Northwestern University, Chicago, USA

    G. Valassopoulo, B.A., King's College, Cambridge, and Licence en Droit, Université de Toulouse

    G. Antonius, B.A., King's College, Cambridge

Note by Four Former Pupils

S. Naggiar, B.A., L.L.B., Trinity College, Cambridge

Victoria College is now in its eighteenth year. Of its foundation, its development and the difficulties against which it has had to contend it is not proposed here to speak at any length. What we, as Old Boys, are more particularly entitled to speak of is the worth, achievement and influence of the School as revealed to us in the light of our personal experience.

In the first place, we value the moral worth of our school training. We were aware, dimly at first, but more clearly now, that what we gained in the class-room was not only knowledge and instruction in certain subjects; that there was also, besides the effort to inculcate knowledge, a constant attempt to exercise the mind, to train the faculties towards drawing conclusions from our studies, that gave that instruction what seems to us to form its real value. We remember how, while still at school, we used to discuss some of our lessons amongst ourselves with eagerness and curiosity. Now on looking back, we realise that that was chiefly owing to two causes: first, because we were made to approach and study those subjects, not so much in their relation to the dreaded examinations, but rather from the standpoint of their human and living relation to the problems of life; and secondly, because our masters had tried to provide us, as well as with the facts of knowledge, with the equipment and desire to acquire more knowledge. We find that the lessons of fifteen years ago stand us in good stead to this day and that they have left a mark on us which is likely to be permanent and for which we are grateful.

In the realm of pure tuition, we can confidently say that our school is on a level with the best of which we know anywhere. In Egypt, where the need of more than one language is a vital one, it is a condition of usefulness that education should be general and should cover a wider range than in most European countries. We think that our school has dealt with this problem with manifest success. It teaches boys the three principal languages of this country simultaneously and approximately on the same level. It prepares pupils, whose mother tongue is usually other than English, for an English examination intended for boys who have completed the course of studies in the Public Schools of Great Britain. It has enabled boys of the same form and of all but identical training to obtain the Oxford and Cambridge Higher Certificate, the Egyptian Secondary Certificate, the French Baccalauréat, and to proceed to British or French or other Universities, there to get their degrees alongside of men from the most famous schools of the world. And later in their careers they have shown their special fitness for the public and professional walks of life, which the special conditions in Egypt require. We do not wish here to boast of the achievements of old pupils of Victoria College: all we wish to say is that any success they may have had is largely due to the excellence of their training at School.

And last but not least we value the influence which our School has had on our lives. The spirit which reigned at Victoria College was marked by a large measure of friendly intercourse between master and pupils. Whether in the classroom or on the playing-field or elsewhere, we were in constant contact with our masters. We knew them, trusted them, and looked up to them, for they were not only teachers but friends and men who, by leading before us and with us lives such as we were taught to aim at, have done more towards our development than anything we have experienced. Now on looking back after the lapse of years, we are able to appreciate their influence. They aimed at forming our characters, not merely by dictating precepts, but also by that most powerful of methods—the method of example. We may be forgiven if we give the first place in our gratitude to our old Headmaster and Masters. If we do so it is because, putting aside all feelings of reverence and affection, we recognise that the influence of their lives and of the example which they set was both deep and lasting. To them we owe the tone and the traditions of the School, in which boys grow up to learn and practise devolution and acquire habits of responsibility and self-reliance, of understanding and goodwill. The lessons of outdoor games and of the monitorial system are things which are to us real and living. They are things of which, little as we may have seen of the world, we can speak with unhesitating confidence: they are our own intimate experience. And on this point we feel all the more strongly as we know that they are things which in this country are yet far from being universally practised or taught, while they are of the very essence of the life at Victoria College.

For all these reasons we are grateful to our School and proud of it; and we wish to do everything we can to help it. The history of the School from its foundation and more particularly during the last twelve years is, in one aspect, a record of financial difficulties. We do not know any of the details of this struggle against bankruptcy; but we know enough to realise that the future of our School has been and perhaps is in grave danger. The actual position, as we know it, is that Victoria College, with a record number of pupils and with extremely high fees, is just (and only just) able, by a policy of continual stinting, to pay its way. How much there lies behind this meeting of the two ends, of close effort and devotion, of anxious moments, of masters bearing too great a burden, of masterships abandoned or for lack of funds remaining unfilled, of promising boys refused, of important improvements postponed, and in general, of wrong but enforced economy, we doubt we could adequately describe. Now we earnestly beg of all those who take an interest in Egyptian education to turn their attention to this serious state of affairs. We think it is serious because we hold, in the first place, that for a public school of this kind to have to eke out a living from its fees is fatal. A school like Victoria College should live without having to rely exclusively on the fees. It should be in a position after paying off its debts to increase its present staff, to afford masters better inducements than they can have now; to be able to exercise reasonably free selection of the boys it accepts, rejecting those who are undesirable and lowering the fees for those more promising boys—and they are not a few—who cannot afford them. This last point, we think, deserves special emphasis. Many boys would otherwise have entered the School with every qualification and promise, are prevented from doing so by the disqualification of insufficient means.

These are some of the much-needed remedies for the existing evils all of which arise out of the fact that the School is almost totally unendowed. There are also needs for such things as the improvement of the playground and the laboratories, the erection of workshops and reading-rooms, which are now lacking, and many others, we believe, which are equally pressing.

Therefore, we have seized the opportunity of the presence in Egypt of the Special Mission who have come to examine conditions in this country, to submit to them this appeal on behalf of our School. We appeal to them to consider the case of Victoria College as part of the great task on which they are at present engaged. Though it may not be for us to point

Appendix E

out, yet we feel that one of the things which this country requires is a training in those qualities, which, as we believe, are best bred in the English Public Schools. We think that the double aim of education in Egypt should be, apart from the tuitional aim, on the one hand to help remove those misunderstandings which "to a greater extent than any solid differences of opinion, do much to further racial animosity"; and on the other to bring up the sons of this country on principles of duty, character and clean living. We firmly believe that our old School carries out those aims. And we hope that our appeal may serve in some measure to awaken the interest of public-spirited and generous men who, by placing the School above its present needs, would enable it to remain what it is now, to use Lord Cromer's words again, "an institution worthy of the great Sovereign whose name it bears."

Appendix F

At Chatalja
The experiences of Ibrahim el Masry (VC 1904–11) in the Balkan war as reported by The Victorian, December 1912

Ibrahim el Masri [VC 1904–1911], at the time of the outbreak of the war in the Balkans, was an undergraduate, in his first term of residence, at Pembroke College, Cambridge. On receiving the news he considered it his duty to hurry to Constantinople to offer himself as a volunteer in the ranks of the Turkish army; and, only informing a few Old Victorians at Cambridge of his intentions, he abruptly departed from the University in the early morning of the 28th October.

The long journey across Europe offered many perplexing problems, for Ibrahim el Masry had but little idea of the route he should follow. In an extremely uncertain frame of mind he reached Paris at 7 p.m. on the day of his departure from Cambridge and decided to stay for the night at the Hotel Terminus. Here he experienced an extraordinary stroke of good fortune. At the hotel he encountered a Greek gentleman who had formerly been in the service of the Sultan Abd el Hamid; Ibrahim el Masry's new friend had left Turkey during the revolution which overthrew the Sultan, but was returning again to Constantinople when the Allied States declared war. Ibrahim el Masry was informed that the Greek had determined to abandon the journey, and that the ticket to Constantinople was at his service if he cared to purchase it. The bargain was at once concluded, the route was fully explained, and at nine o'clock on the same evening, after a stay of only two hours in Paris, Ibrahim el Masry left the city to continue his journey to the East.

After passing through Basle, Buda-Pest and Bucharest, the termination of the overland journey was reached, on the fourth day after leaving Cambridge, at the little coast town of Constanza, on the Black Sea. A day was spent here in awaiting the arrival of the Roumanian vessel which calls at Constanza on her way to Constantinople.

The steamer duly arrived and Ibrahim el Masry embarked upon the last stage of his journey to the seat of war. During the journey he made the acquaintance of a Turkish officer, who, being called home by his Government from Tripoli to the scene of the new Ottoman difficulties, had made his way via Tunis, Marseilles and Constanza to catch the vessel by which they were travelling. This new found friend of Ibrahim el Masry's was to prove eventually of the greatest use to him.

Constantinople being reached without any more exciting incidents than the sighting of some Turkish warships, Ibrahim el Masry proceeded at once to the Minister of War at the War Office in Stamboul. Here he suffered a great disappointment. Despite his earnest entreaties to be allowed to take up arms he was politely informed that volunteers were no longer accepted for the fighting line, although the country would be glad of his services if he would devote himself to the care of the wounded. Such work, however, was not what Ibrahim el Masry desired. Greatly disappointed and a little hurt he left the War Office in despair. It seemed that his long journey across Europe was to be wasted; that all was to end in a polite rebuff.

At this critical moment Ibrahim el Masry suddenly remembered his friend of the Roumanian steamer. By great good fortune he had possessed himself of this officer's address. He at once proceeded to the house, secured an interview, and, to his great joy, was accepted as an unofficial member of the Aly (a troop of 800 horsemen), which the officer commanded. A uniform was at once purchased, and, on the following morning, Ibrahim el Masry was riding bare-back with the troop (although this, of course, was nothing to such a Bedouin as he), without a sword, but otherwise fully armed, towards the famous Chatalja Lines, to which the Bulgarian attack had by this time penetrated.

Chatalja was reached at five o'clock in the evening, and through the whole journey the heavy noise of guns had been in the ears of Ibrahim el Masry and his company [who] proceeded to form a camp where they remained some three days without seeing any really serious fighting. The food supplied consisted of bread, beans and lentils, sufficient in quantity but often of indifferent quality. The water was bad and possessed a very offensive smell. The weather was cold in the extreme but since the Turks slept in very small tents, each of which contained twelve men, the suffering from cold during the night time was not severe.

On the third day after their arrival one half of Ibrahim el Masry's company, in which he himself was included, saw some brisk fighting. After some preliminary rifle fire they were ordered to deliver a charge upon part of the enemy's postion. Four hundred in number, they galloped forward sustaining a heavy fire as they advanced. Suddenly, from their right, there burst out a heavy flanking fire from the Bulgarians. Swept from two sides the little troop quickly melted, wavered, and returned. Four hundred had set out; a mere one hundred and seventy returned, leaving no less than two hundred and thirty of their companions dead or wounded upon the field. The man in front of Ibrahim el Masry was struck by a bullet that pierced his body and struck Ibrahim el Masry's arm with its spent force inflicting a wound severe enough to leave a large scar but, fortunately, not splintering the bone.

Despite his damaged arm Ibrahim el Masry still continued to assist the Turks for some fortnight longer. At the end of that time, however, the officer in command of the troop, sent for him and requested him to leave the Lines and return to his home. This was no doubt due to the fact that the service was exceedingly dangerous and Ibrahim el Masry's friend feared lest this unofficial member of his troop might be slain and severe consequences fall upon himself. Ibrahim el Masry was, therefore, persuaded to leave the front and decided to return to his home in Egypt.

From Constantinople to Jaffa Ibrahim el Masry travelled by steamer. At Jaffa, however, he heard that he might be subjected to seven or even ten days of quarantine at Port Said or Alexandria although cholera had not broken out amongst the Turkish forces at the time of his leaving them. In order to avoid this tiresome delay he decided to continue his journey by land. A horse was procured at Jaffa and the first two days were occupied in travelling from Jaffa to Gaza in company with the mail, which is always well protected by a small force of soldiers. Arrived at Gaza Ibrahim el Masry decided to remain there for twenty-four hours in order to rest, after which he proceeded, by a five hour donkey ride, to the little town of Bof, where he purchased a camel and pushed on as far as the Egyptian frontier. At El Arish, however, his progress was checked by an Egyptian doctor who insisted upon quarantine, an unpleasant process embracing confinement in an unprotected area, exposed to the sun of the desert and a terrible wind. After lasting for a day, however, this unwelcome delay was brought to a close by the arrival of an English inspector who at once allowed Ibrahim el Masry to pass upon his way.

Now began the final stage of this adventure. The formidable Sinai Desert had still to be crossed before home could be reached. Having procured a supply of provisions sufficient for the needs of himself and his animal Ibrahim el Masry set forth. The incidents of this journey were many. At the end of the first day, guiding his camel towards a large fire which he observed in the dusk, Ibrahim el Masry discovered two Bedouins who were engaged in preparing and cooking their food. From them he learned the extremely valuable lesson of how to make a fire from the leaves of palm trees. Camping at night, indeed, was a matter of some danger and throughout the whole journey a revolver was an indispensable companion. Ibrahim el Masry adopted the plan of tethering his camel outside the palm grove which he selected for his resting place, while he concealed himself as much as possible in the shadows of the trees. During the day he endeavoured to follow, as far as he could, the regular caravan route, departure from which would then mean an utter losing of his way and a slow death by starvation and thirst in the desert. In finding his way he was, on the whole, successful, although he sometimes found himself slightly astray, only being saved by chance meetings with other travellers.

On one memorable night, however, to his intense delight, he saw, far away on the horizon, great glares of light which could only be caused by steamships passing up and down the Suez Canal. After such a period of strain and anxiety it is easy to imagine how welcome were these tokens that the conclusion of his wanderings was close at hand. He expressed his feelings in true Bedouin fashion by firing a "feu de joie" of six shots from his revolver and pressed forwards towards the town of Ismailia, which he reached, seven hours later, at ten o'clock in the morning. Here he sold his camel and proceeded by rail to his native village of Dessounes in the Nile Delta.

Such is the tale of the perils endured and difficulties overcome which is told by Ibrahim el Masry. Surely Victoria College may be proud of a pupil of such pluck and dash, and surely the whole school will join with us in heartily congratulating him upon the motives which led him throughout the whole of his adventures.

Appendix G

Random notes by Malek Hanna for Douglas Haydon's proposed history of the school 1976
Courtesy of Christopher Haydon

C.R. LIAS

(1) To C.R. Lias must be given the credit for having laid the foundation on which Reed and his successors built a successful Victoria College. He started from scratch in the face of great odds. He devised courses of study, imported suitable text-books and hired teachers for students he knew nothing about in a country whose Islamic majority had barely emerged from the Middle Ages.

C.R. Lias had a clear vision of what he wanted to accomplish and he had the strength of character to overcome all obstacles that confronted him.

The first of his objectives was to give his students a "liberal education" on English public school lines. "Education," he said in one of his addresses, "is to train minds to think and hearts to feel." But how can you accomplish that without money?

Financial problems plagued him right from the beginning. The school had no endowment money or reserve funds and he had to compete with schools that were already established and richly endowed like the Jesuits or Frères, or government subsidized institutions like the Lycée Français, Italian, German or Greek schools.

When the school moved from Mazarita to its present buildings in Ramleh enrolment was expected to rise, but this did not materialize and the lovely and spacious buildings whose upkeep had risen sharply, were half empty.

Dunlop, the famous or rather infamous, Adviser to the Egyptian Ministry of Education, sensing an easy prey, paid a visit to C.R.L.[ias] and proposed a government subsidy in return for govt. inspection and adoption of certain modifications to the courses of study: C.R.L. politely accompanied him to the door and informed him that future visits would be unwelcome.

V.C.'s financial troubles were eased towards the end of Lias's tenure as Headmaster. Alfred Viscount Milner, Secretary of State for the Colonies, visited the school when he was on his official mission to study and report on the causes of unrest in Egypt after World War I. V.C. was the only place where he was not boycotted and C.R. Lias prompted a few prominent Old Victorians to ask Lord Milner for financial help for the school. Lord Milner as Chairman of the Rhodes Fund granted the school 30,000 pounds sterling.

(2) C.R. Lias the teacher

Mr. Lias taught me English in V.A. (Lower Certificate), Arabic and French translations in the Upper School—School and Higher Certificates—1914–1919. His methods were old-fashioned and at times uninspiring, but his lessons were well prepared and thoroughly executed. He gave us no respite and drove us hard during the whole fifty minutes of each lesson, and if his lessons happened to be the last period in the afternoon, he often kept us going till 5 p.m.

He was a linguist. He was a scholar of no mean calibre in French and in Arabic, and later I learnt that he was also proficient in German.

In Arabic, I can say unreservedly, that he was not inferior to the famous Arabists Professors Gibb and Guillaume. From first hand knowledge, I can say that he was their superior. Yet he was humble and when urged to publish his work and translations of Arabic classic masterpieces, he brushed it aside as unworthy of publication.

The following is proof of his modesty. Albert (Bertie) Shoucair, son of Sir Saïd Shoucair Pasha of the Sudan Govt., accidentally lost an eye in a scuffle between two rival Houses and was sent to Hospital. When the father came to visit him Mr. Lias invited him to lunch. Edward Atiyah and myself were asked to attend—Atiyah because his father was in the service of the Sudan Govt. and a friend of the Pasha, and I was the Prefect of Bertie Shoucair's House.

Appendix G

The Pasha who was an Arabic scholar and proficient in English and French asked Mr. Lias how good was his knowledge of French? Atiyah and I, who attended his French Translation classes, knew the answer. But for a scholar who translated Musset and Vigny from French verse to English verse, Lias's answer was modesty itself: "I admit to a certain knowledge of French, but I am more proficient in German."

His knowledge of German must have been fantastic.

(3) Lias the administrator

Lias was an administrator of the "old school"—he retained all power and delegated little authority to his subordinates. He was in his office at 7.30 a.m.—ate lunch at the high-table (6th Form) and apart from a short break to eat dinner with Mrs. Lias, rarely retired to bed before midnight. He knew every student by name, and he knew what was going on in every corner of the school.

When he was in a good mood, he mixed with us, joked and was affable. But unfortunately, he suffered from a skin disease which made him irritable and his behaviour became unpredictable.

During the war years 1914–1919—with the exception of Reed, all the other teachers joined the armed forces. New teachers were hard to find and Lias had a full-time teaching assignment beside running the school. This had its effects on his health and the doctors advised him to leave the humid atmosphere of Alexandria and go to the drier climate of Helwan.

I have never approved of corporal punishment. In my 30 years in education, as teacher, principal or Director General, I have never used or authorized its use. Lias used the cane freely for disciplinary and other infractions. I was never one of his victims, but boys who had to submit to the indignity told me that he could be brutal when he lost his temper.

In closing this account, I must add a few words about Mrs. Lias.

In Oct. 1911, C.R.L. returned to school with a bride on his arm. She was a highly educated, and kind lady. Boys of my generation will always remember her for the Sunday afternoon tea and games which she gave to the boarders of the Prep. School House. From Oct. 1914 to July 1919, because of lack of staff she acted as Matron and corrected the compositions and other written assignments which Mr. Lias gave us. She even prepared Fareed Bashatly in German for the Higher Certificate.

The last time I saw her was in the spring of 1922 when she paid us a visit at Oxford (Amin Osman, Fares Sarofeem, Kamel Boulos and myself), and we all entertained her in a grand style to repay her for all her kindnesses.

MR. REED

Those of us who were assigned to Reed's House were very fortunate, because he was kind and considerate and he spent a lot of time with us talking about England and Oxford. He was a most entertaining conversationalist and as he had amassed a good library he allowed us to borrow books from it and guided us in their choice.

Here, I would like to make a few remarks about Reed, the teacher. In the classroom, he was a most inspiring teacher and he had the ability of getting the best out of his pupils, whether they happened to be good, average or indifferent students. In the evenings, he spent endless hours going over our essays with us individually. I took History and Arabic as my special subjects in the Higher Certificate, and he was so good at tutoring me that I not only earned a distinction, but also was able to write the History Prelim. of the Honour School of Modern History at Oxford at the end of my first term in residence (Dec.) instead of the end of June. The distinction that I obtained in Arabic I owe to Lias who taught us Arabic Translation of two difficult classics Al-Fakhry (prose) and Al-Motanaby (verse). In spite of the drawbacks at Mazarita, going up and down five flights of stairs several times a day and poor food because of the war, we lived as a happy family in Reed's House. Reed inspired us and Mrs. Bolton mothered us. Our greatest delight came when we returned to the familiar surroundings of Ramleh in June 1919 to spend the last month of our school career and write our final examinations.

One more word about Reed—he took a great deal of interest in his boys. Without his help and initiative Edward Atiyah would not have had the benefit of an Oxford education. He knew that Edward's parents could not afford to send him to Oxford, and he convinced Nicholas Sursock, a very rich Lebanese and Old Victorian to give 300 pounds sterling a year for three years in the form of an Old Victorian Scholarship which was awarded to Atiyah. Two years later, he gave another boy, Emile Abdel-Malek, another O.V. Scholarship of 240 pounds sterling a year for 5 years, to enable him to study Medicine at Birmingham. Some Old Boys contributed minor sums to this Scholarship, but most of it came out of Reed's pocket.

Reed was more innovative than Lias. He sought the advice of the Old Boys about the teaching of Arabic in the school. The course of study in that subject was set by the Oxford & Cambridge Schools Exam. Board and was archaic. The teachers of Arabic were not qualified or trained teachers. The Egyptian boys knew a great deal about English and World History, but were completely ignorant of their heritage. I came face to face with this reality in my third term at Oxford. I received invitations to tea from Prof. Butler and Miss Blackman—authorities on Egyptology and the Coptic Church. Not knowing who they were, I sought the advice of my tutor Mr. Daniel Ogg who informed me that I should feel very proud to be invited by such eminent scholars. My dilemma was that I knew practically nothing about the History of my people, the ancient Egyptians, or the history of my Church, the Coptic Church. I went to the College library and spent days and nights preparing myself for the encounter.

Reed called on me to teach European History to the School and Higher Certificate classes and in the course of many conversations we had on the teaching of Arabic, he asked for my suggestions and nominated on my recommendations 3 graduates from Dar-El-Eloum who had taught for me. I saw the results when my two sons began to ask me questions on the Pyramids, the Sphinx and the Valley of the Kings, and asked me to take them to visit the museum in Cairo. At least they were not as ignorant as I was.

I would like to terminate this by saying that the test of any school system is the ability of the staff to motivate and to develop the different potentialities of the students. Judging by the success of many Old Victorians in many fields, Victoria College accomplished its objectives.

AMIN OSMAN

1. Until the rise of Amin Osman to power and fame, the most predominant students at Victoria College were Levantines—Syrians, Jews, Palestinians and other stateless persons from the cosmopolitan population of Alexandria. Two Egyptian students were exceptions to this rule, Abdel-Rahman Hamada and Mahmoud Abaza, and are worthy of mention here. Hamada after obtaining the Higher Certificate proceeded to Birmingham University and graduated in engineering and returned to teach at the School of Engineering in Cairo and later became the Managing Director of the Filature Misr at Mehalla (the largest spinning and weaving mill in the Middle East and employs 30,000 workmen), and became the first Old Victorian to be awarded the title of Pasha. Abaza, whose studies in Medicine at Edinburgh had been interrupted by World War I, returned to Scotland after the war to complete his studies and was the first Egyptian O.V. in Medicine. While Hamada rarely took part in O.V. activities, Abaza was always prominent.

Amin Osman was two or three years my senior, but owing to the prolonged duration of W. War I and his inability to go to England to complete his education, he remained in school and my group caught up with him. He ended by having 3 Higher Certificates and the Egyptian Baccalaureat—a remarkable record.

2. Amin was the second son of Mohamed Osman Bey—Ex-Secretary-General of the Alexandria Municipality, a man of modest means. The eldest son Mounir, who preceded Amin as Head-boy, was accidentally drowned at Abu-Kir trying to save Amin. His contemporaries say that he was as brilliant if not more brilliant than Amin.

3. Amin had a thorough knowledge of English, French and Turkish, but was not that proficient in Arabic in spite of his Egyptian Baccalaureat. But that was not his fault. Our Arabic teacher in the Upper School was Sheikh Attallah. He hated Amin and kept making disparaging remarks by calling him 'Mr. Amin.' He was so unfair to him that Amin lost interest in learning Arabic. As he generally sat behind me in Arabic lessons, I had to sit up to conceal an English or French novel which Amin read during the lesson. On one occasion he gave himself away. He was reading *The Pickwick Papers* while the good Sheikh was

giving us a dull grammar lesson, Amin suddenly burst out laughing and the Sheikh thinking it was directed at his lesson, sent him to the office. Luckily Mr. Lias was sick that day and Reed saved the situation. Amin apologized, but the apology was grudgingly accepted.

4. When I joined V.C. in Oct. 1911, I was placed in the third form of the Prep. School with a group that had enrolled two years earlier. With a few drop-outs and additions, that group made it to the Sixth form. On the way it made history. In 1912 when Houseden and Preece started the Scouts movement, most if not all the group joined the troop and ensured its success. This was *the first Scout troop in Egypt*. In 1915, without the aid of a Games-Master (because of the war, the school did not have a Games-Master), the group formed the School's first 2nd XI (football) and had two successful seasons before becoming the 1st XI with Amin Osman as its Captain. In 1917 the group formed the first debating society with Amin Osman as its first Chairman. In 1918 the group issued *The Victorian Times* edited by Helmi Makrama weekly periodical of school news. Amin Osman was a contributor. In 1917 the Prefect system was introduced for the first time in the school. This was initiated by Reed in the absence of Lias in Helwan. The school lacked staff and to help with the supervision of corridors, Playground, Prep-rooms and dormitories, Reed nominated 12 prefects—all from that group. The group readily accepted the leadership of Amin Osman—many of us became his lasting friends.

AMIN OSMAN AT SCHOOL AND VARSITY

He was a disciplined student who never allowed anything to distract him from doing his work. Apart from the trouble he had with Sheikh Attallah, which was not of his own making, I do not remember that he was ever sent to the office.

He was a good all-round student—equally proficient in Maths, languages and Literature. He was a voracious reader and developed a taste for English Literature.

Apart from being a model student, he was a fine athlete and he excelled in soccer. He was captain of Games for the first 3 years of his career in school. Anyone who had watched him play could have judged his character. He was absolutely fearless—though short and light in weight, he more than made up for it by his agility and his extraordinary power of sensing his opponents' moves. Above all he was an extraordinary leader who set his team mates the best example of a perfect sportsman. At Oxford (Brasenose College) he won his College Colours in soccer, became Secretary of Brasenose College A.F.C.(a great honour) in his third year and played for the Oxford University Centaurs (equivalent to half Blue). I tried to persuade him to stay on another year to Captain his College team and most probably play for Oxford and earn his Blue. But he knew his father could not afford another year. However, B.N.C. won the Cup (soccer) during his final year and all of us who saw that game were of the opinion that Amin won the cup for B.N.C. I covered the game for the *Isis*—the undergraduate weekly periodical and I said as much in my article. On the way back from the game I heard the newspaper boy say as Amin passed—"Well played Mr. Os."

His stay in England lasted 4 years and he earned B.A. Hons in Jurisprudence from Oxford and L.L.B. Hons from University College London. Amin was held in high esteem by his tutors and fellow undergrads. I attended the dinner to celebrate the Cup victory. Stallybrass, the assistant Vice-Principal of B.N.C. and Amin's Law tutor praised Amin: "Os is not only an excellent football player, but also an excellent student." He proved it by getting a good 2nd Class in his B.A.

Edward Atiyah who had joined Amin at B.N.C. witnessed the following scene. One evening after dinner in the Junior Common Room, one of the undergrads was heard complaining loudly that his admittance to B.N.C. had been delayed for one year because the College authorities had preferred "a bloody foreigner—an Egyptian." One of Amin's teammates who had heard the complaint walked up to him, gave him a knockout saying: "That bloody foreigner is worth ten of your kind."

Here, I would like to add a few little known facts about Amin. (a) He was a devout Muslim—he prayed five times a day—abstained from drinking alcohol and as a vegetarian he did not eat pork or any kind of meat. He also did not develop the habit of smoking until much later in his career. (b) He had to live on a very tight budget. He could not afford to rent a room on his own and I shared one with him throughout our first year in England at Henley-on-Thames and at Vincent Square in London. He was the most considerate and interesting companion one could ever have.

Appendix G

When he entered politics, he had to abandon many of his habits and principles. His career demanded that he attend lunches, dinners, cocktail parties and other social events. He ate a little meat (very sparingly), he drank wine and Martinis, and he smoked cigars. Cigar smoking did not become a habit until after 1936.

The Egyptian Delegation that signed the Anglo-Egyptian Treaty of that year visited the European capitals. In Berlin, Hitler sent Amin (Secretary-General of the Delegation) two bottles of choice champagne and two boxes of fine cigars for each member. Most of the members accepted the champagne, but refused the cigars, and so Amin was left with a dozen boxes of cigars and from then on, he really enjoyed smoking cigars.

RETURN TO EGYPT AFTER GRADUATION

In August of 1919, there was an exodus of Victorians to British universities—9 went to Oxford and Cambridge, 5 to Edinburgh to study Medicine, 2 to Birmingham (one Medicine and the other Engineering). All successfully completed their studies and by 1924 & 25 were back in Egypt. We had done well and were proud of our achievement, but an unpleasant surprise and a big disappointment awaited some of us.

Some of our group came from wealthy families and did not need jobs, others were offspring of the "Egyptian Establishment" and easily got jobs. Amin and I did not belong to either group and we needed government jobs to earn our living. We thought we had good credentials and were entitled to good jobs, but to our dismay we came up against a stone wall. Reed wrote to Sir Reginald Patterson, the Financial Adviser, on behalf of Amin, and all that letter could produce was a LE 15 a month job in the Legal Department of the Ministry of Public Works. As beggars could not be choosers, he had to accept. I still remember the derision with which some govt. employees treated his hard earned law degrees. But this did not break Amin's will. He immediately registered for the "Doctorat en Droit" Course at the Sorbonne in Paris. He passed the Première Partie in Summer of 1925 and the Deuxième Partie in 1926 and became "Docteur en Droit"—a title disdainfully he never used. He had worked hard for four years to obtain his English degrees and exactly two months to obtain his French Doctorate.

As for me, I appealed to the Ministries of Finance and Foreign Affairs. From the latter I received no reply—these jobs were reserved for the lucky sons of Ministers and ex-ministers. The Ministry of Finance considered my application, accepted it and sent me for a medical exam which declared me fit for employment, but nothing came of it. There was a change of ministry after the assassination of Sir Lee Stack and Abdel-Wahab Pasha, the Undersecretary of Finance, who was prejudiced against Copts, simply put my application on file. Luckily I was offered a teaching position at the Morcossia Schools, Alexandria, which I accepted.

Though we couldn't have teas at Groppi, cocktails at Shepheard's and dinners at St. James, we formed an active O.V. Club, played football in the afternoon and met every evening in Kamel Boulos's *dahabia* (Nile-boat)—we were never down-hearted.

The tide turned in the late twenties. Badawi Pasha, the Head of the State Legal Department, became interested in Amin and asked that his case be reviewed—his salary was readjusted to LE 45 (a month), and he was appointed as Inspector of Finance for Alexandria and the Province of Beheira. He was promoted to Director of Receipts at the Alexandria Municipality and just before negotiations for the Anglo-Egyptian Treaty were begun, he was appointed as Secretary-General to the Egyptian Delegation. After the Anglo-Egyptian Treaty was signed he was appointed Under-Secretary of State for Finance and was awarded the title of Pasha and knighted.

Appendix H

*Letter from the Daira of Her Sultanate Highness
the Princess Nimatallah to Mr. Reed*

List of clothes for the Nabil Mohamed Tewfik Tousson

VICTORIA COLLEGE, RAMLEH
ALEXANDRIA.

SCHOOL OUTFITS.

Every Boarder must bring with him to school the following:-

- 4 Sheets.
- 4 Towels.
- 1 Bath Gown.
- 1 Rain Coat or Overcoat.
  Winter and Summer suits. Extravagance in cut or colour not allowed.
- 3 Pairs strong shoes, black or brown. Parti-coloured shoes not allowed.
- 1 Pair of bed-room slippers.
- 12 Handkerchiefs.
- 6 or more Shirts.
- 4 Vests.
- 4 Under pants.
- 6 or more pairs of socks or stockings.
- 4 Suits of Pyjamas.
  Ties. School or dark colours only.

Mohamed TEWFIK TOUSSOUN

4 Sheets
4 Towels
1 Bath Gown
1 " Slip
1 " Suit
1 Rain Coat
1 Overcoat
1 Woollen scarf
2 Winter golf suits
2 " suits long pants
2 Spring suits short
3 Summer suits linen
2 Shorts
1 Navy blue suit for evening
3 Pairs brown shoes
1 " blak evening shoes
1 Bed room slippers
12 Handkerchiefs
4 White shirts for evening
6 Tann shirts
2 Blue "
6 White sport shirts
4 vests Woollen
4 Underpants Woollen
12 Vests white thread
12 Pants " "
12 Pairs stocking brown thread
8 Pairs socks thread
6 Pairs wooll stockings
2 " Navy blue stockings
6 Pyjamas blue and white
2 " wooll
5 Ties
3 Belts
1 Dressing gown

Appendix I

Emir Abdulillah's letter to Mr. Reed

Istanbul,
Turkey
15/10/1933

My dear Mr. Reed

Thank you very much for the telegram of congratulations, which you had sent to Baghdad only two days after I had left for Turkey. When the news of King Feisal's death reached us I and my family were here. To be present at the funeral I left alone and reached home one day before the body. Your telegram was taken with the secretary who left with my father for Europe a few days after me and was only sent to me last week after the Egyptian mail had left.

I wanted to write to you some time ago that the British Ambassador and some other English people decided my father not to send me to the London School of Economics. And now it is decided that H.E.'s wife who is in England should look for a place for me in order to work for the Littlego and enter Cambridge. I think that will take a long time, but I must obey. I am returning to Iraq in less than a month's time to stay there about one month and then leave for England via Egypt when I hope to meet you at the College.

Kahil told me that he saw you before he came to Turkey this summer, but he didn't know if you were spending the summer in Alexandria or in England.

Yours Sincerely,
Abdulillah

Ulusköy - Istanbul
Turkey
15/10/39

My dear Mr Reed

Thank you very much for the telegram of congratulations, which you had sent to Baghdad only two days after I had left for Turkey. When the news of King Faisal's death reached us I and my family were here. To be present at the funeral I left alone and reached home one day before the body. Your telegram was taken with the secretary who left with my father for Europe a few days after me and was only

APPENDIX I

shut to me last week after the
Egyptian mail had left.
    I wanted to write to you
some time ago that the British
Ambassador and some other
English people decided my
father not to send me to the
London School of Economics.
And now it is decided that
H.E.'s wife who is in England
should look for a place for
me in order to work for the littlego and enter Cambridge. I think
that will take a long time, but
I must obey. I am returning
to Iraq in less than a month's
time to stay there about one month
and then leave for England
via Egypt when I hope to meet

you at the College.
Kahil told me that he saw you before he came to Turkey this summer, but he didn't know if you were spending the summer in Alexandria or in England.

Yours Sincerely

Abdulillah

Appendix J

Obituary from The Victorian
Mr. Percy Bolton

January 1946 was a sad month for us for a week after the assassination of Amin Osman Pasha occurred the sad and unexpected death of Mr. P. J. Bolton.

"Percy" had been with us at Victoria College for nearly forty years and was one of those figures, often to be found at English Public Schools, who seem to belong so completely to the establishment that they seem to be part of the actual fabric. But, to us, Percy was much more than that. In his duties as Steward he displayed a knowledge and ability that were little short of astonishing. He knew where everything in the College was and was able to produce, as if by magic, other things that were not. In the speech he made on the occasion of Mr. Bolton's twenty-fifth year at the College, Mr. Reed said that the invariable reply that one gave to any question about the fabric and equipment of the College was "Ask Percy" for Percy always knew. And so it was till the very day before his death. But he was not, like many men of kindred ability, a sort of human machine, doing things automatically when asked and conveying the impression of efficiency and nothing more. There was a kindness and charm about him that made one feel that what he did for one was actually a pleasure, so that all who had dealings with him could not regard him otherwise than as a cheerful and trusty friend. In times of difficulty—and he went through many, particularly during the two world war—she never lost his temper or his nerve and there can be few people in similar positions of whom as much can be said.

Obituary of Mr. Percy Bolton

In his early days at the College Mr. Bolton was a cricketer of no mean ability and even recently he used to play in matches against the School.

His wife and daughter have gone to live in England and carry with them our deepest sympathy and good wishes. The latter will be missed in the Kindergarten where she taught for some time. We were glad to have Mr. Bolton's son—an Old Victorian, now in the Navy—with us for a few weeks during the summer. Mr. Leslie Bolton is an even more distinguished cricketer than his father was.

Appendix K

Letter of authorization from Princess Emina Fazil to Mr. Reed, 1934

CONSULAT ROYAL D'EGYPTE
TRIESTE

Trieste, le 2 Juillet 1934.

N° 220 (35/5)

Monsieur le Recteur,

D'ordre de S.A. la Princesse Emina Fazil, j'ai l'honneur de vous remettre ci-inclus une procuration signée par Son Altesse et legalisée par ce Consulat.

Veuillez agréer, Monsieur le Recteur, l'expression de ma parfaite considération.

Le Consul d'Egypte

Monsieur le
Headmaster R. W. C. Reed
O.B.E., M.A.
Victoria College
Alexandrie.

Letter from Princess Emina Fazil

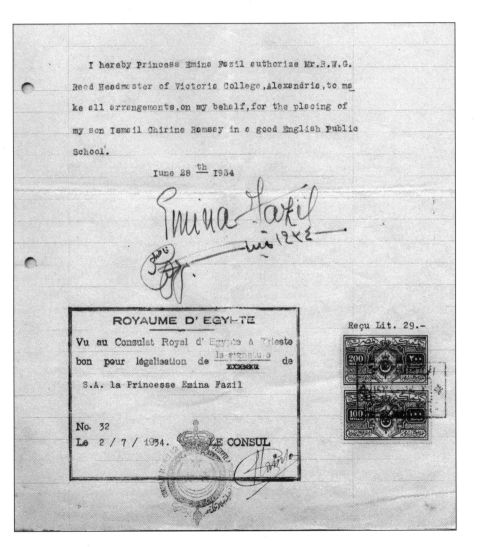

Appendix L

Speech Day, 27 March 1926
Excerpts of speeches published in either the Egyptian
Gazette *or the* Egyptian Mail, *29 March 1926, plus a
transcript of Sir Henry Barker's handwritten draft.*

L ord Lloyd [the High Commissioner], at the outset of his remarks, expressed his gratitude for the welcome accorded him, and his thanks to H.E. Ziwer Pasha [the Prime Minister] for his presence among them. The High Commissioner commented on the various nationalities and creeds which comprise the mosaic of the cosmopolitan city of Alexandria, and said, for the welding of this mosaic into an organic entity there could be no more useful instrument than a great educational establishment, foreign to exclusiveness and intolerance, like Victoria College. Proceeding to sketch the history of the College, Lord Lloyd said:

> Victoria College was founded 25 years ago by public subscriptions, chiefly among the British residents of Alexandria, and it owes its existence very largely to the generosity of Sir George Alderson, whose absence today we all regret so much. A very special interest was taken by my great predecessor Lord Cromer, and in coming here today I do homage to his memory and to the work he did both for his own country and for the country which after his own was the dearest to his heart. Lord Cromer consolidated an association between Great Britain and Egypt, which, whatever may be its changing forms, is so obvious a necessity for both partners that it

SPEECH DAY, 27 MARCH 1926

is bound to continue. In order that the association may be harmonious and in the greatest possible degree mutually beneficent, there exists a great need to strengthen the means at our disposal for mutual interpretation and mutual understanding between the British, the Egyptians, and other communities who have made their home in this country and particularly in Alexandria. In founding Victoria College, and in founding it in Alexandria, this was the main object which Lord Cromer intended it to serve, an object which I am convinced it effectually does serve.

The High Commissioner went on to discuss the history of Alexandria, which he remarked was designed to be the capital of the world its founder, Alexander the Great, knew, and to be a link between the East and the West. This function it had performed, and the link that Alexandria was on a large scale, Victoria College was in miniature. Continuing, Lord Lloyd, said:

Alexandria, as I repeat, is the link city, Alexandria should be the interpreter. It is to her in particular that we should look for the forging of the link of understanding, and for the forging of that link there can be no more useful instrument than a well-conceived College instructing in the ideals of the British the youth of all the races that are to live in daily contact; we are all associated in a general endeavour of mutual comprehension; and the prizes that wait on success are none other than peace, prosperity and progress. It is for these reasons that I welcome so deeply and so sincerely the fact that we meet in the hall of Victoria College: for I feel that here, perhaps more than in any other place, this atmosphere of mutual understanding and mutual comprehension can be especially vivid and penetrating. And what is Victoria College? Victoria College is an English School, open to boys of all nationalities. Here we have a school that despite the unique opportunities it affords is not yet fully taken advantage of nor fully understood by the parents of the youth growing up. It is but fair to all concerned to make public what are the special advantages that this school provides. It has a staff of English masters trained in the principles of English public school life; its achievements in the academic world fully equal those of equivalent schools in England, and many are the honours that have been gained by the boys of the Victoria College in the last few years. Now as to character. The prefect system which we in England believe does so much to develop the sense of responsibility, of honour, of truth, of self-discipline, and of constancy, and consequently is of such inestimable value in providing that quality without which the spirit of good citizenship cannot thrive, this prefect system is carried on here exactly as in England and this despite the varied nationalities of the boys in the school. In games and in cricket and in scouting the corporate spirit is fostered and developed. So excellent the tone has been in this school, that during the troublous years 1919 and 1921 never was there any friction, never was there any ill-feeling between the students. It may interest you to know that to-day the Old Boys represent some 8 or 9 races, and that today in the school some 30% of the boys are Egyptians, some 20% Anglo-Saxon and then there are lesser percentages of Greeks, Israelites, Italians, Armenians, Syrians, Copts, and Abyssinians. All of them, in due course of time, thanks largely to the close personal contact maintained with the boys by the English masters become permeated with the British outlook and the class of boy that this school is turning out at present would, so I am informed on all sides, be a credit to any country, and should prove an asset of considerable value to Egypt. Not only have the problems of to-day been solved between Great Britain and Egypt, but problems will necessarily arise at every turning during the years of intercourse. These I say can only be solved provided we on the one hand and the peoples of this country on the other, have learned to see and appreciate and sympathise with each other's point of view. Gentlemen, I have been immensely gratified at having this opportunity of meeting you all today, and I shall feel that your time and my time has not been wasted if some fraction at least of what I have tried to put before you has had a common meaning for both you and me, so that in future more threads may be woven into that stout bond of sympathy which should with ever increasing strength unite Great Britain with this land of Egypt.

His Excellency the Prime Minister, Ziwer Pasha, who was loudly applauded on rising, spoke in French. He said: "There is no finer conquest than the peaceful penetration performed by the sciences and arts, by education." Modern Egypt realised the necessity for it, when she created schools for the stimulation of the spirit of inquiry of among the unenlightened town and country population. He outlined the progress of education in Egypt during the past twenty years, and remarked that under King Fouad it has reached a standard comparable with the best everywhere. "Our University flatters itself that one of the finest stones which have been laid towards its foundation is Victoria College!" The Prime Minister concluded by impressing on the audience the far-reaching effects of the teaching of Victoria College in the establishment of better and more frank relations between England and Egypt.

APPENDIX L

Sir Henry Barker's handwritten draft (dated 14 March)

No-one can have listened to what [Lord Lloyd] has said except with earnest interest or have failed to notice the great compliment he paid to Victoria College when he said that he hoped that some time soon a similar school may be available for girls. The English Educational system differs from that of other countries. It is often criticised for devoting too much time to games. To some extent perhaps the criticism is justified, but we believe that in order to train the mind you must train the body and the fact that so many other countries are now adopting similar methods, tends to show that the theory is a sound one. The Prime Minister struck a true note when he emphasised the great value of training people to understand each other. Education without understanding, instruction without the training of character, are of doubtful value to anyone, the happiness and prosperity of any country and especially that of Egypt, with its cosmopolitan population, depend upon the ability of its inhabitants to understand each other and to cooperate for the general weal. It was therefore gratifying to hear His Excellency say that the training boys receive here is well calculated to attain this end. If by taking in boys of different nationalities and of different creeds and by bringing them up to recognize there is always a good deal to be said for other people's views, by teaching them the great values of what we call team work, Victoria College succeeds in sending out into the world a band of tolerant, broadminded young men, I think it will have deserved well of the community and will have fulfilled a great mission. The aim of all schools, by making a boy's education a pleasure to him, should in Milton's words be to send youth forth into the world "Enflamed with the study of learning and the admiration of virtue and buoyed up with high hopes of living to be brave men and worthy patriots, dear to God and famous to all ages."

Appendix M

*Invitation to Old Victorian Dinner, 1942,
held in honor of HRH Emir Abdulillah*

OLD VICTORIAN DINNER

HELD AT

VICTORIA COLLEGE, CAIRO,

IN HONOUR OF

H. R. H. EMIR ABDULILLAH,

REGENT OF IRAQ.

30th. December, 1942

Appendix M

Menu

ESSENCE DE VOLAILLE PRINCESSE

MAYONNAISE POISSON IRAQ

FONDS D'ARTICHAUX CUSSY

DINDONNEAU DE FAYOUM DORÉ

POMMES CHAMPIGNOLES

COEUR DE LAITUE MY LADY

TARTE AUX FRAISES

CORBEILLE DE FRUITS

TASSE EGYPTIENNE

Toast List

H.M. KING FAROUK I.
H.M. KING GEORGE VI.

THE GUEST OF HONOUR
Proposed by :- The Headmaster of Victoria College.
Responded to by :- H.R.H. Emir Abdulillah.

THE SCHOOL AND THE OLD VICTORIANS
Proposed by :- Prof. H. S. Deighton.
Responded to by :- Dr. Mahmoud Bey Abaza.

THE GUESTS
Proposed by :- H.E. Amin Osman Pasha.
Responded to by : H.E. Mustafa el Nahas Pasha.

Appendix N

Victoria College application form of Ayesha Osman, 1927

Appendix O

Telegram from Asadig Assenussi, 1952

Appendix P

Letter from the Royal Hashemite Diwan, 1953

Appendix Q

*Invitation from His Majesty King Hussein I
to the 1981 Annual Reunion in Amman*

By Command of our President
His Majesty King Hussein I of the
Royal Hashemite Kingdom of Jordan
The Chairman and Committee of
The Victoria College Association
request the pleasure of the company of

Mrs. Abdel Fattah Loutfi

at the 1981 Annual Reunion
to be held in Amman from
Friday 1st May to Monday 4th May

ADMISSION STRICTLY BY THIS INVITATION CARD
WHICH MUST BE SHOWN ON ARRIVAL AT AMMAN AIRPORT

Appendix R

Victoria College: Meanings in its Architecture
by Mohamed Awad

The intention to create a British school in Alexandria became reality with the formation in 1898 of a limited liability company called the British Schools of Egypt. The project was promoted by the British Consul-General, Sir Charles Cookson, and sponsored by prominent members of the British community in Alexandria. Queen Victoria's death in 1901 prompted the idea of making the school into a memorial, and a plot of land on the eastern harbor, gifted by G. B. Alderson, eventually saw the laying of the foundation stone on 25 April 1901 by Lord Cromer, despite his lack of optimism.

The design of the building in Mazarita was entrusted to a resident British architect, H. Favarger (1855–1922), who, although a fellow of Royal Institute of British Architects from 1901, has been described as having no professional education, and as being previously connected with an engineering business before beginning to practice as an architect in Cairo in 1887. Little is known of his work in Egypt other than the design of the Cataract Hotel in Aswan, as well as an article entitled "Modern Building in Egypt," published in *Transactions of RIBA* (1891–1892, vol. 8, pp. 33–48).

On the Mazarita college, there seems to have been only few architectural influences guiding Favarger's conceptualization of the two-story building, which looked more like a villa than a school. His revivalist Gothic eclectic style, although not affecting the building form except for its wall buttresses, appears to have influenced its detailing in the mock casement arched moldings applied to fenestration and in the balustrade of the external stairs. The choice seems to coincide with high British Victorian architectural tendencies, when historical revivalism was fashionable, especially Gothic, which had developed from the eighteenth century and was promoted in the nineteenth century by such chivalric writings as those of Sir Walter Scott. Gothic revivalism marked many of Britain's nineteenth-century public buildings and particularly its most reputed colleges.

The College opened in 1902 and, in 1903, the basement was operational while a second floor was added to the building to accommodate the boarders. This latter was designed by Mr. Kevork Meramedjian (1860–1918) of the Ecole des Beaux-Arts; the contractors were Messrs. McClure and Dorling.

Victoria College continued to grow in size with the addition of a kindergarten in the 1904–1905 school year. By 1906 it was becoming evident that the school was far outgrowing its facilities. Once again, George B. Alderson stepped in to buy a plot of land in the remote area of the Domaine de Siouf for a new school. Although Mr. Meramedjian was already experienced in transforming and renovating the French missionary girls' school, Notre-Dame de Sion, and had previously dealt with Victoria's extensions, the decision to commission an architect for the new buildings in Siouf was made in favor of the reputed French architect Henry Gorra.

Mr. Lias, the headmaster of the school, and Mr. Gorra are said to have traveled to England for the purpose of inspecting and collecting information bearing on the construction and equipment of British public schools. The visit came at a time when various types of antiquarian expression were prevalent in Britain as also in Egypt. Victorian Britain confirmed a preference for Italian high-style Renaissance; following this movement, public buildings and royal residences were modeled on Italian palaces. In line with these ideas, Gorra had conceived his most reputed building in Alexandria, the elegant premises of the Banco di Roma (1905)—presently the National Bank of Egypt located at the corner of Toussoun Street and Sherif Pasha Street—inspired by Sangalo's and Michelangelo's Palazzo Farnese in Rome.

The foundation stone of the new Victoria College was laid on 24 May 1906 by Lady Cromer. Her husband, now convinced about the prospects of the school, withdrew his earlier reservations as to its potential success.

Gorra's original balanced, rather symmetrical layout still dominates the complex in spite of many successive additions. The two main school blocks are flanked by corner towers, which give the building the monumental aspect of a fortress. The central dining hall building is dominated by the main tower, whose unfortunate collapse during construction had caused much public anxiety (according to the fifth Annual Report, 1906–1907) and delayed the occupation of the new buildings for a year. The Executive Committee therefore referred to the professional advice of Favarger, the architect of the old school, who, after careful examination, embodied his views in a report recommending certain modifications to the original plans. These were carried out under the superintendence of his capable representative, Mr. W.A. Hodges, FRIBA.

The importance of Victoria College's colonial conceptualization lies in the fact that it represents one of the earliest attempts to blend eclectically a local expression with an occidental concept. The post-Renaissance monumental building form remains dominant when compared to the rather superficial application of a neo-Islamic language, which appears in the stalactite detailing of the cornices, friezes, and lintels of the fenestration. The local expression, however suppressed, appears in the Moorish arcades leading to the quadrangle as well as in the central *iwan* of the dining hall portico, but yet again overpowered by the imposing bulk of the occidentalized building structure. The Victoria College experience of neo-Islamic eclecticism is unique in Gorra's professional career, yet justifiable considering his Levantine origins, European education, and the influences of his cosmopolitan milieu.

His choice of a neo-Islamic theme, while seemingly rather in contradiction with the newly introduced secularist education intended at Victoria College, was nonetheless more appropriate than other local revivalist languages, such as neo-Pharaonic, for example. Gorra opted for an architectural expression that would evoke the values of a progressivist Islamic society. Indeed, at the dawn of the twentieth century, Egypt was promoting an Islam of tolerance, accommodating pluralism and, more importantly, not in conflict with modernity. So, while calling upon

APPENDIX R

tradition yet being representative of modernity, Victoria College's architecture may account for its popularity and its preference in the region. The image of the school may thus have promoted its reputation and ensured its success.

There are few British influences in Victoria College's architectural conceptualization. This is not too surprising given that in Alexandria a cosmopolitan, pro-European hegemonic culture had long preceded the direct impacts of the British occupation in 1882. The local eclectic expressionism evident in Victoria College's architecture, although rare in the Alexandrian built environment, was certainly not unique. Yet colonial influences must certainly have directed the choice of the remote location and the spacious site of eighteen feddans around which a whole district developed and took the name of the school. Furthermore, Victoria College introduced to Alexandria a rather unique educational model, with integrated facilities and a diversity of sporting possibilities, on which other schools were later fashioned, however pale in comparison.

The school facilities continued to expand, aided by donations such as those of Percy Carver and Dr. M.A. Ruffer who paid for the construction of the science laboratories and their furnishing with equipment from London (some of it is still in use). The interiors are on the whole standardized without any special feature. Once inside, the Oriental aspect can be easily forgotten and it is interesting to note that, when the library was reinforced in 1912 with four large columns, oak wood was used to cover them in an attempt to make the room look as English as possible.

The misfortunes of the First World War claimed the lives not only of many of the young graduates and staff of Victoria College but also that of Mr. Henry Gorra, architect of its new buildings, killed on 29 October 1914 while on duty near Bethune. He had joined the French colors at the outbreak of the war and was acting as an interpreter, being attached to the British headquarters' staff as officer inspector.

In March 1915, the school became the headquarters of the French Oriental Expeditionary Corps. The school magazine, *The Victorian*, of July 1915 recounts the transformation of the school buildings in April to become British General Hospital No. 17, forcing staff and pupils to return to the old school building at Mazarita, then occupied by the

VICTORIA COLLEGE: MEANINGS IN ARCHITECTURE

Government Survey Department and serving also as a meeting hall for Old Victorians. A large apartment near the school, at 14 Khartoum Street, provided accommodation for the boarders. While some activities had to be disrupted, such as science work, because it was not possible to find space for laboratories, the school cricket team seems to have had an enjoyable season. More than 80,000 patients passed through the hospital before it was returned to the school in July 1919.

The principal event of the post-First World War era was the construction of an additional story and two corner towers to the school block, made possible by the generosity of the British community. Furthermore, in 1928 Edwin Goar donated a plot of adjoining land, and the offices of the General Committee of the New British Schools set aside £10,000 from their subscriptions for the needs of Victoria College. The headmaster, Mr. Reed, described this additional story on Speech Day in 1929, saying that it "completes a hitherto unfinished and unsightly block, and immensely enhances the appearance of the buildings . . . provides accommodation for fifty more boarders . . . as well as urgently needed classrooms and quarters for our increasing resident staff." A grant from the New British Schools Fund made it possible to put all the roofs of the school buildings, regarding which there had been some uneasiness, into a state of perfect repair. All this work was executed under the direction of a resident British architect, Mr. Noel Dawson, FRIBA.

Soon grass replaced the banana trees in the west corner of the school, and everywhere young trees seemed to promise shelter from the sometimes too hot sun (*The Victorian*, 1929); sports flourished in the school. In 1929, Kamel Wassif, then still a pupil at Victoria, provided for the Scout hut, while profits from the school shop, under the direction of Mr. R.R. Parkhouse, reaching approximately LE 200, were used to build a cricket pavilion that housed changing rooms, sports staff headquarters, and a fine viewing platform of the First and Second XI pitches.

In 1933, Mr. K.P. Birley made a considerable donation to the school. It was decided that it should be used for an Assembly Hall, which opened in 1937. Dawson's designs for extensions at Victoria College during the interwar period may be said to blend harmoniously with the existing established character of the original buildings. Unlike his involvement with the British Boys School in 1929, where he is characteristically very British, at Victoria College only his cricket pavilion seems to stem from traditional English country clubs.

The school was again forced to move with the outbreak of the Second World War. This time the move was made to the San Stefano Casino, which was altered by Dawson to suit the function of an educational institution. This displacement, however, was much to the delight of the pupils, who enjoyed the amenities of the adjacent beach and especially, as noted, the filled sandwiches of Philippe, on account of his pretty daughter. The school buildings in Alexandria were turned into a Naval and Military Hospital, with some thirty huts erected by the Royal Engineers to serve as wards. Two of these were retained after the war in 1945 and were converted to classrooms and used as part of the primary school.

In 1948 Noel Dawson designed the south wing to be attached to the classroom block. His extension can be said to have been successful in that it seems to be an integral part of the original design although almost doubling the size of the main school building. In 1949, Edwin Goar gave LE 2,000 to the school for a gymnasium, which was designed by John Prosper Serjeant and Max Zollikofer. Serjeant was an Anglo-French Old Boy, who had qualified as a fellow of the RIBA after studying at University College, London, 1934, and then worked in Alexandria for the Quarantine Board. His long association with the Swiss architect Max Zollikofer began with their collaboration in developing the industrial town of Beida Dyers, a subsidiary of Bradford Textile Industries in Kafr el Dawar near Alexandria. The minimalist pro-modernist approach adopted by Serjeant and Zollikofer marked the end of the eclecticism and a shift to the international style, also adopted in 1949 when the Bassili brothers, Victor, Albert, and Jack, sponsored the swimming pool and changing rooms in conjunction with the gymnasium.

When J.P. Serjeant retired to England, Max Zollikofer was joined by his son Claude, of the Ecole des Beaux-Arts; they were among the few foreign architects still in practice in Alexandria after 1956. Together they proposed three schemes for a new kindergarten, none of which was carried out.

In the early 1960s, much to the dislike of the schoolboys, the present walls and gates were added as a result of a generous donation from Mr. A. Kassem in order to help the school administration stop pupils from leaving the school premises during class hours. It was through the persistent endeavours of Mr. M. Nofal and donations from certain parents of pupils that a new mosque now replaced the small prayer-room and occupied a prime location on the First XI grounds, marking a new era in the school's fate, and maybe in that of the entire country.

A more dense and populist post-1970 Egypt has also had its dramatic implications on Victory College, as the school was renamed in 1956. The Third XI grounds and the tennis courts were cut off to give way to a separate educational facility. Inside Victory, more classrooms were erected. A new building, by the Egyptian architect Omar Mahran of Alexandria University, occupies part of the playgrounds of the preparatory school while more semi-open spaces and the inner courtyards have been transformed to host more than 6,000 pupils, over tenfold the original capacity of the school.

Victoria College—from Alexandria to Cairo
The Cairo branch of Victoria College—or more accurately, however lengthily debated, the independent Victoria College in Cairo—owes its existence to the British Council, its main benefactor. The events of the Second World War precipitated a long-awaited decision pending since the late 1930s, with a move from Alexandria to the relative safety of Cairo becoming imperative. The beginnings of a Victoria College, Cairo, found residence for its kindergarten in a villa in Giza while the rest of the school was housed in the former Italian school buildings in Shubra.

A report entitled "Prospects and Needs of Victoria College," dated 3 March 1947 (Public Record Office file MH 106/1887), records the purchase of land from the Delta Land Company in the remote location of Degla, adjacent to the garden suburb of Maadi.

The school's design was entrusted to the British architect J.W. Poltock, (1903–89), who is described as being familiar with local conditions. He had begun his career as an articled pupil in private practice (1920–25), to become an official with London County Council Architects Department (1925–31) and then with Kent County Architects

Appendix R

Department (1931–49). Poltock served in Egypt during the war as a major in the Royal Engineers, commanding 261 Works Section (1944–45). He then set up his own private practice in Maidstone and, in 1949, became an associate of the RIBA.

Poltock's published works of his practice are few, all of them consisting of school buildings. In 1934 he designed Linton school in Kent, a rather advanced modern building whose construction was delayed but which was nonetheless well received when finally completed. Another major work was the Maidstone Technical School for Boys, also in the county of Kent. Poltock's career seems to have suffered in England; Victoria College in 1947 was possibly his first major commission and has remained his most important work.

The preliminary plans for the college, covering an area of twenty-two feddans, were established to accommodate 150 boarders and 350 day boys. The estimated cost in accordance with specifications set out was £300,000. Poltock was asked to alter his designs and specifications to meet a maximum expenditure of £250,000. At the same time in 1949 the construction of the Maadi school began under Braithwaite Co. Ltd., a British contracting firm. And in 1950 the school's move was hailed on Speech Day by Major W. Fanner, who described it as going "from the din of Shubra to the Eden of Maadi," as Samir Raafat reports in *Society and History in a Cairo Suburb—Maadi, 1904–1962*.

Quite a literature exists on the buildings of Victoria College, Cairo: *Architectural Review*, Jan. 1952, pp.8–22; *Architectural Forum*, July 1952, pp.126–27; *Techniques et Architecture*, vol. 2, no. 11–12, pp.70–74; and in *Architects Journal*, vol. 17 (Jan. 1952), p.73. Poltock's early modern conceptualizations project in the Cairo buildings new forms and structural techniques of space configuration, surface treatment, use of materials and landscaping, featuring a rationale of environmental control and a design sensitive to climate. The college's major design problem became its major design feature. Sun devices, thermal insulation, and natural ventilation experienced in the concept are traced back by H.P.H. West, Poltock's assistant, to Le Corbusier's projected buildings for Algiers. Poltock's design quality therefore transcends the improvization of architectural trends to reach the provision of timeless architecture.

Appendix S

Ceremony and preambles of the memorial service for His Majesty the late King Hussein ibn Talal of Jordan held at the Birley Hall, Victory College, on 19 March 1999.

Programme

Recital of verses from the Holy Koran

Introductory speech by Dr. Mohamed Awad, President of the Old Victorian Association

Speeches by:
His Highness Prince Zeid ben Shaker
His Excellency Sayed Sadek el Mahdi
Dr. George Kardouche

Messages of condolence read by Mr. Armand Kahil from Mr. Freddy Yazgui on behalf of the Old Victorians in Geneva, and from Mr. Samir Zalzal on behalf of the Old Victorians in Canada and North America

Mr. Mohamed Shirazy, a Victory College student, playing a piece from Chopin's *The Funerary March* on the flute

Recital of verses from the Holy Koran

Closing speech by Dr. Mohamed Awad

Appendix T

*Letter from Her Majesty Queen Nour
to the Old Victorian Association, April 1999*

Amman
April 1999

Dear Dr. Awad and members of the Board of the Old Victorian Association,

Thank you for your very kind and thoughtful letter message of condolence.

Our family has taken great solace from the remarkable, moving tributes to our beloved King Hussein, may his soul rest in peace, and from the overwhelming, compassionate support we have received from around the world.

We rejoice in his life and are conscious, much more, of the blessing of having shared it, than of his absence. I hope and pray that those who knew and cared for him, also will find comfort in his eternal, transcendent spirit and presence in all our lives. In his passing as in his life, His Majesty's message of humanity and peace brought our world together and we are committed to keeping his vision alive in all our efforts at home and abroad.

Please always remember him with a smile.

With our sincere appreciation,

Bibliography

ABDEL NASSER, G. *The Philosophy of the Revolution*. Buffalo: Smith, Keynes and Marshall, 1959.
ACIMAN, A. *Out of Egypt*. New York: Farrar, Strauss, Giroux, 1994.
ALDRED-BROWN, R. "Education." In Arnold Wright, ed., *Twentieth Century Impressions of Egypt: Its History, People, Commerce, Industries, and Resources*. London: Lloyd's Greater Britain Publishing Co. Ltd., 1909.
ANTONIUS, G. *The Arab Awakening*. London: Hamish Hamilton, 1938.
ASHOUR, R. *Atyaf*. Cairo: al-Mu'assasa al-'Arabiya lil-Dirasat wa-l-Nashr, 1999.
ATIYAH, E. *An Arab Tells His Story*. London: John Murray, 1946.
AWAD, L. *Awraq al-'umr: sanawat al-takwin*. Cairo: Madbouli, 1989.
BOWMAN, H. *Middle East Window*. London: Longmans, Green and Co., 1942.
CLIFFORD, A. *Three Against Rommel*. London: Harrap, 1943.
COOPER, A. *Cairo in the War*. London: Hamish Hamilton, 1989.
EVANS, T., ED., *The Killearn Diaries*. London: Sidgwick and Jackson, 1972.
FARGHALY, M. *'Ayshtu hayati bayn ha'ula'*. Cairo: Matabi' al-Ahram al-Tugariya, 1984.
GHALI, W. *Beer in the Snooker Club*. London: Serpent's Tail, 1987.
GORST, A., AND L. JOHNMAN. *The Suez Crisis*. London: Routledge, 1997.
HAMPTON, C. *White Chameleon*. London: Faber and Faber, 1991.
HEATH-STUBBS, J. *Hindsights: An Autobiography*. London: Hodder and Stroughton, 1993.

HEIKAL, M.H. *Kharif al-ghadab*. n.p., second edition 1983.
HIRST, D., AND I. BEESON. *Sadat*. London: Faber and Faber, 1981.
LACKANY, R. *Quelques notes de toponymie alexandrine*. Alexandria: n.p., 1968.
LANDAU, J. *Jews in 19th Century Egypt*. New York: NYUP, 1969.
LIAS, C.R. *A Short Account of Victoria College: From its Founding to 1919*. Alexandria: Whitehead Morris, 1920.
LLOYD, LORD, *Egypt since Cromer*, vol. 1. London: Macmillan, 1933.
LOVE, K. *Suez: The Twice-Fought War*. New York: McGraw–Hill Book Company, 1969.
al-Mithaq wa qanun al-ittihad al-ishtiraki al-'arabi, Cairo: al-Dar al-Qawmiya lil-Tiba'a wa-l-Nashr, n.d.
SADAT, A. *al-Bahth 'an al-dhat: qissat hayati*. Cairo: al-Maktab al-Misri al-Hadith, 1978.
SAID, E.W. *Culture and Imperialism*. London: Chatto & Windus, 1993.
SAID, E.W. "Between Worlds." *London Review of Books*, 7 May 1997.
SAID, E.W. *Out of Place*. London: Granta Books, 1999.
SALAMA, G. *Tarikh al-ta'lim al-agnabi fi Misr fi-l-qarnayn al-tasi' 'ashar wa-l-'ishrin*. Cairo: n.p., 1962.
SALIH, T. *Season of Migration to the North*. Trans. Denys Johnson-Davies. Portsmouth: Heinemann, 1970.
SOUTHGATE, G.W. *A Text Book of Modern European History 1830–1919*. London: J.M. Dent and Sons, 1937.
VATIKIOTIS, P.J. *The History of Modern Egypt*. London: Weidenfeld & Nicolson, 1985.
WARBURG, G. *The Sudan under Wingate: Administration in the Anglo-Egyptian Sudan (1899–1916)*. London: Frank Cass & Co., 1971.
ZIKRY, F. *al-Bahariya al-misriya: al-tariq ila Uktubar*. Alexandria: Egyptian Navy Press, 1986.

Notes

1 G. Salama, *Tarikh al-taʻlim al-agnabi fi Misr fi-l-qarnayn al-tasiʻ ʻashar wa-l-ʻishrin*, Cairo, 1962.
2 *Ibid.*
3 *Ibid.*
4 *Ibid.*
5 *Ibid.*
6 J. Landau, *Jews in 19th Century Egypt*, New York, NY UP, 1969, pp. 69ff.
7 Lord Lloyd, *Egypt since Cromer*, vol. 1. London, Macmillan, 1933, p. 159.
8 Lloyd, *Cromer*, p. 161.
9 H. Bowman, *Middle East Window*. London, Longmans, Green and Co., 1942, p. 41.
10 Lloyd, *Cromer*, p. 161.
11 Bowman, *Middle East Window*, pp. 38–39.
12 Bowman, *Middle East Window*, pp. 39–40.
13 R. Aldred-Brown, "Education," in Arnold Wright, ed., *Twentieth Century Impressions of Egypt: Its History, People, Commerce, Industries, and Resources*, London, Lloyd's Greater Britain Publishing Co. Ltd., 1909, pp. 221–23.
14 "There were only two alternatives to choose between in those days: to confide one's children to the religious establishments, they being the only existing schools, or to send the children to Europe at great financial and emotional cost. And the children raised thus too often returned home as strangers, having lost contact and forgotten the gentleness of family life. In such an inventive town as Alexandria this situation had continued for too long and a current of opinion began to form in favor of establishing a school that would be free of any confessional attachments. Meetings were organized and various systems of education were discussed. The system that places equal stress on the exercise of the mind

Notes

and the body was unanimously adopted. . . . An international committee was elected including notables of the different religions and nationalities."

15 G. Warburg, *Sudan under Wingate*, London, Frank Cass and Co., 1971, p. 88.

16 A pic equals approximately 28 inches.

17 The three certificates awarded by the Board were: (1) The Lower Certificate, adapted for candidates of fifteen or sixteen years of age. (2) The School Certificate, corresponding to the French *baccalauréat* and recognized by the Egyptian government as equivalent to its Secondary Certificate. Egyptian pupils who obtained it were eligible as candidates for Egyptian government service. This certificate began to be awarded a few years later. (3) The Higher Certificate, a specialized examination of an advanced character intended for those who are proceeding to an honors course at a university. Later these examinations were replaced by the GCE. O-levels and A-levels, and in the 1990s they became the IGCSE. They were held for the first time at Victoria College in 1906.

18 E. Atiyah, *An Arab Tells His Story*, London, John Murray, 1946, p. 53.

19 P.J. Vatikiotis, *The History of Modern Egypt*, London, Weidenfeld and Nicolson, 1985, pp. 186 and 203.

20 G. Antonius, *The Arab Awakening*, London, Hamish Hamilton, 1938, pp. 411–12.

21 E.W. Said, *Culture and Imperialism*, London, Chatto and Windus, 1993, p. 243.

22 See Appendix D for the list of staff in the first year at Siouf.

23 Atiyah, *Story*, p. 58.

24 *Ibid.*

25 See Appendix F for his adventures.

26 Said, *Imperialism*, p. 137.

27 Said, *Imperialism*, pp. 137–38.

28 The following information on Farghaly Pasha is taken from his memoirs, '*Ayshtu hayati bayn ha'ula*'.

29 Oswald Finney owned land, breweries, and newspapers, and was heavily involved in the cotton business. Amin Pasha Yehia was a member of the Municipal Council and a cotton exporter. The Choremis were cotton exporters. Jacob Rolo of J. Rolo and Co. was a Director of the National Bank of Egypt and was involved in cotton and real estate development. Sir Henry Swinglehurst was a member of the Municipal Council.

30 In 1929 the school treasurers, Messrs. Russell and Co. were replaced by the school bursar, Mr. Ingham.

31 The bus fees for a term were: for the Kindergarten and Prep schools, LE 1.80 from Ramleh and LE 2.40 from Alexandria; for the Lower and Upper schools, LE 2.40 from Ramleh and LE 3.00 from Alexandria.

NOTES

32 A number of Old Boys returned to the school as teachers. Among them are Heidar al Ricaby, Lucien Naudi, George Sylvain, Leslie Fleming, John Towers Abaza, Robert Marco, Charles Hamdy, Hafez Bassoumi, and Adel Tawfik.
33 Farghaly, *Memoirs*, pp. 16, 52.
34 Public Record Office, FO 371/53341.
35 Trefor Evans, ed., *The Killearn Diaries*, London, Sidgwick and Jackson, 1972, p. 209.
36 Evans, *Diaries*, p. 213.
37 Evans, *Diaries*, p. 211.
38 Evans, *Diaries*, p. 213.
39 Evans, *Diaries*, p. 360.
40 See also Chapter 1 for Amin Osman's address to a Zagazig Old Boys' dinner.
41 Letter dated 14 December 1943 to A.J.S. White of the British Council, London. Public Record Office, BW 29/8.
42 Letter dated 22 December, 1942, to Sir Malcolm Robertson in the British Council, London. Public Record Office, BW 29/8.
43 The School offered the Vaux Political Economy Prize, the Ambassador's Most Original Essay Prize, the Clelland Henry Poetry Prize, the Cator Diction Prize, and the Abdel Wahab Memorial Prize. The names of the boys who had won prizes or scholarships were published in the newspapers with the speeches. Mr. Reed gave careful consideration to the prizes, which he ordered from England; he explained that the "books are beautiful in themselves and have been carefully chosen with an eye to the tastes and reading of those who have gained them."
44 Vatikiotis, *History*, p. 317.
45 One feddan equals a little more than one acre.
46 Notes on a meeting of the Council of Victoria College, Cairo, 16 March 1949. Public Record Office, BW 29/35.
47 A. Clifford, *Three against Rommel*, London, Harrap, 1943, p. 315.
48 Vatikiotis, *History*, p. 347.
49 A. Cooper, *Cairo in the War*, London, Hamish Hamilton, 1989, p. 173.
50 The Victory Thanksgiving Fund appeal was launched in 1945 by Lord Killearn with the object of improving and endowing British schools and hospitals in Egypt.
51 British Council files, Education: general 1935–37, Public Record Office, BW 29/3.
52 Public Record Office, BW 29/3.
53 *Ibid.*
54 Public Record Office, BW 29/8.

NOTES

55 Atiyah, *Story*. p. 60.
56 Letter from Reed to A.S.S. White, British Council, London, 2 June 1943, in Public Record Office, BW 29/8.
57 Public Record Office, BW 29/8.
58 Public Record Office, MH 106/1887.
59 *Ibid.*
60 *Ibid.*
61 Public Record Office, BW 29/23.
62 From HM Inspector's Report, March 1949, Public Record Office, BW 29/35.
63 Public Record Office, BW 29/37.
64 *Ibid.*
65 Public Record Office, BW 29/35.
66 Vatikiotis, *History*, 361.
67 E.W. Said, "Between Worlds," *London Review of Books*, 7 May 1997.
68 Hussein, King of Jordan, *Uneasy Lies the Head*, London, Heinemann, 1962, pp. 12–13.
69 Hassan Abou Khebir fondly remembers the old days of Victoria and particularly the presence of the future King Hussein of Jordan. In the 1980s a Jordanian delegation visiting the school was asked by the king to pay his respects to Hassan. They were informed that he was ill with serious eye problems. The king promptly arranged for him to be flown to Jordan, where he was accommodated in a five-star hotel and received the best hospital treatment.
70 Vatikiotis, *History*, 384.
71 Public Record Office, BW 29/44.
72 Said, "Between Worlds,"
73 Said, *Out of Place*, London, Granta Books, 1999, p. 185.
74 Said, *Out of Place*, p. 182.
75 Said, *Out of Place*, p. 184.
76 Mr. Wightman, a master at Victoria College, described Ghali in a letter to Mr. Scovil as "rather a nondescript sort of chap, certainly not clever"!
77 W. Ghali, *Beer in the Snooker Club*, London, Serpent's Tail, 1987, pp. 57–58.
78 J. Heath-Stubbs, *Hindsights: An Autobiography*. London, Hodder and Stroughton, 1993.
79 Heath-Stubbs, *Hindsights*, p. 228.
80 Heath-Stubbs, *Hindsights*, p. 234.
81 See, in this context, Christopher Hampton's play, *White Chameleon*, London, Faber and Faber, 1991. Hampton had been a pupil at Victoria College, Alexandria, in 1953. In an "Afterword," Hampton explains that while he has used "directly autobiographical material" (p. 56), there have been certain trans-

NOTES

positions and modifications. *White Chameleon* traces the Egyptian experience of a character named Christopher, whose father is an engineer at the Cable and Wireless company in Alexandria, from Black Saturday to the aftermath of the Suez War. While Christopher and his mother are evacuated in 1956, the father remains in Alexandria and is placed under house arrest for three weeks, before being expelled from the country. Although Christopher finds "the non-British boys of the British Boys' School [which he joined after leaving VC]... more tolerant than the princelings of Victoria College" (p. 40), there is an incident at the BBS when a boy attacks him. This is later paralleled by the bullying of his classmates in England who call him a "wog-lover" because he "said if they [the British] go to war over the Suez Canal, they need their heads examining. That's what my father says" (p. 46). Finally, Christopher's tarboosh is confiscated and burned by a kindly headmaster concerned about the boy's unpatriotic remarks—an amalgam of two incidents that had occurred to Hampton and his brother, as explained in the "Afterword."

82 Anthony Eden was, of course, to resign in January 1957. In the summer of 1956, after the nationalization of the Suez Canal, Britain and France put pressure on the Suez Canal Company to withdraw its non-Egyptian employees and pilots. Hence, apart from employees who were on leave, "[t]he remaining British, French, Dutch, and Italian pilots applied for their exit visas on 12 September, [and] resigned from the new Suez Canal Authority... They had been told by the company that they would forfeit their pensions if they stayed. They were told by the Egyptians that if they quit they would be blacklisted from ever returning again, even as tourists. Only the Greek government refused permission to its nationals to leave Egyptian service, going so far as to withhold visas to enter Greece (which were needed even by Greeks), and finally instructing Greek consuls to call in the passports of Greek Canal workers," according to Kennett Love's *Suez: The Twice-Fought War*, New York, McGraw-Hill Book Company, 1969, p. 422. For a recent study on Suez, which reproduces and analyzes many contemporary documents, see Anthony Gorst and Lewis Johnman, *The Suez Crisis*, London, Routledge, 1997.

83 For information on the subsequent careers of Dr. Mohamed Aglan and Dr. Hussein Kamaleddin, We are indebted to Dr. Fuad Mounir, an Alexandrian left-wing acquaintance of the two men.

84 Southgate, G.W., *A Text Book of Modern European History 1830–1919*, London, J.M. Dent and Sons, 1937, p. 109.

85 R. Ashour, *Atyaf*. Cairo, al-Mu'assasa al-'Arabiya lil-Dirasat wa-l-Nashr, 1999, p. 29; my translation. Although several of Ashour's foreign teachers left after

Suez, both the Mathematics master and the French language teacher, Mme. Michel, stayed on. Ashour describes the two teachers' contempt for the Egyptian pupils, particularly Mme. Michel who browbeat the young girl.

86 For the change in the name of Victoria tram station, and the tram line named after it, see Radames Lackany, *Quelques notes de toponymie alexandrine*, Alexandria, n.p., 1968, p.20.

87 Many thanks to Mona Anis who, during a conversation in Cairo in 1997, suggested the comparison, and provided information on the construction of the Corniche in relation to the British Embassy.

88 Vatikiotis, *History*, p. 475.

89 A. Aciman, *Out of Egypt*. New York, Ferrar, Strauss, Giroux, 1994.

90 Aciman, *Out of Egypt*, p. 240.

91 Aciman, *Out of Egypt*, p. 283. Emphasis in original.

92 *Ibid.*

93 At the EGC, meanwhile, there were two Jewish teachers. Ms. Hertha Pappo, an Alexandrian Italian–Austrian who taught piano and singing, continued to play a key role in the production of school public events such as Speech Day until her retirement in the 1980s. Dr. Roberts, an Austrian Science Mistress, retired in the 1970s.

94 See *al-Mithaq wa qanun al-ittihad al-ishtiraki al-'arabi*, Cairo, al-Dar al-Qawmiya lil-Tiba'a wa-l-Nashr, n.d.

95 Aciman, *Out of Egypt*, p. 228.

96 The introduction of Sharia as a source of legislation was an amendment, approved by the People's Assembly in 1980, to Sadat's 1971 constitution. For this and other amendments to Sadat's constitution, see David Hirst and Irene Beeson, *Sadat*, London, Faber and Faber, 1981, pp. 331–2. Sadat's constitution, nevertheless, retains articles affirming the equality of all citizens in rights and obligations, irrespective of religion, and warranting freedom of belief and religious practice.

97 L. Awad, *Awraq al-'umr: sanawat al-takwin*, Cairo, Madbouli, 1989, p. 257; my translation.

98 *Old Victorian Association Newsletter*, ed. Armand Kahil, March 1996.

Index

Abaza, John 195, 227
Abaza, Mahmoud 29, 128, 158
Abbadi, Abdel Aziz Hassib 207–08
Abdallah, Gad 76
Abdel Aal, Abdel Moneim 52
Abdel Moneim, Suleiman 52
Abdel Nasser, Gamal 138, 188, 192, 203, 207; bans Muslim Brotherhood 230; chairman of Revolutionary Command Council 173; consolidates power 178; *al-Mithaq* (The Charter) 219; nationalization of Suez Canal 180; and pan-Arabism 225; and President Tito 221–22; on religious freedom 231
Abdel Salam, Mohamed Bey 104
Abdel Salam, Shadi 104, 113–14
Abdel Wahab, Loutfy 198
Abdin 'Incident' 120–22, 146
Abdulillah, Emir 65, 79–81; dinner in honour of 46
Abdullah, Emir of Transjordan 70, 79
Abou Ayana, Fathy 241
Abou Seif, Fawzi 239
Abu al-Ela family 169
Abu Seif, Salah 114
Abudy, Jack 83
Aciman, André 214–16, 228
Adam, Sir Ronald 150
Adham, Kamal 169, 240
Agami, Alain Aslan 216
el Aggan, Hussein 130
Aghion, Behor 10
Aghion, Charles 23
Aghion, Elie 23
Aghion, Fernand 23

Aghion, Isaac 10
Aghion, Maurice 53
Aghion, Victor 23
Aglan, Mohamed 196
el Alamein 122, 133, 141
Alderson, Sir George Beeton 4, 17, 18, 25, 35–36; funds for library 33; generous assistance of 22; sponsor of school 20
Alexanian, "Willy" 141
Alexandria Schools Trust Charity 235–36, 237, 239, 242
Ali, Ahmed Helmy 194, 196, 197, 203
Ali, Baba 78–79, 83
Allenby, Lord 42, 50, 53
Alsagaff, Seyd Hadi 69
Alsagoff, Sayed Ali 69
American University of Beirut 23, 31, 76, 77, 92
Amr, Abdel Fatah Pasha, 147
Anglo-Egyptian Treaty (1936) 50, 97, 119, 138, 161, 170
Anglo-Egyptian Condominium of Sudan, 49, 170
Anhoury, Antoine 53
Annaniantz, Miss A. 212
Antonius, George 29, 30–33, 43, 52, 84
Antonius, Habib 29
Antonius, Michael 27, 29–30, 35, 50
Armaos, A. 212
Arnold, Dr. Thomas 37
Artin, Yacoub Pasha 15
Ashour, Radwa 199
el Askari, General Siam 82
el Askari, Hussein 82

INDEX

el Askari, Ja'far Pasha 82
el Askari, Nazar 82
el Askari, Ziad 82
Atif, Ezz Eldin 101
Atif, Galal 101
Atiyah, Edward 15, 28, 54, 63, 72, 93, 94–95, 128, 129; arrives at school 49; corresponding with Mr. Reed 95–96; in London 158; on Reed 154–55; on solidarity 40; on Speech Day 126; presents play to Lord Milner 42; secures scholarship for Oxford 50
Atiyah, Michael 93–95
Atiyah, Patrick 93, 129
Aubrey, A.E. 22
el Awa, Ahmed 81
el Awa, Safwat Pasha, 81, 83
Awad, Fouad 76, 85, 87, 99, 100, 129, 130, 134; caught cheating 102; on school dinners 105
Awad, Louis 232
Awad, Mohamed 2, 100, 197, 209, 216, 232, 240–41; on boarders 225–26; on discipline 228–29; on *al-Mithaq* 220

Badawi, Miss 215
Baden-Powell, Lord 47, 99
Badr, Emir 70
Bahr, Amm Abdou 194
Baker Pasha, F.D. 132
Balit, Georges 166–67, 173, 181, 185
Balkan Wars 133; Victorians involved 44
Bandas, shop owner 105
el Banna, Hassan 138
Barda, James 45
Barker, H. Alwyn 187, 207, 235
Barker, Lady 100
Barker, Michael 235
Barker, Sir Henry 4, 18, 25, 43, 126–27; addresses EGC 25; campaigning for girls' school 24; dies 149; on foundation of VC 16
Baroudi, Ashraf Sami 51
Baroudi, Kamal 51
al-Baroudi, Mahmoud Sami 51
Baroudi, Mrs. Zizi 51
Barritt, Herbert 14, 102, 160, 179, 184, 185, 189, 193, 195, 206; on Arabic teaching 175; on the dining hall 170; on effect of political troubles 171; on extracurricular activities 163–64; on future of the two schools 151; overseas trip 177–78; pride in the school

164; on problems of VC Alexandria 161–62; resigns 187; on the revolution 172; school open day 172–73; on Shadi Abdel Salam 113
Barron, Mr. 74, 75
Bassili, Albert 163,
Bassili, Antoine 28, 84, 85, 99, 101, 109
Bassili, Jack 163
Bassili, Victor 101, 163, 177
Bassoumi, Hafez 85, 109, 203, 229; on the house feast 227
Baxter, James 58
Behar, Marcel 140, 181
el Beheiry, Maamoun 71
Bell, Kenneth 92
Bevin, Ernest 119, 121, 123
Birley, K.P. 219
Blake, George 20
Blake-Reed, J.S. 160–61
Bliss, Dr. Howard 23
Blomfield, Sir Massie 15
Boddy, Rev. A. 34
Bolton, Leslie 67
Bolton, Mrs., matron 48–49, 105
Bolton, Percy 48, 52, 67, 105, 149
Bose, Professor 155
Bowman, Humphrey 26, 31, 76, 77; on teaching in Egypt 11
Bramley, Major Jennings 143
British Boys' School 87, 235; name change 202
British Council 82, 83, 96, 125, 140, 148, 151, 154, 176, 180, 211; creation of 153; denying responsibility for new school 158; financing of VC 159; involvement in VC 156–57; priorities 155; Mr. Reed as representative 95
Bretton Woods Conference (1944) 58–59
Brooke-Popham, Sir Robert 78
Bru, César 30
Burgess, Miss 48, 49
Burney, E. 140
de Bustros, Alexander 134
de Bustros, Selim Paul 134
Butler, Sir Neville 156

Cairo, burning of 46, 171
Campbell, Sir Ronald: importance of establishing VCC 155–57
Capitulations 138, 146
Carlyle, Thomas 4
Carver, Felix 55
Carver, H.B. 100, 128

INDEX

Carver, P.W. 39
Carver, Ralph 235
Carver, Sydney 18, 25, 55
Chabrit, Albert 216
Chahine, Youssef 133
Chalaby, Mounir 241
Chalhoub, Michel 163, 164
Chamas, Jean 55
Checri, Themistocles 39
Chehata, Yusri 217, 224, 227; on boarders 226
Chirine, Hussein Bey 65, 114–15
Chirine, Ismail 65, 80, 115
Choremi, Constantine 68
Claudianus, Claudius 43
Clayton, Colonel Gilbert 83–84
Clement, Colin 236
Collège Saint-Marc 107, 202
Colley, Arthur 67, 99
Colucci, Mario, 109; on French system 106–07
Connaught, Duchess of 35
Connaught, Duke of 35
Connelly, Neil 236–37
Constantinidis, Michael 212
Cook, Miss 212, 218
Cook, Sir Edward 83
Cookson, Sir Charles 16, 17, 25
Corbett, Sir Vincent 15
Cordahi, Emile 30, 35, 54, 55
Cordahi family 54, 55
Cornwallis, Sir Kinahan 77, 78
Cripps, Vivian 106
Cromer, Lady 16, 35
Cromer, Lord 16, 21, 24, 25, 26, 35, 54; attitude to education 11, 145; founds Gordon College, Khartoum 19; negative attitude to VC 19, 20
Cryer, J. 12 on Douglas Dunlop
Cumming, Brigadier 144

David, A.P. 159
Dawson, Noel 130
Defrawi, Enam 203
Deschambeaux, Jacques 64, 109
DesMeules, J.G. 212
Diab, Emile 53
Doble, Mr. 64, 66, 80
Dolfuss, Englebert, 129
Doyle, Mr. 159
Dumont, Georges 21, 27, 40, 52, 59, 111, 149
Dundas, C.A.F. 154

Dunlop, Douglas 8, 11, 12, 26, 59
Durrell, Lawrence 85

Ebeid, Makram 121
Ebeid, Malek Hanna 2, 47, 50; on effects of First World War on school 47–48
Eden, Anthony 191
Edmonds, Mr. 77, 82
Edward I, King 42
Elliot-Smith, Alan Guy 159, 184, 185
Elmasri, Maher 233
Elmasri, Ramez 233
Emby, Mrs. 197
English Girls' College 190, 202, 203, 227, 231, 235, 237; coeducation at 233; move to Chatby 25; name change 201; opens 24; relations with VC 100
English School, Cairo 20
Evans, B. Ifor 125, 154
Ezzat, Mohamed 217, 227, 229

Fadl, Omar 53
el Falaky, Mahmoud Saleh 57–59,
el Falaky, Mahmoud Hamdy 57
Farghaly, Ahmed Effendi 55
Farghaly Pasha, Mohamed 55–57, 122, 123, 127, 132
Farhi, Henri 77, 128
Farouk, King 112, 120–21, 146, 167
Favarger, H. 21
Fawzia, Princess 115
Fayez, Mr. 109
Fazil, Princess Emina 65
Feisal, King of Iraq 79, 80
Feisal, King of Saudi Arabia 169
Finney, Oswald 68
Fleming, Leslie 67, 79, 103
Florence, Captain 143
Florentis, Litsa 212, 224, 234–35
Forrest, Dr. 104
Forster, E.M. 106
Fouad, King 56
Furness, R.A. 148

Gately, Keith 140
Gawdat Bey 71
George V, King 46, 50, 56
Ghaleb, Hussein 53
Ghali, Waguih 185–86
Ghanem family 169
Ghorayeb, Alexander 168, 170, 182
Ghubril, Fouad 195, 212, 222, 226
Gilbertson, Mrs. 212

Index

Glover, John 193
Goar, Edwin 162
Goha, Mgr. Kyrollis 15
Gordon College, Khartoum 19–20
Gorra, Henri 36
Gorst, Sir Eldon 26
Gould, E. B. 16, 25, 26, 35
Gould, Mrs. 26
Grant, Miss D., matron 36
Green, Mr. 212
Grice, Mr. 77, 78
Griffin, Alfred Edward 193
Guindi, Mr. 192

Haile Selassie, Emperor 73, 75
Halim, Helmi 114
Halim, Princess Abbas 66
Hamada, Abdel Rahman 1, 29
Hamada, Hussein 102
Hamada, Mohamed 102
Hamdy, Charles 52, 109, 190, 191, 192, 193, 195, 198, 200, 203, 204, 221, 230, 231, 232, 234, 237; on changing student body 217; continues traditions 205; on Egyptian teachers 195; faces state security 223; on post-Suez atmosphere 189; on social segregation 196
Hamid, Sheikh Mohamed 21, 22, 35
Hanna, Bushra Bey 45
Hanna, Charles 45
Hanna, Kamel Boulos 74
Hanna, Willie 45
Harari, M. 127
Harari, Nouri Elie 129
Harle, Edwin 22, 29
Hart, Mr. 48
Harûn, Hakham 22
Hassan, Hassan Ahmed *see* Khebir, Abou
Hassan, Mansour 168, 181, 183–85
Hassan, Mohamed 198
Hassanein, Ahmed Pasha 92, 120–21, 123, 146–47, 148
Hassanein, Hisham 147–48
Hassanein, Tarek 24, 147–48
Haydon, Douglas 2, 4, 47, 52, 105, 106, 128, 129; 143–44; on politics 118–19; on theatrics 133
Haydon, Mrs. 105, 129
Heath-Stubbs, John 192–93
Heathcote-Smith, Sir Clifford 74–76, 127
Heikal, Mohamed Hassanein 123
Heikal Pasha 118

Heneikati, Edward 101
Heroui, Blaten Gueta 73
Heroui, George 73, 74
Heroui, Haillou 73–74
Heroui, Michael 73
Heroui, Sirak 73
Highwood, R.G. 52, 66, 69, 82, 86, 106, 109–10, 111, 112; on government intervention 118; on Mr. Lias's desire to return to VC 60–61; moves to Iraq 82–83
Hilali Bey 126
Hill, Mr. 159
Hitler, Adolf 131
Hourani, Albert 88–89
Housden, Mr. 47
Howell, C.D. 176–77
Howell-Griffiths, Stephen 140
Humphreys, Mr. 159
Hussein, Ali 70, 79
Hussein, El Sharif 31, 65, 70, 101
Hussein, Feisal 31, 70; *see also* Feisal, King of Iraq
Hussein, Kamaleddin 200, 202, 204
Hussein, King of Jordan 169, 238, 240
Hussein, Mrs. 228
al Husseini, Haj Amin 31
Hussey, E.R.J. 158

Ibadi, Mustapha Pasha 15
Idris, King of Libya 145
Ingham, Mr., bursar 68, 99
Iskander, Habib 48
Ismail, Khedive 17, 57
Issawi, Charles 2, 87–93, 98, 117, 131; bad attitude 103; and British Intelligence 83–84; on debating in school 106; head boy 105; and OV Club 128; and Rotary Club 127–28
Issawi, Elie Bey 89, 90, 91, 92, 93, 103, 128; on Arabic teaching 115–16

Joannides, Miss A. 212

Kadry Bey 79
Kahil, Armand 28, 238, 239, 240; on French education 107; on OVA 237, 241
Kahil, Raouf 128
Kamal, Usama 237
Kamaleddin, Dr. Hussein 196
Karam, George 45
Kardouche, George 3, 239, 241

Index

Kassem, Ahmed Abdel Rahman 225
Kassem, Usama 217–18, 226
Kato, Ahmed Fawzi Ben 226
Kawalerowicz, Jerzy 114
Keynes, John Maynard 58
Khalafallah, Ann 202, 203, 227–28
el Khalidi, Mohamed 76
el Khalidi, Moustapha Bey 76
Khalifa, Ahmes 240
Khashoggi, Adnan 169
Khebir, Abou 176
Khoury, Robert 101
Khruschev, Nikita 221
Killearn, Lord *see* Lampson, Sir Miles
Kingham, Harry Pugh 18, 25
Kipling, Rudyard 47
el Kirdany, Ibrahim 227
Kitchener, Lord 19–20, 47
Klat, Maurice 42, 54
Klat, Oscar 53, 54
Koreish, Abdel Aziz 218, 224, 234

Lagonicos family 23
Laight, Brandon 158, 173
Lampson, Lady 127
Lampson, Sir Miles 46, 112, 127, 136, 148, 153; and Abdin 'Incident' 120–22, 146; on Amin Osman 119–20, 123–24; launches Victory Thanksgiving Fund 160
Laskaridis, John 53, 54
Laurens, Edouard 35
Lee, H.D. 148
Leeper, R.W.A. 153
Lennox Cooke, Mr. 159
Lewin, Peter 117, 167, 169; on revolution 172
Lias, Charles R. 1, 2, 4, 20, 30, 40, 41, 47, 48, 52, 53, 54, 59, 61, 63, 95; accepted as headmaster 21; chooses school motto 43; describing early years 24; early account of school 22; on education 37–39; establishes Speech Day ritual 26; first Old Boys dinner 45; hiring Cantabrigians 49; introduces Oxford and Cambridge Joint Board Examination 25–26; invites Lord Milner to school 42–43; lamenting absence of girls' school 24; on religious instruction 214; resigns 59; on Siouf site 34–35, 36; starts Kindergarten 25; wanting to return to VC 60
Lias, Miss M.T. 25, 52

Lias, Mrs. 49
Lloyd, Lord 11, 82
London Conference (1939) 31
Lorraine, Sir Percy 153; on failure of British influence 152; on VC 38–39
Loutfy, Abdel Fatah 168, 182; on King Hussein 169
Lowe, C.A.F. 159
Lowick, Mr. 22

MacMahon, Sir Henry 31, 47
Mahdi family 169
el Mahdi, Ismail 168, 181–82; on King Hussein 169
el Mahdi, Sadek 183
el Mahdi, Sir Sayed Abdel Rahman 74
Maher, Ali Pasha 102, 117, 120, 126
Maher, Mohamed Ali 102–03
Mahmoud, Mohamed Pasha 92
Makarius, Shahin 31
Malloy, Mrs. 100
Malloy, S.E. 100
Mansour, Hassan 29
Mansur, Hamid 23
el Manzalaoui, Mahmoud 110
el Masri, Abdel Kerim 237
el Masry, Ibrahim 44
el Masry, Mohamed Ismail 219
el Masry, Taher 219, 228
Mazarita 20, 35, 39, 40, 46, 47, 49, 51, 52, 67, 86; move from 36, 42
McClure and Dorling, contractors 21, 24
Meath, Lord 39
el Medani, Mustafa 3; appeal to OVA 241–42
Menasce, Jacob de 10
Menasce, Baron Jacques de 13, 15, 18, 19, 25, 35; speech at laying of foundation stone 16
Merghani family 169
Michaelidis, John 54
Millar, Miss Ethel, matron 149
Miller, Miss 100
Milner, Lord 42–43, 53, 59, 64
Mires, Alfred 54
Misr el Fatat 138
Moghazi, Mohamed 101
Muhammad Ali 6, 7, 8
Montgomery, General Bernard 141
Montreux Convention 138
Morhig, Mr. 72
Morrison, Alfred 22, 40
Moschovachi, Miss A. 212

INDEX

Moss, Robert 18, 25
Mourad, Mohamed Helmy 232
Moursy, Mahmoud 29, 53
Mouzzouris, S. 212
Muslim Brotherhood 138, 178, 182, 230
Mussolini, Benito 119, 166
Mustard, Ambrose 21
Mustard, V.R. 22

Naggiar, Sydney 29, 43
Nahas, Albert 29, 43
el Nahas, Mustafa Pasha 120–22, 123, 124, 128, 146; attempted assassination 122; attends Old Boys dinner 46
el Nakeeb, Adham 87, 238
Napoleon III 57
el Nashashibi, Rasheed 76–77
Nashed, Mahmoud Tewfick 218
Nasr, Saida 71
Nazer, Hisham 169
Neguib, General Mohamed 172, 178
Nessier, Dr. Richard 239
Niazi, Zeinab 24
Nimatalla, Princess 65
Nimr, Albert 29, 31
Nimr family 31
Nofal, Haj 229–31
Nofal, Mohamed 221, 222, 230
Nureddin, Mohamed Ezzat 203, 205–06, 207–08, 227

Old Victorian Clubs 2, 128; Ahmes Khalifa Fund 240; acquires premises 46; database of students 165; dinners 46, 50–51; first club founded 45; international groups 238; International Reunion 1988 87; OVA reborn 237; world directories 238
O'Rafferty, S.L. 145
Osman, Amin Pasha 2, 24, 52, 55, 63, 70, 71, 72, 74, 87, 96–97, 98, 105, 117, 128; and Abdin 'Incident' 120–22; on Anglo-Egyptian ties 122; and Anglo-Egyptian Treaty 119; assassination of 123, 161; as captain of 1st XI 40; dinners in his honor 45; on patriotism 50–51
Osman, Ayesha 24, 123
Osman, Munir 52

Page, F.J. 48
Parkhouse, R.R. 52, 76, 99, 130, 183, 194; on dress codes 170

Patricia, Princess of Connaught, 35
Peel, Sir Edward 136, 150, 151, 155; on new preparatory school rooms 163
Penglis, E.C. 212
Perkunder, Hans 133
Philby, Harry St. J. 46, 84
Philippe, sandwich seller 130
Photius II (Greek Orthodox patriarch) 15
Politi, Albert 216
Poltock, John 158
Poriasi, Stefy 213–14
Preece, D.E. 47
Preston, Arthur S. 18, 21, 35, 45
Preston, Janie 35
Price, J. Rex G. 52, 93, 94, 140, 144; headmaster VC Cairo 135; resigns 159
Prucher, Signor 40
Psaltis, A.S. 29, 44

Raafat, Samir 238
Ralli, Ambroise 23, 25
Ralli family 23
Ramzi, Ahmed 164
Rashed, Aziza 202
Reed, Mrs. 95, 159
Reed, Ralph 2, 4, 14, 24, 28, 45, 47, 48, 49, 52, 53, 54, 55, 61, 66, 69, 87, 88, 89, 93, 95, 98, 99, 100, 103, 112, 113, 117, 126, 128, 129, 130, 132, 133, 137, 143, 147, 153; advising parents 65; on Arabic teaching 116; attitude to Egyptians 86; becomes headmaster 63; concern for the boys 65, 70–73, 78–79, 79–81, 90–92, 96–97, 101, 115, 134; connections with British Intelligence 83–84; death of 136, 149; on dorm life 40–41; on duration of war 131; on education 63–64; on exams 110; financial arrangements for boys 67, 74–76; frugal lifestyle 84; hiring Oxonians 50; influence on boys 50; ill health 64, 102, 105, 135; *in loco parentis* 104; involved in diplomacy 119; moves school to Cairo 140; networking in Iraq 77, 79–83; political views and activity 124–25; on Speech Day 127; as seen by British Council 154; tribute to Mr. Lias 60
el Ricaby, Ali Reda Pasha 77
el Ricaby, Heider 77, 128
Rider, H.B. 52, 102, 103, 109, 130, 141, 145, 189, 193, 195, 196, 204, 218;

INDEX

acting headmaster 187; on changeover post-Suez 190–91; leaving Egypt 194
Rider, James 189
Ridha, Ali Abdullah Ali 101, 105
el Rifaai, Zeid 169
Roditi, Eugene 216
Rofé, Harry 150–51
Roha, Mr. 190, 191,
Rolo, J. 25, 68
Rommel, Erwin von 141, 146
Rossellini, Roberto 114
Rowden, J. 40
Ruffer, Sir Marc Armand 18, 19, 25, 42, 45, 53
Ruppa, Alexandre 30
Rye, Anthony 189
Rye, Sydney 189

Saba, Farid Joseph 23, 53
Saba Pasha, Joseph 13, 19, 23, 25
Sabbah family 169
al Sabbah, Ali Abdullah al Jaber 188
Sabry, Hassan Pasha 56, 70, 101
Sabry, Mounir Hassan, 70, 101
Sabry, Samir 164
Sadat, Anwar 122–23, 237
Sadek, Ahmed 101
Sadek family 128
Sadek, Ibrahim 101
Sadek, Mahmoud 101
Sadek, Saleh 101
Safwat, Dr. 1
el Said, Assem Bey 76
el Said, Bahai' 76
Said, Edward: on G. Antonius 33; on Omar Sharif 163; on VC 182–83
el Said, Nuri Pasha 46
Said Pasha 10
el Sakkaf, Abkar 70
el Sakkaf, El Sharif Mohamed Said 69–70
el Sakkaf, Mohamed Said Omar 69,
el Sakkaf, Mustafa 69–71, 76
Salih, Tayeb 187
Salvago, Pandely Michel 55
Salvator, Erherzog Ludwig 34
Salvatore, Mrs. G. 212
Sami, Yacoub Pasha 51
San Remo Conference (1922) 32
San Stefano Hotel, 34, 131, 140, 141, 206; school moves to 130, 139
Sandars, Lionel 17, 19
Sarofeem, Fares 1, 158
Sarruf, Yacub 31
Sarwat Pasha 70
Saud, King Abdel Aziz Ibn 31, 46, 84
al Saud, Prince Feisal 217–18
Scheiss Pasha 15
Scovil, W.J. 52, 67, 93, 143, 144, 149; acting Head at San Stefano 131, 140; on Egyptian teachers 195; on growing numbers of pupils during the war 141–42; headmaster at Siouf 136; on problems at VC Alexandria 160; writing to Ali Pasha Maher about son Mohamed 102–03
el Senoussi, Kamal 143–44
el Senoussi, Mohamed 144–45
el Senoussi, Sayed Sadek 144
el Senoussi, Seif el Din 143
Sergeant, A.R.D. 54
Sergeant, Jack Prosper 54
Serroussi, Maurice 106
Shaker, Zeid bin 77, 169
Shama, Clement 86, 133
Sharara, Zahir, 42, 53
Shaarawi, Adel 236
Sharif, Omar *see* Chalhoub, Michel
Sharon, André 239
Shashoua, Roddy 216
el Shazly, Nadia 135
Shehayib, Hassan Sabry 70
Shiber, Mr. 48, 49
Shubra, VC 93, 131, 140, 141, 154, 168
Sid Ahmed, Kamel 181
Sidahmed, Mohamed Zaki 211, 218,
Sidky, Aziz 51
Sidky, Ismail Pasha 51, 58, 87, 117
Simon, Sir John 152
Sinadino, Michel 15
Sirry, Hassan 23
Sirry, Hussein Pasha 56, 120, 146
Sirry, Ismail Bey 23
Sirry, Yusuf 23
Siouf 35, 40, 41, 136, 141, 188; foundation ceremony 15, 17, 19, 35; move to 36, 42; move back after First World War 52; back to after Second World War 142; site purchased 34
Smart, Sir Walter 155
Smith, Lionel 77, 78, 81, 82, 111
Smith, Miss S.A.E., matron 36
Smouha, Joseph 68
Sobhi, Ahmed 239
St. Leger-Hill, Edward 52, 104, 113, 129, 130; sets up volunteer fire service 132–33

Index

Stamboulieh, Gabriel 72
Stamboulieh, Nicola 63, 72–73, 87, 190–91, 195, 212; deputy headmaster 196; on changeover post-Suez 190; resignation 203–05
Sterry, Sir Wasey 72.
Suleiman, Sheikh Mohamed 78
Sursock, Nicholas 54
Swinglehurst, Henry 68
Sykes–Picot Agreement 32
Syrian Protestant College 23, 31 *see also* American University of Beirut

Tadros, Heba 110
Tchidoukdjian, Serge 217, 220, 222
Tegneh, Constantine 74–76.
Tell al-Kebir, Battle of 51
Tenebaum brothers 76
Tewfik, Hussein 122
Tewfik, Khedive 64
Tewfiq, Sheikh Mohamed 52, 71, 115 dies
Thomas, David 236–37
Thompson, Major 143
Thornton, Colonel 132
Tito, Josip Broz 221–22
Tookey, H.C. 40
Tookey, W.J. 53
Tossizza brothers 9
Tousson, Mohamed Tewfik 65
Tousson, Prince Omar 68, 99
Treen, A. 48, 52, 105
Trevelyan, G.M. 38

Uzdi, Mohamed 169
Urabi, Ahmed Pasha 51

Vafris, Spiro 211
Valassopoulos family 23
Valassopoulo, George 27, 29, 43, 44
Vasquez, Señor 26
Vatikiotis, P.J. 209
Verny, Auguste 39
Victoria, Queen 5, 17, 20, 35, 202
Victory Thanksgiving Fund 152, 160, 162
Vlasto, C. 54

Waights, Mr. 192
Wallace, William 42, 43
Ward, Archdeacon 22
Wassef, Hussein Pasha 65
Wassef, Kamel 65, 80
Wassef, Ramsis Wissa 114

Weheiba, Abdel Fatah 197–98
Weisz, Oswald 130
Wightman, John N. 140
Wilson, Sir Henry Maitland 143
Wingate, Sir Reginald 19
Winn, C.E. 48
Wissa family 67
Wollaston, Arthur J. 140
War, Arab–Israeli (1948) 166, 167, 170, 184
War, Arab–Israeli (1967) 231
War, First World 5, 31, 42, 49, 51, 52, 53, 68, 132, 139, 145; effect on school 47–49
War, Second World 9, 19, 46, 58, 86, 96, 101, 120, 122, 129, 131, 135, 137, 138, 143, 150, 169, 182, 206; effect on Alexandria 166; effect on Egyptian economy 142; effect on VC 160, 181; Italy declares war on allies 140; Old Victorians involved 133–34; state of school at end 155
War, Suez 178, 180, 185, 186 188, 190, 192, 198, 212, 235

Yannakakis, Ilios 137
Yassa, Hany 199, 239–41
Yeghen, Adly 117
Yeghen, Midhat Pasha 66
Yehia, Abdel Fattah Pasha 56
Yehia, Amin Pasha 56, 68
Yehia, Imam 31, 70
Yeken, Adly Pasha 57–58, 64, 117
Youssef, El Sayed 203, 207
Youssef, Mahar 168
Yule, Dr. 8

Zaghloul Pasha, Saad 42, 43, 51, 58, 64
Zaidan, Henry 216–17, 220–21
Zananiri, Gaston 96–98
Zananiri, George Pasha 96
Zanati family 67
Zaphiro, Mr. 73.
Zeid, Prince Raad bin 169
Zikry, Fouad 134–35
Zikry, Mohamed Bey 100, 104
Zikry, Saleh 104, 134
Zohdi, Mustafa 101
Zolikofer, Max and Claude, architects 207
el Zorba, Abdel Maqsoud 240
Zulfiqar, Said 181